RETURN AGAIN TO THE SCENE OF THE

CRIME

MARCH 19, 1931. WILLIAM J. ROONEY IS THE MAN ON THE SIDE-
WALK (TOP). THE MURDER SCENE AT 1517 NORTH AUSTIN
BOULEVARD AS IT LOOKS TODAY.

FRONTISPIECE

The Man on the Sidewalk

Readers of my first volume of Chicago crime history (*Return to the Scene of the Crime: A Guide to Infamous Places in Chicago*) were understandably curious about the story behind the photograph on the cover of the book. They say a picture is worth a thousand words, but with more than one thousand unsolved gangland slayings dating back to 1920 to sort through, I was at a loss to explain the unfortunate set of circumstances that had befallen the dead man clad in spats and striped trousers.

The macabre image, so typical of Chicago, seemed very appropriate given the content of the book. The cream-colored building in the foreground of the photograph is instantly recognizable as Chicago architecture to generations of city folk born and reared in bungalow-belt and courtyard-apartment neighborhoods. "The building is up on the Far North Side in Rogers Park," claimed one reader, who swore that he drove by there every day and knew of no murders that had occurred there.

"No, it's down on the South Side," insisted another.

In truth, I did not know where or when this crime had occurred. I chose it because it was an intriguing image that smacked of all things Chicago. It bore the unmistakable imprimatur of Al Capone. That much seemed certain as I sifted through a stack of undated, discarded Chicago crime photos belonging to my friend and colleague William J. Helmer, author of several fine books about John Dillinger and the Prohibition Era.

Intrigued by the mystery of the photograph, retired Chicago Police Officer James Viola, who has an interest in the Prohibition Era, solicited the opinions of the late Frank Pape, a former police captain whose controversial methods dispatched nine felons to the afterlife (whether they deserved it or not). Pape told Viola that he seemed to recall a mob shooting of a union leader out on the West Side in the early 1930s. Viola conducted some independent research and verified that the apartment building was still standing near the intersection of Austin Boulevard and North Avenue.

Next, I examined the lengthy roster of unsolved mob hits arranged in chronological order by the Chicago Crime Commission. Later, with the help of Paul Newey, a former chief investigator for the Cook County state's attorney, I uncovered an astonishing collection of classified field reports filed by the late Shirley Kub. Kub was a clever and manipulative doyenne who was pulling double duty for the Chicago mob while feeding street intelligence about organized crime activity to the Secret Six, the Prohibition Era investigative arm of the Crime Commission empowered to infiltrate the Capone gang.

Kub is one of those unbelievable figures you often run across while researching crime in Chicago—a squat, diminutive, rather unattractive woman with a small mouth, piercing eyes, a gangster moll's glibness, and a good dose of cunning. On the eve of her February 1931 grand jury appearance where she promised to tell all she knew about police corruption, Kub fled Chicago, deciding that a prison stretch was safer than provoking the wrath of the Capone mob. As punishment for her silence, she was thrown in the jug for four months, but after completing her sentence and apologizing to the judge, Kub resumed her sleuthing for the Crime Commission, continuing to throw light on unsolved mob homicides.

In her report to the "Six" dated December 6-7, 1932, Kub fingered the killers of William J. "Wild Bill" Rooney—the man on the sidewalk.

For the last sixteen years of his life, "Wild Bill" Rooney headed the Sheet Metal Workers Union. His brother John was a business agent for the Bill Posters Union, and his brother-in-law Jerry Horan ran the powerful Building Service Employees Union.

Horan and Rooney were business partners for many years, but in 1931, according to published reports, they stood on opposite sides of the political fence, and there was speculation that Rooney's death might have had something to do with poor political choices he had made in the early months of that electoral season.

The Chicago mayoralty was at stake and Horan was a supporter of the corrupt demagogue William Hale Thompson. Rooney threw his rank-and-file support behind Anton Cermak, the powerful West Side Czech politician and president of the Cook County Board. Cermak owned a resort home adjacent to William Rooney's place in Antioch, Illinois, where wife, Isabelle Rooney, and her three children joined Bill for his annual summer holiday and various social gatherings for the benefit of the sachems of organized labor.

The facts of this case were easily verified by John Rooney, nephew of the deceased, who contacted me prior to the publication of this second volume. "He [William Rooney] was responsible for moving the Chicago labor movement away from Thompson and over to Cermak," writes Rooney. He goes on to say that his uncle's murder was due in part to the fact that Capone coveted several unions under Rooney's control. The elder Rooney was warned that he might be marked for a hit, but because he had a tough crew of his own, including his cousins Tommy and Roger Touhy, and had successfully thwarted other attempts by Capone, he wasn't afraid.

At the time, Cermak was charting an ill-advised course to destroy the Capone mob for the benefit of his Bohemian constituents, who desired control of the various "wildcat" breweries established by Italians following the repeal of Prohibition. This seemed to be a *fait accompli* by 1931. Cermak's racket-busting stance undoubtedly cost him his own life in 1933, two years after he decisively trounced Thompson at the polls in one of the most vicious mudslinging, name-calling campaigns in the city's history.

William Rooney had been a big man in Chicago politics and organized labor up to that time. The fact that he was also skilled with a gun, a shiv, and a blackjack was never in dispute. He was tried for the 1916 murder of Joseph Cooney during a bloody union election. Rooney's name cropped up again in 1922 during the murder trial of Thomas J. Walsh, the business agent of the Sheet Metal Workers Union who was accused of killing two men during a drunken melee inside a West Randolph Street wine cellar in December 1921.

Not long afterward, Rooney was feted by his admirers at a huge banquet at a swank downtown hotel. In union circles it seems to follow that the tougher and more fearsome the reputation, the more beloved the man.

When Rooney stepped out of his first-floor apartment at 1517 North Austin Boulevard for the last time on March 19, 1931, he was sporting a diamond ring valued at $1,000 and carrying $417 in his pocket—a tidy sum of money for any man in those dark days of the Great Depression.

As Rooney approached the sidewalk, the driver of a fast-moving automobile drove up to the curb to greet him. "One of the men in the car sang out, 'Hi, Billy!' and the car pulled to the wrong side [the west side] of the street," Emma Wilner, the only eyewitness to the shooting, told police. "Just as Rooney got halfway across the parkway a man in the rear seat poked the nose of the gun out through the window."

William Rooney must have recognized his killers, because he showed no signs of fear. He was strolling toward the vehicle at a leisurely pace when he was peppered with seventeen shots. He didn't have a chance.

In her Crime Commission dispatch, Shirley Kub accused three Capone triggermen. "The killing squad for Wm. J. consisted of Rocky De Grazia, Lefty Louie, and Willie Heeney in Rocky's big Caddy, and two other men, names unknown, in a Ford.

"As W. J. Rooney came out of his house, Rocky tooted the horn, which was a signal to the Ford parked a short ways from there. Rooney walked a few feet and Rocky called to him. He turned and started towards the curb and the Ford car by this time was passing and one of the men in same shot and killed Rooney. Rooney on falling raised to his knees, as if crawling, got out his .38, but then collapsed and fell, his false teeth falling out of his mouth. #14 [Kub's undercover ID number] does not know why he was killed."

The killers sped away, and no one was ever arrested or prosecuted for the murder, though Chicago "street justice" usually finds a way of evening old scores. "His killing by three gunmen whose names I'm not sure I should mention, was avenged within three months," explains John Rooney, who refused to divulge any specifics.

The shooting of "Wild Bill" is a forgotten episode in Chicago's legendary Prohibition Era gangland wars. Shirley Kub's romantic attachment to the gangsters eventually brought shame and disgrace down upon the heads of the Secret Six, forcing an embarrassed Robert Isham Randolph, a respected civic and commercial leader, to dissolve the unit on April 19, 1933. In the ensuing years, the Chicago Crime Commission took a less proactive stance in the war against the mob, electing to withdraw from the field of undercover investigation.

The Austin Apartments are located just south of the intersection of Austin Boulevard and North Avenue. The street has been widened since Rooney's time, and the archway over the sidewalk has been painted red, but otherwise the building is marvelously preserved in a neighborhood that has been battered in recent years by street gangs and poverty.

Richard C. Lindberg
June 2001

RETURN AGAIN TO THE SCENE OF THE

CRIME

A Guide to Even More Infamous Places in

CHICAGO

Richard Lindberg

Cumberland House
Nashville, Tennessee

Published by Cumberland House Publishing, 431 Harding Industrial Drive, Nashville, Tennessee 37211-3160.

Maps reprinted with permission of American Map Corporation.

Cover and text design: Unlikely Suburban Design
Cover photo by Art Bilek, "Incident on a City Street," 1951.

Library of Congress Cataloging-in-Publication Data

Lindberg, Richard, 1953–
    Return again to the scene of the crime : a guide to infamous places in Chicago / Richard Lindberg.
        p. cm.
    Includes bibliographical references and index.
    ISBN 1-58182-167-0 (pbk. : alk. paper)
        1. Chicago (Ill.)–Tours. 2. Historic sites–Illinois–Chicago–Guidebooks. 3. Crime scenes–Illinois–Chicago–History. 4. Criminals–Illinois–Chicago–History. I. Title.

F548.18 .L495 2001
917.73'110444–dc21

                                                                                2001032314

Printed in the United States of America
1 2 3 4 5 6 7 8—04 03 02 01 00 99

Other Books by Richard Lindberg

- *Stuck on the Sox,* 1978
- *Who's On Third: The Chicago White Sox Story,* 1983
- *The Macmillan White Sox Encyclopedia,* 1984
- *Chicago Ragtime: Another Look at Chicago 1880-1920,* 1985; reprinted in paperback as *Chicago by Gaslight: A History of the Chicago Netherworld 1880-1920,* 1996
- *To Serve and Collect: Chicago Politics and Police Corruption from the Lager Beer Riot to the Summerdale Scandal 1855-1960,* 1991; reprinted in paperback, 1998
- *Passport's Guide to Ethnic Chicago,* 1992; second edition, 1997
- *Stealing First in a Two-Team Town: The White Sox from Comiskey to Reinsdorf,* 1994
- *Quotable Chicago,* 1996
- *The White Sox Encyclopedia,* 1997
- *The Armchair Companion to Chicago Sports,* 1997
- *Return to the Scene of the Crime,* 1999

In addition, Lindberg was a contributing author to the following:
- *A Kid's Guide to Chicago* (1980)
- *The Encyclopedia of World Crime* (1990)
- *The Baseball Biographical Encyclopedia* (1990)
- *The Encyclopedia of Major League Baseball Team Histories* (1990)
- *American National Biography* (1999 revision)

CONTENTS

• Tour 1 •

In the Shadows of Skyscrapers: Tales of Downtown Crime   1

To even the most jaundiced eye gazing upon the majesty of downtown
Chicago from the lake, the panorama of the city suggests order and a
unity of purpose with its picture-perfect skyline, prim inner harbors,
and necklace of greenery dividing the shoreline from the streets.

• Tour 2 •

Near North Confidential: The Chicago River to Old Town   85

Burlesque, booze, and barflies. The Near North Side
nightclub district, world renown in former days for seamy
attractions, exists today only in memory.

• Tour 3 •

In Pursuit of Nazis, Gangsters, and Anarchists: North Side Crime Scenes from Lincoln Park to Rogers Park   125

Crime cooks on all eight cylinders. In violent and unpredictable times,
the North Side of Chicago emerged as a kind of film noir, a backdrop
for an oddball assortment of kooks and killers, con men and crazy
women, Nazi spies, and plotting anarchists.

PREFACE: THE *REST* OF THE STORY

In April 2000, a stunning visual display depicting the history of Chicago from prairie frontier town to world-class city entering the new millennium was unveiled in the Sears Tower Skydeck. The curving, interactive exhibit celebrates the contributions of the city's most prominent residents from the time of the French voyageurs. I was particularly pleased that I had been asked to participate in this noteworthy project designed to educate and enlighten visitors from around the world about the promise that is Chicago.

There was a tremendous outpouring of civic pride the night of the gala grand opening, which was attended by a number of city officials and other dignitaries. The historic themes of the exhibit pointed to a triumph over adversity and were mirrored by the city's cultural achievements and exemplified by the two World's Fairs in 1893 and 1933, the poetry of Gwendolyn Brooks, South Side jazz, and the best that life in the peaceful pastures of the "Middle Border" can offer. Notably absent in this celebratory collage of great architecture, the indomitable "I Will" spirit of the city, and Ferris wheel rides on Navy Pier, was the image of Al Capone, Chicago's most enduring and recognizable personage.

Unfamiliar with the subject matter of my most recent book, a representative of the Mayor's Office of Cultural Affairs casually remarked to me that it was a great relief to finally be able to present Chicago to the world without the glorification of the gangster gunplay of the 1920s, the man in the fedora smoking the long cigar, or the "C" word (for Capone) and the infamy it connotes.

"Yes," I said, with a withering smile, as I vacillated between hometown boosterism and the desire to speak the truth about the spirit and character of this city I call home. Chicago is, if anything, the sum of all its parts. Chicago's history reflects a human melody with spiritual and sensuous themes alternating in a syncopating rhythm. In a very real sense, Chicago is resolutely lowbrow, crude, and vital. It is politics, power, and prestige. It is a sucker's game with a preacher's morality. Most of all, it is colorful and outrageous—made so by its fantastic pageant of grifters, reformers, gamblers, deacons, whores, and politicians. It proves that it is possible to be all these things and still be a great city.

I have it on good authority that in other places where tourism fuels the local economy, celebrated shootouts like the Gunfight at the O.K. Corral are reenacted every day before hundreds of applauding spectators, and city officials are less concerned about image than with making history pay off. In London, you can embark on a guided tour of the Whitechapel district at night and prowl the route traveled by Jack the Ripper. None of the chaps down at 10 Downing Street seem to have been put off by it.

Chicago, on the other hand, is embarrassed by the history of its reputation. (There was a book by that same name, *Chicago: A History of Its Reputation* by Henry Justin Smith, which should tell you something.) It is, however, a history that others around the world view with wonderment and awe, or at the very least curiosity.

In Chicago, you will not find the names of Al Capone, Johnny Torrio, H. H. Holmes, or even Marty Durkin inscribed alongside the names of Marshall Field or Jane Addams on the walls in the Sears Tower Skydeck panorama. The City of Chicago is not amused by nor does it pretend to appreciate or value guided bus tours to the scenes of bloody shootouts, or theme restaurants pandering to gangster legends, even if it is all in good fun. So long as the city inquisitors and censors remain in high dudgeon, you will never find a historic marker designating the site of the St. Valentine's Day Massacre at 2122 North Clark Street.

Given this pervasive attitude, it was with some apprehension that I commenced work on *Return to the Scene of the Crime: A Guide to Infamous Places in Chicago* in the spring of 1998. I had had an earlier chance to do this book, but had decided to pass. Then I read Andrew Roth's *Infamous Manhattan*, which I discovered quite by chance in the Savvy Traveler bookstore on Michigan Avenue. I took the book with me to New York on a weekend getaway, and instantly knew that the concept could be adapted to Chicago. Heck, if touring crime scenes in New York City could be this interesting, think what could be done with Chicago's fertile ground.

When my first volume was published in 1999, book reviewers affirmed the public fascination with the notorious. In fact, my retelling of the Richard Speck case inspired *Chicago Sun-Times* columnist Richard Roeper to personally investigate the crime scene in order to satisfy his curiosity as to the present occupants of the building.

It is the darker truths about human nature we all seek.

The collection of stories I selected for the first volume were signature Chicago crime cases. The daunting task was in keeping the book at a manageable length.

I have chosen for this sequel a collection of famous and forgotten stories from yesteryear, real dramas illustrating human conflict. Some of them, like the "Vampire Woman of West Hammond," are outrageous and border on the surreal. They defy convention and logic, but I can reassure the reader that all are true and well documented, albeit forgotten by time and erased from public memory.

Be warned that many are not for the faint of heart or the squeamish.

The reconstruction of events presented herein takes into account the "great unknowable." What actually passed between the perpetrator and the victim in some instances can only be surmised. With this understanding, I have researched and written the anthology with an exacting eye toward the small details that often are the most absorbing. I have tried to flesh out the "story behind the story," prying loose odd facts and bizarre events. What emerged was quite startling.

One example is the famous circus train wreck, which occurred outside Hammond, Indiana, in 1918. For years I have heard the tale oft-told by local ghost hunters about unearthly sounds of trumpeting elephants, baying hounds, and roaring lions emanating after dark from the cemetery that contains graves of the circus performers. The story became an accepted part of our folklore, though it was finally debunked when a brilliant wag figured out that the Brookfield Zoo was located nearby.

But what about the real circumstances leading up to that grim and terrible tragedy? Who owned the train in the first place? Was the train cursed? The story cried out for more detail.

With apologies to Paul Harvey, why skim the surface of the thing, when, with a little extra spadework, we bring forth *the rest of the story*.

ACKNOWLEDGMENTS

A book, like a successful journey to a distant land, is not possible without proper navigational guidance. The author, at the onset of his travels, has in mind a topical guideline that functions as a surrogate road map. As in any journey, the most interesting discoveries are often made quite by accident, or upon the recommendation of local experts in places well off the beaten path. The research and writing of these two crime travelogues have afforded me the opportunity of exchanging information and receiving leads from a number of these local experts on the vast subject of misbehavior in obscure corners of the Windy City. I am particularly indebted to Lawrence Raeder. Together we tramped through South Side cemeteries, the weeds and marshes of Wolf Lake, and the city's busy thoroughfares and quiet side streets to formulate the "then-and-now" cityscapes that make this kind of research so fascinating. Also, Al Schafer, for his perspectives on the death of the "Millionaire Orphan"; R. Timothy Unsworth; Tamara Shaffer; South Side folklorist Bill Wright; Carol Mercado; Ann Lunde; the Des Plaines Historical Society; Paul Newey, former Chief Investigator for the Cook County State's Attorney; Barbara Schaaf; William J. Helmer; John Burke, my colleague at Search International; Antoinette Giancana and her former husband, Robert J. McDonnell. I would also like to express my appreciation to Nic Howell, Public Information Director at the Illinois Department of Corrections (IDOC) and members of his research staff. Carol Jean Carlson edited the manuscript and provided other valuable input. Margaret Graham Tebo shepherded the manuscript to publication with Lisa Taylor of Cumberland House. Wayne Johnson, Chief Investigator for the Chicago Crime Commission, took time out to graciously assist me with photos, along with Arthur Bilek, an esteemed criminologist; James Dilorto; John Binder; and Matt Luzi. Thank you to the many readers who wrote or called regarding story ideas, or to take issue with me on minor technical points. I read every letter carefully and will always continue to welcome comments.

CRIME

In the Shadows of Skyscrapers:

Tales of Downtown Crime

To even the most jaundiced eye gazing upon the majesty of downtown Chicago from the lake, the panorama of the city suggests order and a unity of purpose with its picture-perfect skyline, prim inner harbors, and necklace of greenery dividing the shoreline from the streets.

In this splendid "Garden City," it is difficult to imagine acts of treachery perpetrated on the unsuspecting. But take a closer look. Old-fashioned buildings that have survived the wrecker's ball, vacant lots, and even redeveloped parcels of land, where gleaming office towers of glass and steel obliterate the past, speak to the blemished and "unhistorical" past. On every corner there is a famous or half-forgotten story to tell.

Much like the little boy in the movie *The Sixth Sense* who sees "dead people everywhere," Chicago will never fully escape from the ghosts of its checkered past. The famous crimes, as well as the nearly forgotten darkly humorous vignettes of larcenies, con games, murders, newspaper wars, forgers, fakers, and chiselers, are *everywhere*.

Chicago, as journalist Paul Douglas ruefully observed in 1977, is a city "with a Queen Anne front and a Mary Ann back."

It all begins downtown where great architecture, famous department stores, and the old and new converge in a densely inhabited setting known as "the Loop," so named because of the elevated train tracks that circle, or form a *loop* around, the central business district. Chicagoans of the 1880s coined the nickname, and it has managed to hold up after all these years. Forgotten in the din of screeching CTA (Chicago Transit Authority) cars navigating 90-degree turns over Wabash Avenue and Lake Street is that this most visible symbol of the vitality of downtown Chicago was the handwork of a generation of late-nineteenth-century scoundrels, boodlers, and connivers, who parceled off entire city blocks to avaricious traction magnates in the form of "perpetual franchises."

In Chicago, always lurking in the shadow of every great civic improvement,

1

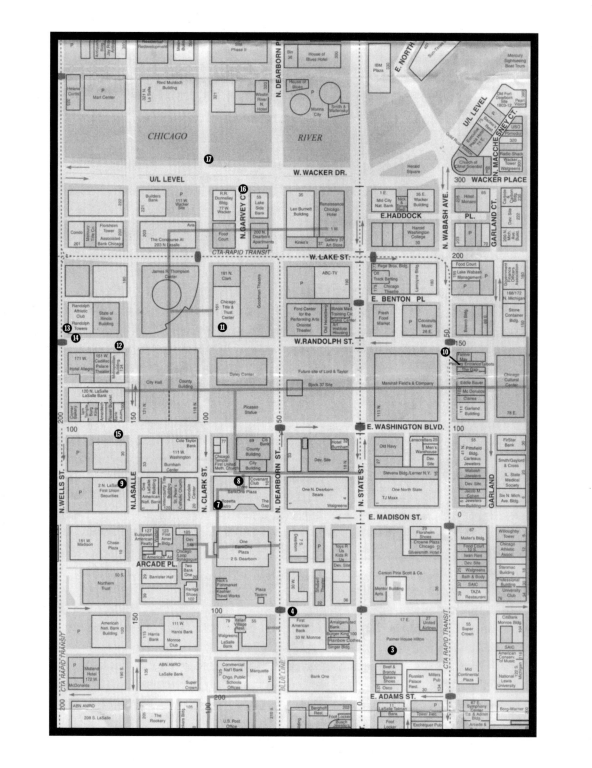

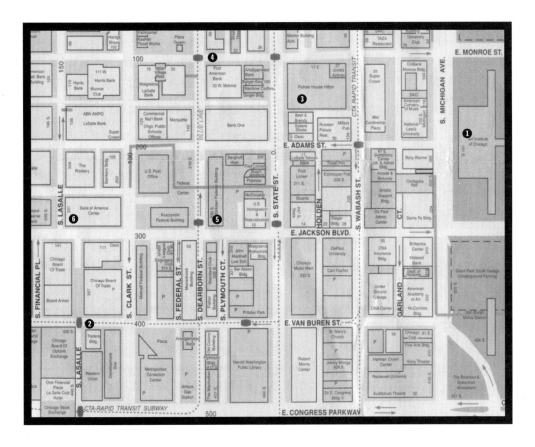

1. Site of Interstate Industrial Exposition Building.
2. LaSalle Atrium Building, where Webster Guerin was murdered.
3. Palmer House Hotel.
4. Gambler's Row.
5. Dirksen Federal Building and site of Great Northern Hotel.
6. Continental Bank (now the Bank of America).
7. Newsboy's Corner.
8. Billy Boyle's Chophouse.
9. Whitechapel Club.
10. Former gambling den, 139 N. Wabash Ave.
11. Judge Fetzer murdered at Randolph St. and Clark St.
12. Palace Theater.
13. & 14. Randolph Towers/Bieber and Brodkin offices/Granata murder.
15. 30 N. LaSalle St.—the drug store murder.
16. Chicago's first Great Fire.
17. Clark Street Bridge. The *Rouse Simmons* docked here.

such as the construction of an urban railway, was the politics of influence, deal-making, self-interest, and alliance-building. Politics and crime are interwoven themes in the city's history, and as we consider the dismal lessons of recent scandals involving the corruption of Chicago's public officials by criminal elements in such well-publicized escapades as "Operation Silver Shovel," "Gambat," and "Haunted Hall," we find that nothing much has changed. Therefore, it is appropriate to begin our tour by stepping back to another time to examine the root of all this rascality.

Our "crime-through-the-ages" tour spans 150 years of city history and begins on Michigan Avenue (formerly known as Pine Street). It is the Gilded Age of American history, and the approximate location is the site of one of the city's most beloved cultural attractions, the Art Institute of Chicago, *before* the world-class museum we know so well evolved.

Michigan Avenue at the foot of Adams Street

OYSTERS ON THE HALF SHELL: CHICAGO'S FORGOTTEN POLITICAL CONVENTIONS OF 1884

Between the crisis of a great Civil War and the dawn of the twentieth century, the City of Chicago hosted eight national nominating conventions, which established the bustling metropolis as a hub of political influence—and gave the city a reputation for windbag oratory and backroom deal-cutting. Three of these gala affairs were held in the electoral seasons of 1880 and 1884 inside the opulent Inter-State Industrial Exposition Building located on Michigan Avenue at the foot of Adams Street. Known to that generation of Chicagoans as the "Glass Palace" because of its majestic crystal ceiling, the expensive hall was built at a cost of $345,927 by a consortium of the city's most prominent captains of industry headed by Potter Palmer, David Gage, and Cyrus Hall McCormick. Aesthetically pleasing to look at in surviving sepia-tone photographs from the 1880s, the huge iron and glass edifice quickly became a financial sinkhole with terrible acoustics and a leaky roof. The Exposition Company hosted livestock shows, art exhibits, and a series of light summer musical concerts conducted by maestro Theodore Thomas, but it failed in its larger mission to consistently lure the important out-of-town conventions once word of mouth reached key decision makers back east. The age of the "robber barons," was in full flower, and with great pageantry and flair Chicago presented to the American electorate of the Gilded Age candidates *who reflected the moral ambiguities of the age and the widening gulf between the "haves" and the "have-nots" in an otherwise quiet time in American politics. The Republicans met at the Glass Palace in 1880. Both parties selected the venue for their conventions in 1884, but after that the building fell into disuse and was eventually abandoned. The short-lived Glass Palace stood forlornly until 1891, when it was razed to make way for the neoclassical Art Institute of Chicago, designed by the Boston architectural firm of Shepley, Rutan & Coolidge. The rest, as they say, is history. But as you stroll past the bronze statues of the lions adorning the Michigan Avenue entrance to the museum, recall, if you will, another time and place when politics took center stage in American life inside Chicago's (un)conventional "Glass Palace."*

The Windy City has hosted more national nominating conventions than any other American metropolis with good reason: Chicago has long stood at the crossroads of the nation and offered convenience and easy accessibility via the network of railroads crisscrossing the restless nation. Visiting state delegations enjoyed the city's unique blend of hospitality and social amenities. The pageantry commenced every four years in the sultry June heat and enjoyed the carnival spirit of a city unhampered by Eastern pomposity and stodgy old-world custom.

In those days, there were saloons on every corner, tawdry dancehalls, and lowbrow theaters catering to prurient tastes. Carrie Watson's world-class "resort" was renown for the beauty of its courtesans, while the racetracks and gambling "hells" afforded enjoyment for the wagering men. Chicago was an alluring and amoral place that jarred the sensibilities. Where else could one go to savor the wicked allure of the western badlands within the sprawl of a great city?

In this Gilded Age, American politics were characterized by bitter factional disputes over tariff reform and a contentious debate over elimination of the "spoils system," something the sachems of the urban Democratic machines and many Republican leaders generally opposed. Civil service would effectively cut off their control of federal and state patronage. Defenders of the spoils system, which included Illinois' favorite son General John A. Logan, were known as "stalwarts."

"The Democratic party cannot be run without a machine or several of them in every city and a boss to manage them," the partisan Republican *Tribune* complained. "Patronage is the alpha and omega of Democracy, and to control and divide that patronage is the purpose of the leaders."

"Mugwumps," "stalwarts," and "half-breeds" (those who supported the adoption of civil service) were colorful nicknames applied to that generation of

American statesmen, who jostled wildly over these issues in the grandest arena of them all, the three-ring spectacle known as the national nominating convention.

The electorate may not have understood the vagaries of tariff reform, but a rousing torchlight parade down State Street by members of a marching club supporting one presidential contender over another provided a festive, circus-like atmosphere. The bantering between rival delegations was an amusing diversion during heated electoral sessions.

Inside the lobby of the Grand Pacific Hotel on the eve of the opening of the 1884 Republican Convention, the noisy supporters of General Logan tramped through the corridors singing the praises of their great "stalwart" leader. When they reached the hotel rotunda, a contingency of James G. Blaine sloganeers (who dubbed their hero "the Plumed Knight," while Democratic opponents belittled him as "the Continental Liar from the State of Maine") surrounded the Logan-ites and for a half-hour bedlam reigned supreme as the two delegations attempted to drown each other out with catcalls, insults, and repeated mockery.

The opening gavel was struck inside the acoustically imperfect Glass Palace on June 3, 1884. In order to improve the sound quality of the building, supervising architect Dankmar Adler installed two enormous "sounding boards" and reduced the seating capacity to less than nine thousand. He also moved the main stage from the north end to the south wing of the building, but it turned out to be an unparalleled security nightmare. A thousand gatecrashers punched and elbowed their way past only eighteen uniformed Chicago police officers into the hall, sparking a chorus of heated complaints from the visiting press delegations. "More Chicago gall!" snarled one unhappy scribe. "I leaned over the table to hand a telegram to a boy and damned if some cuss didn't steal my chair from under me! This is a great city!"

At Riley's downtown "poolroom," where for eleven months out of any given year the sporting men and racetrack idlers placed their typical wagers on the outcome of horseraces and ball games, the betting action was all on the candidates, and business was brisk. Who was it going to be? Blaine or Logan?

James G. Blaine, who had faithfully served the martyred President James A. Garfield as secretary of state, was nominated on the fourth ballot after "Black Jack" Logan cabled the Illinois delegation from Washington and told them to switch their vote. Logan was handsomely paid off by the Blaine forces with the vice-presidential nomination.

"From this hour dates the death of the Republican Party," groaned a dejected Carl Schurz, who bolted the party to support the candidacy of the Democrat, Governor Grover Cleveland of New York. The 1884 Republican turncoats were tarred as "Mugwumps."

A month later, on July 8, 1884, the Democrats descended on Chicago to nominate, after considerable intra-party bickering, the reform candidate Cleveland as their standard bearer. Author and civic booster A. T. Andreas reported that the Democratic convention "far outrivaled the Republican gathering in point of excitement, enthusiasm, fireworks, the noise of the brass bands and the speeches of agitators who endeavored to control the local feeling." Undoubtedly Andreas was referring to the powerful New York delegation from Tammany Hall, who arrived in their specially chartered Pullman coaches at the Lake Shore train depot on July 6. Tammany delegates were met by the tumultuous applause of twenty thousand noisy spectators elbowing their way forward to catch a glimpse of "Honest" John Kelly, the corrupt chieftain of the most powerful and intimidating urban political machine in the country up to that time. The Tammanyites cussed "snivel service." They drank. They whored. And their regimental marching band, festooned in dazzling red-and-yellow uniforms, drew raves as they paraded up and down State Street, creating quite a spectacle with stirring renditions of "Dixieland," "Marching Through Georgia," and "Daisy."

One would not find the bluenosed Frances E. Willard of the Woman's Christian Temperance Union (WCTU) counted among this carnival gathering of scoundrels and ne'er-do-wells. Ms. Willard, waving her "Carrie Nation" fist, was

THE "GLASS PALACE" HOSTED BOTH NATIONAL NOMINATING CONVENTIONS IN 1884. MICHIGAN AVENUE NEAR ADAMS.

unable to secure a ticket to the Republican convention even after much badgering. In disgust, she fled Chicago one step ahead of the invading Democrats.

Kelly was warmly greeted by then Chicago mayor Carter Harrison. Harrison symbolically linked arms with Joseph Chesterfield Mackin ("Oyster Joe"), a First Ward saloon rogue, and his protégé from the Chicago underworld, gambler boss Michael C. McDonald, in a triumphal procession that inched past cheering throngs from the train station down State Street to the special accommodations afforded them inside the Palmer House. The Palmer House was the traditional headquarters of the Democrats during the political season and Mackin's permanent address. "Boss" Kelly solicited Harrison and "Boss" McDonald to help him derail the hated Cleveland, who was perceived to be anti-Irish, anti-saloon, and anti-Catholic in his thinking.

In reality, the portly (300-pound) Cleveland had vigorously opposed the Tammany bosses on civil service reform. But Harrison, a politically ambitious Kentuckian, was neither Catholic nor much concerned about intra-party squabbling among the New York delegates.

The Glass Palace was draped with tricolored bunting and reconfigured to satisfy the egalitarian leanings of the Democrats. Gone were the private viewing boxes patronized by Chicago's business elite during the Republican convention. In their place were substituted rows and rows of ordinary folding chairs for the expected crush of delegates, reporters, and spectators.

Carter Harrison, despised by former Illinois governor John M. Palmer who chaired the state delegation, was accused of "packing the hall" with his Irish ward cronies and Mackin men, whose appointed task was to cheer lustily when Mayor Harrison stood before them on the convention dais to second Cleveland's nomination. In the prime of life, a robust and eternally confident Mike McDonald had marshaled the saloon vote, the flophouse hoboes from Kilgubbin and Conley's Patch, his army of traveling bunco men, and the dancehall queens to lend "moral support" in the hotel lobbies and saloons. By the dint of his brilliant organizational skills, he had successfully fused this ragtag coalition into a solid voting bloc staunchly behind "Our Carter." With their support, McDonald and Mackin went about the business of handpicking the state delegation and rigging the county elections.

Harrison had actively campaigned behind the scenes for the vice-presidential nomination and, though he welcomed the support, Cleveland was not of a mind to ally himself with the powerful big-city bosses whom he knew to be in league with gamblers and the criminal element. He believed he could win without their help, and he did, despite the worst sex scandal to embarrass any presidential candidate up to the time of William Jefferson Clinton in 1992.

On July 21, 1884, the *Buffalo Telegraph*, a Republican paper violently opposed to the Cleveland candidacy, reported that the nominee had sired an illegitimate child a decade earlier with a young woman named Maria Crofts Halpin. Halpin could not be found to corroborate the charge, but all across the land was heard the sarcastic chant, "Ma! Ma! Where's Pa? Gone off to the White House. Ha! Ha!" *The New York Sun* called Cleveland a "coarse debauchee" and predicted that he would "bring his harlots with him to Washington."

The governor responded to the newspaper scandal with low-key honesty and was elected to office by twenty-four thousand votes, becoming the first Democratic president since the end of the Civil War. The voting public equated the Blaine-Logan ticket with the eastern "robber barons" and the unchecked monopolistic greed that symbolized the age.

President-elect Cleveland made a good accounting. He demonstrated independence and a clear head and was gracious under fire. Back in Chicago, where things were never on the square, there was intrigue afoot. The *Chicago Tribune* drew attention to certain voting irregularities in the Eighteenth Ward. At the center of the controversy stood party boss Oyster Joe Mackin, who built a loyal and dependable constituency by dispensing free oysters with every schooner of beer sold to thirsty patrons inside his saloon (thereby introducing the "free lunch" to the city).

Mackin had choreographed every move the Illinois delegation made, secretly ensuring that the voters elected only the approved slate of candidates. The *Tribune*, backed by the powerful social elite and ruling business class, made an issue of the moral character of the Mackin-McDonald crowd and demanded a swift but thorough investigation.

Not long after the final votes were tallied and the results entered into the official record, Oyster Joe was brought up on charges of vote fraud before a Cook County Grand Jury. The wheezy old grafter had brazenly stolen two fistfuls of Republican votes from a ballot box used in the Second Precinct. When no one was watching, he substituted Democratic forgeries ordered from a Chicago printing company days before the election.

Mackin was convicted on a charge of perjury in July 1885. With great reluctance, the trial judge fixed his sentence at five years in the state penitentiary. Within two and a half years, that same judge filed a petition with Illinois Governor Richard J. Oglesby, pleading for early parole for Mackin. The judge argued that the trial evidence did not warrant the jury's conviction. Like many other prominent men of good character and reputation, he personally believed in Oyster Joe and thought him innocent.

Party slate-makers loyal to Joe launched a letter-writing campaign. Armed with the judge's politically expedient decision to get behind the partisan effort to free the boss, the gates of the penitentiary swung open for Joe. Once again beer was flowing freely up and down Gambler's Alley. Once again, the boys were making merry. The Democrats were back in business, and the oysters on the half shell never tasted better.

The Fine Arts Building
410 South Michigan Avenue

As you stroll southward on Michigan Avenue from the Art Institute toward Van Buren Street, detour to the Fine Arts Building at 410 South Michigan Avenue. The vintage Victorian brownstone, formerly known as the Studebaker Building, has remained a center for the performing arts for more than one hundred years. In 1885, architect Solon S. Beman designed the building for the Studebaker carriage company. The archway above the box office of the present-day theater was once the vehicular entrance for the carriage crowd who had come to Michigan Avenue to negotiate the purchase of a fashionable "four-by-four" or "dogcart." In 1898, the show rooms were permanently abandoned, and the building was remodeled into artists' studios. In one of the interior studios in 1900, newspaperman L. Frank Baum, who toiled for the Chicago Evening Post, *penned* The Wonderful Wizard of Oz. *Back at Van Buren and Michigan, turn right and continue to LaSalle Street.*

SIDETRIP

Southeast corner, LaSalle and Van Buren Streets

HELL HATH NO FURY LIKE A "FLORA DORA" GIRL SCORNED: DORA FELDMAN MCDONALD SHOOTS HER TEENAGE LOVER
February 21, 1907

Mike McDonald cast a long and imperious shadow over the city during his thirty-year reign as overlord of the Chicago underworld. Down through the years, legends have been told about how McDonald, the first successful "gambler politician" of the post–Civil War era, ruled the city with outstretched palms. He stood apart from other men, and the oft-repeated phrase, "There's a sucker born every minute," is attributable to "King" Mike." McDonald was an empire builder who solidified his position as the undisputed ruler of dice and cards by purchasing wholesale police protection; publishing his own newspaper, the Chicago Globe; *and electing political can-*

didates to high office who were favorable to his interests. There was very little he failed to accomplish in that graft-plagued era, dictating city appointments, hobnobbing with mayors and presidential candidates, and building the Lake Street elevated railway with money earned from greenhorns and suckers, who foolishly gambled away their meager earnings inside "the Store," McDonald's deluxe downtown casino where hundreds of thousands of dollars changed hands each night. Mike McDonald was infallible, except when it came to affairs of the heart. In the end it wasn't the police, gangland bullets, or even a guilty conscience that killed the old cardsharp. It was his feckless second wife, Dora, whose personal shame was so terrible a burden to bear that McDonald's ticker stopped working. The crime of passion that ultimately sapped his energy and will to live was committed in a private art studio located inside the Omaha Building, a vintage 1884 seven-story office center at LaSalle and Van Buren in the South Loop. The area looks quite different today from when the jealous adulteress stormed into the Omaha Building with a loaded pistol secreted in her purse. In McDonald's day, the LaSalle Street Train Station, which served eight thousand arriving and departing transcontinental passengers a day in its well-appointed waiting rooms under the twin clock towers, stood opposite the Omaha Building on the southwest corner. Today it is the LaSalle Street Metra Station, and the crush of passengers accommodated by the station travel only as far as the Chicago suburbs. Now, observe the modern-day Chicago Board of Trade complex on the northwest corner. In 1907, the Rialto Building, an early steel-frame skyscraper adjoining the city's original Board of Trade Building, stood on the site. The Omaha Building was replaced by the LaSalle Atrium Building at 401 West Van Buren, the oldest surviving structure in the immediate vicinity.

Mike McDonald was lounging comfortably, his breakfast and his *Chicago American* at hand (William Randolph Hearst's morning newspaper with a decidedly liberal Democratic slant), when Dora Feldman, his vivacious and buxom young wife, announced her intention to go out for the day. "I will be going to my office soon," McDonald casually replied as he scanned the financial page for the latest real estate news. In his dotage, the aging crime boss and political dealmaker had given up his gambling rackets and was a respectable man of means. He had amassed a recent fortune by creating new elevated lines and selling the franchise at inflated prices.

Dora had attracted McDonald's roving eye while dancing with the "Flora

MICHAEL CASSIUS MCDONALD (ALIGHTING HIS CARRIAGE) WAS THE FATHER OF
CHICAGO ORGANIZED CRIME.

Dora Sextet" at a firemen's benefit at the old Clark Street Theater one night in 1894. (*Author's note:* The original Flora Dora Sextet was such a popular vaudeville attraction that copies sprang up across the country.) Dora was wearing a Grecian-style chiffon gown with a plunging neckline that accented her shapely form. Mike was enchanted, and at that moment he knew he had to possess the rebellious, quick-witted, golden-haired temptress from Chicago's West Side Jewish ghetto. Sadly, he learned that she was married to Sam Barkley, a gimpy-legged ex–baseball player who had ended his career with the Kansas City team of the American Association five years earlier.

It was rumored that the gambler offered Barkley a $20,000 cash settlement to release Dora from her marital obligations. Barkley, who owned a saloon, adamantly refused. Then, as Dora's pulse quickened with the certain knowledge that so powerful and wealthy a man as Mike McDonald had fallen in love with her, Barkley retained the services of two street thugs to spirit his estranged wife away in a closed carriage to a "low resort," where the washed-up ballplayer, besotted with booze and morphine, pleaded for a reconciliation.

On the strength of this disgusting display, Dora obtained a divorce on the grounds of mental cruelty. The aging gambler king eloped to Milwaukee with the young woman just as soon as the ink had dried on her divorce decree. For McDonald, it was his second marriage. Mary Noonan, his first wife, was an insanely jealous old-man trap, who labored under the illusion that Mike had seduced his pretty young niece who was living in their stately West Side mansion at Harrison and Ashland Boulevard, a few doors down the street from an old friend, Carter Henry Harrison I, mayor of Chicago.

Convinced that Mike was unfaithful, Mary devoted her time and energy to religion, specifically a handsome young Belgian Catholic priest named Father Joseph Moissant, who made a daily pilgrimage to the mansion to attend to her devotions. Soon, Mary demanded that Mike build her a private chapel in a spare room inside the house, where she and Father Moissant could meditate on spiritual matters.

Mike complied with the unusual request, but became suspicious when the priest began locking the outer door to the private confessional. Father Moissant and Mary Noonan were not praying hard enough for the redemption of their almighty souls. The fact is, they weren't praying at all, but engaging in torrid sex while the cuckolded McDonald attended to other matters elsewhere in the house. When the adultery was proved and the scandal a matter of public record, Mary was banished from the mansion.

For the first few years after their nuptials, McDonald and Dora Feldman were happy newlyweds in the Ashland Avenue mansion. (McDonald eventually moved to 4501 Drexel Boulevard in the South Side's millionaire's row.) Mike forsook the Catholic faith, converted to Judaism, and legally adopted Dora's son, Ralph, as his own.

McDonald's eldest son, Guy, despised Feldman, and was observed punching and kicking the woman on the front lawn. McDonald intervened. Dora patched up her differences with her stepson (who was closer to her age than her husband's), and calm

THE SOMBER MATRON

DORA FELDMAN McDONALD.

was eventually restored to the household.

Dora always called McDonald "Papa," referring to the father-like role he had assumed in her life.

Papa's money and tender endearments were one thing, but the difference in age eventually proved to be too much of a liability for the fiery blond showgirl to endure. Dora was in the prime of womanhood and sexually frustrated. She wanted a younger, more virile man, and she found him living across the street from the Ashland Avenue residence. Only this particular young man was a fresh-faced schoolboy about to graduate from short pants to trousers.

Webster S. Guerin, a redheaded youth with artistic ambitions, was only four-teen when he fell under the spell of Feldman, age thirty-two. Dora Feldman lav-ished her young charge with gifts of clothing, jewelry, and cash. In her chauffeur-driven carriage, Dora picked Guerin up at his residence each day for an afternoon canter around the city. She spent the next several years busily directing his life.

"She was forever trying to get him to go into some other line of business. Mrs. McDonald took a particular interest in the appearance of my brother," recalled Guerin's brother Benjamin. "I remember once she objected to his wear-ing a white hat with his red hair. That doesn't become you, Webster," she said.

Webster Guerin entered the haberdashery business after Dora nagged and cajoled him to work hard and become an important man of commercial affairs like her husband.

The clothing business was not, however, to his liking, and the shop suffered while Webster daydreamed of becoming the next Toulouse-Lautrec. That, too, Dora was willing to tolerate, as long as he maintained his devotion and unswerv-ing loyalty to her.

Smothered by Dora's constant affection and attention, Guerin began to feel trapped.

Feldman then set Guerin up in Suite 703 of the Omaha Building—a love nest for Dora, an art studio for Webster, which he shared with his brother Archibald. Often there were violent quarrels overheard by the other tenants. The crashing of furniture was not an uncommon occurrence. The love affair was tempestuous.

The real trouble began when Archibald Guerin invited his eighteen-year-old fiancée, Miss Avis Dargan, a tall, slender, and graceful beauty, to the studio. As jeal-ous and suspicious of Webster as Mary Noonan had once been of McDonald's young niece, Dora fixated on the other woman to the point of hysterical obses-sion. She was convinced that Miss Avis was after Webster, and she brooded over the matter for weeks.

Guerin grew increasingly apprehensive. His mother couldn't help but notice Webster's nervous anxiety. Dora was in the habit of telephoning Webster at odd hours. Discretion was abandoned, Dora threatened reprisals, and the neighbors were gossiping. Still, nothing was communicated directly to Mike McDonald, though Guerin's aunt, Miss Nellie Fitzgibbons, and Webster's mother called on Mrs. McDonald one afternoon to try to convince her to relinquish her hold on the young man.

"Please let that boy alone. He would be good if it was not for your influence," pleaded the mother. "You seem to have cast a spell over him. I can't do anything with him. Oh, won't you let me have him?" Dora McDonald, it was said, drove the two women from the porch, threatening to shoot them down if they persisted in bothering her.

On the morning of February 21, 1907, as Mike prepared to go to his office at the Fort Dearborn Building downtown, Dora Feldman McDonald quietly slipped out of the house. Tucked inside her purse were a gun and a bundle of love letters and poems she had composed. One stanza read:

> *Kill me if you will, for all is well!*
> *I know that in Satan your soul you can't sell!*
> *I have saved you from everlasting hell!*
> *I lifted you up when low I found you;*
> *Slowly but surely you were dragging me down.*

It was a bright Thursday morning. No one seemed to pay attention to the McDonald woman as she swept past the office clerks. By now she was a familiar sight to the tenants of the Omaha Building.

Dora crept into Guerin's studio, closing and locking the door behind her. There was an exchange of angry words. Guerin ordered her out, then suddenly there came the unmistakable crack of a pistol. She had shot her lover through the neck, just below the left ear. Death was imminent. Dora lapsed into hysterics and appeared to be stark raving mad. She smashed out the plate glass in the door with the butt of the pistol. "Oh God!" she shrieked. "Get a doctor! He has shot himself!"

Blood was streaming from her face and hands as three building tenants from a nearby suite burst into the room and managed to disarm her before she could turn the weapon on herself or some innocent bystander.

"If he is to die, I'll say that I killed him so then they will kill me, too," she said, sobbing uncontrollably. Detective Clifton Rodman Wooldridge, who, by coincidence, was on his way to question Guerin about a shady business transaction recently reported to the police, led the babbling, incoherent woman away to the Harrison Street lockup. (*Author's Note:* See *Return to the Scene of the Crime* for a history and description of this famous city jail.)

A few hours later, Mike McDonald appeared at her side. "Put your arms around me, Papa!" she wailed.

"It doesn't make any difference now," McDonald said in a soothing tone, silently nodding to his aide to attend to matters at hand. Dora's personal maid was brought down to the jail to offer succor and comfort.

Dr. Leonard St. John, McDonald's friend since the early 1880s and a party to his many schemes to bilk the city, told police that in his expert opinion the woman was clearly delusional and not in full possession of her faculties at the time of the shooting. Alfred S. Trude, one of the brainiest criminal defense attorneys in the city and another longtime McDonald crony, was pulled out of retirement to act in an advisory capacity. Lawyer Trude put an expert spin to the story in order to spare his old friend public humiliation.

Mike McDonald still loved Dora, and in this high-stakes, life-and-death poker game, he pulled out all the stops to save her from a certain rendezvous with the gallows. Within twenty-four hours, McDonald's friends along newspaper row were publishing a fictitious yarn cooked up by Trude to embarrass and discredit Guerin's family. The papers told how Guerin was blackmailing Dora and how he

THE PARTING OF THE WAYS FOR DORA M'DONALD--WHICH WILL IT BE?

Sketch by Chicago American Staff Artist Paleriske, Illustrating the Future Before the Guerin Tragedy-Defendant. She Has No Chance for Liberty. Her Relatives Assert That Even if She Is Acquitted She Will Be Sent to an Asylum for the Insane.

ASYLUM OR PRISON?

NEITHER, AS IT TURNED OUT.

CARTOONISTS FOR THE YELLOW

PRESS FOLLOWED EVERY MOMENT

OF THE SENSATIONAL TRIAL.

COLONEL J. HAMILTON LEWIS, DORA M'DONALD'S ADVOCATE, DISPLAYING REVOLVER THAT KILLED WEBSTER GUERIN.

COURTROOM DRAMA AT THE DORA McDONALD MURDER TRIAL. DEFENSE ATTORNEY J. HAMILTON LEWIS BRANDISHES THE WEAPON USED TO KILL WEBSTER GUERIN.

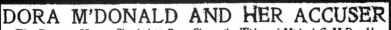

DORA M'DONALD AND HER ACCUSER

This Dramatic Moment Sketched in Court Shows the Widow of Michael C. McDonald Facing Archie Guerin, Vengeance-Seeking Brother of the Man She Is Accused of Killing.

A TEST OF NERVE. DORA STARING DOWN HER VICTIM'S BROTHER.

had "stalked" her all the way to California during a recent vacation junket. It was reported that Guerin was in possession of scandalous photographs he had taken of Dora in flagrant dishabille and had threatened to go public, though the existence of these scintillating images remained a closely guarded secret until after the trial commenced.

The blackmail theory was supported by Guy McDonald, who said that he always "stood by" his stepmother. She had no other choice, he said, but to defend the honor of the family. Guerin was shot in an act of self-defense. Since no one had actually witnessed the altercation, a seed of doubt was planted.

The *Inter-Ocean*, a Republican newspaper that was neither subservient to nor afraid of McDonald's political clout within Democratic Party circles, countered the hypothesis by directly quoting Guerin's mother and brothers, who told of Dora's repeated threats.

The questions raised by Trude caused a coroner's jury to return an open verdict. They failed to find Dora responsible for Guerin's death, but the Cook County Grand Jury indicted her on murder charges nevertheless.

Mike's millions and his considerable influence in the halls of justice undoubtedly helped save her life, but ultimately it cost him his own. The gambler king died from grief at St. Anthony's Hospital on August 8, 1907. As he was passing to his death, there crept into his hospital room a white-haired woman who had come all the way from Newark, New Jersey, where she was engaged in charity work rescuing "fallen" girls like herself for the Crittenden homes. The woman was McDonald's first wife, Mary, who now answered to the name "Grashoff." She held Mike's hand and begged for reconciliation, while Dora sat outside in the hallway, suddenly realizing that her star was fading fast. With the gentle urging of the Catholic Church, Mike McDonald was obliged to forgive Mary and accept consecration in a Catholic graveyard.

Found among Dora's accumulated love letters to Guerin was an unflattering reference to Mike, in which she called him a "slob." More than anything, that personal insult, and not the marital infidelity of two wives, was said to have killed him. "Plainly speaking it was from a broken heart," opined Dr. St. John. "It was sorrow that brought the old man to the grave."

Mike McDonald's last will and testament was signed and dated on July 10, 1907. He bequeathed a large sum of money for Dora's legal protection. The executors of the estate forked over a $25,000 retainer to Colonel James Hamilton Lewis, who would actually try the case, and another $30,000 to "Asa" Trude, the behind-the-scenes wirepuller. Together they succeeded in convincing a judge to release Dora from jail on a $50,000 bond.

For a brief period of time, Dora was confined to the Laura C. Buck Rest

Sanitarium, where it was hoped she would begin to regain her senses. Progress was noted, and Dora was soon released to her mother's care at the family homestead at 8680 South Calumet Avenue. However, her mental state continued to deteriorate. Dora was prone to fits of hysterical shrieking. The neighbors would gather outside, whisper among themselves, and shake their heads knowingly until the police wagon was summoned and the crowd of gawkers politely dispersed.

Dora once attempted suicide twice within a day. Dora pirouetted on the second-floor windowsill one afternoon but, through the quick action of her brother, she was pulled to safety. She accused the trustees of Mike's estate of conspiring to kill her. "They will not give me so much as the bread necessary to keep me alive. I have not even a dress to wear!" Guy McDonald and his brother Cassius had cut her off from the money pot with the connivance of Trude and Lewis. Then, in a pitiful attempt to draw attention to her reduced circumstances, she tried to commit suicide with the gas pipe later that same day, but was revived before the deadly fumes could release her from this veil of tears.

Dora McDonald's repeated bouts of hysteria delayed the start of the criminal trial until January 20, 1908, when jury selection finally began. Her spirits crushed, she sat implacably in the court, day after day, with her nurse attending to her every need. Time and time again she fainted, as one witness after another testified that they had seen Guerin and Dora in intimate embrace all across town, from banquet board to theater box.

There were fears that Dora would not live through the trial. A physician was on call at every moment. At one point, Dora began whistling Irish folk tones. Unperturbed, Avis Dargan smiled maliciously down at Dora from the witness stand and told of the wild flights of fancy and insane jealousy she had observed. Presiding judge Theodore Brentano had all he could do to maintain order.

Would it be prison or the asylum for Dora? The gentlemen of the press and the jury puzzled over one question, the key to the whole thing. Was Guerin the innocent victim of an obsessed crazy woman, or was he a scheming blackmailer? After six hours of deliberation the jury on February 11 returned a "Not Guilty" verdict, citing the lack of an eyewitness to the shooting.

It could have been deliberate murder, but then again maybe darling Web had killed himself after all. Or was it self-defense? If the trial were held in England under English law, instead of under Chicago's "politics of influence," the jury undoubtedly would have come back with a verdict of "Not Proven."

"I felt sure that God was with me all along if nobody else was," a remarkably composed Dora said afterward. Having miraculously recovered her sanity with the reading of the verdict, she went on with her life as best she could, minus Mike's fortune.

MC DONALD FAMILY

MAUSOLEUM AT

MT. OLIVET CEMETERY.

NO ROOM FOR DORA.

(Photo by author)

Dora lived out the remainder of her days peacefully, but was unable to realize her dream of erecting a permanent shrine to the memory of Mike McDonald, the man whose patience and forgiving nature spared her the rope. She said she could not afford to build such a monument on her meager subsistence.

The gambler boss was laid to rest inside the family mausoleum at Mt. Olivet, a South Side Catholic cemetery. In 1917, Mike was joined by Mary Grashoff, his first wife, then later by two of his three sons from the first marriage. There was no room at the inn for Dora Feldman, who disappeared into the vapors of history.

Meanwhile, Avis Dargan had married Archie Guerin, and they lived happily ever after.

Webster Guerin, the young gigolo with the paintbrush and the empty wallet, was interred near his aunt, Ellen Fitzgibbons, in an unmarked grave at Calvary Cemetery in Evanston. Either the family could not pay for a suitably inscribed stone, or they simply decided the shame was too great a burden to bear.

No one goes there now. It all happened so long ago, and time has a way of erasing memories of the most brutal incidents of the past.

State

Street

entrance,

south of

Monroe

Street

CATTY WORDS KILL A BRIDE
AT THE PALMER HOUSE
June 30, 1946

The Palmer House at 17 East Monroe Street in the heart of the Loop has remained a symbol of luxurious Chicago hostelry for nearly 130 years. Inside the gilded, French-inspired lobby with chandeliers copied from the palaces at Versailles and Compeigne, the chair-lounging newspaper reader, ducking inside for a cool respite from the blazing July city heat, can be made to feel like a king, even on a Burger King budget. As long as you are suitably presentable and do not gape in awe at the famous personages checking in at the front desk, the house detectives will generally leave you alone. Enjoy the ambiance of yesteryear, the historic furnishings, and the thirty-five-foot ceiling and always try to remember that there was a time when the hoi polloi were definitely not welcomed in polite company such as this. There have been three Palmer Houses lending pomp and dignity to State Street since Potter Palmer, the social arbiter of taste, formality, and refinement opened his cozy inn on September 26, 1871—less than two weeks before the Chicago Fire destroyed the entire city. The hotel was a $3.5 million gift to his young wife, the famous socialite Bertha Honore, who ruled over an obedient flock of Chicago society matrons for nearly forty years. The second Palmer House borrowed an original design from John Van Osdel, Chicago's first architect, and was constructed on the present site in 1873, after Palmer borrowed $2 million from an insurance company—the largest sum ever loaned to a private citizen up to that time. Palmer's personal marker was always good in Chicago, even though he suffered the ignominy of being arrested and charged with keeping a gambling house at 178 State Street. At the time of his arrest on March 7, 1882, Potter owned three-quarters of a mile of prime State Street property. The loan was paid back on time, and the hotel remained a profitable operation until it was razed in 1926 to make way for an even more ostentatious hotel forever immortalized in the Broadway musical Showboat. *For many years the third Palmer House, built at a cost of $40 million by Honore and Potter Palmer II, was advertised as the largest hotel in the world, with 2,268 guestrooms, 2,268* *baths, and 2,268 "servidors." The fabled Empire Room above the main lobby was an elegant nightclub featuring the top names in show business for many years. The hotel and nightclub were sold to Conrad Hilton in 1945. Today it is the Palmer House Hilton. What happened on the sixth floor of the third Palmer House that humid afternoon in 1946 was not a front-page story or terribly significant in the larger scheme of things, especially when weighed against mounting concerns over postwar unemployment, price controls, and the Communist takeover of Eastern Europe. But this one-act melodrama played out at the Palmer House brings to mind the social pressures brought to bear upon the young women of that era, and how far we have advanced as a society, and as a people.*

Vickey Heyman married medical student Bernard Rumsch in a New York City wedding that spared no expense. Heyman was a nineteen-year-old, starry-eyed Hunter College undergraduate who had lived in the same apartment house as Rumsch.

Vickey Heyman was also a very nervous and insecure bride.

At the wedding reception on Saturday, a thoughtless remark from a meddling old biddy sent the young woman into a dizzying tailspin of depression. "She isn't good enough for him!" Heyman overheard the remark and took it to heart.

"See! I'm not fit to marry you!" Vickey wailed to her husband.

Bernard Rumsch attempted to soothe the jangled nerves and guilt-plagued conscience of his pretty young wife by assuring her that everything would be all right once they managed to escape from the clutches of the washday gossips and head west on a glorious honeymoon (with a quick stopover in Chicago).

They flew to Chicago from New York the night of June 30, checking into the Palmer House at 5:00 P.M. After they had settled comfortably into their sixth-floor room overlooking State Street, Rumsch finally relaxed. He believed Vickey's wedding jitters were over, and that she had put the unfortunate episode behind her. "I'm going out for a shave and a shoeshine," he announced. "Be back in a little while." Vickey seemed happy and in good spirits, but then she asked him not to go. But Rumsch was becoming agitated with her at this point and fled from the room.

Rumsch, wearing a sports jacket and a white shirt open at the collar, went out to check on his airline reservations to Denver. The honeymooning couple were staying in Chicago just this one night, and he was anxious to reach Colorado.

Bernard Rumsch was gone for less than half an hour.

THE SECOND

PALMER HOUSE

(ABOVE) LASTED

FROM 1873 UNTIL

1926, WHEN THE

PRESENT HOTEL

(LEFT)

WAS BUILT.

When he returned, a crowd of rubbernecking pedestrians had formed a tight knot in front of the hotel and were staring at a formless shape lying on the sidewalk just below the Rumschs' room. Rumsch could not quite make out the object of curiosity. He brushed past the throng of people and proceeded through the doors of the State Street entrance and down the corridor of the hotel, where he heard that a woman had plunged to her death. In a sudden panic, he raced up the stairs toward the house phone, brushing past the bellhops and matrons. When Vickey did not answer he raced outside and found the crumpled body of his wife lying on the sidewalk.

According to eyewitness Harry Levin, the woman cast a long glance toward the sky, pausing for just a second before taking the fateful plunge from the sixth-floor ledge and landing on the sidewalk in front of the A. S. Beck shoe salon (now Mysels Furs). In her fall, Vickey narrowly missed hitting a pedestrian from Willoughby, Ohio.

Bernie Rumsch stared in sickened disbelief. An ill-chosen remark . . . a thoughtless decision to go out for a shave . . . and now his life was in tatters. What could he say to the folks back home?

Jack W. Heyman, an engineer, said his daughter had expressed concerns about the impending nuptials, but he had talked it over with the girl, and she had decided to go through with it.

"She married that boy because she loved him and I know the boy loved her," Heyman said, but there was no ready explanation for Vickey's sudden and unexpected action.

The police dispersed the crowd. "Gwan' home now! Nothing more to see! Show is over." The Palmer House cleaning crew wiped the fresh bloodstains from the pavement. And, in only a few minutes the entire matter was completely forgotten in the hubbub of downtown Chicago on a warm Sunday night in June.

THE BOX TRICK: HOW THE GREENHORNS WERE ROBBED OF THEIR MONEY ALONG "GAMBLERS ROW"
November 23, 1880

Dearborn and Monroe Streets

Downtown Chicago in the 1880s was a haven for card-sharps, bunco artists and tinhorn gamblers blowing into town from Natchez to the Great Divide. In the years following the Civil War, the gentlemen of "the green cloth trade" found safe haven in the bosom of gambling boss Mike McDonald's empire of dice and cards on Monroe Street stretching between Dearborn and Clark

Streets. Games of chance were played long into the night at deluxe casinos like McDonald's "Store" at Monroe and Clark. For the convenience of the less affluent workingmen, the disreputable "dinner pail" resorts advertised crooked games of faro, roulette, hazard, and poker for only two bits. Chicago was a noisy, dusty, and congested frontier town in 1880, luring men of imagination, along with wily, unscrupulous cardsharps and mountebanks plumbing the lower depths. "Dance halls, concert saloons, and disreputable houses of every description abounded and flourished," wrote John Phillip Quinn of Chicago in the 1870s and 1880s. "Toughs of every grade walked the streets without fear; and the bunco men, brace dealers, Monte players and crooks of high and low degree openly plied their vocation." The bunco artists of the 1880s comprehended the foibles of human nature better than most men, and exploited the inherent weaknesses and greed of the "greenhorns" in clever and daring ways. The following dispatch filed by a Chicago Tribune *reporter for the November 24, 1880, morning edition provides a colorful and fascinating glimpse into one such con game luring the unsuspecting into a money trap along the downtown boulevard then known as "Gambler's Row." It is recognizable to modern-day Chicagoans as the Bank One Plaza.*

"Considerable amusement was created on the corner of Dearborn and Monroe streets yesterday afternoon by the antics of a young man who wore an air of overconfidence and great grief, as well as a butternut suit and big boots. He stood on the corner and poured forth his woes, at the same time clutching frantically at five little cardboard boxes, into which he peeped from time to time and then uttered prolonged wails of agony. Naturally, a crowd soon gathered and when an inquisitive spectator asked him to disclose the cause of his grief he did so amid great sobs. It appears that he had been 'taken in and done for' to the tune of 5 dollars on the 'Prize money pasteboard game.' This is a simple little game, yet wonderfully successful in catching greenhorns.

"An individual stands upon a street corner and proclaims to the crowd which soon gathers that he is in a great bonanza, that he is liberally rolling in wealth and is seeking an outlet for it in order to benefit suffering humanity, and the way he does it is this: He gets a lot of little pasteboard boxes, generally seven or eight in number, and in one he inserts a small piece of canceled revenue stamp that resembled a greenback. The other boxes are empty. The prepared box he places among the rest, and then he holds up to the startled and surprised gaze of the loiterers, a ten-dollar bill, and though not extending it far from his grasp, he

FAMOUS STREET CORNER CONFIDENCE GAMES IN LATE 19TH CENTURY CHICAGO.

gives them all a chance to see that it is genuine. 'See,' says the orator, 'you observe before me these seven little boxes. Now gentlemen—they are all empty, but—' and he suits the word by the action, 'I shall take one of them and in it I shall place this ten-dollar bill. I then, gentlemen, place the box back with the remainder,' — and does so, 'and mix them all up so; and now gentlemen, where once there were seven empty boxes, there are now six empty boxes and one that contains Uncle Samuel's note for ten dollars.' He then proceeds to state that he will allow any gentleman to take his pick of the seven boxes and select five, and if he gets this one containing the ten-dollar bill he may keep it, and all he has to pay for his five chances out of seven is a five-dollar bill.

"Now this game takes remarkably well among the gullible. As a matter of fact the ten-dollar bill is good, *but*—as a matter of fact, it never goes into one of those little boxes. A sleight of hand movement places the bill up the operator's sleeve, and then in mixing up the boxes, he manages to open it slightly, the one containing the canceled revenue stamp so that a piece of it is exposed, and the desired investor in the pasteboards observes it, thinks that the operator neglected to close the box effectively, and that the showing is unbeknown to him, and that there is a grand chance to 'coin a fiver.' He accordingly rakes around in his clothing, produces an original five, and handing it to the operator, takes his five boxes, opens them and finds that one contains the canceled stamp; the other four are blanks. Of course a series of blanks would be proper to give the expressions of the duped party in full, but he only has himself to blame for his loss."

Dearborn Street and Jackson Boulevard

A NOVEL WAY TO SUPPRESS CRIME: CLOSE THE BARBERSHOPS! THE BARBER'S REVOLT AT THE GREAT NORTHERN HOTEL
October 1895

In the days of horse-drawn streetcars and bicycles built for two, the Great Northern Hotel, located at the northeast corner of Dearborn Street and Jackson Boulevard in the heart of the downtown commercial district, towered above the busy thoroughfare with a quiet dignity befitting the famous eastern hostelries. In his book Chicago Interiors, *author David Lowe praised architect John Welborn Root for "carrying forward this brilliant economy of material first evidenced by Root in the Montauk of 1892 and brought to full fruition in the Monadnock designed in 1889." The Monadnock, an astonishing edifice on the opposite side of the street from the hotel, still stands. The Great Northern, an early example of steel and wrought-iron frame construction, does not. Erected in 1891 at a cost of $1.15 million, the Great Northern featured 500 guestrooms, 8 dining rooms, a cafe, 6 elevators, a barbershop that is the focus of this story, and a "plan of entertainment" that was "strictly European." Impressive in its graceful proportions and subtle beauty, the hotel was part of*

a larger complex featuring an adjoining theater and office building that last-
ed only until the mid-twentieth century. The Chicago White Sox baseball team,
owned and operated by Charles Comiskey, and the American League of pro-
fessional baseball clubs were both founded in one of the stately clubrooms on
the upper floors of the Great Northern on October 11, 1899. Before that pivotal
moment in local baseball history, there occurred a lesser known incident of
note, the arrest of fifteen barbers in open revolt against the civil authorities.
And what of the hotel where this infamy occurred? With casual disregard for
the passing of tradition and the Chicago school of architecture, the Great
Northern was thoughtlessly demolished in 1940. The playhouse and office
building were razed in 1961. Today, the twenty-seven-story Everett McKinley
Dirksen Federal Building, designed by Ludwig Mies van der Rohe, occupies the
site at 219 South Dearborn, where FBI men, U.S. attorneys, prosecutors, judges,
bailiffs, bondsmen, marshals, and clerks converge each day to confront the
more transcendent horrors of modern society reenacted in the criminal justice
system.

A series of general directives aimed at suppressing crime and moral turpitude in downtown Chicago in the fall of 1895 sparked widespread comment and
a near riot inside the barbershop of the Great Northern Hotel.

Fifteen barbers were hauled off to jail for thumbing their nose at a
Republican-sponsored blue law. The problem was traced to a recent escalation in
crime. It therefore followed that barbershops must be vicious and low places,
where idle men congregated to speak of sports, read the lusty newspapers of the
day like the *Police Gazette,* and muse over the charms of the opposite sex while
awaiting tonsorial work from one of Chicago's expert hair trimmers.

On October 20, Superintendent John J. Badenoch of the Chicago Police
Department, a civilian appointee of George Swift, the Republican mayor who was
alarmed over a sensational trolley-car robbery and a series of after-hours holdups,
ordered that every person observed walking the streets after midnight would be
arrested and brought to jail if he failed to provide a strict accounting of himself.
"All well-known thieves and crooks should be arrested on sight!" intoned
Badenoch, a former grain merchant and member of the school board. In 1895, a
person could be escorted to jail merely "on suspicion" if it pleased the arresting
officer.

The Republicans must have considered Sunday afternoons to be especially
perilous, for the state legislature had recently directed that all barbershops be

"STAYING AT THE

GREAT NORTHERN

HOTEL AND HAVING

A WONDERFUL TIME!"

closed out of respect for the Sabbath. The edict was met with a storm of furious protest coming from representatives of the Barbers Aid and Protective Association, who pointed out that Sunday was their most lucrative day.

Trying to enforce such a wretched law was another matter. A week later, fifteen barbers showed up for work at the Great Northern. Hearing of their affrontiveness, the chief dispatched his most able men to enforce the Sunday closing. Following a minor scuffle with Badenoch's bluecoats, the fifteen were marched over to the Bridewell, where they were each forced to post a $150 bond. You can well imagine the look of bemusement on the magistrate's face.

Reconsidering the matter sometime later, the judiciary declared the law unconstitutional, and the barbers were allowed to return to their chairs.

The lamentable Mayor Swift completed only one term of office. Badenoch, well-intentioned but lacking sound judgment, was turned out by the incoming

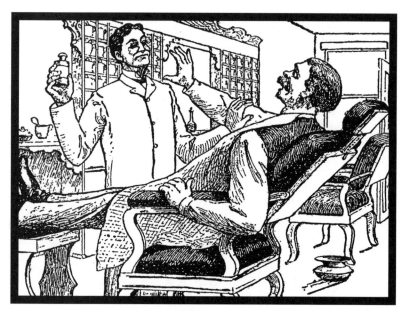

"BARBER'S REVOLT" AT THE GREAT NORTHERN HOTEL, 1895.

Democratic regime in 1897. Badenoch had fired every Democratic police officer left standing on the departmental rolls in 1895 (597 in all), only to suffer the ignominy of seeing them all reinstated by his successor, Joseph Kipley, two years later.

A shootout at the Everett M. Dirksen Building

THE VIOLENT AND TWISTED SAGA OF A "SUBURBAN BONNIE AND CLYDE"
July 20, 1992

The steel-and-plate-glass slab, named in honor of the gravelly voiced and flamboyant former U.S. senator from Illinois, is the crown jewel of Chicago's Federal Center Plaza in the South Loop. The Dirksen Building at 219 South Dearborn Street looks out on a fifty-three-foot Alexander Calder sculpture called Flamingo. *The artwork hardly resembles the common conception of a flamingo, but it provides a sense of balance to the spacious plaza adjacent to a low-rise post office, the Dirksen Center, and the John C. Kluczynski Federal Building, named after another longtime Chicago politico of note. The twin towers designed by Ludwig Mies van der Rohe, arguably Chicago's most influential architect of the postmodern age, were completed in 1975.*

Eight days before Jeffrey Erickson's suicidal flight from justice, his mother, June Erickson, asked her son's defense attorney, Richard Mottweiler, for a moment of his time. Mrs. Erickson had been carefully observing her Jeffrey's nervous mannerisms inside a Dirksen Building courtroom where he was on trial for a string of suburban bank robberies committed with his wife, Jill.

"Please tell the marshals that Jeff is talking unusual," the mother was quoted as saying. "I think he may try to make a run for it. He's looking around too much." Trusting a mother's instincts, the lawyer relayed her concerns to the U.S. marshal responsible for transporting federal prisoners to and from court each day.

Only after the bloody carnage had ended did questions begin to surface concerning the adequacy of courtroom security at the federal courthouse. How was Erickson able to breach the security of this supposedly impregnable fortress so easily? When asked, U.S. Attorney Fred Foreman refused to comment.

In 1991 the Chicago banking community was under siege. An unprecedented ninety-two stickups had occurred in the six-county metro area during the preceding twelve months, setting new standards, while the FBI and various suburban task forces doggedly pressed on.

The Ericksons were responsible for at least eight of these daring daylight bank heists beginning in January 1990 and continuing right up until the fateful moment on December 16, 1991, when Jeffrey was nabbed by FBI agents.

Erickson was seated in a stolen Mazda in a shopping plaza where Wise Road and Irving Park intersect at the south end of Schaumburg, that vast, unchecked suburban "mall sprawl" northwest of O'Hare Airport. The Ericksons' two-year crime spree, which would end in murder and suicide, brought to mind similar exploits of the famous southwestern "Dustbowl" desperadoes, Bonnie Parker and Clyde Barrow.

Jeff Erickson, an "all-American" boy from Morton Grove, Illinois, was an ex-marine who had served briefly as an auxiliary police officer in suburban Rosemont and Hoffman Estates from 1985 until 1987. Erickson was a uniform-and-gun nut, obsessed with motorcycles and firepower, but his departmental evaluations on his last job were substandard, forcing his resignation.

One shudders to think just how many other psychopaths with gun fetishes manage to slip through the testing safeguards and wind up out on the street in uniform.

And yet, while it seemed completely out of character for this type of individual to open a used book store and capably represent himself before a cerebral clientele of bibliophiles and Book-of-the-Month aficionados, Erickson was warmly regarded by his customers as well versed in the classics and possessing a superior mind.

Erickson closed his store on Mondays—setting aside that one day of the week to rob banks. He disguised himself with a phony beard, drove stolen Japanese imports, carried an assault rifle into the poorly guarded suburban banks, and threatened to kill everyone in sight who failed to cooperate. His adoring wife, Jill, whom he affectionately referred to as "Gorgeous," drove the backup getaway car.

The two of them were believed to have forged a "death pact." They would not be taken alive to face the sting of incarceration, and they had vowed to end their own lives if they were cornered by police or placed in a tight situation where escape was not possible.

Dubbed the "suburban Bonnie and Clyde" by reporters, the thrill-seeking Ericksons undoubtedly reveled in all of the publicity and media attention until the long arm of the law literally reached out and grabbed Jeffery by the collar, just before he could carry out his next bank job. FBI and suburban law enforcement had been tracking the couple's movements for weeks. A task force had been formed, and they had kept Erickson's Hanover Park apartment under twenty-four-hour surveillance.

Observing the arrest of her husband while seated behind the wheel of a battered Ford Econoline van, Jill Erickson whirled the vehicle around, deciding to make a run for it. She led the cops on a wild ten-mile car chase through the Northwest and Western suburbs, firing over her shoulder as she plowed through dense traffic with the Feds and as many as forty patrol cars in hot pursuit. The chase ended at Bear Flag Drive, a residential subdivision in Hanover Park.

Her tire shot out, and struck by police gunfire, Jill realized the hopelessness of her situation. Surrender was not an option. She turned the weapon on herself. It was lights out for the "Yuppie Bonnie Parker." She died at Humana Hospital that night.

Meanwhile, husband Jeff was hustled off to the Dirksen Building, where he was booked on federal bank robbing charges. In a newspaper interview just a few months later, the cynical and bemused ex-cop turned stickup man ridiculed the booking procedures and security lapses and recommended that the Marshal's Service conduct an emergency officer's safety training session. He boasted that it would have been easy for him to snatch a gun from the detention officer's holster and walk scot-free through the Dearborn Street revolving doors and into the safety of the pedestrian throngs.

"When I was fingerprinted they told me they were going to put me in prison for life. But the number one wrong thing to do they did. You never hand-cuff palms together, hands in front and that's what they did," Erickson said, literally diagramming for a reporter his intended plan of escape. The FBI, the Marshal's Service, and court security should have been paying closer attention, but they were not. "They put me in civilian elevators. That's how they take guys out of the lockup area."

There had been minor incidents before. In 1983, one Keith Garth Richardson held nine lawyers hostage and threatened to blow up the building with a bomb he claimed to have hidden in a blue duffle bag. Richardson eventually freed his hostages and gave up, but the hostage situation prompted the Feds to install airport metal detectors near the bank of elevators. Was it enough to forestall a similar attack?

The day of reckoning came on July 20, 1992—the sixth day of Erickson's criminal trial before Judge James Alesia of the U.S. District Court. At 5:30 in the afternoon, just as thousands of homeward-bound Loop office workers poured out of their offices and were on their way to the commuter train stations and CTA Rapid Transit lines, Erickson, dressed in a blue suit, was riding an elevator to the underground parking garage of the Dirksen Building from which he was scheduled to be transported to his cell in the Metropolitan Correctional Center (MCC), just a few blocks away.

While standing inside the garage elevator, Erickson managed to squirm out of his handcuffs and seize the firearm belonging to Terry Pinta, a female Deputy Marshal. He turned and fired two shots at deputy marshal Roy Frakes, who had no chance to defend himself. New to the job, Frakes collapsed to the floor with wounds to the head and back. He died at Northwestern Hospital less than half an hour later.

"I'm going to jail!" raged Jeffrey Erickson in a blind fury. "I'm going to jail! I'm going to die anyway! I'm going to take everybody with me!" Erickson raced through the garage toward the auto exit ramp leading out of the Federal Building and onto eastbound Jackson Boulevard with its dingy passport-photo studios and doughnut shops.

Standing between Erickson and freedom was Harry Belluomini, a retired thirty-one-year veteran of the Chicago Police Department, who had left the job with the rank of detective and an honorable career on the streets already behind him. At the time of the Erickson trial, he was employed by the General Security Services Corporation (GSSC) as a security guard. The Marshal's Service had hired GSSC to supply court security officers, and the government paid them an hourly rate, in what was widely seen as a cost-cutting measure.

Belluomini, who had earned many commendations in Chicago and was looking forward to retiring to Wisconsin with his wife once his Chicago house was sold, stood in the direct line of fire. Before he could release the safety, Erickson drew down.

Fatally wounded, Belluomini managed to fire off one round at the fleeing gunman with his dying breath. Erickson dropped to the narrow sidewalk, twenty-five feet shy of the street. Though his wound was probably not fatal, the bank robber realized that his last chance to escape was squandered. He had saved a final bullet for himself, thus fulfilling his end of the death pact made with Jill, whom he had adored.

Belluomini's quick reaction undoubtedly saved Judge Alesia's life. By coincidence, Alesia was driving out of the garage with his two sons the exact moment Erickson shot Frakes and bolted for the street. In all likelihood, the gunman would have attempted to commandeer Alesia's car or a civilian's car on Jackson Boulevard.

Harry Belluomini was cited for his heroism. The section of Dearborn Street passing the Dirksen Building was appropriately renamed "Harry Belluomini Way" by the Chicago City Council. The brown-colored sign is affixed to a pole that stands about five hundred yards west of the underground ramp where Erickson fell. Everyone agreed that Harry was a hero, and rightly deserving of every honor due him.

Milly Belluomini mourned the loss of her husband. She retired to Wisconsin, keeping faith with Harry's original plan for living out the "golden years" in the country. But without that added $515 a month, she was forced to take part-time waitressing and bartending jobs at the northern vacation resorts.

In their infinite wisdom, the U.S. Labor Department had decided to cut off her federal survivor benefits in 1996 on the dubious grounds that because a private security guard company had employed Harry at the time of his death, he was technically not an "officer of the law."

A hero who saved the life of a federal judge was thus reduced to the status of "rent-a-cop," the disparaging and condescending term often applied to private security guards by police unions and members of the rank and file.

How tragic. How typical.

HIGH FINANCE AND MISDEMEANORS: THE
DECLINE AND FALL OF THE CONTINENTAL BANK
1982–1994

LaSalle Street

and Jackson

Boulevard

(231 South

LaSalle)

Go now to the heart of Chicago's financial district; one block west of the Federal Building, to Wall Street in miniature, where wild speculation and cautious conservatism collide in unexpected ways, and where carefully laid plans and fanciful dreams of empire die hard. Behold the impressive Romanesque façade of the somber-looking, twenty-one-story structure looming over the intersection of LaSalle Street and Jackson Boulevard. It is for the moment the Bank of America, but over the magnificent Corinthian columns that tower above the main entrance, the name Continental Illinois Bank Building remains etched into the limestone, a less than subtle reminder that once, not so long ago, the most admired financial institution in America was headquartered here. During the palmy 1970s, Continental was the nation's sixth-largest bank, until greed, mismanagement, and shady dealings with a flim-flamming storefront banker in Oklahoma City killed the golden goose, and sent nervous federal regulators scurrying to the rescue with Uncle Sam's open checkbook in hand. The city block, spanning LaSalle from Jackson Boulevard north to Adams Street, has an interesting but checkered past. Following the devastation wrought by the Chicago Fire, architect John Van Osdel designed the temporary City Hall that stood on the southeast corner of Jackson and Adams from 1872 until 1885. Inside, a succession of Chicago mayors (at least one of them actually desiring to do something more for the city than hatch fresh grafting schemes with Mike McDonald) governed their flock through some hard economic times in the city's history. In 1885, when a more permanent City Hall was erected, the old building was razed to make way for the Rookery, designed by the renowned architects Daniel Burnham and John Welborn Root. The name is believed to have derived from the nineteenth-century slang term "rooking," connoting the corruptive acts of politicians and scoundrels so closely identified with McDonald's "Gaslight" Chicago. The Rookery at 209 South LaSalle (just north of Quincy Street, a narrow alley/street) is a preserved antique; one of the rare architectural gems from earlier times that has managed to survive the onslaught of city planners and wrecking companies in the modern age. In the 1980s, when the building was still owned by the Continental Bank and in desperate need of refurbishing, the $26.6 million required to restore the luster of the old Rookery was simply not available

*because of the precarious financial position the bank was in at the time. L. T.
"Tom" Baldwin III bought the property in 1987, and the restoration finally
went through. The Rookery was saved, to everyone's considerable relief. Next
door to the Rookery, the Continental Illinois Bank Building occupied the same
parcel of ground where the Illinois Trust and Savings stood in July 1919 when
the lighter-than-air dirigible* Wing Foot *crashed through the skylight roof,
killing thirteen people.* (Author's Note: *See pages 36–38 of* Return to the Scene
of the Crime *for a complete description of this tragedy.) Very few people outside a small circle of historians and Chicago trivia experts have ever heard of
the terrible gasbag disaster, but everyone in Chicago at one time or another
has probably cashed a check drawn on the Continental Illinois Bank. The
bank, a tottering giant that might have inflicted permanent damage on the
banking system of the United States were it not for an eleventh-hour bailout,
was the result of a series of complicated mergers in the 1920s involving several
powerful financial institutions, including the Illinois Trust and Savings Bank,
the Corn Exchange National Bank, and the Illinois Merchant's Trust Company.
In 1924, the present-day structure now housing the Bank of America was completed. The regal ostentation of the building is evident everywhere, from its elegant paneled offices to the Grand Banking Hall, and up to the second-floor
chairman's office, styled after a sixteenth-century English castle.*

I n the 1970s, when the rest of the country suffered under the strain of soaring gas prices, rampant inflation, a soft job market, and a general economic
malaise that the political pundits of the Nixon-Ford-Carter years labeled "stagfla-
tion" (stagnancy plus inflation equated to a decade-long hangover), the
Continental Bank was seen as a model of efficiency and resourcefulness, reflecting the unbridled confidence of its dynamic in tandem leadership.

While Mayor Jane Byrne, the erstwhile "snowstorm queen of 1979," was alien-
ating the Chicago business community and distancing herself from the coalition
of independents, African Americans, trade unionists, and lakefront liberals who
elected her to office, she kept the phone lines open to Continental Bank executives. Continental was the bank of choice on the fifth floor of City Hall, even as
Chicago's bond rating suffered its worst pounding since the Great Depression.

Under the aegis of Chairman Roger Anderson and President John Perkins,
who took over in 1973, the bank loaned more money to American business than
any other institution in the country, and often very unwisely.

In one famous incident that underscores the carelessness of Continental's

THE CONTINENTAL BANK BUILDING, LASALLE AND JACKSON.

loan department, a con man convinced the bank to front him several million dollars to build a suburban strip mall. After paying the first eight monthly installments on time, he asked the loan officer for an additional loan, which the banker, of course, was more than happy to give. Then, mysteriously after six weeks, the "developer" could not be reached. The only known phone number was disconnected, and urgent appeals sent certified from the bank were returned, "No such address." The police were called in, but it was already too late.

The developer had already flown the coop, along with several million dollars of Continental loan money in hand, leaving a worthless, overgrown weed lot as "collateral." The loan officer had never bothered to drive out to the suburbs and physically inspect the property where the proposed shopping center was to be built, nor had he done much more than the most cursory background check before approving the paperwork.

The bank was "bullish" on Chicago, and continued to gamble with rising and falling interest rates like a Las Vegas card counter unable to lay 'em down and walk away. When the rates plummeted in the late 1970s, the bank earned higher revenues from its loans than what it was paying for its deposits. But that could only last so long.

"Conservative but aggressive" was the shop motto—a cheerful phrase coined by Anderson and Perkins in better days. But Continental's house of cards soon came tumbling down. As interest rates climbed, the bank invested heavily in energy, agribusiness, and real estate, none of which held up well in the unfolding era of "Reaganomics."

Public scandal and a myriad of lawsuits were soon to follow.

A global recession in 1982, reflected in a worldwide reduction in oil demand and exploration, drove many of Continental's borrowers into bankruptcy, fueling demands for immediate accountability. The scandal that knocked Continental to the mat, however, accompanied the July 5, 1982, collapse of the little-known Penn Square Bank, located in a storefront location in an Oklahoma City shopping center. Continental acquired $1.05 billion in loans originated by Penn—many of them awarded to flimflamming, good-old-boy con men in cowboy getup, brandishing ten-inch cigars and unsecured collateral.

When Texas oil went bust, so did the bank, leaving Continental executive John R. Lytle to shoulder the blame. Continental began writing off $326 million in bad Penn Square loans.

Lytle, in charge of energy lending in Oklahoma, pleaded guilty to an indictment charging him with defrauding Continental of $2.25 million. The government accused Lytle of pocketing $585,000 in kickbacks for approving risky loan applications that any other banker would have tossed in the wastebasket. In 1988, the humbled executive was sentenced to three and a half years in a federal prison by Judge Milton Shadur. Lytle insisted that he was made the scapegoat for the bank's larger failures, which may be partly true.

Continental's problems went well beyond Lytle's deal-cutting with wheedling Texas oil plungers. Analysts pinned the disaster on the entire corporate culture, wherein the obscenely overpaid management elite placed a premium on gambling with other people's money in order to outshine the principal competition—in this case, the First National Bank of Chicago. Stockholders filed a class-action lawsuit charging that a coterie of privileged Continental insiders had deliberately misled investors about the bank's position.

In July 1984, the Federal Deposit Insurance Corporation (FDIC) bailed out the floundering Continental Illinois Bank for the second time in its history. Teetering on the precipice once before, the Reconstruction Finance Corporation stepped in and bought $50 million worth of the banks' preferred stock in December 1933, staving off a Depression-era calamity that would have set back the timetables of Franklin Roosevelt's National Recovery Act (NRA).

The situation was not nearly so dire in 1984, but a global run on the bank's assets in May of that year precipitated an FDIC restructuring. Fearing a collapse of the entire banking system, the government pumped $1 billion into Continental, and bought $4.5 billion in bad loans, thus acquiring 80 percent ownership. The rescue package drew fire from many quarters, not the least of which were the angry taxpayers forced to foot the bill for banking incompetence and greed. But the loyal Chicago gossip columnists were delighted to hear that John E. Swearingen, the retired chairman of Standard Oil, was signing on as chairman and chief executive officer of the new Continental.

Barely a day would pass in the 1970s and 1980s without some yawning mention of a charity ball, library fundraiser, or art gallery opening attended by John Swearingen and his table-hopping wife, Bonnie. The Swearingens were the closest approximation to royalty in a smokestack kind of town where grace, decorum, and a sense of style are often measured by the size of one's investment portfolio.

"John Swearingen is deservedly respected in the business community and should help to shore up Continental's reputation. Optimists will prefer to treat it as the first chapter in the story of Continental's rebirth," glowed the *Chicago Tribune* in an op-ed piece.

Neither Swearingen's inventive genius as a turnaround specialist nor the *Tribune*'s unfounded confidence in Continental's shaky future could safely deliver the bank to the threshold of the new millennium. On September 2, 1994, following months of negotiation, the San Francisco–based Bank of America Corporation completed its $2 billion buyout of Continental.

After 137 years in business, Chicago's oldest financial institution, organized back in 1857 by William Butler Ogden and Cyrus Hall McCormick as the Merchants Savings, Loan and Trust Company, ceased to exist. Size always mattered to proud old Continental, so it must have come as quite a shock to casual observers in 1994 when it was reported that Continental was dwarfed by the First Chicago Corporation. How the mighty had fallen.

Was it the end of the story, however, or just the beginning? If one is of a mind to subscribe to far-flung conspiracy notions, Sherman Skolnick, founder of the Citizens' Committee to Clean Up the Courts and a veteran Chicago community activist, alleges on his Web site (http://www.skolnicksreport.com) that Continental cultivated secret ties to the Papacy, the Royal Family of England, and Japanese gangsters (the *yakuza*) and may have even played a sinister, underhanded role in the plot to assassinate President Abraham Lincoln when the institution was still called the Merchants Savings, Loan and Trust Company.

Believe it . . . or not.

Northeast

corner of

Madison

and Clark

Streets

"SELL 'EM OR EAT 'EM." JIMMY "THE JOKER" HENNESSEY, LOOP NEWSBOY
1892–1932

In the good old days of Chicago journalism, let's say around 1910, when there were nine competing morning and afternoon newspapers in the city and the bloody circulation wars of that decade exacted a more human toll, Jimmy "the Joker" Hennessey was the most famous newsboy of them all. For nearly forty years, Jimmy managed to survive the gales blowing in from Lake Michigan, the heat of summer, and the attacks of the "bootjackers" (armed thugs who forced the dealers to buy one newspaper over another). His customers knew him as "Jimmy the Joker," a warm-hearted wiseacre who peddled his papers and clocked bets on the side underneath the lamppost at Madison and Clark Streets. The newsstand is long gone, of course. You will find a Loop office tower with a street-level UPS service center there now. But each little corner of Chicago has a story to tell, and on the northeast corner of Madison and Clark it happens to be Jimmy's story.

Jimmy Hennessey died a poor but contented man on March 8, 1932. It was the worst year of the Depression with bank failures galore and suicides reported every day in the newspaper.

The very same day the members of the Chicago Newsboys Association took up a collection to give Jimmy a decent burial, a forty-two-year-old Polish man named John Progdiuska hanged himself from a steam pipe in his basement at 4732 South Avers because a $286 tax bill had come due. He had been out of work for months and did not know how to pay the bill, or feed four hungry children. It was hard times, and people were desperate. Jimmy Hennessey made a fortune and gave it all away. If he had known Progdiuska, he might have helped him out, too. Money was always incidental to the larger joys of living, and Jimmy cheerfully donated his roll to whoever touched him for a loan.

Hennessey came to Chicago from Buffalo around the time of the World's Columbian Exposition—the 1893 World's Fair—when the city beckoned wayfarers and adventurers from around the globe. A stocky, ruddy-faced Irishman, Jimmy set himself up in business as a newsboy, hawking *Tribunes, Inter-Oceans,* copies of the *Daily News,* and a half-dozen other forgotten Chicago papers that came and went with the blink of an eye, and, of course, the racing scratch sheets.

Jimmy loved the ponies. With the money he saved from his newsstand, he bought an oatburner named "Babe." They said that Jimmy kept Babe inside his apartment, which was a lie, of course. Babe lived in a fancy stable on Illinois Street and pulled Jimmy's newspaper wagon to and from the post office. Babe never won a race. He turned out to be a better delivery horse than track thoroughbred. But Jimmy kept his customers informed about Babe's progress, and the morning line on the nags out at Hawthorne. It was considered good luck to buy a scratch sheet from Jimmy on race day.

Jimmy had an instinctive flair for the news business. He was the first dealer in Chicago to sell out-of-town papers, which he made available to customers at a second newsstand he opened at State and Monroe. Most of the old downtown crowd knew Hennessey simply as "Jimmy the Joker," because of his quick wit and the clever quips he told.

Jimmy's affairs were looked after by Alderman Michael "Hinky Dink" Kenna, boss of the First Ward and protectorate of the Levee vice district for nearly four decades. Kenna shielded Jimmy from harm when Andy Lawrence turned his sluggers loose on uncooperative dealers who refused to push the *American* over the *Tribune*. In those days, a dealer had "to sell 'em or eat 'em," or risk deadly reprisals. Many of the dealers were driven out of business. Jimmy the Joker persevered.

In his many years on the street, Hennessey amassed a small fortune— pegged at $100,000. With his savings, he bought two homes in Los Angeles for his sisters. Both of them died during the First World War. Later on he gave away his stand at State and Monroe to two old friends as a reward for their loyalty.

Jimmy lived alone in a rooming house at 348 North State. He was sixty-one years old when he suffered the unfortunate accident that cost him his life. He slipped and fell on an icy patch on stairs leading to a basement barbershop near the familiar lamp pole at Madison and Clark. His head struck the pavement, causing a fracture of the skull. The tab for his funeral was picked up by a female acquaintance who bought his papers every day. He had managed to outlive his horse Babe, who passed away two years earlier.

Calhoun Place, midway between Dearborn and Clark Streets

BILLY BOYLE'S CHOPHOUSE: A PLACE IN AN ALLEY TO EAT, DRINK, AND GAMBLE
1870s–1890s

Calhoun Place, named for Chicago newspaper publisher John Calhoun (1808–1859), isn't much to look at anymore. Once a street of gaiety, larceny, and occasional villainy, Calhoun Place is today a dreary back alley that bisects State Street and runs one way from east to west over to South Wacker Drive. Billy Boyle's Chophouse was situated between Dearborn and Clark Streets. That narrow little roadway, where Boyle's aged steaks and lamb chops satiated the palates of the Gilded Age's "sporting crowd," is flanked today by the Citibank skyscraper on the north and the 10 North Dearborn building on the south. Other than the occasional cursing garbage-truck driver attempting to navigate his rig through the sunless passageway in order to empty the trash dumpsters, I suspect that few Chicagoans are aware of this obscure little street, now more of an alley, or its picturesque history.

Billy Boyle, a flamboyant Irish restaurateur sporting an enormous walrus mustache, a large forehead, and a sad but penetrating gaze, drifted into Chicago from his home in Utica, New York, in the mid 1870s. Gambling was running wide-open up and down Monroe, Clark, and Madison Streets in those days, thanks to Harvey Doolittle Colvin, the mayor of Chicago who imposed a "liberal form of government" upon the populace following the puritanical reign of Joseph Medill, the blue-blooded publisher of the *Chicago Tribune*. Medill tried to impose Sunday closing laws during his short but unhappy term of office. Under Colvin, the Goddess of Chance was permitted to return, much to the chagrin of the church deacons, reformers, and Committee of Seventy (a group of laymen opposed to the open tolerance of vice).

Boyle was no puritan. He was a "showman of the culinary arts," and his instincts told him that gamblers, like anyone else, needed a good public house to repair to once the workday was over. And the end of the workday happened to coincide with the burning of the midnight oil.

Because there were only two all-night eateries in Chicago in the 1870s, Batchelder's on South State Street and Lonny Freeman's place out on the West Side, Boyle recognized a good hand when he saw one and was eager to cash in.

In 1878, or thereabouts, he opened his famous epicurean resort in back of the Chicago *Inter-Ocean* newspaper offices on Calhoun Place, just west of Dearborn Street. The eatery stood on the north side of the alley/street.

Thus, assured of a steady clientele of hungry overnight reporters from the good, gray Republican-leaning *Inter-Ocean*, who were sure to spread the word that Billy's steaks and chops were the finest in the Midwest, the business seemed destined to grow, and grow it did. Because so many wagering men from the first-class houses and the more infamous "gambling hells" scattered throughout the downtown area favored Billy with their after-hours presence, Calhoun Place became known far and wide as "Gambler's Alley."

Among the nightly habitués sipping brandy and smoking cheroots at Billy Boyle's place were pugilists, politicians, musicians, and showmen; just about everyone who was anyone, with one notable exception. Boyle did not permit the ladies to enter his restaurant. Undoubtedly he did not endear himself to a generation of feminists and suffragettes, but that was his rule, and he abided by it.

Among the more famous diners dropping by from time to time were the famous detective William A. Pinkerton, General Philip Sheridan, *Daily News* publisher Melville Stone, and the stage actor Edwin Booth. Nearly every late-nineteenth-century mayor of Chicago, with the exception of the teetotaling Medill, dined at Billy's at one time or another, and undoubtedly they found themselves seated within spitting distance of gambler boss Mike McDonald and his flock of roving cardsharps and tricksters. "Blind" John Condon; "Prince" Harry Varnell; Billy "the Clock" Skakel, who dabbled in Democratic politics; "Mockingbird" Whalen; Pat Sheedy; Kirk Gunn; and the four terrible Hankins brothers (one of whom was killed by a defective folding bed) were all regular customers.

Varnell, acting on behalf of the gambling fraternity, had the less than solemn duty of slating John "Bathhouse" Coughlin as the best candidate to represent their interests in the City Council during one particularly riotous bull session in Billy's second-floor loft during the 1892 electoral season. Politics and gambling were always the topics of conversation.

No steak was ever broiled for a customer unless it had hung at least six weeks in a refrigerator, and no smart-thinking customer dared challenge Billy on the quality of his meats. Mike McDonald, according to legend, preferred salt pork and truffles to the chops.

Boyle staked many down-on-their-luck gamblers to a free meal. He was a first-class sport, and a gentleman who tried in vain to keep the curse words to a minimum. His generosity, in general, knew no bounds. But when mounting public pressure forced Mayor Carter Harrison II to close down the last of the faro and roulette games still operating in the Loop after the close of the 1893 World's Fair, business conditions along Calhoun Place deteriorated. Billy moved his chophouse to the south side of the alley, but his debts were rising and creditors were calling in their IOU's, which totaled nearly $25,000. Times were changing, and the old crowd was drifting away.

Horseracing was the rage in the early 1890s, and a new generation of gamblers was busy fleecing the greenhorns out at the suburban tracks, abandoning the once fashionable downtown casinos of the 1870s and 1880s. When the sheriff arrived to wrest control of the restaurant from Boyle to satisfy a raft of creditors pressing their demands, the front door key could not be located anywhere. "This place hasn't been closed once in more than twenty years," Billy whispered, choking back tears.

The sport of kings was Billy's passion, but his horseracing debts to bookies and touts at every track finally forced him to take a position as restaurant manager at Chapin & Gore's on Monroe Street, arguably Chicago's most famous eatery of the "Gay 90s." But the Chapin & Gore crowd was slightly more reserved in manner than the raucous gamblers and show people he had known so well back in the palmy days of the "Alley." Later, Boyle managed a chophouse at Wabash Avenue and Adams Street. However, by this time, he was a nearly forgotten figure from the faded Gaslight Era. In 1916, Robert Sweitzer, an unsuccessful mayoral candidate, gave him a job in the Cook County clerk's office. Billy was broke and living with his niece. He had to do something to cover his outstanding markers.

Billy toiled anonymously in the clerk's office right up until the moment of his death on November 5, 1921. In the days and weeks following, Boyle and his chophouse were eulogized by the famous *literati* of the day. The venerable *Daily News* man and poet of the streets, Eugene Field, composed a tribute to Billy:

> It is likely that Boyle's has played in its quiet way a more important part in the history of the town than you might suppose. It was here that the lawyers consulted with their clients during the noon hour; politicians came hither to confer with one another and to devise schemes by which parties were to be humbugged. It was here that the painter and the actor discussed their respective arts; here too, in the small hours of the morning, the newspaper editor and reporters gathered together to dismiss professional cares and jealousies for the nonce, and to feed in the most amicable spirit from the same trough. Jobs were "out up," coups planned, reconciliations affected, schemes devised, combinations suggested, news exploited, and scandals disseminated, friendships strengthened, acquaintances made—all this at Billy Boyle's—as you see it would have been hard to find a better field in which to

study human nature, for here came people of every class and kind with their ambitions, hopes, purposes and eccentricities.

Southwest Corner, Calhoun Place and LaSalle Street, between Washington and Madison Streets

THE WHITECHAPEL CLUB: A PLACE OF PROMINENCE
1889–1895

J ohn Drury, an author and radio commentator who wrote eloquently about old Chicago houses in the days when there were still more than a few of them left standing, told his listening audience that in all his days he had "never found anything to equal the Whitechapel Club.

"It was the weirdest, most fantastic organization I ever heard of," he said, with an admiration generally reserved only for odd and eccentric curiosities dug out of sarcophagi or found in an emperor's tomb. "It even went to the extent of becoming gruesome."

Gruesome in a good-natured, gallows-humor way, of course. That was the reputation of the Whitechapel Club, founded by the literary wags and editorial geniuses of Chicago's "Fourth Estate" in 1889.

The literary scene in those days was dominated not by the brilliant minds of poets and essayists, but rather by the ardent spirits marking time in the city newsroom. Among the honored ninety-four welcomed into membership were Finley Peter Dunne ("Mr. Martin Dooley"); Brand Whitlock, who was later elected mayor of Toledo; poet and novelist Wallace Rice; *Tribune* cartoonist John T. McCutcheon; Frederick Upham Adams; Opie Read; Eugene Field; George Ade; and Hobart Chatfield Chatfield-Taylor, society dandy, world traveler, and a cofounder of the Society of Midland Authors.

The only entrance into the Whitechapel Club was through a heavy oak door leading into the basement of Henry Koster's Saloon, located at the southwest corner of Calhoun Place and LaSalle Street. This western exposure of Calhoun Place was then known as "Newsboys' Alley," out of respect to the reporters, cartoonists, and editors from the nearby offices of the *Herald* and the *Times* who gathered there. To the east, of course, was Boyle's Chophouse in "Gambler's Alley," serving a different sort of crowd.

Above the doorway of Koster's, a stained-glass window was inscribed with the chilling warning: "Abandon hope, all ye who enter here!"

The Whitechapel Club came into being a year after Jack the Ripper commenced his bloody reign of terror in the Whitechapel section of London. The archfiend of late Victorian society does not, however, seem to figure prominently in the name. Rather, it appears that the great public stir created by the murder of Irish nationalist Dr. Patrick Henry Cronin in Chicago in May 1889 inspired Charles Goodyear Seymour, a noted *Herald* sportswriter, and his colleagues on the crime beat to repair to a little out-of-the-way place where they could compare notes over lager and crackers. It was a fitting tribute to the hated English that these native sons of Ireland who made their living scribbling prose should name this place "Whitechapel."

Thus was born a true "blood-and-guts" drinking club, decorated by artifacts from the "Black Museum" of Chicago crime history. John Kelley, who covered the crime beat for many years, helped launch a Whitechapel tradition by donating a rare and unusual snakeskin, measuring twelve feet in length. Thereafter, members tried to outdo each other in ghoulishness by importing an astonishing array of revolvers, swords, hangmen's ropes, and even a spent bullet removed from the stiff corpse of "Doc" Haggerty, slain in a duel by "Bad" Jimmy Connerton, one of Chicago's most notorious Gaslight Era criminals.

A collection of skulls, said to be the prized possession of Dr. John C. Spray of the Elgin State Mental Hospital, were donated to member Chrysostom "Tombstone" Thompson to do with what he pleased. Dr. Spray had conducted a clinical study of the skulls of the insane to determine if there were differences in shape and size compared to the skulls of supposedly "normal" people. "Tombstone" let the members of the club decide for themselves by converting the skulls into globes for the gas jets by boring holes through the tops.

The most famous adornment bequeathed to Chatfield-Taylor and his merry men was the skull of "Waterford Jack," a post–Civil War madame who prowled the back alleys north of the Chicago River. Born Frances Warren around 1840, "Waterford Jack" supervised a stable of prostitutes. She was known among the habitués of Monroe Street as the "Millionaire Streetwalker," though a less flattering description appeared in the pages of the racy *Chicago Street Gazette*. Madame Waterford Jack was called a "pug-nosed, ugly-looking little critter."

A large table fashioned into the shape of a coffin was added to the clubroom. Here, amid the raucous sounds of laughter in the smoke-filled cellar reeking of spit and old beer, members sang a jolly chorus of "There'll Be Murder Here Tonight."

The club welcomed two future presidents, Governor William McKinley of Ohio and Theodore Roosevelt; the great bare-knuckles prizefighter John L. Sullivan; author Rudyard Kipling; and many other visiting celebrities to the weird

"GRUESOME IN A GOOD-NATURED KIND OF WAY." THE POETS AND PUNDITS OF THE
WHITECHAPEL CLUB, CIRCA 1890.

rituals and customs of the Whitechapel Club.

The laughter and merriment abruptly ended in 1892 when Koster moved down the alley to larger quarters. With the passing of *Chicago Herald* publisher James Wilmot Scott in 1895, the show was officially over. Scott had coughed up the necessary cash each month to pay the rent. Whitechapel members adopted a political platform calling for "No gas, No water, No police, No rent, No taxes." Scott respected that.

The corporate charter was canceled in 1902. Seven years later, Koster's original saloon was demolished in order to make way for the La Salle Hotel. The final death knell sounded in 1921 when the superior court of Cook County formally dissolved the club.

Years later, what was left of the Whitechapel Club—the grisly paraphernalia, the beer schooners, and the photos on the wall—was transferred to the lobby of the new LaSalle, where a "Whitechapel Pub" was opened in memory of those former times.

Avery Brundage, czar of the Olympic Games, was in charge of the La Salle Hotel at the time and had an appreciation for the absurd. By then, however, the Whitechapel Club was a dim echo of a lost age. Its famous members had all crossed the great divide, but memories were kept alive by Charles A. Dennis of the *Daily News*, who published his recollections in a thirty-six-part newspaper serialization in 1936.

Let us hope that the worthy Whitechapel men were greeted by more pleasant sites in heaven than leering skulls dripping candle wax in some dimly lit underground room.

139 North Wabash Avenue (Randolph Street and Wabash Avenue)

OH YES, SHE'S SHOPPING! FOR WHAT, A HORSE BLANKET?" THE COPS RAID A DOWNTOWN GAMBLING DEN
September 16, 1937

A stroll northeast through Chicago's emerging theater district leads us to a dilapidated five-story, bay-windowed building with supporting ornamental columns across the street from Marshall Field's department store. The facade of 139 North Wabash is sandwiched between the Fanny May Candy Store on the southeast corner and the Alfred Mossner Building two doors down. A "For Lease" sign is tacked to the empty storefront window. Dust and grime coat the glass. The upper floors appear to be empty. Obviously the structure has seen its better days and is a rather pitiful reminder (need we say it again?) that buildings pay a price for the infamous acts of their owners that occur inside.

A city election was on the horizon, and the incumbent Cook County State's Attorney Thomas Courtney needed a campaign issue to drum into the minds of the voters. The eternally ambitious prosecutor desired to step up in the world and challenge the incumbent mayor, Edward "Big Red" Kelly, patron saint of the Eleventh Ward Chicago Irish.

Courtney, identified as a friend of the crime syndicate by Shirley Kub, undercover investigator for the Chicago Crime Commission (see "J. Edgar Hoover in

A PRIVATE GAMBLING DEN

FOR THE LADIES WAS

HIDDEN BEHIND THE

ROMANESQUE COLUMNS

AT 139 NORTH WABASH.

THE BUILDING IS

BOARDED UP TODAY.

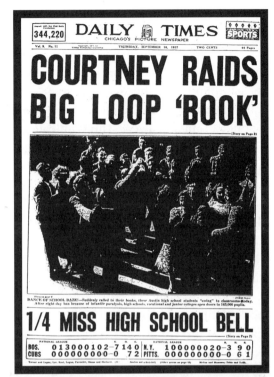

Uptown" in Tour 3), had turned a blind eye to illegal bookmaking during much of his time in office.

Therefore, it must have come as something of a surprise when the state's attorney put the mayor on notice that unless he did something to rid the city of its "gambling hells," he, Courtney, would close down every wireroom, betting parlor, and handbook in the city, one by one. Chicago's gambling rackets were worth a cool $11 million a year. The syndicate bosses squirmed. The politicians fidgeted.

Chief Investigator Dan Gilbert, tagged as "the Millionaire Cop" because of his many shrewd "investments," told the boys not to worry. "He's got a plan. That's all. Sit back and enjoy the ride."

Gilbert was a street cop. He knew the places around town that were hot and the ones that should be left alone. Accordingly, he tipped off his boss about a big game going down across the street from Marshall Field's. "Who's the operator?" Courtney demanded, knowing that the "independent" operations were always fair game.

"John P. Shaw," came the reply. "And there's more betting windows in that place than at Lincoln Fields!" Gilbert beamed. (Lincoln Fields was a thoroughbred track in south suburban Crete.)

"Who?" Shaw's name did not chime in Courtney's fertile brain. "Well then, go get 'em, Danny!" The splashy raid was guaranteed to pull a front-page headline in the *Daily Times*, a Democratic paper sympathetic to his aims.

Armed with a boatload of state's attorney police officers and a detachment of Chicago cops under the command of Captain Martin Mullen, the boys in blue barreled through the front door with guns drawn at the height of the afternoon rush hour, catching six hundred gamblers red-handed. The air-conditioned upstairs room was gaily decorated with oil paintings, stuffed sofas, and easy chairs.

Two-thirds of the patrons were women. Not the usual dime-a-dance floozies or B-Girl hustlers from the Rush Street nightclubs. Inside this "gambling hell," betting the grocery money at the two-dollar windows, were the housewives, young mothers, and elderly grandmas of Chicago. Many carried Marshall Field's shopping bags loaded with treasures from an afternoon of downtown shopping.

In the mass confusion of the raid, there were heard the anguished sobs of women being led away to the paddy wagon parked outside. "I can't stay here! I've got to get home and get my husband and children their dinners!" cried one unlucky bettor, elbowing her way past the crush of frightened women toward the door.

The raid was a spectacular triumph for the headline-hunting Courtney, who chuckled at the mayor's acute embarrassment the next day. And to think the big game was going only two blocks from his office in City Hall.

INSANE WRITER MURDERS A JUDGE
October 26, 1935

Clark

and

Randolph

Streets

With only slight exaggeration, it may be said that Randolph Street is indeed a street with a shadowy past—from its foot at Michigan Avenue, where Tribune *reporter Jake Lingle was cashiered by the mob in June 1930, to Des Plaines Street, where the Haymarket bomb claimed the lives of seven police officers in 1886. Infamous acts occurring inside the dimly lit interiors of theaters, wine rooms, honky-tonks, boarding houses, and even the anterooms of the most stately office buildings suggest that early patterns of criminal behavior are likely predictors of future ignominy. On every corner up and down the street, if you look hard enough, there can be found the faint footprints of horror stories from the past. This one concerns the murder of a shady ex-judge and a stalking gunman with a long memory, whose suicide note denounced all who would "ignore human principle." A murderous rampage in a public place is a contemporary crime. It jars our senses, especially when carried out with numbing precision. It is the kind of crime we hear about too often on the evening news. But it is not unique to this time and place or generation. Randolph Street provided the backdrop for such a Depression-era killer. The shooting of Judge William R. Fetzer occurred in the twelfth-floor corridor of the Ashland Block, one of the then most populous commercial centers in the Chicago Loop. The Ashland Block was an important early skyscraper, a fifteen-story Burnham & Root brownstone creation situated on the northeast corner of Clark and Randolph Streets from 1892 until 1949. It housed many lawyers, architects, and designers. The Justinian Society of Advocates, a legal fraternal association, was founded there on October 17, 1921. But in 1949, city planners ordered the Ashland Block demolished to make way for the Greyhound Bus Terminal, which would in later years become a seedy hangout for hustlers, down-and-outers, and criminal panderers. The bus terminal came to symbolize the blight that had overtaken the area around Clark and Randolph, and the once famous intersection was forced to relinquish its boastful title of "the World's Busiest Nightlife Corner." The Greyhound Bus Company abandoned the derelict terminal in the 1980s. It was eventually razed, and today Chicago Title and Trust occupies the gleaming new office tower standing on the site.*

Three attorneys were seated quietly inside one of the law offices fronting a bank of elevators in the center of the Ashland Block building. It was the noon hour, and the receptionist had just gone to lunch, when suddenly they heard the discharge of a gun coming from down the hall. Seconds later, the doors to the office were thrown open, and a red-haired man appeared, brandishing an automatic pistol.

The gunman marched through the unprotected outer office. Stopping short of an inner doorway, he drew down on Attorney William Hawthorne, who stared at the stranger in dumbfounded disbelief. Before Hawthorne had time to flee, two bullets pierced his back and head, and he fell to the floor mortally wounded. Bert Lannon slammed the door shut, while Charles Horgan, a veteran attorney who shared offices with the two men, frantically pushed pieces of furniture up against the door to prevent the shooter from entering the room.

"I grabbed the telephone and tried to get the police," Horgan patiently explained to the cops and a swarm of reporters who gazed down at the mortally wounded Hawthorne. "Then we heard another shot. After a moment we heard another shot and we opened the door cautiously—and there was the fellow who did the shooting lying on the floor."

Less than five minutes earlier, a forty-two-year-old epilepsy sufferer and ex-convict named Raymond Lanning had casually stridden into the twelfth-floor law offices of William R. Fetzer. "He asked to see the judge," said stenographer Florence Levy, who told him that Fetzer was tied up at the moment. The man in the brown-suede coat carrying a portfolio introduced himself and chatted pleasantly with Levy. He was calm and composed, providing no hint of the deadly rampage he was about to unleash.

When the unsuspecting Fetzer and a second downtown attorney named Nathan Weintroob emerged from the inner office, they were suddenly fired upon. Lanning discharged two of the eight bullets from his .32-caliber automatic into Fetzer before dropping the portfolio he had carried into the office.

Bent on carrying out wholesale slaughter, Lanning turned the gun on Weintroob. "You don't like me either, so I'll kill you, too!" he hissed. Lanning then raced down the hall, firing several errant shots before shooting Attorney Hawthorne.

When the smoke from this inexplicable rampage had cleared, Lanning was removed to the Bridewell infirmary, where doctors removed a suicide note from the dying man's pocket. His motive was easy to ascertain. "A too severe judge,

PHOTODIAGRAM

OF THE

SHOOTING

RAMPAGE

INSIDE JUDGE

FETZER'S

ASHLAND

BUILDING

OFFICE.

sticking to the letter of the law and ignoring human principles, has taken my life," Lanning wrote, "his own through me, and the lives of several others, perhaps, through me. I too, am severe, cruel now, because I find the majority of people that way."

Judge Fetzer, who had sentenced Lanning to the Bridewell six years earlier for criminal assault with a knife, now became the victim of the vengeance killer, who had had the time and the inclination to obsessively brood over past injustices.

Raymond Lanning, who had a record of petty criminal offenses, had been released from the custody of the psychiatric ward only a few weeks earlier. During his long period of incarceration, he blamed his epileptic seizures on Fetzer. Lanning had composed a convoluted eighty-five-page typewritten autobiography titled "Rust," which he eventually hoped to publish with a respected New York literary magazine.

A 1932 CHICAGO REAL ESTATE LISTING SHOWS RETIRED JUDGE WILLIAM FETZER MAINTAINING LAW OFFICES IN ROOM 601 OF THE ASHLAND BLOCK. A GLEAMING NEW OFFICE TOWER STANDS ON THE SITE TODAY.

The title was symbolic of Lanning's perception that Fetzer was "eating away" at his life. Lanning referred to himself in the third person as "Rusty." In his rambling "eye-for-an-eye" tome, the killer vowed to carry out the assassinations of Chicago Mayor Edward J. Kelly, Judge Fetzer, and anti-vice crusader Reverend Philip Yarrow, as well as the destruction of the Union Stockyards by an arson fire he alone intended to ignite.

Whether or not Lanning intended to see these terrible acts through or if they were just the wild fantasies of a demented mind will never be known.

Lanning's sister Gloria told police that her brother had been subject to seizures ever since his wartime service, and she related that he acted queerly at times, but had never spoken with animus toward Fetzer. "He was brilliant and had done a lot of writing," she said. "But," she sighed, "that's the way Ray wanted it, so it's better that he died."

It was all too familiar a lament, repeated over and over again by bewildered and grief-stricken relatives to generations of cops and reporters who had been given the unenviable task of piecing together the essential facts of a gun tragedy.

William R. Fetzer was elected Seventh Ward alderman in 1917 after a bitter election fight with Professor Charles E. Merriam, a failed reformer and political idealist from the University of Chicago. With the backing of downtown political hacks loyal to Mayor William Hale Thompson, Fetzer was declared the winner by just *three* votes following a recount.

A political satrap bought and paid for by the corrupt demagogue Thompson during his mayoralty in the ragged Prohibition era, Fetzer was elected to the municipal court bench in 1920. He was at best a machine judge of dubious distinction, drawing the ire of the Chicago Crime Commission and the Chicago Bar Association for discharging syndicate hoodlums and a suspected bomber in possession of one hundred pounds of dynamite.

In 1921, observing the proceedings in Fetzer's "Branch 27" courtroom, a Crime Commission court watcher keeping tabs on suspected judicial bribe takers noted: "The judge uses technicalities as a pretense to excuse guilty persons. Judge is too lenient. So many fixers are so prominent that city prosecutor Bombaugh in the court said that he was ashamed of it."

A rumor gained currency that the distinguished and grandfatherly Fetzer was a "syndicate judge," a mob mouthpiece who protected bigshot hoods from prosecution, while throwing the book at small-fry crooks like Lanning, in order to build a formidable, but mostly false, image as a dedicated crime fighter and friend of the people for the benefit of the Cook County electorate.

The judge earned the nickname "Cash Register" Fetzer for payoffs received from professional bondsmen loitering inside his chambers. For this and other misdeeds during his twelve years on the bench, he was often subjected to "severe criticism" from Chief Justice Harry Olson. Fetzer discharged scores of syndicate hoodlums accused of racketeering and running gambling operations in the vice-ridden Maxwell Street Police District, where the "Terrible Genna Brothers" gang held sway. In September 1930, Fetzer received unwanted publicity for a decision in which he held that betting on a horserace was not a game of chance but of skill.

At his death, the gentlemen of the press described "Cash Register" Fetzer's judicial career as a "stormy one." They probably suspected that his judicial idiosyncrasies were far from the respectful review of his life and times and guarded praise that they were forced by their editors to heap on the slain judge.

Fetzer was accorded full Masonic honors at Oakwoods Cemetery on the South Side and mourned by friends and colleagues alike. Death has a way of elevating sinners to saints.

151 West

Randolph

Street

SEALED LIPS AND THE KISS OF DEATH: MURDER AT THE RKO PALACE

February 25, 1942

Mayor Richard M. Daley is understandably proud of the ongoing revitalization of Randolph Street from State Street west to Franklin. The dedication and grand reopening of the Ford Center for the Performing Arts/Oriental Theater in 1998 signaled an exciting and glorious rebirth of Chicago's once flourishing entertainment district, which had sadly deteriorated once the marquees of the famous movie houses and former vaudeville theaters lining Randolph Street darkened in the 1960s and 1970s. The Greyhound Bus Terminal and a depressing collage of $3 steak houses, pinball arcades, and wholesale electronics dealers sprang up like ugly weeds in a dying rose garden. Their appearance in the 1950s and 1960s slowly choked the life out of a once vibrant east-west corridor of live entertainment. Pushing forward with his plan for the creation of a new Chicago theater district to restore the nighttime luster to the Loop, Daley and his city planners were beaming when the reincarnated Cadillac Palace Theater finally opened inside the Hotel Allegro (formerly the old Bismarck Hotel) in December 1999 with the musical Aida. *Renovation costs were pegged at a cool $20 million. The Cadillac Division of General Motors graciously purchased the naming rights for an unspecified sum. After all, it* was *the Palace, and a Cadillac is still the symbol of American automotive luxury. What better imprimatur than the Palace, the most regal-sounding name in the show-biz galaxy, to promote a line of cars? Until you played the Palace you were nothing, or so Judy Garland would have had us all believe. New York had a Palace, and for many years so did the city of Chicago. In its heyday, the RKO Palace (housed inside the Bismarck Hotel on the southeast corner of Randolph and LaSalle) featured a succession of vaudeville acts, newsreels, and first-run movies. Opened in October 1926, the majestic old theater was the flagship of the Orpheum circuit until first-run motion pictures supplanted vaudeville in 1931. The theater featured an orchestra, dress circle, and balcony, and was*

modeled after Louis XIV's Palace of Versailles in France. In 1942, for sixty
cents, a patron could spend the entire day or night at the movies and never be
rousted by an usher or a floorwalker—one reason why many of the small-time
crooks and gunmen on the lam hid out inside the downtown movie houses.
With the disappearance of the RKO studio name in the 1950s, Emil and Karl
Eitel added their names to the marquee. In the final two years of its existence,
the theater was simply known as the "Palace," advertising three projectors,
twenty-seven speakers, and Cinerama, a 1950s wide-screen innovation.
Despite modern advances, the venerable old Palace Theater closed in 1962,
reopening a few years later as the "Bismarck," which featured a mix of movies
and live performances. Sadly, the Bismarck did not last, and when the entire
operation closed down in the 1980s, it signaled a profound shift in the public
taste away from spending Saturday evenings in the city to spending Saturday
evenings at dull suburban cineplexes. Maybe when all is said and done, the
Palace had a curse attached to it, suggesting once again that where infamy
occurs, bad luck is certain to follow. The popcorn matinees invited all types of
scoundrels with evil intentions, and sometimes bad things happened to the
unsuspecting—even inside a once glorious Palace.

I n the shadows of the darkened Palace Theater a teenage suitor kissed his sweetheart goodbye then killed her in a jealous fit of rage. "Why did you do it, kid?" asked Coroner A. L. Brodie hours later. The shooter, seventeen-year-old Clarence McDonald of west suburban Berwyn, was pensive. He ran his fingers through his brilliantined hair and answered: "I killed her because I didn't want anyone else to have her."

As McDonald combed his wavy hair, a squinty-eyed Chicago cop leaned over and whispered to the boy, "It's too bad when they have to cut that hair off!" The cop was referring to the standard procedure of shaving a condemned man's head before walking the final thirty paces to the electric chair.

McDonald was suddenly contrite, now that he had had time to think about the *real* reason he had decided to fire a .38-caliber slug into the side of pretty Dorothy Broz seconds after kissing her goodbye in a final gesture of love.

McDonald, a handsome blond youth, and Broz, a schoolmate of McDonald's at J. Stirling Morton Township High School in Cicero, had been dating off and on. Citing religious differences and a loss of interest, the pretty high schooler decided to call off the romance and abandon any premature promises of marriage that she had made to McDonald. Bright and ambitious, Dorothy had turned her atten-

P RETTY D OROTHY

B ROZ NEVER MADE

IT TO GRADUATION

DAY.

(Photo courtesy of Tamara Shaffer)

FULL OF REMORSE,

C LARENCE

M C D ONALD WENT

ON A HUNGER

STRIKE INSIDE

HIS JAIL CELL.

(Photo courtesy of Tamara Shaffer)

THE PALACE

THEATER,

CIRCA 1925.

FEBRUARY 1942 ADVERTISEMENT

FOR "SEALED LIPS" SHOWING AT

THE RKO PALACE.

DETECTIVES PREPARE TO TRANSPORT DOROTHY BROZ FROM THE PALACE THEATER

BALCONY TO THE COUNTY MORGUE.

(Photo courtesy of Tamara Shaffer)

tion to college. She planned to attend either the University of Chicago or Steven's Beauty College in the Loop.

It was common knowledge in the hallways of Morton High that McDonald did not take kindly to the rebuff, and on one earlier occasion had pointed an unloaded gun at Broz inside Lanke's ice cream store in Cicero. In a fit of anger, he had also allegedly punched her in the face. And two weeks before the tragedy, McDonald had placed a $5 bet, wagering that Dorothy "would never graduate." "Just kidding—a joke, that's all," the youth said with a chuckle.

The murder weapon was stolen from the Great Western Railway freight yard where McDonald had been employed as a messenger during the previous Christmas holiday.

Apparently unconcerned about McDonald's aberrant behavior toward her, the trusting girl made a date with him to attend a downtown matinee. They left the high school campus at 12:45 P.M., arriving in the Loop about a half-hour later. Dorothy and Clarence killed time until the next show by browsing for sweaters at the Carson Pirie Scott department store at State and Washington. They walked over to the Palace at two o'clock, just in time to catch the matinee-showing of *Hellzapoppin'*, a rollicking, slapstick comedy starring Martha Raye and Olsen & Johnson, a nationally known vaudeville act.

As they sat together in the lower balcony in the midst of fifteen hundred other movie patrons, McDonald coolly cradled his loaded .38 inside his left suit pocket, waiting for the right moment. At 4:26, following a *March of Time* newsreel, the film noir crime picture *Sealed Lips* rolled through the opening credits. Two minutes later, amid the clamor of an onscreen depiction of a prison riot, McDonald planted a firm kiss on Dorothy's sealed lips and pressed the .38 into her left side.

The girl's sudden scream was barely audible above the movie gunshots and mayhem. "My God! He's got a gun!" Then a muffled shot, and the girl slumped over. McDonald composed himself and quietly retreated to the upper balcony where he blended in with the crowd. Lingering for just a moment, he then made a hasty retreat down the stairs and exited through an alley door before the audience could fully comprehend what had just happened. Eyewitnesses told police that they assumed it was just a promotional stunt tied in with the whiz-bang, shoot-'em-up antics in *Hellzapoppin'*. By the time the police arrived to seal off the exits, the killer had fled.

McDonald caught the Douglas line elevated train at Quincy and Wells (the antique train station still stands, a block west of the Rookery Building) and returned to his sister's home. Feeling no guilt, or simply dazed by the awful knowledge of what he had done, the boy took in another double feature at the

Olympic Theater in Cicero with a schoolmate companion before retiring. He concealed the murder weapon in the garage behind the house.

The expected knock on the door came at 3:45 the next morning after police had questioned girlfriends of the deceased.

Police learned from the accused's sister that McDonald's family life was in shambles. Clarence's father hanged himself inside the Marquette District Police Station on September 3, 1936, after he was accused of raping his thirteen-year-old daughter, Phoebe. Police feared that Clarence would follow his father to the grave in a similar fashion following his arrest. "There's nothing more to live for since Dottie's dead," he wailed after the tough Chicago detectives helped strip away his bravado.

Put on a twenty-four-hour suicide watch, McDonald was taken back to the Palace the next morning, where he was forced to reenact the shooting for the benefit of police, reporters, and the county coroner. That was standard police procedure in those days. Afterward, the boy gave a full confession to Captain Thomas Duffy in the interrogation room of the First District Police Station. He said that he had thought about "doing away" with Dorothy for three days before he actually worked up enough nerve to pull the trigger.

After the dead girl's indignant uncle punched the killer in the face during the inquest, McDonald's sister, Mrs. Robert Wagner, pleaded for sympathy and understanding. "He was full of hate and anger and it grew in him until he had to get it out some way. He was taunted by a relative who repeatedly told him, 'Your father was insane and killed himself. Someday you will be insane too!'"

Jaded by one too many homicides, the Chicago press corps dubbed the teenage killer, "Kiss of Death" McDonald. Before the grand jury, the boy's lawyer described his client as "a seventeen-year-old Penrod gone berserk." (Penrod was the incorrigible boy created by Booth Tarkington.)

Penrod he wasn't, but Clarence McDonald was obviously a troubled youth who was a puzzle to the psychiatrists who testified for the both the defense and the State during the trial.

The jury convicted him of murder on May 22, 1942, setting the penalty for the crime at life in prison. Clarence McDonald served eighteen years of the original sentence at the Pontiac, Illinois, reformatory before receiving parole on March 17, 1961.

188 West

Randolph

Street

HACKED TO DEATH IN THE SHADOW OF CITY HALL
October 8, 1948

The Randolph Tower is a weather-beaten downtown office and apartment building that has seen better days. Built in 1929, it stands like a silent sentinel directly across the street from the Hotel Allegro and the newly refurbished Palace Theater. It is one of the few vintage graystone Gothic-revival skyscrapers still remaining. People have rushed by the building every day without giving it much thought. That is until February 2001, when the City of Chicago called the Randolph Tower a "danger zone" and ordered protective netting installed over the seventeen top floors in order to protect pedestrians below from falling chunks of terra cotta. Telegraph Properties, the current owner of the building, was dragged into court by the City in an effort to compel them to vacate sections of the upper floors. In March 2001, the City closed Wells and Randolph Streets and the adjacent el lines because of the hazard, causing tremendous inconvenience. I am sure the time is fast approaching when the wrecking ball will batter down the Randolph Tower, and a gleaming new hotel high-rise with an atrium and five salad-bar–fitted bistros financed by a politically connected North Michigan Avenue real estate consortium will arise in its place. Until that day arrives, we will remember the Randolph Tower as the unfortunate location of one of the most grisly and stupefying election-year murders in the long history of the seamy criminal alliances and dealmaking forged between gangland heavies and their vassals in local government. It is hard to predict just how far William John Granata might have advanced in state Republican politics if only he had the good sense to look over his shoulder before attempting to enter his building through the revolving doors at 188 West Randolph Street. If he had lived, he might have attained far greater political rewards as a future Illinois governor or senator. Or maybe the gods would have made it impossible for him to escape from his destiny as another victim in a long line of unsolved mob homicides. Go there now and step back through time, past the same set of revolving doors where Granata met his doom. On the exterior wall of the building, there is an advertisement for the "Randolph Athletic Club, 27th floor, founded 1927." As it was in Granata's day, there is a doorman waiting to welcome you.

It was shortly after midnight when two vicious swipes from an assassin's meat cleaver split open William Granata's skull and cut his jugular vein. Collapsing to the pavement, the forty-two-year-old Republican candidate for circuit court clerk gasped for air. Words formed in his mouth, but no one inside the Randolph Tower could hear him. At this late hour, the normally busy intersection of Wells Street and Randolph was virtually deserted. A full five minutes would pass before the Tower elevator man, Nick Salm, came to his rescue. By that time, blood covered the sidewalk and it was too late. William John Granata was dead upon arrival at Henrotin Hospital.

Granata's twenty-eight-year-old wife, Violet, babbled incoherently when she gazed at his lifeless form prostrate on the emergency room operating table. "It should have happened to Sheriff [Elmer] Walsh and not him!" she shouted, referring to her husband's friend and political sponsor—the only political figure in Cook County history to ever defeat Richard J. Daley in a head-to-head election.

Granata had effectively managed Walsh's election win over the up-and-coming Dick Daley who would eventually rule Chicago as mayor for twenty-one years. "I can't imagine what she meant," the sheriff said later. "William Granata was a clean-cut fellow if there ever was one. Granata was a capable lawyer. He and his brother Peter C. are powerful in West Side politics. I'm at a complete loss as to why anyone would want to kill such a fine fellow."

The cops were in a perpetual fog. Chief of Detectives Walter Storms assigned twenty of his best plainclothesmen, but mob murders of this kind are never solved in Chicago, either through design or outright incompetence.

To say that the Granata brothers were a "power in West Side politics" understated their importance. William's rise to prominence paralleled the immigrant struggles of many dirt-poor Italians living in the Hull House section of Chicago's Near West Side. When barely past his fifth birthday, young Granata was sent to work peddling newspapers at Van Buren and Franklin Streets, while his widowed mother, Rose, carried on her late husband's import-export business from inside the family home on Forquer Street in the poorest section of the Italian quarter.

William completed his law school studies at De Paul and Northwestern, becoming active in Republican politics at an early age. Clinging to the coattails of his older brother Peter, who was elected to the state legislature from the Seventeenth District, Granata in 1940 received a patronage appointment from Governor Dwight Green to lead the Illinois Industrial Commission. At the time of his sudden demise, he was the Republican committeeman of the Twenty-seventh Ward—an enormously important post in city politics, because the committeeman controlled all of the jobs and local appointments.

Before thousands of poor southern blacks (who began pouring into Granata's Twenty-seventh Ward in the 1940s) finally had had enough and elected candidates more favorable to their interests, the district was a "political plantation," a stamping ground for syndicate hoodlums, and a bloody battleground that had already witnessed the assassination of one aspiring African-American politician named Octavus Granady.

In order to maintain their tenuous grip on power, the Granatas forged an uneasy alliance with the West Side Bloc, a cabal of gangster-politicians who controlled patronage, appointments, gambling games, and vice interests in nine crucial West Side wards from the era of Al Capone up through the 1970s. The bloc sponsored Democratic aldermen in Chicago and Republican legislators down in Springfield who were favorable to their interests. The bloc consistently voted down any piece of legislation threatening to curb vice conditions in Chicago. Political designations were largely meaningless in those days, and those who stood in the way of the syndicate were dispatched to another world.

Operating through the First Ward of Chicago, the "Blocsters" delivered large pluralities to cooperative politicians willing to "play ball." State Representative James Adduci, arrested eighteen times between 1920 and 1934, was the boss of the Seventeenth District for the West Side Bloc mobsters. Adduci, a close friend of hoodlum "Dago" Lawrence Mangano, was elected to the state house for the first time in 1934.

While brother Peter cooperated with Adduci—up to a point—William Granata hedged his bets. According to author Ovid Demaris in *Captive City*, Adduci's brother Joe had warned Granata that his leanings toward reform were not appreciated. "Watch yourself, you're getting too big for your pants!"

The police recovered a list of thirteen names from inside the dead man's pocket. The "mystery list" created quite a stir in the morning papers, but any hope the cops had of identifying the killers was quashed by Sheriff Walsh, who reported that the names were those of "special deputy sheriffs" sponsored by Granata.

RANDOLPH

TOWERS: AN

OLD MURDER

AND FALLING

TERRA COTTA.

(Photo by author)

The awarding of badges and guns to unqualified political hacks and civilians who generously donated to the sheriff's election campaign was a time-honored tradition in Cook County, predating Walsh and continuing through the 1990s.

The police interrogated Granata's chauffeur, Amoth C. Cope, a Republican precinct worker with a petty criminal record who was the last person to see his boss alive. Cope told the cops that he had driven Granata to several dances and political rallies in three West Side wards that night before dropping him off in front of the Randolph Tower, where he maintained an apartment with his wife and four-year-old son on the forty-second floor. "Granata got out in front of his place, waved to me, then crossed the street for his paper. I drove to Ogden and Madison for coffee and later dropped into several Madison Street taverns to talk with my precinct workers."

Three men in a black sedan were observed cruising around the block shortly before Granata was slain. A twelve-inch butcher knife left behind by a "mystery woman" was found by three youths in the back seat of a taxicab at Randolph and Wells minutes after the murder. Police determined that the knife was not the actual murder weapon, but it may have been one of several that had been taken along just in case something went wrong in the planning of the execution. The coroner determined that the instrument of death was a "bayonet-type weapon" wielded by a powerfully built man. That man was never found.

These were the only tangible clues to emerge from the month-long investigation into the slaying, but they bolstered the belief that the killing was somehow linked to the Granata brothers' unwillingness to trade votes and grant influence to Jake Guzik and Paul "the Waiter" Ricca, who had marshaled control of the Capone syndicate following the suicide of its second boss, Frank Nitti, in March 1943.

It was business as usual in Chicago. Within a few weeks of the murder, Granata's driver, Amoth Cope, set aside personal differences and went to work for Adduci as his full-time chauffeur and lackey.

Representative James Adduci, Peter Granata, and the West Side cabal ruled their fiefdoms for many more years, until their power base was eroded by increasing numbers of African Americans and Hispanics who refused to elect any more white hoodlum politicians to office.

"THE MOTION TO FIX." THE LAW OFFICES OF BIEBER & BRODKIN
Prominent from the 1920s through the 1970s

Mike Brodkin was the cautious procedural member of the team. His law partner, George Bieber, was a Rush Street first-nighter who lavished his enormous expense account and legal fees on booze, broads, and Châteaubriand in Las Vegas, Miami Beach, and Hollywood. Brodkin spoke with a heavy Chicago neighborhood accent and came up the hard way. Bieber, on the other hand, was educated, refined, and a real man about town, who always operated on the premise that life is too short and you could wind up on the slab any moment if you weren't careful. Bieber was no fool. He had seen firsthand what happened to Bill Granata, the ruler of the West Side "Patch" and a fellow tenant in the Randolph Tower.

Taking into account the rogues gallery of gangsters, con men, and hoods that these two represented during their storied fifty-year partnership, it's no wonder Bieber chose the life of *bon vivant*. As "Paddy" Bauler wryly observed, "What's it all mean? Nuttin'! All you get out of life is a few laughs."

The enormous political clout this "Burke & Hare" of local jurisprudence wielded, with their ability to suborn judges and influence editorial coverage of their cases, was no laughing matter to federal prosecutors. Paul Newey, chief investigator for the late Benjamin Adamowski, Cook County state's attorney from 1956 to 1960, blames them for the failure of the reformers to mend the tattered cloth of Chicago municipal government.

"They *invented* 'the motion to fix.' When Brodkin heard that he was going to be indicted," Newey recalls, "he conveniently set fire to his office at the Randolph Tower. All the files we needed to prosecute were destroyed and that ended the case against him."

Attorney Robert J. McDonnell, former husband of Antoinette Giancana and legal counsel for many top hoodlum leaders during the salad days of the late 1950s and early 1960s, said that the B & B Boys' influence extended all the way into the Illinois Supreme Court, where they "controlled" two justices.

After Ben Adamowski charged Bieber, Brodkin, and fellow "B-Boys" Herb Barsey, Charles Bellows, and Harry Busch with receiving "special treatment" from Cook County judges, George Bieber in characteristic high dudgeon replied: "That's a lie! I gotta go now. I'm due in Felony Court to file a motion to fix!"

In a letter to the Chicago Bar Association, Adamowski calculated that between them, the five "B-Boys" handled 98 cases in the Cook County Criminal Court from September 2, 1958, through July 30, 1959. Of these 98 cases, 74 were tried before the same four judges. Half of them were assigned to Judge Joseph A. Pope, censured by the Chicago Crime Commission for leniency in cases where the crime syndicate had a vested interest.

George Bieber grew up in world of racketeers, union sluggers, and political fixers. He remembered the ".38 Caliber Circulation Drive" of 1910, when William Randolph Hearst and his Chicago business manager, "Long Green" Andy Lawrence, sent into the field a paid army of street toughs to harass and intimidate newsdealers refusing to carry the morning *Examiner*. Lawrence employed the terrible Gentlemen brothers, Gus, Peter, and Dutch, and a young up-and-comer named Dion O'Banion to wreak havoc on *Tribune* delivery trucks and news-stands. "Our job was to dump over the other guys' delivery trucks," Bieber happily reminisced with Eddie Baumann.

The famous partnership of Bieber and Brodkin was launched during Prohibition days when they filed a damage suit on behalf of William "Billy"

BEMUSED MOBSTER

SAM "GOLF BAG"

HUNT (LEFT)

AWAITS GEORGE

BIEBER'S "MOTION

TO FIX."

Skidmore, a West Side horse-and-wagon junk peddler who was much more powerful than his humble pushcart business would suggest. Skidmore was a master fixer, professional bondsman, and political wheel horse with links to the police commissioner, the mayor, and the entire gambling apparatus of Cook County, numbering ten thousand street bookies.

"Boys, how would you like to go to work for me?" Skidmore's word-of-mouth referrals put the B & B Boys in business, representing dice shakers and syndicate whores in vice court. It was low-end work, but the word soon got around that the B & B Boys could fix anything that needed fixing. They traded on the weaknesses of human nature and bribed greedy prosecutors and judges with great skill. Every hoodlum of consequence called on them sooner or later. Mike Brodkin was riding along one night in 1944 when Jake "Greasy Thumb" Guzik was pulled over and dragged from his car outside Willow Springs by rival gangsters. Brodkin negotiated the $250,000 ransom and served as an honorary pallbearer when Guzik passed away in 1956.

Bieber and Brodkin's lengthy client list included Tony Accardo; Murray "the Camel" Humphreys; L.A. crime boss Mickey Cohen; Bill Kaplan, the horserace handicapper; jewel thief "Pops" Panczko (whom they represented pro bono because he "amused" them); "Milwaukee" Phil Alderisio; Paul "the Waiter" Ricca; and Dave Zatz, a small-fry bookie who was shot to death and stuffed in the trunk of a car. Bieber was one of his pallbearers—then turned up in court the next day as defense counsel for the murder suspect.

Stymied at every turn by syndicate judges, Newey and Adamowski considered planting wiretaps to prove their allegations that the fix was always in. "Most of their (Bieber's and Brodkin's) time was spent in the newsroom at the Criminal Courts Building at Twenty-sixth and California," Newey recalled. "They used the public pay phone on the fourth floor next to the pressroom. I was always tempted to tap that phone, but was reluctant to do so because there were too many snitches in the state's attorney's office including some of my own policemen."

Justice sold was justice denied, but unfortunately there was little else the state's attorney could do to thwart the "Habeas Corpus Twins" except wait for them to retire, get sick, or die.

In 1971, a year after the B & B Boys dissolved the partnership by mutual agreement, Mayor Richard J. Daley stunned the legal community by appointing Brodkin as an assistant corporation counsel. Daley responded to critics by gently reminding them that "Abraham Lincoln defended criminals, too." Unfavorable publicity caused Brodkin to resign after only week on the job. He died penniless in a nursing home on March 7, 1974. Those who knew him intimately chuckled, posing the most logical question, "Where's the loot?"

Brodkin had always played it close to the vest. He never picked up a dinner tab when he didn't have to, and the fortune, if it existed at all, had vanished into thin air. The IRS sent in agents to investigate the trail of the missing money, but, of course, Bieber wasn't about to squeal on his old pal.

Partially blind and semiretired, George Bieber put in an appearance at 188 West Randolph and his other favorite haunt, the coffee shop of the Bismarck Hotel across the street, every day right up until the bitter end on July 23, 1981.

One colorful and outrageous era had ended, but a new generation of "fixers" were already hard at work putting into practice the lessons their forefathers, the B & B Boys, had taught them.

In 1983, the "Operation Greylord" judicial scandal broke in Cook County, sending to jail a score of corrupt defense attorneys, bribe-taking judges, and courtroom hangers-on. The whole rotten system patted and nurtured by the B & B Boys decades earlier was on the verge of collapse.

LaSalle Street

and

Washington

Boulevard

A SHORT WALK FROM THE ASYLUM TO THE GALLOWS: THE SAGA OF THE SCOTT BROTHERS, THE CITY HALL DRUG STORE BANDITS
April 1924 to October 1927

The insignificant little drugstore standing across the street from City Hall at 30 North LaSalle Street is gone now. Once, there were dozens of soda fountain drugstores just like it in the Loop, in the days when the neon marquees of the Randolph Street theaters blazed into the night and people were not afraid to stroll around downtown well after dark. The City Hall Drug Store, owned and operated by Charles H. Edison, and similar establishments scattered up and down State, Randolph, and Washington were a delight for late-night moviegoers desiring little more than an after-hours feast of grilled cheese sandwiches, fries, lime phosphates, or cherry colas. From time to time, crime visited such places, until eventually the battle-tested storeowners decided it wasn't worth it any longer and dimmed their lights following the six o'clock exodus of the office workers retreating to bungalows and two-flats scattered safely outside the inner city. When the show places vacated downtown, many of the other all-night businesses followed suit. With the gradual disappearance of the movie houses and theaters by the 1970s, there remained a perfect urban still life of darkened buildings and quiet streets. The empty canyons of the Loop provided a solitary backdrop of shadows and isolation. In the distance, the lonely echoes of police sirens, the forlorn sound of the horn blown by the last commuter train pulling out of the Northwestern Station, and the omnipresent gusts of wind blowing off Lake Michigan were accents to life on the streets, an unhappy struggle for survival of those unfortunate souls forced to scavenge for change.

Minutes after the Randolph Street theater crowd let out following the last performance, three well-dressed men, one of them wearing a derby, a blue overcoat, and gray spats, approached the soda fountain where the owner, Charles Edison, was preparing for the later evening rush. "I'd like to get paper and string, so wrap this up!" said one, pushing a package across the lacquered countertop.

As Edison momentarily diverted his gaze, two men pulled concealed pistols from their coats and drew down on the owner and his two clerks, Elizabeth Davis and Joseph Maurer. "Down in the basement, all of you!" At gunpoint, they complied with an order to face the wall, hands in the air.

One of the robbers, who had hovered near the safe upstairs, summoned Maurer to come up and crack the combination. The twenty-year-old clerk refused to do their bidding and scuffled with one of the gunmen. Within seconds, the soda fountain was wrecked. A shot was fired, and Maurer slumped over with a bullet lodged in his back. By now Loop theater patrons had heard the sharp report of a gun, and a crowd was forming outside the door.

Thwarted in their efforts to slip away unnoticed, the robbers panicked and ran off. (One of the robbers fled into the crowd and was never apprehended. He was not thought to be the shooter.) The safe was never opened. In their wake, they left behind the crumpled form of Maurer, who, desiring to be noble and steadfast in the face of danger as so many an impetuous youth is want to do, sacrificed his life in order to save the contents of his employer's safe from plundering by thieves.

As pedestrians rushed to the aid of the fallen drugstore clerk, two of the would-be robbers hailed a cab and drove over to the Drake Hotel to see what was going on among the sports and society gals of Michigan Avenue. Later they headed down to the Lexington Hotel at 2135 South Michigan Avenue for a late-evening nightcap. The Lexington, of course, is where the Al Capone gang established headquarters in 1928. (*Author's Note:* See the "South Side Sinners" chapter in *Return to the Scene of the Crime* for a description of this famous gangland locale.)

It wasn't hard for the police to guess the identity of the prime suspect in the Mauer shooting once they properly identified a carelessly discarded overcoat belonging to one Robert S. Scott, registered at the Brevoort Hotel as a guest from New York.

Scott's room key was found tucked inside the pocket of the coat draped over a chair in the basement of the drugstore. Hours later, brother Russell was taken into custody by Chicago police, commencing a long and emotionally charged Cain-and-Abel drama that tested the limitations of the insanity defense in the criminal justice system and the patience of a politically ambitious Cook County state's attorney.

The question boiled down to: Who shot Joseph Maurer? Was it Robert Scott or his older brother Russell, the philandering father of three young children who was arrested inside a West Side flat belonging to his girlfriend, Helen Bullard Conley? With $6,000 in traveler's checks, the pair were preparing to flee the city and take their chances on the open road.

In better days, Russell Scott had stood tall among the brilliant young men of East Coast finance. He was once vice president of the R. T. Scott Company, Ltd., a Toronto brokerage firm that had failed in 1923 due to mismanagement. At his arraignment, Russell boasted of his business acumen, but he also told of serious setbacks. It seems that he had promoted the international bridge spanning the Detroit River from the United States into Windsor, Canada, until the asset was seized and taken over by U.S. Steel Corporation.

He told Chief of Detectives William "Shoes" Schoemaker that he was driven into a life of crime and bootlegging after knocking about the lower echelons of the underworld for several years following the shame and disgrace of financial ruin. Scott had drawn his younger brother into his robbery schemes. From every corner of the city, scores of drugstore proprietors came forward to finger the brothers.

There were no creditable eyewitnesses to the shooting of Joseph Maurer, and the accused killers' father, Thomas Scott, encouraged his boys to be vague and evasive to detectives. The father, who had come down from Detroit, faced indictment for complicity.

The Scott brothers, however, lost their resolve and provided a detailed confession to the police. "What a mess I've made of things, and when I think of the chances I've had," said a sobbing Russell, his finely tailored clothes having lost their press after hours of grueling police interrogation.

On June 15, 1924, through his attorney, Walter Stanton, Russell Scott entered a plea of guilty to the charge of murder, throwing himself at the mercy of Judge William J. Lindsay. Lindsay had no mercy to spare. When he reached the part of the sentence calling for Scott to "hang by the neck until dead," the befuddled dollar-an-hour defender broke out into long pitiful sobs, and begged the judge to allow him to change the plea to one of not guilty.

Lindsay had hard words for Stanton, but after considering the matter for a few moments, he allowed the plea to stand. Three exacerbating trials followed, resulting in three death-sentence convictions for Russell—all of them artfully overturned by lawyers pleading the insanity defense on behalf of their client.

Once, Russell Scott was only hours away from the gallows when his execution was stayed by Judge Joseph David, who was roused from his bed at 2:00 A.M. Retried for a third time, the court eventually ordered Scott to the Chester, Illinois, prison for the criminally insane.

Robert Scott had refused to testify on his own behalf, fearing that it might "cast reflections" on Russell. Defense Attorney William Scott Stewart said that "Robert would even risk the imposition of the extreme penalty rather than gain mitigation by testifying against his brother."

This courtroom maneuvering greatly perturbed Assistant State's Attorney Charles J. Mueller, but it helped keep Russell alive for another day. "If Robert is saved from the noose and as soon as he is safely away in the penitentiary he will broadcast in the world that it was he and not Russell who really did the shooting. This will be used to save Russell from the gallows," predicted Mueller.

Twenty-five-year-old Robert was sentenced to life in prison on July 15, 1927, by Judge William Nelson Gemmill, who was convinced that it was the older brother who had fired the gun during the struggle. "Robert did not seem to be the leader," he said, noting Russell's apparent willingness to blame Robert for firing the fatal shot.

"He is seven years younger than his brother, was in Russell's employ, and came to Chicago at his request. If Robert was as bloodthirsty as most of the robbers we try here every day, it seems to me that with a revolver in his hand during the struggle, Robert could have killed Maurer at any time, but he made no effort to do so."

Acting on orders from the state supreme court, the warden returned Russell Scott to Chicago to undergo another sanity hearing. The high court held that his mental condition justified a new inquest. Public sentiment was gradually building for the accused killer. Florence Scott, the impoverished wife who was forced to place her children in an orphanage while she remained in Chicago to fight for her husband's life, raised a large contingency fund. Her efforts created reasonable doubt in the public mind, and an outpouring of sympathy, which resulted in many more court continuances. But they only served to postpone the inevitable.

State's Attorney Robert E. Crowe, a political lackey of Mayor William Hale Thompson, lost face during the 1924 Loeb-Leopold trial when the brilliant courtroom tactician Clarence Darrow aroused heartfelt sympathy for the two youthful "thrill killers," who were spared the death house. It was a ringing blow to Bob Crowe's public image as a tough prosecutor. Of course, Darrow was handsomely paid off by the families of Nathan Leopold and Richard Loeb, whereas the Scott brothers, by dint of their reduced circumstances, were forced to settle for the average garden-variety lawyer.

Without Darrow, or someone like him, tugging at the moral coat sleeves of the community, Crowe relentlessly pursued Russell Scott. He was never beyond Crowe's grasp and that of the state's attorney, even though the courts had already passed judgment three times in the matter.

The fourth time out of the box doomed Russell Scott. Believing his case to be utterly hopeless even though another sanity hearing was on the docket and the final determination was yet to come, Russell Scott committed suicide on October 8, 1927, in the old Cook County Jail at Hubbard and Dearborn Streets. (*Author's Note: See Return to the Scene of the Crime* for the interesting history of this building.) He was found at 11:05 P.M. by Deputy Warden Otto Schuler.

Shortly before he fashioned the belt of his trousers into a hangman's noose, Scott was visited by Florence. She found her husband billeted in the "Gold Coast" section of the jail, a high-security compound kept under constant vigil ever since the midget bandit Henry Fernekes blew a hole through the wall with a stick of dynamite. (See Tour 3.) The ex-millionaire-turned-robber was an unruly and quarrelsome prisoner, testing the warden's patience. There were concerns Scott would make a break for it. No one suspected he had suicide on his mind, however.

"Russell had been sick for more than a week," the wife related. "And I went to the jail yesterday with a basket of food that I thought might appeal to him. We talked together about thirty minutes and he seemed somewhat despondent about his illness (bronchitis)."

Bottling the extreme anger and rage he felt at the moment, Attorney Stewart pointed the finger at Crowe and the system of justice that conspired to execute a man whose sanity was in question. "It shows he was crazy," decried Stewart. "We knew he was not sane. But we thought he had a superiority complex; delusions of grandeur. He had come to believe that he would escape all punishment and become a financial wizard."

Showing not the slightest hint of compassion for the widow and her fatherless brood, Crowe exulted: "Scott did what the law should have done years ago!"

One system of justice permanently ended in Cook County with the final resolution of the Scott case—execution by rope. Henceforth, condemned prisoners faced a newer and more efficient horror awaiting them at the end of their final walk down the long corridor. The electric chair, otherwise known as "Old Sparky," would be put to the test the very next time, on February 20, 1929.

THE FIRST CHICAGO FIRE:
"THE PALL OF THE GREAT CALAMITY"
October 19, 1857

Wacker Drive

between

Dearborn

and Clark

Streets

Not far from the entrance gate at Graceland Cemetery (Clark Street and Irving Park Road), as you stroll past the gravesites of some of Chicago's most notable and most obscure citizens, there stands a weather-beaten limestone memorial to a long-forgotten Chicago firefighter. The marker honors the memory of John B. Dickey, foreman of the Liberty Hose Company, who perished in the rush of flame that consumed three downtown blocks on October 19, 1857. The fire on Water Street (now Wacker Drive), between Dearborn on the east and Clark on the west, occurred long before the more famous conflagration of October 8, 1871, that reduced Chicago to miles of smoldering ash. The death of John Dickey and seventeen others in this earlier tragedy pointed to the weaknesses and inefficiencies of the city's volunteer firefighting brigades. In 1857, the City of Chicago lacked a full-time paid fire department. Volunteer companies responded haphazardly—or not at all— when the alarm bell was struck. Very often the citizen-firemen were drunken criminals who plundered the contents of the burning building before training their hoses on the blaze. Forgotten by time, John Dickey rests beneath a five-foot-high white monument with a fireman's helmet carved in relief on top. One has to look closely in order to read the eroded inscription on the limestone. Time and the elements have taken a toll. In a few years, the inscription will probably disappear altogether. Within the many walking tours of this historically important cemetery founded by Thomas Bryan, an associate of Senator Stephen Douglas, there is scant attention paid to the crumbling Dickey marker commemorating this event in the early history of the Chicago Fire Department. The intersection of Dearborn and Wacker, where the fire broke out in the small hours of morning, is today part of a busy commercial thoroughfare located just south of the Chicago River. The 1857 boundaries can no longer be distinguished because the configuration of streets since that time has been dramatically altered. There is no plaque or marker affixed to the Lake Side Bank Building east of 77 Wacker Drive (where the worst fire damage is believed to have been) to remind the current generation of the loss of lives and the suffering of those early Chicagoans whose personal sacrifice helped make the city what it is today. And that is a shame.

T he cool autumn night passed quietly. Then, around 4:00 A.M. on Monday morning, the nineteenth of October, 1857, Michael Joyce, the bell ringer at the Cook County Courthouse, heard the plaintive cry, "Fire!" coming from one of two men standing near the Clark Street Bridge, which spans the Chicago River. Joyce observed plumes of smoke curling toward the sky. At first he thought a river tugboat was in trouble, but then he saw the flames shoot from the roof of one of the buildings at 100 Water Street. At that moment, he began to ring the courthouse bell, summoning the volunteer hook-and-ladder companies to action.

Low-slung four- and five-story, marble-fronted dry goods stores, hatters, stables, and rooming houses lined Water Street, even then a thriving commercial thoroughfare situated on the south bank of the Chicago River. The Water Street merchants from Dearborn on the east to Clark on the west had paid careful attention to the appearance of their storefronts, but the fancy marble pillars and Greek Revival ornamentation they had installed to advertise their business locations and wares disguised the shoddy wooden construction of the interior walls. The entire city was a tinderbox, and it was a wonder that Chicago had been spared the plague of the firebug up to this critical moment of its history.

The fire spread, whipsawing from building to building, trapping sleeping residents living in the rented rooms in the upper floors above the stores. Many of these residents were creatures of the night who reserved the airless, whiskey-stained cubicles by the hour to entertain gentlemen clients. They were forced to jump from rooftop to rooftop to avoid the advancing wall of flames.

After what seemed to be a hellish eternity, the first of the volunteer brigades arrived on the scene, by which time the conflagration was well out of control, and the sidewalls of many of the buildings were collapsing. It was noted on the editorial page of the *Chicago Times* the following afternoon that the conduct of the firemen contributed to the tragedy that left eighteen people dead, many more homeless, and half a million dollars in commercial damage. "We account for the disappointment by the unusual amount of drunkenness and rowdyism in which the firemen indulged. Simultaneously with the work of the engines, the drinking commenced and long before the time for cool and energetic action had passed, scores of men in firemen's garb were too far gone to know whether they were really at a fire or wedding. Of course there was disorder, fighting, rowdyism, and ill-directed and abortive effort because where whiskey is, there good sense is not."

Others, who were not a party to the shenanigans of hooligans, displayed uncommon valor in the face of death. John Dickey, a twenty-six-year-old bachelor

WATER STREET (WACKER DRIVE) DESTROYED BY A WALL OF FLAMES,

OCTOBER 19, 1857.

WEATHER-BEATEN GRAVE MARKER OF FIREFIGHTER JOHN DICKEY AT GRACELAND CEMETERY.

(Photo by Carol Jean Carlson)

who lived with his parents at 118 Monroe Street, charged into Edward Hempstead's wholesale grocery store at 115 Water Street with hose in hand. He was caught by a falling wall and crushed. His lifeless form was dragged from the ruins of the store and returned to his mother's tired embrace within an hour of the sounding of the first general alarm.

By sunset the entire block was flattened, and the grisly search for human remains entombed beneath the embers and ruins had begun. It was noted with disgust and revulsion by the *Chicago Tribune* that "a gang of a hundred boys of all sizes from the urchin of ten summers to the loafer of twenty . . . were down on their bellies clawing through the dirt and among the hot bricks and charred beams in search of unburned property. When one of them would find a quantity of articles a half-dozen others would set upon him and divide it among themselves. When a body would be removed a score would make a rush for the hole to dig and root, scramble and quarrel, brawl and curse. We could not help but think as we turned away from this scene of depravity, what awful neglect of family government and moral training must exist in the households of which those lads and young men belonged."

Nearly twenty thousand people jammed the court house square at Randolph and Clark on October 21 to pay final homage to the eighteen fallen volunteer-brigade men and others whose remains were accounted for in the tragedy. Businesses were closed for the day, and black crepe bunting was hung from the rooftops and windows of the city. The procession passed by the scene of devastation, as the solemn strains of a dead march and the ringing of the courthouse bell filled the air. Throngs of weeping women lined the sidewalks.

In the days that followed, coroners' inquests were held behind the closed doors of the courthouse, and countless rumors and accusations into the nature of the catastrophe circulated through the city. A "dissolute female" quarreling with her paramour over "the price of her shame" in his private fifth-floor room at 113 South Water was held to account. The woman swore that if she was not paid the agreed-upon sum she would set fire to the lodging house. According to one contemporary account, she ignited the man's bed with a candle, driving them both from the room.

The hue and cry was raised in the editorial pages for the common council to follow the lead of Boston and other New England cities and permanently abolish the volunteer fire brigades creating havoc in the streets in favor of a trained citywide force paid for their service to the community.

The scandal accompanying the big fire that long-ago afternoon resulted in the formation of the Citizen's Fire Brigade of Chicago on November 19, 1857. Less than a year later, on August 2, 1858, the first paid fire department took to the streets with the latest equipment. The engine house was headquartered on LaSalle Street where City Hall now stands. At great expense, steam engines and the fire-alarm telegraph were purchased by the city to combat the menace of fire.

Reflecting on the terrible tragedy, the *Tribune* expressed a commonly held sentiment: "Let us hope that God in His mercy will spare us another exhibition so fraught with the utmost human misery." But of course, the greater fire tragedy lay nearly fourteen years in the future, when once again this terrible sorrow would revisit the people of Chicago.

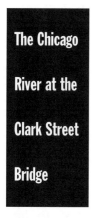

The Chicago

River at the

Clark Street

Bridge

THE WRECK OF THE *ROUSE SIMMONS*: DEATH IN THE FOAMING WAKE, AN EPITAPH FOR THE LOST CHRISTMAS TREE SHIP

November–December 1912

The old trestle bridge spanning the Chicago River at Clark Street was a bridge of legend. Turning on its mighty pivot, the rusting iron expanse, in its slow inimitable way, yielded the right of passage to the impatient skippers of the Lake Michigan schooners, barges, grain boats, wooden scows, and pleasure craft attempting to navigate the "baffling, erratic, reversible river of contradictions," as Henry Hansen termed Chicago's busy commercial waterway. Until it was replaced with a more efficient and technologically superior suspension bridge in 1929, the old Clark Street Bridge had borne silent witness to the last desperate act of hundreds of nameless souls who, upon seeing no alternative to their present miseries, took that final fateful plunge into the sluggish, murky depths. Bridge tender Martin Jeffers was on duty the day the greatest nautical disaster of them all occurred, the 1915 capsizing of the Eastland, claiming 812 victims who had been looking forward to a carefree excursion to Michigan City, Indiana, before tragedy struck. There was little to be done for the drowning passengers of the Eastland, except an offering of prayers to the Almighty. The tragedy of the Eastland brings to mind a similar story of another ill-fated river vessel, the schooner Rouse Simmons, *regularly moored to an ancient dock situated behind a collection of uninspiring commission houses that once fronted the southwestern exposure of the bridge where skyscrapers and a "River Walk" with many charming outdoor cafés now stand. The* Rouse Simmons *was a ship of enchantment, bringing delight to several generations of Chicagoans during the Christmas season until it vanished forever in a bitter Lake Michigan gale; a storm so fierce that the history books record the squall as one of the worst on record.*

Apart from the many abandoned copper mines and ghost towns dotting the region, Michigan's densely forested Upper Peninsula yields a rich harvest of second-growth pine and balsam trees. Beginning in early November, the local woodcutters and lumbermen commence shipment of Christmas trees to the inhabitants of Milwaukee, Chicago, and the lesser cities and towns dotting the shorelines of the lower Great Lakes.

In the early years the task of delivering the fragrant spruce trees via Lake

Michigan was the province of Captain Herman Schuenemann and his brother August, who in 1887 conceived the idea of hauling the bundled cargo, each bundle measuring six to eight feet, by lake schooner.

With his load of pines secure in the hold, Schuenemann sold Christmas trees and hand-fashioned wreaths from his mooring at the Clark Street Bridge. The tallest trees drawn from the lot were presented to the grateful proprietors of the downtown theaters. In return, the brothers received complimentary season passes.

Herman Schuenemann, master of the *Rouse Simmons*, his wife, and three young daughters lived in a tiny flat at 1638 North Clark Street, a little more than a mile north of the river. The eldest daughter, Elsie, was devoted to her father and had recently taken an active interest in his seasonal business.

By 1912, Chicagoans had become accustomed to buying the well-shaped trees from the jovial Schuenemann for prices ranging from seventy-five cents to a dollar. It was as much a cherished holiday tradition as the Fourth of July fireworks celebration and the Taste of Chicago would become to future generations of city dwellers.

Herman affixed a hand-painted sign to the wharf, reminding his customers that he had ventured deep into the snow-covered woods of Manistique and Thompson, Michigan, and had personally selected and chopped down only the finest trees for his friends and business associates back in Chicago.

The shipment of Christmas trees via the Great Lakes was not without risk. The month of November was particularly treacherous for the Lake Michigan merchantmen. High winds and gale-like conditions had sent many a good craft to the bottom. The maritime sailors bitterly recalled the disappearance of the passenger ship *Chicora* in the heavy seas of January 1895. The only traces of the vessel were two bottle notes that washed ashore four months later, purportedly written by the doomed sailors moments before sinking. In 1898, Captain Schuenemann's brother August went down with all hands while manning the fifty-five-ton schooner *S. Thal* in the churning waters off the north suburban Glencoe shoreline.

The threat of dangerous weather conditions failed to deter Herman Schuenemann, who purchased an eighth interest in the *Rouse Simmons* in 1910 with fellow navigator and Chicagoan Charles Nelson. The *Rouse Simmons* was fitted for duty in 1868 by McLelland and Company of Milwaukee. Measuring 123.5 feet in length, the wooden schooner carried three masts and was intended primarily for the lumber trade.

With a crew and passenger list of 16 and between 27,000 and 50,000 trees tied up and bundled below deck, Captain Schuenemann set sail from Manistique, Michigan, on November 22, 1912, bound for Chicago. Skies were overcast and

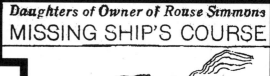

Above—Elsie Scheuneman.

Below—Two other little daughters of Captain Herman Scheuneman, owner of the Rouse Simmons, who was on board the ship.

The diagram of Lake Michigan shows the supposed course of the boat and spot where wreckage was found.

LOST IN LAKE MICHIGAN.

THE *ROUSE SIMMONS*

(ABOVE).

CAPTAIN HERMAN

SCHUENEMANN'S

DAUGHTERS NEVER LOST

HOPE THAT THEIR

FATHER, THE SKIPPER OF

THE "CHRISTMAS TREE

SHIP," WOULD SURVIVE

THE RAGING GALE OF

LAKE MICHIGAN.

high winds were predicted. The *Rouse Simmons* headed straight into the open waters of the lake, heedless of the ominous weather reports. When the storm broke, the ancient wooden craft found itself hopelessly trapped. The flag of distress was hoisted, but there was little the coastal rescue vessels at Sturgeon Bay and Kewaunee could do to assist the imperiled ship traveling in such bad weather. The ship foundered in the rough water before the ice-caked masts and the sails blew out. Shortly thereafter, the *Rouse Simmons* disappeared.

Eighteen days of anguish, fear, and worry passed. In a dingy little room at South Water and Clark Street overlooking the Chicago River, Elsie Schuenemann held out hope that her father's schooner would eventually appear on the distant horizon. She was weaving Christmas garlands, said to have come from the splintered trees recovered by coastal residents of Wisconsin where the trees had washed ashore. Facing destitution, the daughter of Captain Schuenemann and her grief-stricken mother sold the garlands to the public. Every dollar the family possessed was tied up in the boat. The *Chicago Inter-Ocean* newspaper, with the cooperation of the Lake Seamans Union, organized an emergency relief fund for the family.

"I am going to make an attempt to carry on father's Christmas tree business," vowed the brave young woman. "I will get friends to help me and send my trees by rail to Chicago and sell them from the foot of Clark Street. Ever since I was a little girl Papa has sold them there, and lots and lots of people never think of going any other place for their trees."

W. C. Holmes Shipping, for whom Schuenemann skippered a vessel in his younger days, placed the schooner *Oneida* at the family's disposal. It was moored at the Clark Street Bridge where the *Rouse Simmons* had stood for years, and was laden with Christmas trees recovered from Sturgeon Bay and shipped to Chicago. A cherished Yuletide tradition would remain unbroken.

Meanwhile, the U.S. Treasury Department dispatched the revenue cutter *Tuscarora* to search the small islands in Lake Michigan for survivors and clues as to the precise location of the doomed *Rouse Simmons*. The hopes and prayers of sixteen bereft families went with them but quickly faded.

Back in Chicago, a seaman who had signed on with the *Rouse Simmons* related a strange story. Hogan Hoganson, a superstitious Swede who lived at 413 North Milwaukee Avenue, had relied on his instincts and lived another day. He said that he refused to make the homeward voyage to Chicago after he observed several rodents leave the ship and scurry for cover in the shelter of the docks. It is a tradition of the sea that when a rodent abandons ship, disaster is lurking.

"The boys laughed at me," said Hoganson. "They laughed at me for they mostly were not old sailors. To them the rats leaving meant nothing—but to me, who have heard of this strange thing for years—well I'm glad I got the hunch and came back by rail."

Two bottle messages were reportedly retrieved. The first one was pulled from the beach at Sheboygan, Wisconsin, on December 13, 1912. "Friday. Everybody goodbye. I guess we are all through. Sea washed over our deck load Tuesday. During the night, the small boat was washed over. Ingvald and Steve fell overboard on Thursday. God help us. Herman Schuenemann."

Ingvald Newhouse was a deck hand taken on board just before the sailing. Stephen Nelson was the first mate and the son of Captain Charles Nelson, also lost.

A second bottle note from Captain Nelson was reportedly found in 1927. "These lines were written at 10:30 P.M. Schooner R.S. ready to go down about twenty miles southeast of Two Rivers Point, between fifteen to twenty miles off shore. All hands lashed to one line. Goodbye."

From time to time other curious artifacts, including a human skull believed to have come from the lost Christmas tree ship, would be caught in fishermen's nets. On April 23, 1924, Captain Schuenemann's wallet containing business cards and newspaper clippings was recovered at Two Rivers Point. But the precise location of the *Rouse Simmons* remained a Great Lakes mystery until October 1971, when diver G. Kent Bellrichard of Milwaukee found the remarkably well-preserved wreck lying under 180 feet of water off the coast of Two Rivers. The anchor was raised and placed on display at the Milwaukee Yacht Club. A signboard and porthole are on public view at the Milwaukee Public Library marine room.

As to the fate of the surviving Schuenemanns, Elsie and her mother made good on their promise to continue with Papa's business. A Christmas tree ship was moored at the Clark Street Bridge every holiday season thereafter until 1933.

The tragedy of the *Rouse Simmons* was forever immortalized in verse by *Chicago Daily News* reporter and book author Vincent Starrett.

The Ballad of the Christmas Tree Ship

This is the tale of the Christmas ship
that sailed o'er the sullen lake;
And of sixteen souls that made the trip,
And of death in the foaming wake.

Near North Confidential:

The Chicago River to Old Town

Burlesque, booze, and barflies. The Near North Side nightclub district, world renown in former days for seamy attractions, exists today only in memory. The scarlet procession of B-girls, backroom gambling setups, dopesters, hipsters, and G-string peelers vanished in the night. Who took the "toddlin'"out of Chicago, that "toddlin' town?" When *did* that happen?

Such transformations do not occur in a day, a month, or even a decade, but rather in a slow, steady process of decline. The era of bawdy mayhem really began to fade with the arrival of television and air conditioning. People stopped going to nightclubs as a means of escaping the drudgery of their factory jobs; the humid, stifling July nights; and the dull sameness of bungalow living. There was no need to dress up for an evening of live entertainment and excitement in the city, not with Milton Berle on the tube, a cold Meister Brau in hand, and a Polk Brothers window unit whirring on the windowsill.

That which technology and changing societal tastes did not directly kill, atrophied and died during the flowering of the Daley Dynasty. From 1955, year one of Richard J. Daley's two-decade monarchical reign as mayor of Chicago, up until the bitter end in 1976, the Near North Side of Chicago was obliged to shed its honky-tonk reputation and assume a more dignified appearance. Taverns closed. The Rush Street hot spots followed suit, one by one, until even the venerable Mr. Kelly's, which showcased headline acts direct from Hollywood, suspended operations.

Clark Street, a vice-laden hellhole since the 1880s, also succumbed to urban renewal. Syndicate vice lords like Jimmy "the Monk"Allegretti and Caeser DiVarco were made to understand the simple unvarnished truth about Daley's Chicago based on the lessons of life taught to the mayor while he was growing up in his insulated Irish-Catholic parish in Bridgeport. Sex was no good unless it was for the purpose of making babies with your wife. But, stealing votes to sway presidential elections and court favor with a certain Irish-American presidential aspi-

1. The Kinzie Street flood at Wolf Point.
2. Marina City Apartments, 300 N. State St., Nov. 23, 1965.
3. Old Criminal Courts Building, Dearborn & Hubbard.
4. Lee Miglin murder site, Scott St. west of Astor.
5. Shirts Unlimited, a mob boutique, 843 N. State.
6. Connors Park in Connorsville, Chestnut, Wabash & Rush.
7. Mark Twain Hotel, 111 W. Division St.
8. 1982 Tylenol poisoning case, 1601 N. Wells St.
9. Paddy Bauler's saloon, North Avenue & Sedgwick.

rant, appointing unqualified ward hacks to sensitive city posts, building express-ways to segregate one group of people from another, awarding no-bid contracts to the friends of "the man on five," protecting greedy cops while they chiseled bribes from motorists during routine traffic stops—these were understood to be essential components of Chicago's political landscape. Call it clout. Call it "the City That Works." Call it what you will, but first make sure that Alderman Paddy Bauler has enough votes to square accounts with "the boys" in his latest re-zoning scheme. In "Clout City," you take care of the people you know and screw all the rest.

From its inception, this devout-Catholic, blue-collar, union town was locked in the horns of a great moral dilemma. Flaunting virtue was an affront to decen-cy, the church, the teachings of the nuns, and the members of your own family. But on the other end of the spectrum, Chicago had also given rise to *Playboy* magazine, the "Mickey Finn," the one-way ride, and Sally Rand's fan dance. Daley may have succeeded in ridding the Near North Side of its Sodom-and-Gomorrah reputation, but he left behind a cultural dry gulch. The lights went out in a num-ber of Chicago theaters during his long feudal regime. The arts were on a steady, and seemingly irreversible, decline through much of the 1960s and 1970s. In the city of smokestacks, only the paving contractors, wrecking companies, and real-estate plungers like Arthur Rubloff squared accounts.

Try to catch a glimpse of the Near North Side as it appeared to bleary-eyed, out-of-town conventioneers in the unbridled days before Daley, and you are like-ly to be disappointed. A collection of parking lots, condominiums, and Walgreens drugstores supplanted the fabulous cafés and nightclubs of Rush Street and the seedy dives to the immediate west on Clark Street.

Nevertheless, the Near North remains a place of stark contrasts. Michigan Avenue is the Magnificent Mile. The Newberry Library, Bughouse Square (Washington Square Park), and the Catholic archbishop's mansion at 1555 North State Parkway add to the mosaic of the Gold Coast, the traditional boundaries of which extend from Lake Michigan on the east to LaSalle Street on the west, North Avenue and Lincoln Park on the north end, and the pricey boutiques of Oak Street on the south.

Within this pastiche of diverse lifestyles, there are areas of extreme wealth and pockets of poverty. The residents of transient hotels and housing projects mingle with patrons of the most expensive shopping and dining establishments.

Stroll past lavish mansions, the carefully preserved graystones dating back more than one hundred years, and discover for yourself how the other half lives. The next question: Which half would *you* like to see?

The Chicago River Near Wolf Point

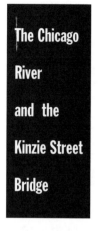

The Chicago River and the Kinzie Street Bridge

THE FLOOD OF '92
April 13, 1992

The iron-girder bridge spanning the murky green depths of the Chicago River near Wolf Point (where the north and south forks of the river diverge) connects two disparate worlds. The factories and ribbons of railroad track snaking along the west bank of the river recall a vanished city of industry, the landscape of which was dominated by smokestacks, grain elevators, and cold-storage warehouses. Crossing over the Kinzie Street Bridge in the eastbound lane, the corroded industrial core of another age is left behind. To the left, the East Bank Club, a "members only" workout room that is this generation's answer to the 1970s singles bar, is a casual reminder of the times in which we live. The Park Condos next door provide urban adventurers the subdued elegance they require amid industrial chic. The old factory buildings in and around Wolf Point have all been torn down or converted to condos. At the Holiday Inn Mart Plaza nearby, the names of the banquet rooms honor the city's earliest settlers who erected their clapboard houses on Wolf Point, a sparse and desolate location in the 1830s. Here stood Wolf Tavern and Sam Miller's Public House, not far from the city's first hostelry of note, the Sauganash, opened by Mark Beaubien in 1831. The rugged frontiersmen in buckskin ensured that a grog house, and not the church, should become the city's first important public meeting place. And thus was born the City of Chicago, and the history of its reputation.

In the early morning hours of April 13, 1992, before the Monday morning rush hour kicked into high gear, Chicago sprang a mighty leak—resulting in not your average garden-variety water-in-the-basement kind of flood, but rather a disaster of epic proportions, which tested the mettle of commuters and forced an increasingly flustered and peevish Mayor Richard M. Daley to call it "one of the most dramatic chapters in Chicago history."

When it was over and calm restored to the city merchants, the loss of dollars from the three-day flood was pegged at a staggering $1.95 billion.

The prelude to disaster began in May 1991, when the City contracted with

KINZIE STREET BRIDGE, NEAR WOLF POINT.

the Great Lakes Dredge & Dock Company to replace clusters of aging timber pilings (telephone poles banded together to fortify bridges and prevent boats from
colliding with piers) around the downtown bridges. The work was to be completed in anticipation of an expected tourist boom and a corresponding increase
in sightseeing boats applying for licenses to traverse the navigable waterway.

On the morning in question, workmen near the Kinzie Street Bridge were
extracting the old pilings from two river barges, one barge supporting an
immense crane, the other the pilings.

There had been a major misunderstanding, it seems, between the project
team from the City that was overseeing the work and Great Lakes Dredge & Dock
concerning the placement of the new pilings. The company later claimed that
the City had failed to advise them of the existence of an abandoned underground
tunnel that had connected many of the downtown retail stores and businesses
beginning in 1899. Deliveries of coal and freight to the buildings utilized electri-
fied cars that navigated the narrow-gauge track in this subterranean maze. One
section of this antiquated fifty-mile tunnel system ran right below the water line
at Kinzie Street.

As a means of conveying freight to and from downtown locations, the tunnel system had outlived its usefulness by 1959. Miles of electrical wire and
cabling were installed in the tunnels in subsequent years, and when an inspector

observed a slow drip from the ceiling, he took pictures of the perforated wall and returned to the office. While the inspector was filing his report, the tunnel simply gave way, and river water poured into the shaft at a rate of 250 gallons per second. By 7:00 A.M., the sub-basements of the department stores and Loop office buildings were already flooded. The water was rising at the rate of four feet an hour.

Power was lost. Elevators were damaged. The downtown streets were choked with traffic. Two CTA subway tunnels were forced to close down. Opening day of the new baseball season at Comiskey Park was pushed off the front page. All in all, it was one hell of a morning, and panic time at City Hall. The building was ordered evacuated, and the Mayor's Office of Information was transferred across the street to the Daley Center.

It took city engineers about an hour to trace the source of the leak. A whirlpool observed in the river at Kinzie Street brought an armada of tugboats loaded with sand, gravel, and concrete to stem the flow. Plugging the hole in this fashion, however, proved ineffective.

The U.S. Army Corps of Engineers and the usual experts who appear in a time of crisis were hastily summoned forth to do battle with Mother Nature and her menacing river. There were plenty of suggestions made, ranging from the sublime (propping up mattresses to stem the flow of water) to the ridiculous (filling the flooded tunnels with Jell-O).

John Kenny Jr. of the Kenny Construction Company was green-lighted by the mayor to head efforts to plug all leaks. And wouldn't you just know it, the press dubbed him the "Flood Stud."

The crisis was solved when Kenny and his colleagues settled on a more sane course of action: plugging the shafts east and west of the river and filling them in with concrete. But it took another five and a half weeks to pump out all the remaining water from the tunnels.

No one died or was seriously hurt in the calamity, but someone had to take the fall while the City prepared to file the usual negligence lawsuits. Nine city workers were discharged for failing to properly respond to reports of leaks months earlier. The litigation would drag on for another seven years.

The Chicago River-Michigan Avenue Area

Chicago
River and
300 North
State Street

FROM MARINA CITY TO THE COUNTY MORGUE: THE END OF THE LINE FOR MURRAY "THE CAMEL" HUMPHREYS
November 23, 1965

Marina City, Bertrand Goldberg's sixty-two-story, "corn-cob" high-rise creation, features cantilevered balconies that afford residents a sweeping panorama of the Chicago skyline, the Chicago River, and points beyond. The twin towers are a succession of circular disks resting on columns, with the first eighteen floors reserved for automobiles. Marina City apartments are pie-shaped, so there is no place to hide when the Feds come knocking at the door. Murray "the Camel" Humphreys, elder statesman of the Chicago mob, learned the painful truth of the matter when his beautiful pad on the fifty-first floor of the east tower was invaded by G-men who had come bearing warrants, not gifts.

In the twilight of his life, Murray Llewelyn Humphreys' daily routines had become an open book to members of the FBI's "Top Hoodlum Unit," otherwise known as C-1. The syndicate's top "connection guy" was placed under 24/7 surveillance as he made the rounds of the Gold Coast nightspots with his wife, Betty Jeanne Neibert, a former Chicago dice girl once betrothed to an unlucky gambler named Irving Vine, who rolled snake eyes and came up dead after tangling with Humphreys. (*Author's Note:* More about Irving Vine in Tour 5.)

Murray "the Camel" Humphreys married Betty Jeanne in 1957. She was only thirty-two at the time, and he a robust fifty-eight. The marriage ended unhappily in 1964 when Betty Jeanne moved to Key Biscayne, Florida.

The only Welshman in the Chicago mob, Murray Humphreys was a grammar school dropout who graduated to bigtime burglary and armed robbery following World War I. He rose to prominence in the 1930s as the principal liaison between the underworld, labor union bosses, cops, politicians, and judges. Witty, urbane, and highly articulate, he was a Rush Street habitué and proprietor of a popular Lake Shore Drive grillroom.

Succeeding Jake "Greasy Thumb" Guzik as the Chicago mob's political point man in 1956, Humphreys was a frequent visitor to Washington, D.C., where he

MURRAY "THE CAMEL" HUMPHREYS (CENTER) FLANKED BY THE "MOTION TO FIX"

BOYS, MICHAEL BRODKIN (LEFT) AND GEORGE BIEBER (RIGHT).

(From the collection of John Binder)

conferred with "friends" on Capitol Hill, most notably Congressman Roland Libonati from the Seventh Illinois District who looked after the Capone interests in the House of Representatives. In the days of "Camelot," they spoke of many things. The Chicago police board needed "fixing." This guy and that guy were not "playing ball." In jest (but sometimes in anger), they called Mayor Richard J. Daley "Porky Pig." President John F. Kennedy was a "sweetheart," his brother Attorney General Robert Kennedy turned out to be a pain in the ass, but the outfit managed small victories nevertheless.

"I killed six of his bills," gloated Libonati on October 23, 1962, while FBI agents listened in. "The wiretapping bill, the intimidation of informants bill . . ."

Humphreys' ability to suborn lawmakers and engineer "the fix," by simply walking into Libonati's office or a judge's chambers in Cook County and whispering the magic word, made the dapper, well-spoken hood indispensable to a succession of crime syndicate bosses in Chicago.

In 1935, Humphreys languished in a federal prison on an income tax evasion rap, when a jailhouse snitch named Byron Bolton fingered him as one of the four shooters who entered the garage at 2122 North Clark Street on Valentine's Day, 1929, and slaughtered seven members of the "Bugs" Moran gang. The hit team also included Claude "Screwy" Maddox, Gus Winkler, and Bolton, a former U.S. Navy machine gunner who required no "on the job" training.

FBI Director J. Edgar Hoover downplayed the seriousness of Bolton's charge and refused to investigate the matter any further, leaving it up to the Chicago police to deal with Humphreys as they pleased. The "Camel" (the nickname was a press invention; associates often called him "Curly") escaped prosecution, but would spend the next two decades paying the Internal Revenue Service $71,000 in back taxes.

Dragged before federal grand juries numerous times in his racketeering career, Murray Humphreys always invoked the Fifth Amendment—his stonewalling technique could never be breached.

On November 23, 1965, the last day of Humphreys' life, a federal grand jury returned an indictment against him charging him with perjury in an attempt to avoid a grand jury subpoena. Immediately following the indictment, FBI agents Maz Rutland, Denny Shanahan, and Tom Parrish went to the Marina City apartments to arrest Humphreys.

"Don't come in here, or I'll kill you!" Humphreys shouted through the door.

Denied entrance, the three burly G-men crashed through the entranceway only to confront the gangster holding a loaded .38. The gun was pointed right at them. "If you guys had been coppers, I would have killed you!" Humphreys chaffed, slowly lowering his weapon.

The agents commenced a search of the apartment. Humphreys boiled over. He rushed toward them, viciously biting one of the agents in the hand before he could be subdued.

The FBI agents detained the enraged Humphreys for nearly two hours in the lockup. His lawyers and bondsmen could not come up with the necessary 10 percent deposit on the $4,500 bond. They had to borrow the sum from a downtown restaurateur to spring "the Hump." The humiliating ordeal was just too much to bear for the proud, aging mobster who supped with congressmen and judges. He had a weak heart, and this kind of excitement was not good for the ticker. "Here we go again!" he said disgustedly, as he scrawled his signature to the bond.

It had been a grueling, emotional day. Finally left alone in his Marina City apartment, Humphreys pondered the situation. In one corner, there were his estranged wife, a perjury indictment, and tax problems. And, in the other corner, the specter of Feds probing into old, unsolved murders. The life of a Chicago gangster was not all frills and fast times.

After tidying up the place (vacuuming his carpet calmed his jangled nerves), Murray Humphreys felt a sudden rush of pain in his chest and collapsed to the floor. A resident Marina City physician, answering an emergency call from Humphreys' brother Jack Wright, who found the master fixer stretched out on the floor later that evening, listed the cause of death as coronary thrombosis, nothing more.

The doctor noted the presence of a mysterious laceration behind Humphreys' earlobe, prompting unfounded rumors that an assassin might have injected poison into Humphreys' brain. This was not the case, however. Humphreys had banged into the coffee table on the way down.

THE DEVIL'S APPRENTICE: THE CRIMES OF JOHANN HOCH, SIDEKICK AND HENCHMAN OF H. H. HOLMES
February 23, 1906

Cook County Jail, 54 West Hubbard Street (Dearborn and Hubbard Streets)

Readers of my first crime guidebook will likely recall our first visit to the old Cook County Criminal Courts Building and jail annex, located north of the Chicago River, and the many famous criminal cases and public hangings occurring there between 1891 and 1929, when the prisoners were removed to newer, more spacious quarters at Twenty-sixth and California on the West Side. The limestone, Romanesque-revival building on Hubbard, designed by Otto Matz, is now the Courthouse Condominiums. Beautifully preserved for the modern generation to enjoy, the walls of the old courthouse speak to the past and an amazing assortment of career criminals who paid with their lives on the courtyard gallows to the immediate rear of the building, where the Chicago Fire Department Prevention Bureau now stands. Married twenty times, bigamist and murderer Johann Hoch was executed on this site in 1906. Before he was dropped into eternity, Hoch condemned the court and his executioners and charged them to "remember his death," knowing that his name would haunt them for the rest of their days in this world and possibly the next.

Mystery still surrounds Johann Hoch, a squat, balding, and unassuming little man who seduced and married (often concurrently) more than twenty middle-aged women for their dowries and the comforts of life they could provide. An arsenic poisoner with a cheery disposition, Hoch displayed a sweet and gentle nature to Cook County jailkeeper Whitman and Hoch's spiritual adviser on death row, the Reverend A. W. Schlechte. How could such a pleasant man, who was no trouble to anyone, commit foul murder? Undoubtedly, there were many women who had fallen victim to his flattery over the years who were asking themselves the same question.

Hoch quoted Scripture and spoke with love and respect about his old mother back in Germany. "A man's best friend is his mother," he often proclaimed with a sob. "She will never lead you astray with bad advice and she will stick to you when all other friends fail."

The arch-bigamist was born Jacob Schmidt near Harweiler-Bingen, Germany, a small town on the banks of the Rhine River. He prepared for the Lutheran clergy to satisfy his mother's intentions for him, but withdrew from religious life forever to be joined in wedlock with Christine Raub, who bore him three children. For reasons known only to himself, Hoch abandoned the family hearth to become a world traveler, embarking for Australia from Africa in 1882 aboard the steamer *La Forisa*. The ship caught fire and everyone on board was lost, except for the resourceful Hoch, who was rescued by a fishing schooner and delivered safely to Capetown. What acts of mischief he carried out in South Africa are lost to history.

Hoch moved to Chicago around 1892, beginning the criminal phase of his Midwestern career in the employ of the prototypical fiend Herman Webster Mudgett (aka H. H. Holmes), the monster of Sixty-third Street who murdered dozens of young women inside his "torture castle." (*Author's Note:* See *Return to the Scene of the Crime* for more details.)

"I feel certain that Hoch was the janitor of Holmes castle, and that if he did not actually operate with Holmes, he learned the latter's methods pretty well," theorized a Chicago police lieutenant.

Witnesses came forward to validate the Holmes-Hoch connection, although there was sharp disagreement as to whether Johann Hoch was actually the building janitor or a junior apprentice to Holmes, trained to mix poisons and swindle insurance companies. It was generally agreed that a man calling himself "Jacob Schmitt" (one of Hoch's many aliases) was seen lurking about the castle.

Hoch was a compulsive womanizer who seduced scores of women through a variety of deceptions. He had an uncanny knack for reciting romantic poetry and demonstrating musical sensitivity. Rocking back and forth, he played the zither and practiced hypnosis on his love-starved victims, lulling them into a romantic stupor. That was how he gained access to their bank accounts.

Hoch employed a variety of assumed names and clever disguises aimed at concealing his background. He was known in various cities and towns as Alfred

JOHANN HOCH WAS
HANGED IN THE REAR OF
THE OLD CRIMINAL
COURTS BUILDING (NOW
THE PRICEY COURTHOUSE
CONDOMINIUMS) AT
HUBBARD & DEARBORN.

Busteberg, Jacob Hek, John Hock, C. C. Meyer, DeWitt C. Cadney, Charles Bartels, John Dotz, Henry Bartels, John Adolph Schmidt, Adolph Hecht, and Jacob Huff.

His marital adventures over the next ten years touched many states. The premature deaths of the middle-aged widows and spinsters he married were ascribed to nephritis. The presence of arsenic in embalming fluid prevented police from detecting its usage as a poison administered by Hoch. Thus, he was able to get away with murder for many years.

No one was completely certain of just how many women Hoch had disposed of in his lifetime. However, investigators assembled an astounding chain of events and a trail of brokenhearted women dating back to 1895, based on Hoch's own statements and the statements of eyewitnesses, jilted ex-wives, and relatives of the deceased.

• December 16, 1895. Hoch married Julia Steinbrecher of 333 West Belmont Avenue. The woman expired within weeks, declaring that she had been poisoned. Hoch ran off with her life savings—$2,000.

• April 1896. Hoch married Martha Hertzfield of 197 Ontario Street, Chicago. After four months, Hoch borrowed $600 on the pretext of going to Germany to claim an inheritance.

HE UTILIZED THE MUSIC, POLICE BELIEVED, TO DISTRACT THE ATTENTION OF HIS VICTIMS WHILE HE PRACTICED THE SUBTLE EVIL OF HYPNO- TISM UPON THEM. ONCE IN HIS POWER, HOCH WAS ABLE TO MOLD THE WILL OF HIS VICTIMS TO HIS OWN AND THEY DID HIS BIDDING WITHOUT QUESTION.

How Johann Hoch, As An Expert On the Zither, Practiced Hypnotism

THIS IS THE WAY JOHANN HOCK TRIED TO HYPNOTIZE MRS KUMMERLE ACCORDING TO HER STORY

"THAT MAN WAS A HYPNOTIST AND A GOOD ONE. HE TRIED TO HYPNO- TIZE ME ALL NIGHT. THE POLICE BETTER LOOK OUT. HE WILL HYPNOTIZE THEM THE FIRST THING THEY KNOW AND GET AWAY!"
—MRS. KATHERINE KUMMERLE OF NEW YORK, FOLLOWING JOHANN HOCH'S ARREST.

(the New York World)

HOCH WRITING A LETTER TO MRS. HANNAH REICHEL

John Hoock
1104 Clay Street
San Francisco
California

WHILE LIVING IN SAN FRANCISCO IN 1900, HOCH WROTE A LOVE LETTER TO MRS. HANNA REICHEL OF 158 MILWAUKEE AVENUE IN CHICAGO PROPOSING MARRIAGE. HE WAS ALREADY MARRIED TO A MRS. LORENZ, PROPRIETRESS OF A SAN FRANCISCO BAKERY SHOP.

(Chicago American graphic)

• August 1896. Hoch married Mary Horley in Wheeling, West Virginia. She died three months later, supposedly of nephritis.

• Fall 1896. Hoch married Clara Bartell, widow of a Cincinnati saloonkeeper. Three months later she also died. Hoch disappeared without paying the undertaker's bill.

• January 1897. Hoch married Julia Dose in Hamilton, Ontario, then ran off with $600.

• 1897. Hoch married Callie C. Andrews while posing as DeWitt C. Chudney. He stayed with her less than a day before running off with her life savings.

• April 29, 1898. Hoch was arrested in Chicago for selling mortgaged furniture belonging to Strauss & Company in his flat at 1006 West Fifteenth Street. He was imprisoned for one year and released on July 31, 1899. Soon after, he repeated the same offense and was jailed for another twelve months.

• 1900. Hoch married Mary Schultz in Argos, Indiana. The woman and her daughter both disappeared.

• November 20, 1901. Hoch married Mrs. Elizabeth Goerhke of 102 Eugenie Street in Chicago, took a job at the Pullman factory on the South Side, then disappeared again on March 10, 1902, after failing to secure money from his latest wife.

• 1902. Hoch married Sophia Fink in Aurora, Illinois.

• April 8, 1902. Hoch married a St. Louis widow named Mary Beaker, and remained with her until March 16, 1903, when he returned to his job in Pullman. Beaker died the following March under suspicious circumstances.

• January 1904. Hoch married Anna Hendrickson, stole $1,000, and absconded.

• 1904. Hoch traveled to Philadelphia where he married Caroline Schaffer. A week later, he stole $1,000 and fled.

• November 16, 1904. Hoch rented a cottage at 5430 Union Avenue. On December 3, he placed a lonely hearts ad seeking a wife in a German-language newspaper. Forty-year-old Mrs. Marie Shippnick Walcker of 12 Willow Street responded to the ad and married Hoch inside her candy store just three days later.

• December 20, 1904. Marie Walcker, a plump, matronly looking woman, took sick. She expired on January 12, 1905. Cause of death, nephritis.

• January 17, 1905. Hoch married Marie's sister, Amelia Fisher, while Marie's corpse was still warm in the coffin. "The dead are for the dead; the living for the living. That is man's moral," Hoch patiently explained as he asked for her hand. After securing $750 in cash, Hoch disappeared . . . again.

Two days after her husband's disappearance, Amelia Fisher reported the circumstances of Marie's death to Inspector George Shippy of the Chicago Police Department. An order of exhumation was obtained, and the coffin was removed from Oakwoods Cemetery for a postmortem examination. Coroner's physician Dr. Otto Lewke detected the presence of arsenic grains in the stomach. There could be no further doubt. Arrest warrants were issued, and an intensive nationwide manhunt for Johann Hoch began.

By now, Hoch was already in New York and hiding out inside a boarding house belonging to a German woman named Mrs. Catherine Kimmerie at 546

West Forty-seventh Street in Manhattan. After only a few hours had passed, Hoch offered to peel the potatoes for the evening supper, believing this sincere form of flattery would appeal to the delicate nature of Mrs. Kimmerie. Then he popped the magical question to the astonished landlady. Johann Hoch was a creature of bad habits. "Why, I haven't known you long enough!" the poor woman stammered.

Her suspicions were aroused by the stranger's decidedly cheeky presumption. A photograph of Hoch appearing in William Randolph Hearst's *New York Evening Journal* caught her attention. She instantly recognized the poisoner of Marie Walcker as her brazen boarder, and the police were summoned to investigate. By nightfall on January 31, 1905, Hoch was stewing in a New York jail cell awaiting extradition back to Chicago.

A white powder that turned out to be arsenic was found inside the barrel of a fountain pen that Hoch always carried in his vest pocket. As the news of Hoch's arrest reached newspapers far and wide, dozens of women from around the country came forward claiming to be one of his abandoned wives.

Returned to the Windy City, Hoch was tried for the murder of Marie Walcker and convicted on May 19, 1905, after thirty days of trial. In his defense, Hoch claimed Marie was a habitual drug user and had died by her own hand. "It was suicide," Hoch said, but the jury was unconvinced.

Efforts to save Hoch from the gallows hinged on whether or not it could be proved that the courts acted improperly by extraditing him for the crime of bigamy, but then prosecuting him for murder once he was secure in the lockup.

The condemned man exhausted his appeals, but never seriously believed he would swing from the rope. "Johann Hoch was never born to die upon the gallows," he said, speaking of himself in the third person. "And I tell you I will not!"

After three stays of execution, the wife murderer was led to the gibbet at 1:28 P.M., February 23, 1906, after Federal Judge Kenesaw Mountain Landis (best remembered for barring eight Chicago White Sox players for life in 1921 for throwing the 1919 World Series) denied the defense team's final motion.

Hoch asserted his innocence right up to the final moment and marched to the gallows unafraid, quoting Bible verses. Evoking the words of Jesus, he said: "Oh Lord, our Father, forgive them. They know not what they do! I must die an innocent man!"

He spoke kindly to his jailers, but warned them that they would have to live with the consequences. "I will soon be dead and can forget," he said. "But not so with them. They will have occasion to think of poor old Johann Hoch many times in the days to come."

Astor Street—North Dearborn Area

Scott Street, west of Astor

THE LEE MIGLIN MURDER: ALL THAT GLITTERS IS NOT GOLD
May 3–4, 1997

Crime preys upon people in all walks of life, and is not always confined to gang-ravaged inner-city neighborhoods. The murder of real-estate mogul Lee Miglin by a sybaritic spree-killer named Andrew Cunanan underscores the inescapable fact that even the high and mighty are not safe in their genteel manses protected by iron-picket fences, security doors, and hidden camera surveillance. Out of respect to Marilyn Miglin, wife of the deceased, we will not publish the address of the property where Cunanan murdered her husband for sport. The handsomely remodeled town homes, mid-rise condominiums, and bay-windowed brownstones at Astor and Scott Streets stand as mute testament to the sumptuous lives of the elite, who began filling in this area in the 1890s when the Prairie Avenue district on the South Side was being taken over by the Levee flesh peddlers and vice merchants. Scott is a one-way, east-west residential street, situated one block south of Goethe. Astor is a block east of State Parkway, running north and south. By far, this is the richest, most affluent slice of Chicago Gold Coast living.

Free from the whirling violence of the city that surrounds them, the residents of the Astor Street community look after one another in the same way that neighbors and friends living along a quiet country lane in Surrey may choose. Wealth is *assumed* and taken very much for granted. There is no need for vulgar ostentation or excess, because everyone who is *anyone* on Astor Street attends the same art gallery openings and charitable events. It is understood that the Rush Street bistros to the immediate south and west provide amusement for the hoi polloi—a nuisance one is forced to endure with hushed stoicism if the full benefits of Astor Street living are to be reaped.

One can well imagine what was being whispered inside the luxury parlors and sitting rooms of the Gold Coast mansions the morning of May 5, 1997, when the residents of Astor and Scott Streets opened their morning *Tribune* to read the awful headline, "Real Estate Tycoon Found Slain."

Unlike many of his tony neighbors who were merely the caretakers of old family fortunes, Lee Miglin, the victim in this puzzling and disturbing crime, came up the hard way. The son of a Lithuanian immigrant, Miglin devoted his early years to work. He was not idling away the hours on the polo fields of some East Coast prep school, but was toiling in a Danville, Illinois, mine, shoveling coal to the surface. In every respect, Miglin was a modern-day Horatio Alger, who parlayed wit, common sense, and his life savings into a thriving commercial real estate consortium he founded in 1982 with business partner J. Paul Beitler.

The firm of Miglin-Beitler is familiar to most workaday Chicagoans through clever billboard advertising lining the expressways leading to and from the central city.

Wife Marilyn was a former Marshall Field's fashion model before striking pay dirt with her own exclusive cosmetics business. The civic-minded socialite and glamour queen owns a megabucks boutique at 112 East Oak Street. She is affectionately known to her intimate circle as "Queen of the Makeovers," and is still out there pitching "Pheramone," one of the top-ten–selling fragrances sold in department and specialty stores. Not so long ago, Oak Street was given the honorary designation of "Marilyn Miglin Way" by the Chicago City Council.

What peculiar set of circumstances brought a predatory hustler like Andrew Phillip Cunanan into the Miglins' insulated world of perfumes and property acquisitions can only be surmised. The salacious rumors, innuendoes, and many unanswered questions will continue to haunt this case for years to come. As yet, there are still no real answers, only speculation. The savagery of the attack against Lee Miglin by Cunanan is the thing that leaves investigators cold. This was not the average robbery-and-assault case that police are accustomed to dealing with in a night's work.

Marilyn Miglin was in Canada doing a promotional spot for the Home Shopping Network at the time when this slaying went down. When she arrived at O'Hare Airport that Sunday morning, Lee was not there to greet her at the gate. How unlike him. Alarmed, she rushed home to find the house disturbed and things out of place. The front gate was unlocked. In a neighborhood of multimillionaires residing less than a mile east of the gin joints and housing projects, no one would dare to be so careless.

Inside, Marilyn contemplated a half-eaten sandwich and dirty dishes in the sink. Lee Miglin was a tidy man. What had happened?

Marilyn found a replica 9-mm handgun resting on a bathroom vanity. It did not belong to the family, and only then did Marilyn decide to call the Eighteenth District to report her husband missing.

At 10:00 A.M. that Sunday morning, the body of Lee Miglin was discovered lying underneath a car in a detached garage at 26 East Division Street. He was tightly wrapped in a green plastic garbage bag, with masking tape covering his entire face and head. The tape was soaked in blood. Miglin had been brutally slashed across the neck with a hacksaw, and the evidence suggested that he had been tortured long before that. Police believe he was led at gunpoint from the Miglin townhouse into the garage where (according to later reports) Cunanan reenacted a scene from his favorite S&M movie, the grisly *Target for Torture*.

Then the killer decided to rest and make himself at home before fleeing the crime scene the following morning with about $2,000 in cash, some gold coins, and a stolen credit card. The condition of the townhouse suggested to police that Miglin invited his killer in through the front door.

The identity of the murderer was easily established by Chicago police two days later through a license plate check of an illegally parked Jeep Cherokee that had been ticketed on Astor Street, eighty-five paces from the Miglin home. The vehicle was traced to Andrew Cunanan, a narcissistic twenty-seven-year-old gay man from San Diego who had a yen for wealthy older men to finance his dissolute lifestyle of greed and consumption.

The Jeep belonged to Cunanan's former lover, Minneapolis architect David Madson, whose mangled body was found in an abandoned farmhouse near Rush Lake, Minnesota. Cunanan was also charged with the murder of Jeffrey Trail, another acquaintance from his underground life, whose remains were wrapped in a rug.

Cunanan drove Miglin's 1994 Lexus to New Jersey where he spontaneously shot and killed a cemetery caretaker named William Reese. His motivation for this crime is another puzzling aspect to the case.

Cunanan's tortured path ended in Miami Beach, where he murdered fashion designer Gianni Versace on July 15, 1997, for the shabbiest reasons, before taking his own life aboard a houseboat. The Versace murder provided Cunanan with the coast-to-coast media publicity he so desperately craved, but his suicide cheated the state of Florida (where capital punishment has become something of a local sport) from executing a national menace.

Back in Chicago, the frantic pace of business never slowed down. Miglin's sudden death foretold change. The former chairman's name was quietly dropped from the corporate masthead in 1998, following a reshuffling that brought new investors into the fold. Today the company is known as Douglas Elliman-Beitler.

Lee Miglin was eulogized in death as a kind and philanthropic man, despite persistent rumors of having led a double life. These charges about his personal life have never been sustained.

Marilyn Miglin tied the knot with international business consultant Naguib Mankarious in June 1999, but lost her chance for permanent happiness when he expired on the operating table less than six months later while undergoing (can you believe it?) facial cosmetic surgery. "We were madly in love, and he never looked more beautiful," reflected Marilyn. Bitter, bitter irony.

In a harrowing, often brutal world, life along Astor Street has nonetheless returned to its normal rhythms. Residents are more cautious than they used to be, however, and at last report, attendance is up at the Eighteenth District's beat meetings. But on any Sunday morning you can observe the rich on parade in casual chic; walking their dogs, jogging up and down the streets of the Gold Coast, and doing the other kinds of things the rich and well-born are known to do in order to keep up appearances for the sake of appearance.

Rush Street Area

843 North State Street

"HEY, MISTUH! YER SHOITS IS READY!" THE OUTFIT OPENS A GOLD COAST BOUTIQUE
1966–1970

Beginning in the 1950s, the Chicago "outfit" stepped up efforts to infiltrate legitimate business in the belief that this was the only viable way to deflect attention from the more traditional revenue streams of loansharking, prostitution and vice, labor union shakedowns, numbers, and drug peddling. The bitter lessons of the past had taught the wise guys one essential truth and that was that nothing draws more unwanted heat from the federal government than gangland violence—the "trunk music" of bullet-riddled, ripe corpses locked inside abandoned Lincolns and Caddy Coup de Villes in the O'Hare Airport parking garage. Lower-echelon hoods opened hot dog stands, started beer distributorships, and launched wholesale jewelry businesses—anything to deceive Uncle Sam at tax time. The underbosses and crew chiefs took over car dealerships. They muscled in on union locals. But in the "Swinging '60s," the Chicago outfit jumped headlong into the clothing business, peddling designer threads imported from London's Carnaby Street and the New York garment district at "Shirts Unlimited," a modest storefront address on State Street, a few doors south of Chestnut on the trendy Gold Coast. The place was under constant FBI surveillance and received a lot of publicity from the Chicago Crime Commission. Virgil Peterson, the fearless Executive Director of the CCC, identified it as a "clearing house" for mob business. The boutique closed long ago; such places rarely remain open for more than two or three years under wise-guy owners. The little storefront on the east side of State Street is barely distinguishable as you walk by it today. It is Sally's Beauty Supply, a cosmetics store selling hair-care products and lotions.

In the summer of 1970, when the nation was at war in North Vietnam and the American public was bitterly divided over the escalation of the Southeast Asian conflict, the North Side haberdashery Shirts Unlimited provided a most unusual setting for an entirely different kind of military summit; one aimed at restoring peace and harmony between two warring crime factions.

At stake for the Chicago outfit was their tenuous hold over their South Side gambling and policy rackets. These had been an important source of revenue since the early 1950s when the last of the uncooperative African-American gambler bosses were assassinated by white hoodlums after refusing to relinquish control of their games to Sam Giancana.

The mob meant business, but this was before the tough inner-city street gangs rose to power in Woodlawn, Englewood, and other South Side neighborhoods ravaged by poverty and a deteriorating infrastructure.

The rise of Jeff Fort's paramilitary gang of thugs, the Blackstone Rangers, signaled a new ruling order in the South Side badlands, and a serious threat for two entrenched Rush Street bosses who had a stake in the gambling action.

Joseph "Caesar" DiVarco and his lieutenant, "Big" Joe Arnold, oversaw loan-sharking, extortion, illegal gambling, prostitution, and porno bookstores in the Eighteenth Police District, which encompassed the heart of the Near North "Gold Coast"—a rich harvest of graft, sleaze, and vice until Rush Street lost its cachet as the epicenter of Chicago nightlife in the late 1970s.

"Joey Caesar," as DiVarco was known to mob associates, was "the man to see" on Rush Street. His career began in the early 1950s when he clocked bets, screened the "26 girls" for employment in syndicate controlled dives, and moved stolen goods in and out of a cigar shop at 808 North Rush Street. Joey Caesar, in business with Jimmy "the Monk" Allegretti, supplied fresh meats to nightclubs and restaurants through C&B Meat Provision Co., a mob-fronted business at 1137 West Randolph Street. Jimmy Allegretti's chauffeur in those days was Joe Arnold, a 270-pound gorilla who was elevated to a position of importance after Allegretti was indicted on federal hijacking charges in 1964.

In December 1966, Arnold and DiVarco opened Shirts Unlimited, and used the boutique as a "front" for the real business, the collection of "juice" loan pay-

"BIG" JOE ARNOLD.

IN MARCH 1980,

HE WAS SHOT TWICE

INSIDE 913 RUSH

STREET. FEARING

RETRIBUTION, THE

WOULD-BE ASSASSIN

FLED TO EUROPE.

(Photo courtesy of the Chicago

Crime Commission)

ments and street taxes from the strip clubs and porno book stores. If a place happened to be owned by a mob "associate," the crew "skimmed" directly from the cash drawer; that is, they took a percentage of the gross every month.

The backroom of this long, rather narrow storefront at 843 North State was outfitted with plush lounge chairs and a television set. Over the next few years, the FBI observed dozens of well-known hoodlums coming and going from the place at all hours. In January 1969, agents of the Illinois Legislative Investigating Commission arrested DiVarco and charged him with failing to register the business under the Illinois Assumed Names Act.

"What's the beef? I'm a legitimate businessman now!" snorted the hoodlum boss.

Wary of the FBI and the ILIC sticking their nose into mob business, DiVarco and Arnold also had to figure out a way to maintain the peace with Fort and his lieutenants, who guaranteed armed violence against the outfit's network of policy runners and street tax collectors on the South Side unless accommodations of an unspecified nature were made.

Rather than see it all slip away, DiVarco called for a peace parley to be held at Shirts Unlimited, just north of the Eighteenth District police headquarters on Chicago Avenue. Jeff Fort, who had marshaled a small band of hero-worshiping, inner-city black youth into an army numbered in the thousands, sent in Mickey Cogswell and Charles Cranshaw as his personal emissaries to the mob.

After much negotiation, the outfit agreed to invest in the future by financing Ranger operations through a series of scheduled payments of $25,000 to $50,000. The mob bought the peace, but the days of the policy rackets were quickly coming to a close. Times were changing, and African-American residents of the South Side refused to spend their money on rigged games of chance.

In 1968, Joe Arnold was arrested and charged with child abandonment in Cleveland, his old home town. Twelve years earlier he had walked out on his wife and two hungry children in order to make his bones with the Chicago crime syndicate. A Cuyahoga County judge ordered him to make restitution to the family, and he managed to avoid prison, but his freedom was short-lived.

A few years later, Arnold and DiVarco were both convicted on income-tax evasion charges and incarcerated in Minnesota's Sandstone Federal Prison. DiVarco eventually died of natural causes behind bars, while his former business partner tried to adjust to life under a new boss, Vincent Solano, labor racketeer and overseer of the Rush Street "crew," one of seven identifiable crime groups comprising the Chicago outfit after the rackets were reapportioned following the imprisonment of Al Capone in 1931.

In March 1980, Arnold was shot and wounded by one of his disgruntled loansharking victims in the basement of the Candy Store, a famous Rush Street strip joint that remained a Gold Coast eyesore until neighborhood gentrification and soaring real-estate values closed the place down during the Reagan era.

Two bullets pierced Arnold's girth, but he held fast to the code of silence and declined to press charges.

Meanwhile, a "For Sale" sign was already tacked on the door of Shirts Unlimited. Pricey Gold Coast rents proved too much, even for the mob.

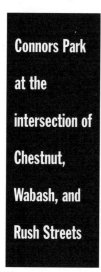

Connors Park

at the

intersection of

Chestnut,

Wabash, and

Rush Streets

IN LOVING MEMORY OF "BOTCHIE"
CONNORS, "KING" OF THE 42ND WARD
1930–1961

With its freshly planted trees, wrought-iron fence, and dignified-looking wooden pergola, Connors Park is a wonderful suburban setting in the dense Near North corridor, jammed with taxicabs, BMW's, Jags, hotel transport buses, and the ebb and flow of shoppers and daily commuter traffic. The real history of Rush Street, apart from its present-day cigar bars, horse-drawn carriages, and chichi restaurants catering to bigtime spenders from out of town, is one that is written in blood. It is a story of crime and corruption; political bosses and Gold Coast Mesdames; gamblers and B-girls; hustlers and hookers. The prima facie evidence of those earlier times is right here in Connors Park, which honors the memory of a man who regulated the goings-on along "Strip Row" and the "miserable mile" extending from Grand Avenue north to Division for more than thirty years. William J. "Botchie" Connors was the potentate of the 42nd Ward, beginning as a deputy bailiff in the municipal court before working himself up to floor leader of the Illinois State Senate. Connors was to twentieth-century Chicago what "Hinky Dink" Kenna and "Bathhouse John" Coughlin were to the nineteenth, that is, a textbook case of "benevolent bossism" in a "wide-open" part of town that did not cotton to the intrusions of reformers or church deacons. His Democratic ward organization was powerful and unbending. Gambling and vice ran in open defiance of the law, and the cops knew better than to interfere. Writer Herman Kogan called this Near North sin-strip "Honky Tonk U.S.A." To others, it was simply "the Roaring 42." The "Magnificent Mile" designation came much later. It is rather curious that at this late date, the City of Chicago would go to the trouble of putting in a park named after Connors at such great expense. Why Connors? Why now? We can only surmise that time has a way of cleansing the sins of the past and forgiving the men who were a party to them.

A *Chicago Daily News* reporter had it on good authority that William "Botchie" Connors, otherwise known as "the King," visited the East Chicago Avenue Police Station each and every Saturday night to give Captain Andrew Barry "the lowdown" on who was to be "pinched" and who was to be left alone during the coming week. The year was 1934, and the *Daily News* called it a "rotten scandal."

"The lawyer, the merchant, the bail bondsman, the panderer, the precinct captain and such characters of the district as 'Big Teresa,' 'Little Mac,' and the proprietor of the dismal hole known as Harry's Place openly discuss in their respective circles how the 'King' directs the affairs of the police station as well as affairs of the ward," the paper noted.

The *Chicago Sun-Times* was even more damning in an October 1950 exposé, calling for a general cleanup—which, of course, fell on deaf ears. "But still the streets of degradation and filth course through a district which also boasts expensive hotels, palatial apartment buildings, and towering office buildings."

Educated in the public schools during the horse-and-buggy era, the ruddy-faced Connors early on aligned himself with Dorsey Crowe, whose reign as an alderman stretched from the beginning of the Prohibition era up through the 1960s. Crow and Connors were vigorously opposed by reform groups who correctly linked them to the West Side Bloc, a cabal of hoodlum politicians who delivered solid Democratic pluralities at election time, while making sure that the vice rackets were left unmolested.

By the time "Botchie" Connors was elected to the Illinois House in 1932, he

WILLIAM "BOTCHIE" CONNORS (CENTER) SIZING UP A RISING YOUNG STAR IN THE

DEMOCRATIC PARTY PANTHEON, RICHARD J. DALEY (LEFT).

had already assembled his own team of "organization men," who were kind and respectful to the old people, the indigent, and the needy, thus ensuring their voting loyalty at the polls come election day. Connors's annual Christmas duck dinners, his willingness to "help out," and his cheerful countenance shone down on the little people at tough moments in their lives, making him a much-admired and even beloved figure.

Meanwhile, the empire of sin and sleaze was being capably administered by George Kries, a former bootlegger pal of George "Bugs" Moran. Kries, indicted for assault with intent to kill after shooting a waiter at the Lido Club, collected the nightly payoffs from "Ma" Kohn, proprietress of the K-9 Club on Walton Place, the largest gambling den in the Near North. When "Ma" was slow to pay, Kries ordered a police raid. Shutters were bolted to the windows, the patrons driven out, and the place closed until "Ma" and her flock of dice shakers wised up.

Other organization men included "the Collector," thick-lipped Eddie Sturch, the tough-guy bodyguard of Connors who pounded lumps on a Winnetka businessman inside the Diamond Cocktail Lounge at 650 North Clark one night. "I don't like your looks!" bellowed the drunken Sturch before laying the man out. Up until that moment, he had never laid eyes on the poor man.

Sturch was released by Municipal Judge Thomas A. Green, a crime syndicate appeaser singled out by the Crime Commission as one of the worst examples of a public servant, guilty of habitual malfeasance on the Cook County bench. The cops who arrested Sturch were all transferred out of the district—"sent to the woods," in police parlance.

In a famous 1921 robbery case involving Connors's most trusted associate, Sturch held up the Benjamin Sugarman Fur Company at 1103 Berwyn Avenue, bound and gagged the elderly husband and wife who ran the place, then emptied the contents of the safe—$230.

Brother John Connors, also known as "Duke de Keno," was an oddsmaker and gambling czar who once owned the C & O Restaurant, former headquarters of the Bugs Moran Gang. John operated a deluxe casino out of the second floor of the Seymour Building, 133 East Ohio, under the business name "Ohio-Michigan Pleasure Club."

Walt Rogers ran the brothels, strip shows, and all-night saloons lining Clark Street and extending east to Rush. If the proprietors of these establishments wanted to stay open until 4:00 A.M., they had to "pony up" with a generous contribution to the ward organization. In the Forty-second Ward, the harlots, whores, and "26 girls" (so-called because of a dice game they played with customers) solicited most every night at the Spa, 921 North Rush Street; Talk of the Town, 1159 North Clark; the Celebrity Lounge, Clark and Oak; and the Broadmount

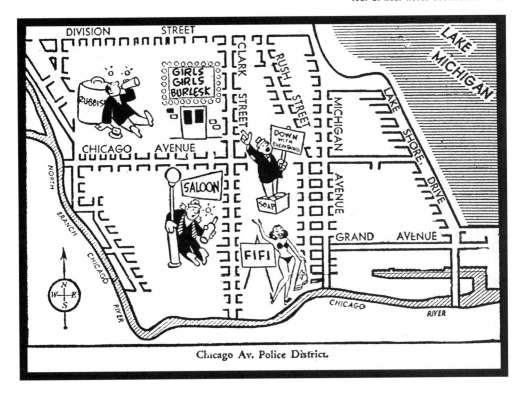

Chicago Av. Police District.

Lounge, 620 North Clark. These places advertised "glamorous girlies" for playful conventioneers. Many of these girls were underage.

Dope dealing was common practice. A "stick of tea" was always available. Conditions were as bad here as they had been in the notorious South Side Levee during the Gaslight Era.

Despite ongoing newspaper exposés and a spate of negative editorials, Senator Connors was returned to the Illinois Senate seven times. Governor Adlai Stevenson chose him as his floor leader in 1949. Connors directed judicial appointments, fought for trucking licensing, and generally kept things afloat for the Chicago "Machine" in Springfield through four mayoralties.

When he died at age sixty-nine on June 25, 1961, eulogies from friends and foes alike poured in. The *Daily News* had railed against his methods for years, but acknowledged that "even a grand jury could not figure out exactly how State Senator William J. Connors did it, but he was a powerhouse in Chicago politics, and an example of the good fortune that gives every man two sides."

Welcome to "Connorsville!" A Bump & Grind Tour of Clark Street Hot Spots, Circa 1948–1959

1. The Playhouse, 550 North Clark (northwest corner of Clark and Ohio). Promising more than the usual fashion parade, the Playhouse was the longest surviving "risqué show house" along strip row. "Long line of lovely scan dolls, call WHI 9615-16." Outside, photographs of the scantily clad ingenues were pasted to the walls, beckoning lonely men from out of town to come in from the cold and sample the attractions. Update: *Not much to see these days. The precise location of the old Playhouse is now the parking lot for the Best Western River North Hotel, one door north of Blue Chicago, a blues nightclub for more eclectic tastes.*

2. French Casino, 641 North Clark Street (northeast corner of Clark and Ohio). Looking for a good time? Telephone DEL 0368. "Chicago's largest floor show. New and lovely terraced theater-restaurant starring a company of well-known and beautiful girls. Open until 4:00 A.M." The conventioneer's guidebook that advertised this misleading enticement neglected to mention that many a brave man who swapped swizzlesticks with the beautiful B-girls inside the bucket of blood ended up on the sidewalk, punched and dazed with pockets picked clean. Update: *The good times ended with a bulldozer and a wrecking ball. The French Casino vanished years ago. A Walgreens drugstore and a parking lot mark the spot today.*

3. Paradise Show Lounge, 1015 North Clark Street (located north of the Newberry Library between Maple and Oak on the east side of the street). Sleaze, sin, and decadence were for sale every night of the week in this tough Gold Coast joint back in the late 1950s. Virgil Peterson of the Chicago Crime Commission filed the following report in 1959: Captain Russell Corcoran, who was then commanding officer of the Thirty-Fifth Police District, personally conducted an investigation in this establishment. Upon entering the place he ordered a bottle of beer at the bar and was charged one dollar. Almost immediately he was approached by a girl who persuaded him to order her a "shot of whiskey" for which he was charged another dollar. The girl then suggested that he retreat with her to a booth where she promptly ordered champagne. The price was $25. Having made this progress the girl offered to perform an act of sexual perversion for a price. At this point Captain Corcoran revealed his identity, exhibited his police captain's star and stated "You are all under arrest." Even this turn of events did not completely dismay the brazen management of the place. Instead, the bartender boldly assaulted Captain

ANOTHER PIT STOP FOR VISITING CONVENTIONEERS ALONG THE CLARK STREET "RED LIGHT RIALTO:" THE NOTORIOUS FRENCH CASINO (LEFT).

1948 PROGRAM ADVERTISEMENT INVITING "LOYAL ORDER OF THE MOOSE" DELEGATES AND CONVENTIONEERS TO COME AND PLAY AT THE "PLAYHOUSE," A BUMP-AND-GRIND SHOW SPOT IN THE HEART OF CONNORSVILLE.

THE OLD PARADISE SHOW LOUNGE AT 1015 N. CLARK IS NOW A FORTUNE- TELLING PARLOR.

Corcoran, striking him in the nose, after which Corcoran fled through the door. Update: *Paradise lost. The sagging, four-story Depression-era commercial building with upstairs apartments stands opposite Dave & Buster's but the ladies of the night retired or moved on eons ago. The Astrology Boutique, a fortunetelling operation, occupies the storefront address today.*

4. Talk of the Town, 1159 North Clark Street (northeast corner Elm and Clark). "Star-studded all-girl review, shimmering G-strings and flimsy bras." *Every Moose, Elk, or Shriner worth his fez dropped in on this famous cabaret at one time or another.* "Of course you get something for your money," *commented* Tribune *reporter E. R. Norderer during a January 1951 visit.* "When $20 has been spent in a half an hour on the red-headed mistress of ceremonies, she stands on her head on the bar. She gets 25 cents on each 75-cent drink of cheap wine purchased by her personal customers and she doesn't trust the bartender. No, she doesn't worry about splinters." *Update:* Nothing to talk about anymore. It's an asphalt parking lot for an Osco drugstore.*

The Mark Twain Hotel, 111 West Division Street

IN LIVING COLOR: TV PREACHER BLAMED FOR FATAL FIRE IN A FLOPHOUSE

January 26, 1986

Hidden away in the darkened corners of the big cities, weather-beaten transient hotels service society's splintered remains—elderly people without means; low-income, unskilled workers; and the physically and mentally impaired who were jettisoned from health-care facilities (ostensibly for cost-cutting reasons) back in the 1980s. We find so many of Chicago's unfortunates who are unable to cope with the daily grind of living ending up in places like the Mark Twain Hotel, a Gold Coast institution (or eyesore, depending on how narrowly one views such places) located on Division Street, a few doors west of Clark where the neighborhood poor and rich historically have converged. All of this is certain to change, what with the arrival of Starbucks, fresh-produce stores, Blockbuster Video, and the ever westward expansion of the Gold Coast. Once the Cabrini-Green housing project is flattened, it is likely we will also witness the disappearance of the remaining currency exchanges, Near North SRO (single-room occupancy) buildings, and transient hotels like the Mark Twain. The Mark Twain is a threadbare five-story flophouse renting for $130 a week. The sparse lobby, though its tiled floor is swept clean, reeks of old soap and the accumulated funk of human habitation—draw your own conclusions. The desk clerk sits behind a panel of bulletproof glass and informs you in a bored monotone that you must present two recent paycheck stubs and be prepared to fully disclose your "circumstances" in a written application if you want to live at the Mark Twain. For your money you get a bed, a bath, and a roof over your head.

Evelyn Johnson was having a bad TV day. In a fit of anger she picked up her television set and hurled it to the floor. The set exploded and ignited a deadly fire inside room 339. As dense black smoke billowed through the third-floor windows, Johnson raced down the stairs, out through the narrow corridor of the Mark Twain Hotel, and east toward Michigan Avenue, screaming "Fire!" as she ran.

The blaze spread quickly throughout the floor, trapping residents behind a curtain of flame. The brave actions of Lt. Edmond P. Coglianese of the Chicago Fire Department saved two residents. But the forty-two-year-old father of three

A ROOF OVER

YOUR HEAD.

THE MARK TWAIN

HOTEL.

died, trapped by flames when he returned to the third floor to search for others left behind. Four other firefighters, a Chicago police officer, and three residents of the hotel were injured in the blaze.

Evelyn Johnson (aka Evelyn Lucas) was originally charged with involuntary manslaughter, but the Cook County state's attorney's office changed this to an indictment for murder.

Appearing before Criminal Court Judge Themis Karnezis, the accused was asked if she had an attorney.

"Only God," came the reply.

Evelyn Johnson had several cases pending against her ranging from criminal damage to property to assault. The woman had also spent some time in a mental institution.

"The public defender will be appointed to assist God," quipped Judge Karnezis, who had heard it all before.

Old Town

WHO PUT THE CYANIDE IN THE TYLENOL?
September 29, 1982

Bustling Old-Town, once a tie-dyed rhapsody of incense-burning head shops, a Ripley's Believe It Or Not Museum, the Royal London Wax Museum, alternative eats, and a mass celebration of 1960s youth culture, has lost its Piper's Alley cachet and with it much of the old unrefined spirit. What remains is the Second City Theatre, an incubator for comedic talent in the United States, Barbara's Book Store, and not much else worth seeing. The arrival of a Starbucks coffee house, directly across the street from the Walgreens Drugstore that is at the center of this story, reminds us that idealized neighborhoods, much like a beautiful bouquet of fresh flowers, eventually wither away and die.

Over the years, there has been much speculation about the lifestyle indicators of the individual responsible for the Tylenol poisonings.

What is still not known after nearly two decades of careful forensic research and analysis is the motive or identity of the killer responsible for the deaths of seven Chicago-area residents who ingested cyanide-laced Extra-Strength Tylenol in the last days of September 1982.

Criminal profilers pegged the murderer as a white male in his early to mid-twenties, reasonably intelligent, but a textbook-case, socially dysfunctional loner. Homicide investigators know, for example, that the tampered products were likely placed on store shelves on Wednesday afternoons, suggesting that the offender worked erratic hours, or had no job at all. No apparent motive for the product tampering has ever been determined.

One cannot walk up to the counter of a local pharmacy and purchase cyanide. However, the compounds are readily available in industrial plants, metal-plating companies, photography labs, and plastics and metallurgical processing factories. It is quite possible, therefore, that the subject purloined quantities of the substance while working in a factory or laboratory. Police theorize that the killer took it to his home where he emptied the Tylenol capsules of their contents and refilled them with crystalline potassium cyanide. His work was clumsy and done in haste, an indication that he was an amateur carrying out a vendetta against society.

The pattern of killings suggested to veteran homicide detectives that the person responsible for this fiendishly random crime spree was a Chicago resident carrying out his madness in suburbia in order to deceive the police task force.

Six of the seven victims swallowed capsules from bottles purchased at Jewel Food Stores in Elk Grove Village and Arlington Heights; an Osco Drug in the Woodfield Mall in Schaumburg; and Frank's Finer Foods in west suburban Winfield.

The Tylenol crisis began with the death of a junior high school student from Elk Grove Village named Mary Ann Kellerman, who took the deadly capsule to ease cold symptoms.

Elk Grove Village postal carrier Adam Janus swallowed a Tylenol pill to ease chest pains. While grieving for his brother, Stanley Janus and his wife Theresa perished in Adam's home—minutes apart—after ingesting capsules from the same contaminated bottle that had taken Adam's life.

The next day, twenty-seven-year-old Mary M. "Lynn" Reiner of Winfield became the sixth person to die after taking two poison capsules. She had only recently returned home from the hospital after giving birth to her fourth child. While Mass was being conducted for Mary Reiner, friends and relatives of Mary McFarland, an employee of Illinois Bell and the mother of two, were gathering in another part of Cook County for a memorial service to honor her memory. McFarland was victim number five. It was only after the deaths of Kellerman and the three Janus family members that suburban officials were able to link Tylenol to the mysterious deaths. Lt. Philip Cappitelli and Richard Keyworth, two off-duty firefighters, compared case notes and discovered that the Tylenol bottles from Elk Grove Village and Arlington Heights had come from the same lot (MC2880).

The first six killings seemed to indicate a clear and concise method of distribution, until a Chicago resident, thirty-five-year-old United Airlines stewardess Paula Prince, became the poisoner's seventh and final victim.

Prince was a native of Omaha, Nebraska, who rented a Gold Coast apartment for the enjoyment of fast-paced, big-city living. But with a demanding flight schedule, there was not much time for her to live out the life of a carefree single. Prince had just returned from Las Vegas and was set to fly out the very next morning. Returning to her place at 1540 North LaSalle Street the evening of September 29, Prince complained of a headache and chronic fatigue.

Before settling in for the evening, the unlucky flight attendant walked the short distance to the Walgreens Drugstore at North and Wells (just around the corner from her apartment), where she bought a bottle of Extra-Strength Tylenol containing the fatal cyanide-laced capsule. An ATM video-surveillance camera actually captured her on film as she paid the cashier for the bottle.

Paula Prince collapsed in her apartment moments after swallowing the headache remedy. The open bottle of Tylenol and the sales receipt were found on the washstand the following evening by the victim's sister.

With the news of this latest poisoning death, the city of Chicago was thrown into a frenzy. One city hospital received seven hundred Tylenol-related phone calls in less than twenty-four hours.

"The victims never had a chance," explained Dr. Thomas Kim of Northwest Community Hospital. "Death was certain within minutes." The latest incident marked the first time the killer had struck within city limits.

As a result of the Paula Prince murder, Mayor Jane Byrne ordered all Tylenol products removed from the shelves of local stores, urging residents to turn in their bottles to police. In the coming days, investigators from the city and suburbs found even more cyanide bottles in area stores, and the first reports of "copycat" poisonings began to trickle in from around the nation. In the first

PAULA PRINCE BOUGHT POISONED TYLENOL CAPSULES

HERE THE NIGHT OF SEPTEMBER 29, 1982.

month following the Tylenol deaths, the Food and Drug Administration recorded 270 separate incidents of product tampering.

The red-and-white poison capsules had come from four different manufacturing lots. But spokesmen from McNeil Consumer Products, a manufacturing division of Johnson & Johnson, convened a press conference to advise the media that strict quality-control standards had been observed at all times. The tamperings could not have occurred until the product reached Illinois. Johnson & Johnson faced a public-relations disaster of nightmare proportions.

Suspects were questioned and an arrest was made, but no one was ever officially charged with committing the seven diabolical murders.

Former tax accountant and real estate salesman James Lewis was convicted of extortion after sending a letter to Johnson & Johnson executives demanding $1 million to stop the killing. Lewis lived in Kansas City and had been implicated in the 1978 murder of an elderly man named Raymond West who was also a client and family friend, but the charges in that case were dropped because evidence had been illegally obtained.

Lewis and his wife operated a storefront tax service until law enforcement began sifting through their records for evidence of fraud. With an arrest warrant hanging over their heads, the flimflamming couple fled to Chicago where they remained until September 4, 1982. The extortion letter arrived at the offices of Johnson & Johnson from a New York address a month later. Lewis was seized inside the New York Public Library not long afterward.

James Lewis was a compelling but unconvincing suspect. He served nearly ten years in a federal penitentiary for the crime of extortion before receiving parole from a federal penitentiary in El Reno, Oklahoma, on October 13, 1995. Journalist Joy Bergmann located him in Cambridge, Massachusetts, where he spends much of his time these days puttering on his home computer.

Up until 1982, Tylenol had been America's best-selling pain reliever. Dire industry forecasts foretold the disappearance of Tylenol products from the shelves, but the company hunkered down and launched a sizzling public relations and marketing campaign that is still studied by young ad executives seeking the magical blueprint to success in a competitive industry.

The first step was to unveil new and improved safety measures. Triple safety-sealed bottles thought to be tamperproof were introduced to ease consumer anxiety.

The investigation soon faded from public view. Tylenol products successfully recovered their market share, but then Diane Elsroth of Yonkers, New York, died from another poisoned capsule in February 1986. In the next five days, five more cyanide capsules were located not far from where Elsroth had purchased the contaminated bottle.

None of the seals protecting the supposedly "tamperproof" bottles recovered in New York showed evidence of being punctured or disturbed.

VIOLENCE AND POLITICAL MAYHEM AT "PADDY" BAULER'S SALOON
December 18, 1933

Southeast corner of North Avenue and Sedgwick Street

Forty-third Ward alderman Mathias "Paddy" Bauler was a watery-eyed sot from years gone by who was charming and perfectly delightful in his cups. Belly up to the bar, boys, and observe the master boss Democrat in his element; a schooner of cold Pilsner clenched in his right hand; a silk top hat perched atop his fat, round head; a lusty beerhall melody droning in the background; and words of wisdom spouting from the mouth of your genial host. "Them new guys in black suits and white shirts and narrow ties; them Ivy League types, them goo-goos. They think the whole thing is on the square!" No one understood better than Bauler that in Chicago poor but honest men go to heaven (independents, idealists, and Republicans mostly), but the political connivers, grafters, and wirepullers are nolle prosequi-ed in the court of last resort. In 1933, the year Bauler was elected to his first term as alderman of the Forty-third Ward, he opened a saloon and political clearing house inside the Immigrant State Bank Building at 343 West North Avenue. Later, Bauler opened another public house directly across the street in a graystone at 403 W. North Avenue, which remained until the beer spigots yielded their last foam on Halloween night, 1960. The building was then converted into a real-estate office. It's still functioning as a law office, but without benefit of a marker, engraving, statue, or tombstone to commemorate Paddy's boisterous presence. Paddy Bauler's original saloon at 343 became the most famous tavern on the North Side. George Cardinal Mundelein, Archbishop of Chicago from 1916–1939, was known to drop in for a beer or two from time to time. Like everyone else, he enjoyed the antics of Paddy Bauler, a celebrated bon vivant whose riotous election-night parties were talked about for many years. It was never a question of did we win; the real question on the lips of the precinct captains, sewer inspectors, and ward heelers staggering into the backroom after the polls closed at seven was, By how much? And while the memory of Paddy and those rollicking good times lives on, there is nothing more to say about the bank that became a saloon. It was torn down; all of it, that is, except for a tiny fragment of the original building left standing on North Avenue east of Sedgwick at Orleans Street. Today it's a hot dog stand known as the North Avenue Deli. The intersection of North and Sedgwick remained vacant for a considerable period of time, until a strip mall, featuring a Dunkin Donuts, and a currency exchange were put in by a developer in the 1990s. Rather sedate, wouldn't you say?

Christmas is for the kiddies, and out of the goodness of his aldermanic heart, Mathias "Paddy" Bauler threw open the doors of the Plaza Theater at 320 West North Avenue to raise money for the tots. (Originally located across the street from the saloon, the former theater is a parking lot for the North Park Towers today.) It was Paddy's annual gala charity event, and as alderman and committeeman of the Forty-third Ward, he hired the famous vaudeville comedy team of Olsen & Johnson to headline an all-star cast. The young ones would not be disappointed, not this year anyway.

Chicago's Mayor Edward Kelly and a swarm of political bigwigs from every Democratic stronghold in the city were on hand to lend encouragement. Baskets of food were donated to the indigent, and the beer flowed right up to midnight.

When only a small coterie of Bauler's closest political allies remained, Paddy suggested they repair to his saloon across the street for a late-night toddy. By now it was already past one in the morning. The outside doors of the saloon were locked tight. That night, Paddy was in rare form, happily crooning his time-honored melodies of love for his private entourage until he was rudely interrupted.

It was about three-thirty when a roadster driven by an off-duty Chicago cop from the Damen Avenue station named John J. Ahearn glided to a stop outside the Bauler saloon. Ahearn, his partner Edward Hayes, and May Tyler, a female companion from Evanston, had been making the rounds of the North Side resorts during an all-night, barhopping binge. Both Hayes and Ahearn were former bodyguards of the late Mayor Anton Cermak, who was murdered by a sniper in Miami earlier that year.

The door of Paddy's place was bolted shut when they arrived. Inside, Cook County Sheriff William D. Meyering and a dozen other public officials, who probably should have had the good sense to have gone home to bed, were enjoying Bauler's conviviality well past the acceptable hour. Ahearn was spotted in the vestibule trying to get their attention. Paddy, his .38-caliber Smith & Wesson revolver concealed inside his vest pocket, uttered a curse word and waved the strangers away.

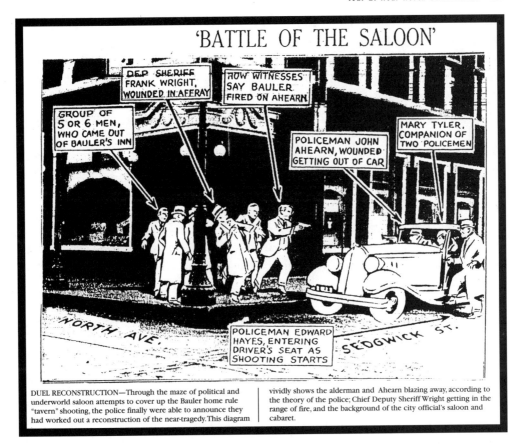

'BATTLE OF THE SALOON'

DUEL RECONSTRUCTION—Through the maze of political and underworld saloon attempts to cover up the Bauler home rule "tavern" shooting, the police finally were able to announce they had worked out a reconstruction of the near-tragedy. This diagram vividly shows the alderman and Ahearn blazing away, according to the theory of the police; Chief Deputy Sheriff Wright getting in the range of fire, and the background of the city official's saloon and cabaret.

But Ahearn had spotted Sheriff Meyering sipping beer inside and was resolved to gain admittance. Hayes and Miss Tyler had retreated to the car. Their instincts told them that this had not been a good idea to begin with.

Bauler, who took his nickname as a young man while trying to break into the boxing world (the adoption of an Irish name was essential to success in the fight racket), was not to be trifled with. For all his bluster, ribald jokes, and expressions of mawkish sentiment on election day, Paddy was as mean and ill-tempered as a cobra when provoked. According to one version of the now famous story, Ahearn uttered a profane epitaph upon being refused admittance the second time. "He swore at me and called me a fat Dutch pig," Bauler told journalist Len O'Connor years later.

In the exchange of gunfire that followed, Ahearn shot and wounded Chief Deputy Cook County Sheriff Frank Wright, who told the press the next day that he "couldn't remember who shot him and he was just innocently walking along the sidewalk at the time."

In fact no one seemed to recall who fired first, or that a shooting had even occurred. Sheriff Meyering, whose reputation for dishonesty and inefficiency was revealed by Roger Touhy in Touhy's published memoirs, likewise "saw nothing." It was as if the whole bloody fracas never occurred, except that a slug had passed through Wright's lung, and Ahearn was laid up with a bullet lodged in his spine at Alexian Brothers Hospital.

Fortunately neither man died, but Paddy Bauler was indicted later that month by a grand jury on a charge of assault with intent to murder. The saloon was ceremoniously padlocked by order of Police Commissioner James Allman, but neither the criminal charge nor the revocation of Paddy's liquor license stuck. Afterward, Bauler said he was going to draft an ordinance requiring cops to leave their guns at work.

When questioned by reporters after he had time to think things over, Officer Ahearn had this to say: "I was always a good friend of Paddy Bauler's. We had been at Charlie Weber's place and we decided to go to Bauler's because we wanted to spend some money and help him with his Christmas fund."

Raising his bottomless beer stein and flashing that famous toothy grin, Bauler observed: "What's it all mean? Nuttin'. All you get out of it all is a few laughs."

ALDERMAN MATHIAS

"PADDY" BAULER OWNED

AND OPERATED HIS LAST

SALOON IN THE BUILDING

SHOWN TO THE LEFT.

HE CLOSED THE BUSINESS

IN 1960.

(Photo by author)

In Pursuit of Nazis, Gangsters, and Anarchists:

North Side Crime Scenes from Lincoln Park to Rogers Park

C rime cooks on all eight cylinders. In violent and unpredictable times, the North Side of Chicago emerged as a kind of film noir, a backdrop for an oddball assortment of kooks and killers, con men and crazy women, Nazi spies, and plotting anarchists.

The entire North Side along the lakefront is awash in colorful true crime stories. The locales of some of the most sensational and brazen murders, bizarre intrigues, and insidious plots from the last one hundred years have been saved from the wrecking ball, but only because the property values in the area have soared since the early 1980s. Baby boomers were quick to recognize the investment potential of old houses in traditional urban neighborhood settings, particularly those in and around Wrigley Field.

Yuppies (for want of a better word) bought these derelict properties at fire sale prices, chasing away the poorer people. In Roscoe Village, for example, retired pitchmen and carnival sidemen who toiled at the old Riverview Amusement Park lived on fixed incomes, until rising property taxes forced them out of their homes. The Yuppie invasion succeeded in turning ramshackle worker cottages into million-dollar town homes. This pattern of residential displacement is being repeated all over the city.

The ethnic identity of the North Side has mostly been lost. The Germans are gone from Lakeview. The Swedes of Andersonville died off or moved out, and the Jews of Rogers Park are fewer in number these days than before. In their place, a restless café society has emerged. Adventurous, affluent young bohemians, transplanted from the suburbs and elsewhere, take the CTA Red Line to their downtown destinations each morning, and return to the Belmont Avenue stop every evening to their coffeehouses, workout rooms, storefront theaters, and heavy-metal rock clubs.

The CTA Red Line provides visitors to Chicago a fascinating bird's-eye glimpse of the North Side and its eclectic mix of poets, street people, stockbrokers, activists,

125

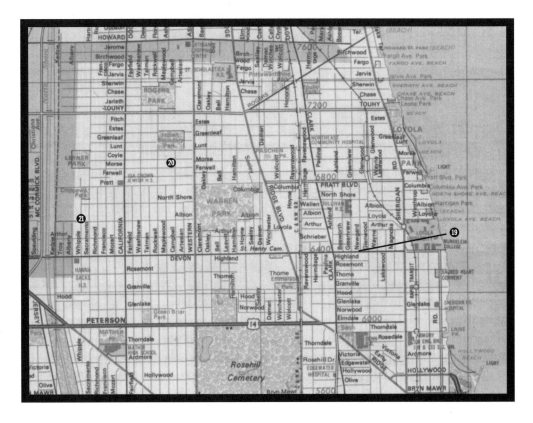

1. Haber Factory fire, 908–914 West North Ave.
2. Emma Goldman's hideout, 2126 Sheffield.
3. House of the Nazi spies, 2234 North Fremont.
4. Kiyo's Restaurant hostage drama, 2827 North Clark St.
5. "Nails" Morton's one-way ride, Clark & Wellington.
6. Dancehall collapse, 3233 North Clark St.
7. Charlie Weber home, 3601 North Wolcott.
8. William Drury murder site, Wolcott and Addison.
9. 1929 drug store holdup at Clark and Roscoe Sts.
10. Dunkel-Lang murder house, 731 West Barry St.
11. Residence of Blanche Dunkel, 1212 Waveland Ave.
12. Monterey Restaurant street fight, 3422 N. Broadway.
13. Lake Michigan tidal wave, Montrose Harbor.
14. Yellow Kid Weil's hotel, 4526 North Sheridan Rd.
15. "Two-gun" Louie Alterie slain at 922 Eastwood.
16. Uptown Theatre, Broadway & Lawrence.
17. Roger Touhy seized here, 5116 North Kenmore.
18. Dr. Harold Cassidy, John Dillinger's plastic surgeon, 4957 North Wolcott.
19. Midget desperado seized at Devon and Newgard.
20. Residence of "Big Tim" Murphy, 2525 Morse Ave.
21. Dr. Peacock's doom, 6438 North Whipple Ave.

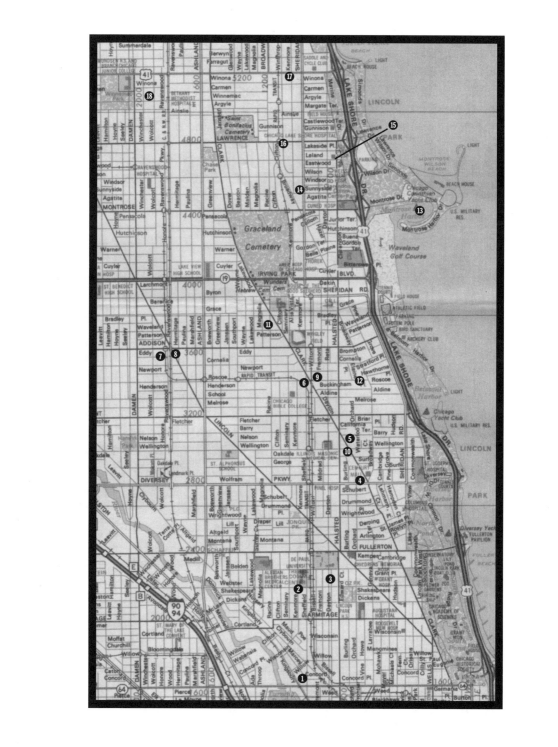

set designers, writers, and grunge musicians, many of whom are likely to sport tattoos, think liberal, and vote for the Democratic Party.

In the days when vaudeville was in full flower and jazz was king, the North Side of Chicago beckoned transients and thrill-seekers to its door and asked no questions. High-rise apartment buildings with lakefront views that sell for millions today were rooming houses renting by the week.

Because there was always so much to see and do, and even more ways to get into trouble, a room with a lakefront view was often nothing more than a place to crash for a few days, or maybe even a month.

Lincoln Park, the Clybourn Corridor

908–914

West

North

Avenue

THE HABER FACTORY FIRE: THIRTY-FIVE IN THE MORGUE
April 16, 1953

Once, not so long ago, manufacturing plants and industrial factories were a staple of urban life—the sustaining, principal element of neighborhoods, helping to define the working-class character of the city as a whole. Chicago had always been a factory town. From Calumet City to Zion, the factories belched thick black smoke into the air, polluted the waters, and killed off, often by inches, the spirits of the downtrodden working stiffs who toiled in meaningless jobs year after monotonous year. You don't hear much of horrific factory fires anymore. That's because the manufacturing plants most susceptible to fire calamities by now have been either slated for the wrecking ball or neatly transformed into chic condo lofts priced in the six figures. The manufacturing jobs have all gone overseas where labor is cheap, and sweatshop conditions are tolerated. There is not much call anymore for punch press men or polishing machine operators. Maybe it is just as well, because factory fires, occurring with alarming regularity in the old days, are largely a thing of the past. As you drive to the site of the old Haber Factory at 908–914 West North Avenue, one block west of Halsted, you will note the presence of a gleaming new Crate & Barrel and the Container Store anchoring an upscale shopping and theater district. An asphalt parking lot separates these two rather imposing retail emporiums that cater to the young urban aesthetes prowling the area for trendy home furnishings. The parking lot marks the exact location of the long-forgotten Haber fire tragedy. It follows, does it not, that when a disaster or crime of magnitude occurs on a site, the site will remain undeveloped for years to come? This section of North Avenue was once a grimy, industrial corridor. It remained that way for many years, until the onslaught of Yuppies and real-estate speculators permanently altered the character of the neighborhood. Continental Can and Gibson Spring were two vintage industrial plants flanking the doomed Haber plant. They are gone now, but several representative examples of crumbling and derelict factories stand rather forlornly on the streets to the immediate west. Buildings like these are more than just casual remnants of Chicago's vanished industrial age. They serve as sullen reminders of the greed, venality, and utter lack of concern for the have-nots, whose lives were considered expendable. When safety was barely a secondary concern to the factory owners, sudden death was not an altogether unexpected outcome.

"**E**verywhere I looked, there were human torches around me with their clothes and hair and bodies on fire! I still don't know what happened!"

His faltering voice betraying a normally placid demeanor, Assistant Fire Commissioner Anthony J. Mullaney wiped the sweat and grime from his face. For the moment, his gaze was riveted on a blackened corpse lying among the smoldering bricks and timber of the fire-ravaged Haber Corporation. "This is horrible," he said. "This proves that management should know more about their employees' safety. They should be more responsible . . ." His voice trailed off. Some things were best left unsaid.

The Haber Corporation built machine parts for food mixers and other small appliances manufactured by Dormeyer, the parent company located at 837 West North Avenue, just down the street. The plant employed eight hundred unskilled assembly-line workers, most of them Eastern European war refugees and Mexicans struggling to understand a new language and unfamiliar customs.

Fortunately, a reduced work force was on duty the morning of April 16, when at around 8:50 A.M. an enormous explosion rocked the plant, and a fireball swept upward from the northwest corner of the first floor. A spark rising into the air from the slipped grinding belt of a polishing machine, operated by Joseph Loverde, ignited a fatal mixture of dust particles, lint, and aluminum shards. Factory inspectors were unanimous in the opinion that the blast had occurred within the exhaust system.

Within minutes the entire plant was a raging inferno. Workers found themselves hopelessly trapped in the upper floors of the Haber plant because someone had unwisely ordered the removal of an emergency stairway and a fire

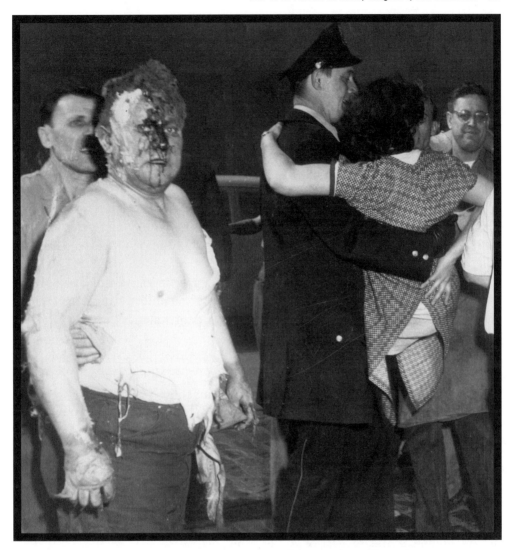

BLEEDING AND DAZED FIRE VICTIMS (ABOVE). THE HABER

FACTORY IN FLAMES (FACING PAGE). YOU WILL FIND A PARKING

LOT FRONTING THE CONTAINER STORE THERE TODAY. STRETCHER

TEAMS CARRY THE INJURED TO SAFETY.

(Photos courtesy of Art Bilek)

escape. The Ragnar Benson construction firm had been hired to re-model the façade of the aging four-story structure, but a rusted fire escape stood in the way of the carpenters and masons. Before work could begin, the troublesome fire escape was taken down on orders from Harry Brady, the director of safety, who (ironically) ended up on a slab in the county morgue alongside thirty-four other victims who perished in the deadly fire.

Screaming women, the hair on their heads on fire, plunged to their deaths from the third-floor ledge after a shipping-room ladder proved inadequate. The positioning of bodies indicated to Deputy Coroner Harry Glos that the roaring flames simply halted fleeing victims in their tracks.

Bodies were pinned under heavy machinery. Charred embers were strewn about like toothpicks. "The sight was awful. It was a fury," commented Third Battalion Chief Frank Thieman. "A sheet of flames shot out of all fourteen second-floor windows facing the street."

Coroner Walter McCarron, a political hack whose incompetence and overall lack of experience compromised several major homicide investigations later in the decade, indignantly tore into company president Kalman Tanko at the City Hall inquest that followed. "Violations were running wild—such as violations of the no-smoking rule. If the fire escape had been there, lives would have been saved!"

Stairwells blocked with boxes of Haber machine parts further impeded escape routes. When it was over and the bodies all counted, the Haber Corporation was cited with ten violations of the fire safety code.

Key Haber Corporation executives failed to show up for the inquest. The families of the dead and dying demanded accountability, but both Tanko and the owner of the property refused to accept responsibility. The owner was vacationing with his wife in New York.

Ownership of the property was traced to Titus Haffa. Haffa was a notorious saloon politician and professional bail bondsman who was sentenced to two years in Leavenworth for federal violations of the Prohibition laws the very same day in 1929 when seven of his friends belonging to the "Bugs" Moran gang were lined up against the wall of a Clark Street garage and machine-gunned to death.

Titus Haffa was the Republican alderman of the 43rd Ward, a North Side domain of organized crime and vice. Before Al Capone forced the Moran gang to dissolve, Haffa relied on gangsters like Ted Newberry to supervise his network of distilleries, which formed the axis of a $5 million bootlegging ring. Haffa generously provided them with all the necessary firepower to protect his interests from "interlopers." In those days, financing arrangements were coordinated through the Haber Company, which Haffa bought for a song in 1921.

Branded a "betrayer of the public trust" by Judge Walter C. Lindley, Alderman Haffa served only seventeen months of his two-year sentence. An unrepentant lawbreaker to the end, Haffa shifted the blame for his predicament to the judge. "I am the victim of circumstances." Haffa then filed a petition for bankruptcy, deciding he would not pay the court-imposed $11,000 fine. After that he turned "respectable," exchanging prison stripes for a gabardine suit.

Haffa recouped his fortune during World War II, buying up old factories and handling war contracts. Always protective of his family, Haffa transferred the title of the Haber plant to his two sisters, Doris and Pauline, who lived off their brother's generosity inside a musty Victorian mansion that once belonged to Robert Todd Lincoln at 1240 Lake Shore Drive. Devoted to Titus, the Haffa sisters called this place home well into the 1960s.

By the time of the Haber fire, Titus Haffa's shady past was forgotten. The bootlegging wars were of another day. Haffa reveled in his newfound status as an admired Chicago business leader and honored member of the Horatio Alger Association of Distinguished Americans. The accolades poured in, and then came the fire, and suddenly the false mask was stripped away.

Surrounded by executives of his $50 million manufacturing empire, the former alderman spoke to the sufferings of the Haber victims in a mournful tone, but he cautiously sidestepped any questions about liability. "No man's grief is greater than mine in all this," he said. "Those who lost their lives were not just employees but friends whom I knew by their first name."

Titus Haffa solemnly vowed that the dead would never be forgotten. As soon as the Speedway Wrecking Company had finished clearing away the last of the fire debris, he solemnly advised community leaders that he would build a playground on the site—a little patch of green in the dense urban sprawl to memorialize the suffering of the victims for future generations. "The material loss is nothing," he said. "I would gladly bear it all if I could bring back one of the dead."

The community awaited further action on Haffa's part, but there was only silence. The months and years rolled by. By this time, the realization had slowly sunk in that there would be no park, no swing set, no monument of any kind. There is only an asphalt lot recently added for the convenience of Crate & Barrel shoppers hurrying to claim their treasures. It is doubtful any of them could possibly suspect the horrible human calamity that occurred here once long ago.

Lincoln Park, the DePaul Area

2126 North Sheffield Avenue (formerly 303 Sheffield)

"THE PRESIDENT IS SHOT! FIND EMMA GOLDMAN!"
September 10, 1901

In the parish of St. Vincent DePaul, a modest four-story graystone building with a garden apartment stands squarely in the middle of the block between Dickens Street on the south and Webster on the north. The unremarkable Sheffield Avenue address might easily be bypassed in the rush to get through the front door of the late-night bars awaiting the students of DePaul University if it were not for this historical footnote. We do not know who lives at this address just now, but the current residents might be interested to know that Emma Goldman, America's "Queen of Anarchy," was arrested inside the third-floor flat on September 10, 1901. The charge: inspiring a mental defective who called himself a "disciple" of Goldman to murder the president of the United States.

In 1901, thirty-two-year-old Emma Goldman was considered by many to be the most dangerous woman in America. Waging class warfare with her comrades from abroad, the Russian exile Angelica Balabanoff and Rosa Luxemburg of Germany, in a few short years Goldman emerged as a player on the stage of international anarchy. Goldman proudly wore the red badge in the days when the mere mention of an anarchist brought forth frightening images of pitiless, wild-eyed men with flowing beards hurling bombs at the homes of kings, magistrates, and heads of state.

As a young Russian émigré, Emma Goldman bore witness to the evils of the American factory system. At the age of seventeen, she worked from dawn to dusk in a shirtwaist factory in Rochester, New York, where she observed firsthand the suffering of the laboring classes.

Her politics were molded by the plight of the four Chicago men who eventually swung from the scaffold in retribution for the 1886 Haymarket Riot, arguably the bloodiest chapter in nineteenth-century labor history. The anarchists were convicted and hanged for setting off a bomb in a column of policemen on May 4, 1886. Upon hearing the news, Goldman flung a pitcher of cold

LOVERS AND ANARCHISTS. EMMA GOLDMAN (LEFT) AND HER CHICAGO PARAMOUR HIPPOLYTE HAVEL.

water in the face of a woman who dared to utter contemptuous words against the memory of the "martyrs." From that moment forward, Goldman waged continuous class warfare with a sense of purpose borne out of fury.

Her celebrated love affair with Alexander Berkman, a Russian-Jew who attempted to assassinate Henry Clay Frick, manager of the Carnegie Steel Mills in Homestead, Pennsylvania, in 1892, brought Goldman into national prominence. However, with Berkman locked away in his prison cell, Goldman cultivated a new lover, a dark-haired Bohemian radical from

EMMA GOLDMAN HID FROM THE POLICE IN THE THIRD FLOOR APARTMENT OF THIS BUILDING ON SHEFFIELD AVENUE, DEPICTED IN 1901 AND TODAY. THE SMALLER FRAME HOUSE TO THE LEFT HAS BEEN RAZED AND IS AN EMPTY LOT.

Chicago named Hippolyte Havel who, like Goldman, believed in neither government nor law. Havel was her adoring "Putzy," and his love letters to Emma were used by the Chicago police as evidence of a plot to kill the president.

In spite of her diminutive stature and plain looks, Goldman was a fluent speaker and a political firebrand who was fearless in her denunciations of the American capitalist system. Even her most strident foes on the conservative right were forced to acknowledge her superior oratorical skills.

Wherever the cause of the oppressed led her, the lecture halls and athenaeums of the industrial North were certain to be packed. Goldman preached equality for women, free love, and a doctrine of unencumbered living that horrified the new American middle class. "Her name was enough in those days to produce a shudder," wrote Margaret Anderson, editor of the influential *Little Review*, published out of Chicago.

Though Goldman did not seem to approve of the extreme measures employed by Berkman and others desiring to overturn the fabric of society with gun and bomb, her expression of sympathy for this class of men inspired Leon Czolgosz to acquire a weapon and travel to the Pan-American Exposition in Buffalo, New York, for the avowed purpose of shooting the president of the United States, the placid and unassuming William McKinley.

On July 12, 1901, Emma Goldman was in the midst of a lecture tour that swung through Chicago. At the same time, Czolgosz arrived in the city to hear her speak on "The New Phases of Anarchism."

Leon Czolgosz, a twenty-seven-year-old Polish drifter, rented a room for fifty cents a night at Esther Wolfson's boarding house at 525 Carroll Avenue (now in the 1500 block, following the 1909 city street renumbering), due north of the old Maxwell Street Jewish ghetto. Czolgosz badgered the other lodgers to reveal information about "secret meetings," and asked his new acquaintances for money but was turned away. The police kept tabs on this side of town. It had long been a seedbed of sedition, and the Carroll Avenue premises were under periodic surveillance.

"There is said to be a larger number of anarchists in Chicago today than at the time of the Haymarket Riot," observed the morning *Inter-Ocean*. "They live in the territory between Carroll Avenue and Twelfth Street and Ashland Avenue and Halsted Street." Anarchist gatherings were often held at the Turner Hall on West Twelfth Street (now Roosevelt Road). The "Red Menace" was pegged by Chicago police as ten thousand strong. It was an exaggeration perhaps, but reflective of the ever growing paranoia of foreign-born revolutionaries.

Czolgosz was a stranger to this particular group. He said he was from Cleveland, but had spent time in Ft. Wayne, Indiana, just before coming to

Chicago. He had signed the guest book at the rooming house "Mr. Schloss." But in Ft. Wayne, he traveled under a different pseudonym, "Fred C. Niemann." Well dressed in a tailor-made suit, Czolgosz, alias "Schloss," was strongly suspected of being a government spy by Goldman's suspicious followers, who had also taken lodging in the Carroll Street address that July. Czolgosz acted queerly and seemed distracted. The anarchist camp considered him a crackpot.

Emma Goldman spoke only briefly with Czolgosz that afternoon before returning by train to her sister's home in Rochester, New York. She did not know until much later that "Schloss" had followed her to the depot and was peering at her as she boarded an eastern train. She thought nothing more of the matter, until news reached her in St. Louis on September 6 that President McKinley had been shot twice in the abdomen while greeting well-wishers in a reception line at the Buffalo Temple of Music.

It was the disturbed young man known as Leon Czolgosz who fired the bullets from a .32-caliber Iver-Johnson revolver.

The gunman was seized immediately and led away for interrogation. "I am a disciple of Emma Goldman," he announced to Buffalo police with an air of casual defiance. "What started this craze to kill was a lecture I heard her make some little time ago. She set me on fire."

A receipt for alterations from a tailor shop at Twelfth Street and Ogden Avenue was found in the assassin's pants pocket. The Chicago police were put on alert.

An arrest warrant was drawn up for Emma Goldman. Convinced that Goldman, Havel, and the rest of the anarchist flock had hatched a presidential murder plot right there in Chicago, the cops rounded up a dozen persons with close ties to the movement. The prisoners were herded into cells at the Harrison Street lockup without being formally charged.

Jane Addams of Hull House called upon Mayor Carter Harrison II to demand that the anarchists be permitted to consult with legal counsel. In a mood of growing public apprehension, Addams represented a soothing triumph of reason. Harrison, a reasonable man, relented.

Meanwhile, Chicago police had intercepted a telegram from Goldman notifying a female acquaintance in Chicago of her intention to return to the city.

On September 10, Captain Herman Schluetter, the city's most celebrated sleuth, raided the Sheffield address belonging to one Charles G. Norris, a wealthy preacher who was not affiliated with the anarchist movement, but personally sympathetic to Emma Goldman. The fashionable North Side address was a good cover for Goldman, who tried to pass herself off as a Swedish servant girl when the cops arrived. It was a futile gesture. She was hardly convincing.

Breaking through the door of the third-floor flat, they found Goldman passively seated in a rocking chair, wearing Indian moccasins and a white shirtwaist, and smiling at them pleasantly. "You are under arrest for the conspiracy to murder the president!" bellowed Schluetter once her identity was established. A personalized fountain pen lying nearby blew her cover.

Goldman was taken to the Harrison Street annex (part of the fortress-like police compound at Harrison and Van Buren known as the Armory until it was razed in 1911), where Mayor Harrison and Chief of Police Frances O'Neill took charge of the interrogation. She was candid with them. "If Czolgosz is irresponsible—weakminded—must I bear the blame? I can see not even circumstantial evidence against me from any point of view." While she defended (in principle) the anarchist objectives Czolgosz purported to represent, she also volunteered to attend to the wounds of the dying president as a nurse's aide.

Goldman underwent far more rigorous questioning once the mayor had left the station and at one point she was slugged in the mouth after objecting to the rough tactics administered by the Chicago bluecoats against another prisoner.

The president died of his wounds on September 14, and a national day of mourning followed. The mood of the country was somber, but in Chicago there was much ill feeling directed toward those who were held accountable for the tragedy. Another witch-hunt, similar to the suspension of civil rights that had occurred in the dangerous days following the Haymarket bomb explosion, seemed imminent.

Emma Goldman was held without bail amid thieves, murderers, and footpads, but she retained her customary stoic composure at all times, even as rumors circulated outside the jail that a lynch mob was forming. Fifty police officers formed a tight circle around the building to protect her.

Goldman remained in her cell until September 24, when charges were dropped for want of evidence. Leon Czolgosz, sullen and filled with hatred toward the American system of government, admitted at his trial that he acted alone and involved no one else. With no other recourse, the police were forced to release Goldman and the twelve other anarchists.

Czolgosz was executed at Auburn Prison on October 29, 1901, leaving behind many unanswered questions. Chicago authorities were not entirely convinced that McKinley's murder was the random act of a lone assassin. They held fast to the belief that the Carroll Avenue group formed the plan and directed Czolgosz in his work every step of the way. These charges were never sustained.

Though Emma Goldman had publicly censured the actions of the murderer, she published an article in the journal *Free Society* later in the month pleading sympathy for Czolgosz who, with each passing day, was becoming more and more her personal martyr to the cause. Many of Goldman's former friends and associates were outraged by her cant and withdrew from her inner circle, fearing more police reprisals. On the fifth anniversary of his execution, she devoted an entire issue of her publication, *Mother Earth*, to the memory of the assassin.

NAZI SPIES ARRESTED IN CHICAGO
June 27, 1942

2234

North

Fremont

Street

The former residence of Mr. and Mrs. Hans Haupt, parents of the Nazi saboteur, is today a beautifully preserved three-story "walkup" located between Belden and Webster, one block west of Halsted Street. The red-brick, iron-gated building is on the west side of Fremont Street, in an area where property values have soared in recent decades. In this serene, tree-lined setting inhabited by wealthy young geniuses who earn their fortunes starting up software companies or trading hog bellies at the "Merc," there exists a real sense of pride in community. Vast sums of money have been expended sprucing up the old homes, whose property deeds date back to the last century. If you want to buy a vintage gray- or brownstone on Fremont Street, it will set you back. But in old homes there are stories to tell, some of them famous and forgotten, others buried in the shrouded mists of time. The story of the Nazi spies and "Bundists" who lurked in the shadows of Fremont Street during the darkest days of World War II is one of them.

In the fall of 1937, the *Chicago Times* drew sharp attention to Nazi sympathizers in Chicago, attempting to alert an apathetic and indifferent citizenry to the menace posed by the German-American Bund (also known as the "Friends of the New Germany"), an ethnic fraternal movement dispensing propaganda and promoting cooperation with Adolf Hitler's government through parades, picnics, youth programs, rifle drills, and beer hall rallies.

Alarmed by the inflammatory rhetoric of these groups, the newspaper assigned a trio of top-notch reporters—James J. Metcalfe, William Mueller, and John C. Metcalfe—to pose as Nazi sympathizers and infiltrate the Bundist movement for the purpose of obtaining secrets and assessing the level of the threat to American security.

John Metcalfe went to New York, where he became a close confidant of Fritz Julius Kuhn, the fanatical "*Bundesfuhrer*," and Hitler's national spokesman in the U.S. James Metcalfe, a former "G-man," infiltrated the secret world of George

Froboese, truculent leader of the *Midwest Amerikadeutscher Volksbund*. At the end of each day, James Metcalfe filed his daily dispatches with Mueller, the outside contact.

The *Times* reporters presented their startling findings to the nation on September 9, 1937, concluding, among other things, that a movement was afoot to recruit American boys of German parentage for sensitive spy missions against the U.S.

Isolationists were outraged, accusing the paper of unnecessary saber rattling and attempting to lure American interests into dangerous foreign entanglements. The nation, including official Washington, ignored the growing threat, because they were in no mood to provoke Hitler's wrath in troubling economic times. America was locked in the grip of the Great Depression, and the acrid memories of World War I were still fresh in people's minds.

The *Times* message was never clearly understood until June 27, 1942, when FBI agents seized twenty-two-year-old Herbert Hans Haupt and another man, Hermann Otto Neubauer, age thirty-two, and charged them with spying for Nazi Germany.

Haupt was arrested in a third-floor flat rented by his parents, Hans and Erma Haupt, at 2234 North Fremont. Bureau agents had kept the place under continuous surveillance from 10:30 A.M., June 22, until the arrests of the saboteur, his parents, and an aunt and uncle were effected on June 27. Within the next twenty-four hours, fourteen other German-Americans in Chicago were seized for lending aid and comfort to the spy ring.

The story broke the next day, alarming a tense and overwrought city that had already become, in the opening months of World War II, accustomed to receiving bad news from the frontlines. Piecing together the essential facts of the case, the press learned from FBI sources that Haupt and Neubauer were part of a team of eight men who had been recruited and specially trained for spy duty by Lt. Walter Kappe of *Abwehr 2* (Intelligence-2), a resident of the U.S. from 1925 to 1937.

Young Haupt was born in Stettin, Germany, but had immigrated to Chicago in 1925 with his mother when he was only six. Herbert was remembered by teachers and former classmates in Chicago as a dullard, completing just enough of his assignments to scrape by. They recalled how impressed he seemed to be with uniforms, military protocol, and the youthful pomp and circumstance of high school ROTC. He enlisted in the corps while attending classes at Amundsen and Lane Tech on the North Side. His mother recalled how her son liked to strut around in full dress uniform outside the house pretending to be an American soldier. Later, he joined the Bund and donned a more sinister-looking getup.

In 1939, as the war clouds over Europe gathered, he was apprenticed to the Simpson Optical Company in Chicago, a manufacturer of lenses for military instruments including parts for the Norden bombsight. Herbert's experience working in this wartime plant made him especially valuable to his Nazi handlers.

On June 14, 1941, Haupt resigned his position, kissed his mother goodbye, and dashed off to Mexico City with fake papers identifying him as "Sgt. Larry Jordan," a name borrowed from a school acquaintance from Chicago. In the company of two fellow Bundists, Haupt called upon the German Consulate, announcing his intention to volunteer for service to the "Fatherland." From Mexico City, Haupt proceeded to Tokyo aboard a Japanese barge, and from there to Bordeaux, France, on a German blockade breaker.

Making contact with Walter Kappe in Berlin, Haupt was assigned to the German espionage school at Quentz Lake, Brandenburg, outside the capital. The estate once belonged to a wealthy Jewish family, until they were forcibly evicted at the hands of the Nazis.

Hermann Neubauer had already settled in Germany after fleeing the U.S. in 1940 with the help of the German Consulate in New York, who paid his traveling expenses. While in Chicago, Neubauer had worked as a cook at the Palmer House Hotel for $5.75 a day. In 1936 he went to work as a cold-meat chef at the Bismarck Hotel, where his bosses remembered him as sullen, quick-tempered, and a "poor man to argue with."

Married to an American girl, Neubauer resided at 2849 North Burling and 933 West Belmont Avenue. Though active in the Bund, he had no police record and kept to himself. Wounded on the eastern front while serving in the German *Wehrmacht,* Neubauer was recruited into the spy service by Kappe as he convalesced in an army medical center near Vienna, Austria.

The saboteurs received three weeks of intensive training in the manufacture of explosives and the theoretical and practical techniques of sabotage. Their assignment was to infiltrate industrial plants in New York City and Chicago crucial to the German war effort. Haupt was to return to Chicago to try to win back his old job as an apprentice optician.

The spies were divided into two groups of four. The New York faction departed from a German submarine base at Lorient, France, on May 26, 1942. Haupt and Neubauer were aboard a U-boat destined for the coast of Florida two days later. They landed at Ponte Vedra Beach, south of Jacksonville, on June 17.

Haupt, Neubauer, Edward John Kerling, and Werner Thiel buried supplies of blasting caps, detonators, and timing devices in the sand; changed into civilian clothing; then dispersed at the train station. Haupt and Neubauer continued to Chicago, Thiel and Kerling went on to New York.

Unknown to Haupt and his fellow spies who were put ashore in Florida was the presence of the FBI, which was charting their course almost from the second they changed clothes on the beach. The spy ring had been sold out by George John Dasch, leader of the New York faction, who hopped a train to Washington to reveal the inner workings of the plot to the FBI. Perhaps out of sheer cowardice, or the realization that the plan was foolhardy and destined to fail from the start, Dasch told Director J. Edgar Hoover everything he needed to know to effect an arrest.

Agents from the Chicago FBI office kept close watch on the Fremont Street apartment house. It seemed very apparent to the G-men that Haupt's father was complicitous in the plot. He accompanied Herbert to the Simpson Optical plant

THE NAZI SPIES

HAVE LANDED!

JUNE 30, 1942.

CHICAGO TIMES

EDITORIAL

CARTOON.

CONDEMNED NAZI SPY HERBERT HANS HAUPT WAS SEIZED INSIDE HIS FATHER'S APARTMENT AT THIS BEAUTIFUL FREMONT STREET ADDRESS ON THE NORTH SIDE.

to help him obtain employment. Hans negotiated the purchase of a 1941 Pontiac automobile for his son, and had foolishly confided to acquaintances that he would never permit his son to join the American army, vowing to return his family to Germany once the Nazis had succeeded in winning the war.

Hans Max Haupt's incriminating remarks contradicted earlier statements made to the FBI that he had encouraged his son to register for the draft and had gone down with him to the recruiting station. "I had registered. I thought it was his duty, too," he said. The father was a veteran of the First World War and had served in the German army.

The arrest of Herbert Haupt stunned twenty-four-year-old Gerda Melind, a hotel beautyshop operator who accepted his marriage proposal after a night of dancing and romancing at the *Haus Vaterland*, a German-American Bund hall located at 2349 West Byron. (*Author's Note:* The beer hall stood at the corner of Byron and Western Avenue in Ravenswood and was owned by Dr. Otto Willumelt, leader of the Chicago Bund. It was closed within hours of Haupt's arrest and was eventually torn down. A used-car lot occupies the site today.)

Gerda's love quickly turned to hate after being summoned to Washington, D.C., where she was grilled by FBI agents."Now I am ashamed of him and don't want anything more to do with him," she said, choking back the sobs. Her father, a German-born janitor, said he never trusted the boy."He was always a four-flusher. He could talk you blue in the face, but at the end he was telling you nothing," the man recalled, understandably worried about being drawn into an ever tightening noose.

Chicago's German-American community expressed a love of country and disavowed any connection with spies or Bundists. They lived in fear of the dreaded knock on the door in the middle of the night.

Neubauer and Haupt were whisked away to Washington under tight security. Tried before a military commission at the U.S. Justice Department on July 8, all eight saboteurs were found guilty and sentenced to death. Attorney General Frances Biddle implored President Franklin D. Roosevelt to commute the sentences of the cooperative Dasch and coconspirator Ernest Peter Burger, who revealed the plot to the FBI. Both men were granted clemency by President Harry Truman in April 1948 on the condition of deportation.

They were fortunate, indeed, to be spared the fate of Herbert Haupt and the remaining six, who were sequestered at the District of Columbia jail until they were hanged by the neck on August 8, 1942. Three days later, the bodies in the morgue were taken out and buried in unmarked pine boxes at Potter's Field, Blue Plains, D.C. Only numbered stakes placed above the gravesites marked the location.

And so ended Nazi Germany's only serious attempt to sabotage the military-industrial complex of the United States.

For the family and friends of the Haupts, matters would drag on for many more years. For sheltering his son in the Fremont Street flat and uttering seditious words, Hans Max Haupt was indicted and convicted on twenty-nine overt acts of treason against his adopted country and was sentenced to life in prison. His wife, Erma, was confined to an internment camp until the end of the war, and an uncle named Walter Froehling received a five-year sentence for misprision (contempt).

There would always remain lingering doubts about the correctness of jailing an indulgent father for the sins of his child. Public opinion concerning the father of the spy was evenly divided while attorneys grappled with the meaning of "treasonable intent" as it applied to Hans Haupt. By its very definition, persons found guilty of the crime of treason must have committed "overt acts." Parental devotion, however misguided, did not seem to fit that description.

Reversed on appeal, the final fate of defendant Haupt was decided by the U.S. Supreme Court on March 30, 1947. Constitutional issues aside, the memories of the Nazi horror in the postwar world seared the public conscience. They had no other choice but to uphold the guilty verdict and send the haggard-looking, middle-aged man to prison for the rest of his days.

Lake View

SHAFT'S BIG SCORE: HOSTAGE DRAMA AT KIYO'S JAPANESE RESTAURANT
August 30, 1972

2827 North

Clark Street

(just north

of Diversey

Parkway)

Kiyo's was the place to go if you savored Japanese tempura and other delights from the Pacific Rim. The restaurant was a neighborhood institution for many years, until the owners closed shop in early 2000. Standing opposite the Century Theater complex on the east side of Clark in a densely packed residential and commercial corridor, where it is virtually impossible to park a car, you will find that Kiyo's is now Mokomo Ltd., a jewelry emporium.

At Kiyo's one night, a pensive-looking man approached one of the Asian waitresses, asking for a glass of water and the right to use the washroom. Of course, maître d's in the better restaurants deeply resent the hoi polloi treating their establishment as a public washroom, but in the interest of maintaining decorum, lest they risk an embarrassing verbal outburst, few are, in fact, turned away.

On this particular August evening in 1972, the waitress told the man that he couldn't use the restroom. It was for customers only. It was ten-thirty in the evening, and the dinner crowd was thinning out.

An hour later, three angry, cursing men brandishing a sawed-off shotgun and pistols stormed into the restaurant, ordering eight customers and nine employees to lie down on the floor. Unnoticed by the heavily armed robbers was Daniel Smith, the seventeen-year-old son of the owner of Kiyo's. Smith fled through the back door and ran east to Broadway. Frightened to the point of hysteria, Smith flagged down a police car driven by Officer Harold Brown. The boy gestured wildly in the direction of the restaurant.

Within moments, a horde of reinforcements screeched to a halt in front of Kiyo's, demanding that the gunmen surrender. The cops sealed off the Clark Street entrance, an action that sparked a potentially deadly ninety-minute hostage standoff inside Kiyo's. Outside, an estimated crowd of six thousand onlookers milling about formed an impenetrable wall of humanity, escalating tensions to the breaking point.

Two shotgun blasts were heard from inside the restaurant as attempts to negotiate the release of the restaurant patrons failed. A kimono-clad waitress was pushed through the door to present their demands. From inside, the police were told that a robber had just shot someone, and to please back off. In truth, this was a bluff, but the cops were suddenly inclined to treat matters more delicately.

Deputy Police Superintendent Walter Vallee negotiated terms with the hostage takers, who demanded among other things that a getaway car be provided and safe passage out of the restaurant guaranteed. With that agreed to by the police, four female hostages piled into the green car at the point of a gun.

What the gunmen did not know was that one of the Chicago police officers had smashed the car's taillights so the vehicle could easily be ID'ed in traffic. The car sped away.

In the confusion of the moment, the robbers suddenly realized that they had left behind $650 in cash and items of jewelry taken from the hostages. "Man," the driver said, "you got the bread?" They looked at each other dumbly, then started cursing and accusing each other of screwing up.

"Turn around, man, we'll go back in and get it. They don't dare stop us with the hostages!"

They had no money and were nearly out of gas.

Mrs. Lorraine Gilkison, who was celebrating her birthday at Kiyo's before the merriment ended on a sour note, persuaded the three stickup men that their best course of action was to dump the car and make a run for it. The barrel of a loaded shotgun was pressed against her neck, but there was a growing sense that these three African-American men, given their youth and inexperience, were just as scared and vulnerable as their prisoners.

Overhead, the sound of a Chicago police helicopter could be heard.

The hostage takers led police on a wild, two-hour, crosstown chase that proceeded north on Clark Street to Irving Park Road, then west to the Kennedy Expressway. They drove erratically from the North Side to the South Side, exiting at Adams, going west to Halsted, and then south, ducking through back alleys and down one-way streets.

At 555 East 61st Street, east of the Dan Ryan Expressway and in the middle of an area well known to Chicagoans as "the projects," they refilled the gas tank and sped off once again.

Shots were exchanged at 63rd and Michigan after two police officers from the Grand Crossing District spotted the car traveling the wrong way on a one-way street.

Unable to shake loose from the relentless surveillance of the overhead helicopter, the panicky driver ended up in the northbound lanes of the Ryan, where a police vehicle driven by Richard Ehrman of the canine unit pulled alongside. His partner, Officer Laurel Redman, waited until they were abreast of a grassy knoll before drawing his service weapon. He aimed the gun an inch below the driver's brain. The decision to shoot was a difficult one, but he had no other recourse.

The bullet found its mark. The car skidded up the embankment and came to a halt, but gasoline was trickling from the tank and an explosion was imminent.

The robber cradling the shotgun was struck by a bullet as he attempted to run away from the burning wreckage of the crashed automobile. On that note, a night of terror ended with a whimper.

The traumatized female hostages were released unhurt. Gunman Louis Tarver, a youth of twenty, was taken into custody. Tarver told police that he and his two companions, Michael Jones, age seventeen, and eighteen-year-old Michael Griggs, had boarded a CTA elevated train bound for the North Side earlier that day. He said he knew the other boys from the neighborhood around Fifty-ninth and Michigan.

Appearing before Judge Albert S. Porter at Wentworth Boy's Court, the lone surviving member of the teenage stickup gang related his story. He told a Damen Avenue detective that they had recently seen *Shaft's Big Score!* at a downtown movie house, and the shoot-'em-up antics of Hollywood had captivated them and made their botched holdup attempt seem like a good idea at the time.

Shaft's Big Score! was playing at the Century Theater, directly across the street from Kiyo's, the night of the robbery.

There was another side to the story. After being refused a glass of water, Jones decided to rob the restaurant patrons because he figured that it was the easiest and fastest way to score money to buy some new clothes . . . for school.

The northwest corner of the Clark Street and Wellington intersection

THE NAIL IN THE COFFIN: A HORSE TAKES "NAILS" MORTON FOR A ONE-WAY RIDE
May 13, 1923

The "murder" of North Side gangster Samuel "Nails" Morton by a rambunctious steed is one of many great "tales of Chicago." It has been told and retold over the years, but like so many colorful vignettes of city life, the true facts of the case have collided with urban myth. Even the most knowledgeable devotees of the Prohibition Era often get it wrong and place the approximate location of the accident along the bridal path inside Lincoln Park. "Nails" actually met his maker at the southeast corner of Diversey Parkway and Clark Street. For dramatic purposes, however, we will revisit the spot where the ill-fated afternoon canter began, the Brown Riding Stables, 3008 North Clark, the northwest corner of Clark and Wellington. The horse stable disappeared long ago; horses have no place in congested Lakeview. But the building that remains in the 3000 block of Clark is recognizable to most modern-day Chicagoans as the old Ivanhoe Theater.

Samuel Morton earned his famous sobriquet fighting bullies in the old Maxwell Street ghetto and not from battling the "Bloody Hun" in Flanders field where he led a company of discouraged Yanks "over the top." Sam was "hard as nails," and he earned the respect of scores of gamblers, pugilists, and gunmen prowling the vicinity of Halsted and Maxwell.

The son of Jewish parents scraping out a living in a miserable cold-water flat, "Nails" did his mitzvahs for God and country during the Great War. He was awarded the Croix de Guerre for heroism in combat and was a much-talked-about figure back home.

Assigned to the 131st Infantry, the old "Dandy First" or Rainbow Division, Morton sustained a bullet wound in the arm and shrapnel to the leg. Laid up in a field hospital, he begged his commanding officer to allow him to rejoin the unit. He led a raiding party against the kaiser's army and was the only one to return to base alive. For this bit of gallantry, he was promoted to lieutenant and sent home to Chicago a full-fledged war hero.

Well spoken, refined, and a natural leader of men, he chose to renew acquaintances with his Irish gangster pals from the North Side rather than pursue a more respectable career in business.

An inveterate gambler, Morton joined forces with Dion O'Banion, Louie "Two-Gun" Alterie, Hymie Weiss, and other familiar faces on the police rolls. Together they organized a profitable gambling and bootlegging syndicate.

It was the dawn of Prohibition, and the North Siders decided to cash in on their associations with politicians and beer distributors. "Nails" Morton presided over the roulette wheel at one of his after-hours gambling dens, and could be seen placing ringside bets at the Friday night fights. "Bet five grand on the man in my corner!" "Nails" cried out, knowing that he would double his wager on a "tanked" prizefight within minutes of the sounding of the bell.

Within two short years, "Nails" Morton had moved in to the Congress Hotel and was enjoying the high life. At age twenty-nine, he was wealthy, powerful, and, through adroit political maneuvering, invulnerable to prosecution.

In October 1921, Morton and "Herschie" Miller, retired municipal court bailiff and part-time gangster, were acquitted on charges of murdering Police Officers William Hennessey and James Mulcahy inside the Pekin Inn, a notorious South Side jazz and gin cabaret. Charges that the eyewitnesses to the shootings had been "bought off" by attachés of Republican State's Attorney Robert E. Crowe were never sustained. A "thorough investigation" ordered by Crowe turned up nothing, and the two men skated.

In early 1923, deciding that it was to their advantage to lend legitimacy to the operation, Morton and O'Banion took on a new business partner, William F. Schofield, proprietor of a florist shop at 738 North State Street, across from Holy Name Cathedral. The famous flower shop was to become the command post of the North Side mob.

GANGSTER "NAILS" MORTON GOT OFF ON THE WRONG FOOT AT THE BROWN RIDING STABLES (CLARK AND WELLINGTON), WHERE THE IVANHOE THEATER NOW STANDS.

(Photo by author)

Not long after the ink had dried on his agreement with Schofield, Morton made a date for an early morning ride with Dion O'Banion, his lovely young wife, and a mutual friend, Peter Mundane. Immaculate in his green sport coat, cream-colored trousers, and riding boots, Morton mounted a frisky young colt O'Banion had named "Morvich," after a famous jockey of the day.

The plan that morning was for "Nails" to jog east down Wellington toward the Lincoln Park bridle path where he would rendezvous with his companions, but the nervous and mettlesome horse had other ideas.

As "Nails" rode away from the stable, Morvich suddenly bolted south down Clark Street. Near the intersection of Diversey and Clark, Police Officer John Keyes noted the fast approach and tried to curb the animal when it became apparent Morton had lost control.

Then suddenly the left stirrup gave way and fell to the ground. Morton clutched the animal by the neck, then decided to chance it and leaped to the ground. He crash-landed headfirst on the street.

On the way down, a kick from the horse's hind hoof struck Morton in the head, inflicting a basil skull fracture that proved fatal. The police officer rushed to the aide of the fallen rider lying unconscious on the ground. "Why, it's 'Nails' Morton!" he said in amazement. "He was my lieutenant in France!"

Morton was rushed to the hospital but expired on the operating table. Within hours, hundreds of friends and associates began arriving at the undertaking parlor at 4936 North Broadway to pay their respects. The ex–war hero was remembered as a likable, friendly fellow.

A crime like this could not go unpunished. Within twenty-four hours, the hapless steed responsible for the outrage was (allegedly) executed at gunpoint by Louis "Two-Gun" Alterie.

Of course, that part of the story may be apocryphal, or merely the clever invention of a Hollywood scriptwriter. The fictional "Nails" Nathan in the gritty 1931 crime noir *The Public Enemy* was based in part on Morton's rise to prominence in the underworld. When Tom Powers (played with a snarling menace by Jimmy Cagney) discovers that his boss has been kicked to death on a bridle path, he visits the stable and shoots the horse.

The Ivanhoe Theater

The Ivanhoe dinner theater, constructed to resemble a medieval English fortress, withstood a powerful bomb blast the evening of August 12, 1964. The explosion ripped a hole in the main entrance, tearing out a stained-glass door on Wellington, just west of Clark. Luckily, no one was hurt, but the incident suggested an emerging pattern of union shakedowns. The Ivanhoe blast was the third bombing of a popular Chicago restaurant in less than a month. Owner Richard Jansen, the director of the Chicago and Illinois Restaurant Association, did not believe the bombing was the result of union trouble, but affidavits dating back to the 1940s were produced showing that his father strongly believed that hoodlums and racketeers had infiltrated the restaurant locals. "It's idiotic to think that all of us restaurant owners are sheep," the son countered. "This is not 1929 Chicago. People aren't afraid to help the police."

SIDETRIP

ST. PATRICK'S DAY DANCEHALL DISASTER
March 17, 1948

Lake View Hall, 3233–3239 North Clark Street

Up and down the major North Side thoroughfares of Broadway, Clark Street, and Ashland Avenue, generations of Chicagoans congregated inside the fraternal lodges and public ballrooms to drink, dance, and socialize among peers. The north-south streets were honeycombed with places like these— red-brick, terra cotta buildings spanning the length of a city block, housing a bowling alley, dance floor, meeting rooms, and small, street-level retail shops. Now, there are only a few of them left. In those bygone days, landlords could sustain a healthy profit renting public space to immigrant groups, first to the Swedes of Clark Street, then to the Germans of Lincoln Avenue, and most notably to the Irish. All of them gathered in places like these to celebrate their ethnic heritage and the fragile bonds between the old country and the new. It was the era before television, air conditioning, suburban movie houses, and shopping malls; a simpler time when people were unafraid to follow their hearts and venture out into the night for romance and pleasure. The Lake View Hall, where more than a hundred St. Patrick's Day revelers tumbled three floors to street level in one sickening moment that they would remember the rest of their lives, is long gone. What remains is a fenced-in weed patch awaiting *redevelopment. Until some land developer can figure out what to do with this disputed property, it will remain a blight on the neighborhood and another stirring reminder that old crimes and forgotten disasters leave behind an indelible mark.*

It was the deafening crack of wooden flooring, and the astonishing sight of grown men and women tumbling through the floor like playful children on a water slide, that eyewitnesses to this tragedy would remember the most.

The fact that it occurred on a night of merriment—a festive night that the Irish-American residents of Chicago had been looking forward to all year—deepened the sense of despair and the feelings of outrage that accompanied the news of the licensing scandal that followed.

It was the annual St. Patty's Day party at Lake View Hall. The Connaughtmen's Social Club rented the larger third-floor ballroom, and the Yankee Division Club of Chicago, the smaller space. Two Irish bands were hired to play dance music in the adjacent rooms, and everyone seemed to be having a corking good time. Patrons of the second-floor bowling alley and billiard room could hear the echoes of Irish folk music and the stamping of happy feet coming from above, but none could possibly imagine that the party was about to crash down upon their heads.

The first warning of the impending cave-in occurred at 10:10 P.M., moments after one of the bands had returned from a brief intermission. A "whooshing" sound, proceeded by a loud and ominous cracking noise, was heard throughout the building. A section of the flooring at the north end of the larger ballroom gave way, tearing down portions of the roof. The floor collapsed at a 45-degree angle, sending men and women spilling onto the lunch counter of the floor below, which was occupied by the Lakeview Bowling Alleys.

In what can only be described as a massive "human pileup," 106 people were injured, but only one person fatally. The blood-covered mass of moaning and dazed survivors were taken to Illinois Masonic Hospital at 836 Wellington, while rescuers wielded electric saws in an effort to pry loose Mrs. Ann Hunt, a native of County Galway, who was pinned to the crumpled floor by a section of the roof. For two hours firefighters struggled to remove the debris. They used chairs to prop up the space between the collapsed ceiling and floor, but by the time they freed the woman she was already dead.

The *Chicago Sun-Times* launched an investigation into the dancehall disaster, and uncovered evidence of a massive city licensing scandal. At least 298 pub-

RESCUERS ARRIVED TOO LATE TO SAVE THIS WOMAN, CRUSHED BY THE COLLAPSE OF THE OVERHEAD CEILING AT THE LAKE VIEW HALL, MARCH 17, 1948.

(Photo courtesy of Art Bilek)

lic places were operating without a license and had not been cleared by the zoning board or the police, fire, or health departments. Many of these places had been denied a license because their structures were found to be defective or were operating on city-issued receipts for payment of the fee, even though the license was never formally issued.

In other words, corrupt city inspectors were pocketing bribes all over town, and were looking the other way while dangerously unstable facilities remained open for business.

John R. Jenkins, the manager and one of the owners of the Lake View Hall, never bothered to apply for a license. What was the point? The entire City Hall apparatus had a "For Sale" sign attached, from the traffic cop down to the lowly sewer inspectors, and all the way up to the judges of the criminal court.

Mayor Martin Kennelly, the well-meaning former moving-van executive, had changed the rules so that the city would take no money and issue no licenses until the violations were corrected.

The Kennelly rule was universally ignored. The mayor could never expect to enforce such meaningless dogma in a machine town like Chicago, for it would effectively cut off an important source of graft for the men who padded and oiled that machine. The righteous Kennelly was not cut out of the same cloth as the man who would ultimately succeed him in office, Richard J. Daley.

He was not the "boss," and the old-line politicos like crafty Joe Gill, clerk of the Municipal Court, always knew it and never respected him. Behind his back, the boys in the organization called Kennelly "Fartin' Martin," as their City Hall underlings allegedly listened in on his phone calls. Gill answered to other masters and, in fact, conducted his 46th Ward political meetings in the unlicensed Lake View Hall.

Meanwhile, John Jenkins feebly tried to explain that "he did not know" what the capacity of his building was supposed to be, but he "guessed that it was around 500 people, give or take." City records showed that his second-floor bowling alley had been refused a license a year earlier for failing to meet minimum safety requirements.

West Lakeview

THE STRANGE DEATH OF ALDERMAN CHARLIE WEBER
August 16, 1960

3601 North

Wolcott

Avenue

(Wolcott

and Addison)

Homes of politicians, athletes, and show business celebrities are often set apart from the rest of the neighborhood by the fences their owners erect to keep away autograph chasers, fans, and curiosity seekers. In Chicago, where there are many more politicians than actors (thus the politicians enjoy a quasi-celebrity status), six-foot-high brick walls surrounding a property usually signify that this is a residence belonging to an alderman, a county commissioner, or a judge. The yellow-brick bi-level house situated at the northeast corner of Wolcott Avenue and Addison Street (a half-block west of the Ravenswood elevated line in the St. Andrew's Parish section of Lakeview) is distinctive from the surrounding two flats because of the presence of an imposing security wall, effectively cutting off all but an obstructed view of the roofline. Undoubtedly when 45th Ward Alderman Charles Weber lived there, he must have harbored grave concerns for his personal safety and that of his third wife, Emma, to have constructed such an unfriendly barrier. And with seemingly good reason. Inside the home, this powerful saloon politician with connections to the Chicago underworld perished, either by accident or design. The mystery has never been resolved.

On the wall of his ward office at 2922 North Southport, Charlie Weber framed a favorite saying that was his personal credo: "Kids are like apples. Pick 'em up and wipe 'em clean and they won't go bad." Weber loved dachshunds and children. Every year, at the end of August, he threw an enormous party for the neighborhood waifs at Riverview, the fabled North Side amusement park in which he held a one-fifth interest.

Alderman Weber represented the colorful "old guard" of the Democratic machine of legend. For thirty years, beginning in 1922, he served this heavily German-American voting district in the Illinois legislature. He was elected committeeman in 1926, and alderman twenty-nine years later (1955). Between 1952 and 1955, he was a Cook County commissioner. Weber amassed a fortune in real estate and through his ownership of a tavern at 2933 Southport (which would later become the famous Zum Deutchen Eck restaurant). "I spend my money as fast as I get it," he joked.

During one reelection campaign, Charlie sent every female voter a dozen roses and a card urging them to come out and vote the ticket. Each eligible male voter was awarded $5, and the women in an adjoining precinct were given silk babushkas for their support.

A proponent of the "wide-open town" and legalized gambling, Weber never made any bones about his warm association with gangsters and bootleggers. It was simply a matter of "expediency."

In large measure, he was the "P.T. Barnum" of Chicago politics, a party to the many graft schemes hatched by his closest friend and confederate in the Chicago City Council, Alderman Mathias "Paddy" Bauler. Weber was an outspoken critic of Republicans, reformers, and teetotalers, though he himself never consumed anything stronger than a chocolate soda.

During Prohibition, Weber openly flaunted the dry law by operating a beer distributorship at 1414 Roscoe. On October 9, 1933, gangster Gus Winkler was shotgunned to death outside the entrance to the place. Winkler was rumored to have been one of the masterminds of the St. Valentine's Day Massacre. Weber denied any personal involvement with Winkler or receiving illegal revenue, but in her divorce action filed against Charlie in 1930, first wife Eleanor Weber said that "liquor and gambling activities" earned him upward of $100,000 a year.

Weber kept the streets of the ward swept clean, fought for educational reforms, and faced no serious challenges from good-government types for many years. But in early 1960, Weber broke ranks with Mayor Daley and other Democratic regulars over their choice for the Democratic presidential nomination, John F. Kennedy.

Weber distributed eighty thousand copies of his newspaper, the *Lake View Independent*, urging his constituents to support the candidacy of Senator Lyndon B. Johnson, who had just been invited to attend the 1960 "Kid's Day" outing at Riverview.

Weber was unafraid of Daley, and Weber's personal attitude toward Kennedy was hostile and vindictive. The alderman had been receiving sensitive information from the mob's political "fixer," Murray "the Camel" Humphreys, that this young Massachusetts upstart was "not on the square." According to author Len O'Connor, the outfit kept a "John book" recording the mating habits of political figures and celebrities. After hearing the salacious details, Alderman Weber decided that members of the Kennedy clan were not "our kind of people."

All of this raises an interesting question. Did Charlie's behind-the-scenes politicking contribute to his death?

On the night of August 16, 1960, Weber returned to his walled fortress at 3601 North Wolcott at around 11:30. He pulled his new Cadillac into the adjoining garage and retired for the evening. Emma Weber, his wife of twenty years, had come back from a hospital visit and was already asleep.

Between midnight and 4:00 A.M., Mrs. Weber stumbled out of bed. Investigators theorized that she had called to her husband, complaining of sudden illness. Charlie was attempting to go to her assistance when he collapsed to the floor. Both of them succumbed to carbon monoxide poisoning. A member of the Roman Catholic teaching order, and a family friend, found them lying on the floor next to each other the next morning. The police were summoned, and the property was hastily cordoned off.

In the garage, Chief of Detectives James McMahon discovered that the Webers' 1960 Cadillac had been left running all night. The alderman habitually left his car keys in the ignition, but even if he had forgotten to turn the Cadillac off on this one instance, there was still no creditable explanation as to why the trapdoor in the ceiling of the garage was left open. Coroner Walter McCarron ordered an autopsy, but there would always be lingering doubts as to whether Weber died accidentally or was the victim of a cold, diabolical murder plot carried out with precision by the mob.

Charlie was up in years and wore a hearing aid. But he had already taken it off for the evening and could not possibly have heard the rustling of a prowler switching on the ignition then slipping away into the night, if in fact that is how it all went down.

It should be noted that in the thirteen months leading up to Charlie Weber's death, three other prominent citizens with Chicago connections had also died of carbon monoxide fumes from automobile exhausts.

1843

West Addison

Street

(Addison and

Wolcott

Avenue)

RACKETS BUSTER KILLED BY THE MOB
September 25, 1950

Now, let's cross Addison Street and go back to September 25, 1950. The two-story, brown-brick home facing the Weber property on the south side of Addison (two doors east of Wolcott) was once the home of William Drury, one of Chicago's most highly revered and decorated police captains. Drury grew up in that house and continued to live there with his wife and parents. Charlie Weber must have known Bill Drury and undoubtedly valued his friendship ... and the protection his presence in the neighborhood afforded. Drury was a tough street cop and a man of integrity. He feared no one and, unlike the late Frank Pape, whose itchy trigger finger killed nine men, Drury never had to machine-gun a crook in the back to drive home that point either. Drury tried mightily to expose grafters and right the old injustices in "machine town." Ultimately, his crusading stance against organized crime cost him his life. The Drury case illustrates some fundamental truths about the enormous corrupting power of the Chicago crime syndicate in the postwar years. By 1950, the outfit was as strong and invincible as Caesar's legions, maybe even more so.

In June 1930, a time when gangland killings escalated to frightening proportions, Chief of Detectives John Stege suddenly reassigned his "Watchdogs of the Loop" to "the woods." In police vernacular, that meant that the officers were exiled to the hinterland for being too efficient at their jobs. The order came from "up above," meaning from Al Capone to Mayor William Hale Thompson, then down to Chief Stege, who was alleged to be on the Capone payroll.

William Drury and John I. Howe were the "Watchdogs of the Loop." Assigned to the shoplifter detail, they preferred to ruffle the feathers of the underworld rather than roust pickpockets from the State Street department stores at Christmastime. For more serious offenses, Drury and his partner arrested Harry Guzik, Hymie "Loudmouth" Levin, and other agents of Alphonse Capone in the beer rackets.

"Drury and Howe were interested in arresting persons whose reputations would ensure newspaper publicity," came the feeble explanation from Lieutenant Morris Byrne, who headed the detail. The Chicago Crime Commission spoke to the outrage of thousands of city residents perceptive enough to realize it wasn't the police who were calling the shots.

Bill Drury, a slight man who weighed only 130 pounds when he joined the Chicago PD in 1924, was feted for gallantry on numerous occasions. He won the department's coveted Lambert Tree Award for disarming a team of bandits and

CHICAGO POLICE INSPECTOR EXAMINES THE BULLET-RIDDLED WINDSHIELD OF MURDER VICTIM BILL DRURY'S CAR INSIDE THE GARAGE WHERE DRURY WAS EXECUTED.

(Photo courtesy of Art Bilek)

was widely respected for his poise, personal charm, and unflinching courage under fire. He was promoted to lieutenant in May 1938, and acting captain of the North Side Town Hall District in 1943.

Though reserved in nature, controversy and bad luck hounded Drury's waking moments and marred an otherwise exemplary career. He was one of six police captains suspended from the force in June 1944 for failing to suppress citywide gambling. The specific charges against Drury may have been engineered by the crime syndicate as revenge for his attempt to frame Rocco Fischetti, a cousin of Al Capone, for the brutal 1943 slaying of the glamour queen Estelle Evelyn Carey. (See *Return to the Scene of the Crime* for coverage of this sensational murder.)

All six were restored to full rank two years later following a long court fight. Then in 1946, Drury turned a routine murder investigation of the aging racing news czar James Ragen into a personal crusade. Believing he owed Ragen a debt for offering him employment while still under suspension, Drury and his new partner, Tom Connelly, used extralegal tactics to pin the murder on a trio of hoods from the "Jewish faction" of the Chicago crime syndicate—Lenny Patrick, Dave Yaras, and Willie Block.

Drury and Connelly were accused of coercing witness testimony and conspiring to bring about a false indictment, although the charge against them at the civil service hearing was a simple refusal to waive immunity before a grand jury. Both men were discharged in 1947, and not even the U.S. Supreme Court was willing to consider the mitigating circumstances.

Embittered by the turn of events, Drury kept insisting he was "railroaded" out of the police force and, in hindsight, he probably was. The former Loop "Watchdog" made the mistake of arresting syndicate bigshot Jake Guzik on suspicion.

After that, Bill Drury slid down a slippery pole. The *Chicago Herald-American* hired him to cover the crime beat from a historical perspective. For two years, he provided readers with a scintillating look at the city's most infamous crimes, told from a cop's perspective. When the paper dropped him in 1949, Drury caught on with the *Miami Daily News.* The insider material brought forth in Jack Lait and Lee Mortimer's tome, *Chicago Confidential,* was supplied firsthand by Drury.

All of this was done with a single-minded purpose: to vindicate himself in the court of public opinion. The more Drury revealed about the inner workings of the Chicago crime syndicate, the less likely it became for the mob to turn the other cheek.

When Senator Carey Estes Kefauver (D-Tenn.) began lining up witnesses for the Chicago phase of his nationwide organized crime investigation in the fall of

1950, Drury supplied the committee with pages of oral and written testimony. The Kefauver hearings cast a searching spotlight on illegal gambling in the Windy City and elsewhere, but before the actual deliberations began, the Chicago mob took the necessary steps to silence the one man in town who dared defy them.

Hours before his death, Bill Drury turned up at his lawyer's office in an agitated state. He said he had had a premonition of his own death. "I'm awfully hot," he said. The lawyer telephoned Senator Kefauver's chief counsel, who signed the papers authorizing a bodyguard detail for Drury that very afternoon. But it was too late.

At 5:00 P.M. on September 25, 1950, Anabel Poloma Drury was cooking her husband's evening meal when the telephone rang. On the other end, Kefauver Investigator George Robinson called to say that the request for twenty-four-hour protection had been granted. "Please have him call me back around seven," he said.

The call was never made. There was no point. At 6:45 P.M., Drury backed his new Cadillac into the garage. From her kitchen window, Anabel heard the sharp retort of a car backfiring, and observed two automobiles speeding west out of the alley. Anabel thought nothing more of it until 7:35 P.M., when she went out to the garage, flashlight in hand. The lateness of the hour was cause for concern. The single beam of light revealed her husband thrown back against the seat of the car, dead. Drury was torn apart by ten small pellets fired from a shotgun at close range.

That same day, across town, lawyer and politician Marvin Bas was also shot to death in gangland fashion. He had been gathering data about the crime syndicate to aid John Babb, Republican candidate for Cook County sheriff, in his election battle against Dan "Tubbo" Gilbert, the "Millionaire Cop" who conspired to frame Roger Touhy on trumped up kidnapping charges in 1933.

From Washington, Senator Kefauver demanded speedy results from the Chicago Police Department. "It shows the savagery of the Chicago gang. His killers must be brought to justice!"

Senator Kefauver was too busy mounting a presidential campaign to understand that things just don't work that way in Chicago. Bill Drury's killers would *never* be brought to justice.

Wrigleyville

DRUGSTORE HOLDUP SENDS TWO COP KILLERS TO THE ELECTRIC CHAIR: "OLD SPARKY" CLAIMS HIS FIRST VICTIMS

April 27, 1928, and February 19, 1929

3404

North Clark

Street

(Clark &

Roscoe

Streets)

The reason why the Chicago Cubs are so popular in this town has nothing to do with the game of baseball or the quality of the team on the field, which, in any given decade, ranges from mediocre to lousy. (In truth, discerning fans who understand baseball and appreciate the gentle rhythms of the national pastime cheer for the Chicago White Sox.) The team's popularity lies in the quaint charms of the old ballpark and the ambience of the surrounding Wrigleyville neighborhood, a happening place for the twenty-something generation since at least 1984. The Cubs are so boring and predictable that most of the fans in attendance are not paying attention, let alone keeping score. A visit to the bleachers is all about getting drunk and acting stupid, or gabbing with the neighbors about investment portfolios, the next promotion, the cost of daycare, or where to go in the neighborhood for dinner. Among the many fine places in Wrigleyville to repair to after the seventh-inning stretch is Fly Me to the Moon, a piano bar and restaurant at Clark and Roscoe. As you pass by, look closely at the exterior of this old building and observe the bricked-in area next to the main entrance where there was once, long ago, a display window. The color and age of the cream-colored brickwork do not match the originals, telling us that the large window disappeared years ago. Urban archaeology is a subject of endless fascination, and old Chicago commercial buildings like this one speak volumes about the individual tastes of succeeding owners down through the years, while retaining enough physical clues to suggest original usage. This unassuming corner building has no doubt hosted many businesses over the years, and has probably been remodeled dozens of times. Now it is a chichi restaurant for wine-sipping Yuppies and Wrigleyville singles on the make. Back in 1928, it was the Community Drug Store belonging to Jack Termin, who watched a man die during one of the city's frequent crime waves.

Charles Walz and Anthony Grecco were not yet old enough to vote when they began sticking up drugstores to finance their profligate lifestyle. Walz was the tough guy. Always quick with a joke and very sure of himself, he planned the nightly capers. Grecco would not have had the nerve to go it alone. He possessed a sensitive nature. In an era made famous by society's "thrill killers," these two were the poor man's Leopold and Loeb. Too bad a juvenile officer did not get a hold of them sooner.

Walz and Grecco were responsible for twenty armed robberies. Greed and lust motivated the duo. They had recently taken up with a couple of chippies named Dolly Kazor and Gertrude Piatkowski, alias "Trudy Ryan." The women were in their mid-twenties and worldly in their outlook. Walz was only seventeen, and Grecco, eighteen. The boys came from South Side working-class families (Walz's brother was killed in 1926), but the perfumed scent of the two Jazz Age flappers was a marked contrast from the poor neighborhood factory girls with whom they had previously kept company.

The stolen loot from the drugstore robberies paid for a suite of rooms at the Wacker Hotel, where the two drank and whored contentedly for a period of two months. It might have gone on like this for many more weeks had the querulous, ill-humored Walz not gotten careless with a gun.

On the night of April 27, 1928, the underage robbers left their girlfriends at the hotel and proceeded to the Community Drug Store where they bound and gagged owner Jack Termin, his brother Louie, and a customer from Evanston who was forced to hand over a wallet containing $26. Just as they finished securing their prisoners to a chair in the backroom, they heard the unmistakable shuffling of a customer coming in through the front door.

Crouching low behind a counter, Walz suddenly arose and fired three point-blank shots, suspecting that the man might be a cop. His instincts were right. The victim turned out to be a plainclothes police officer named Arthur F. Esau of the Town Hall District. Esau collapsed and died instantly.

A senseless act, born out of stupidity and desperation.

Ten days later, the killers were nabbed on the South Side, after detectives located their personal effects and memoranda at the Wacker Hotel listing the dates of their previous holdups and the address of Dolly Kazor's sister Ida at 7706 Catalpa Avenue. The drugstore owner and his brother picked them out of a line-up, and the robbers were indicted on murder charges.

Dolly turned state's evidence, telling detectives that Walz returned to his home that night, and that she had watched him closely as he calmly cleaned the gun and described in graphic detail the murder of Officer Esau.

By copping a plea, the girls avoided a lengthy prison sentence, and possibly a date with the newly installed electric chair in the old Cook County Jail at Hubbard and Dearborn.

On February 19, 1929, just five days after the St. Valentine's Day Massacre, Walz and Grecco, two faceless young hoods, became the first prisoners in Cook County to die in the chair after Governor Louis J. Emmerson refused to grant a reprieve or an eleventh-hour stay of execution.

Anthony Grecco showed genuine remorse for his actions. Hours before his death, he penned a simple verse for his brother and sisters, but got no further than a little plaintive that ran:

In sadness and despair
Sitting here so lonely ...

FORM FOLLOWS FUNCTION, DOES IT NOT? THE COMMUNITY DRUG STORE OF 1929 (SCENE OF THE WALZ-GRECCO HOLDUP) IS NOW THE FLY ME TO THE MOON RESTAURANT OF WRIGLEYVILLE.

"Junk! Where's my dinner?" snarled Walz, unfazed.

The *Chicago Tribune* praised the efficiency of the killing machine. "A faint whining sound was heard. It grew in volume as the throb of a huge vacuum cleaner. Scarcely six minutes were required for the execution of each youth."

For the record, no member or associate of organized crime has ever been put to death in Cook County.

MY SON-IN-LAW, MY LOVER: A WEIRD TALE OF LUST, BETRAYAL, AND MURDER IN WRIGLEYVILLE

July 6, 1935

Crime scene at 731 West Barry Street, residence at 1212 Waveland Avenue

An ex–burlesque queen and a mother-in-law obsessed with her daughter's charming young husband, as well as a Chinese hatchet man, are the players in this grisly one-act melodrama set against the backdrop of a deadly crime wave in the sticky summer months of 1935. The "torso murder" inspired one afternoon newspaper to go so far as to hire a numerologist to analyze the personality traits of the victim and his killers. Chicagoans were shocked and horrified, but clamored for more of the salacious details of the murder. The "yellow press" willingly obliged, day after day. I cannot imagine a more bizarre Chicago murder than the Dunkel-Lang case, as you soon shall see. The victim was lured to his death inside a three-story graystone apartment house located three doors east of Clark Street at 731 West Barry. The building still stands, on the south side of the street near the LaSalle Bank Building. The May-December romance leading up to the tragedy sprouted inside a common brown-brick apartment building at 1212 West Waveland, a half-block west of Racine. The address is the back apartment.

Blanche Dunkel loved much, but not wisely. The forty-two-year-old, ash-blond veteran of four failed marriages lived under the same roof as her daughter Mallie and son-in-law Ervin J. Lang, a grocery store clerk who could not afford a place of his own in those rugged depression days. Blanche, an eighth-grade dropout with an IQ of 79, kept them all fed by working in the linen supply room of Passavant Hospital.

MIDDLE AGE CRAZY. BLANCHE
DUNKEL IN CUSTODY WHILE THE
COPS COMB CHINATOWN FOR
CLUES TO THE WHEREABOUTS
OF EVELYN SMITH, THE
HIRED KILLER, AND HER
ETHNIC CHINESE HUSBAND.
JULY 12, 1935.

In her airless, dingy Waveland Avenue flat, Mrs. Dunkel was swept off her feet by Ervin's attentiveness to her daughter; his gentle, refined nature, and the many kindnesses he showered upon them both. "My God, it was selfish of me, but no one will ever understand the thrill I got when I looked at that boy." Night and day she fantasized about the dashing, dark-haired twenty-eight-year-old clerk making love to her. "I had to fight with myself to control my anger, my jealousy when I saw him with her."

Mallie Lang was nobody's fool. She was wise to the intrigue. Refusing to share her husband, she scolded her mother and threatened to move out unless her mother agreed to desist in her schoolgirl crush. Blanche called her bluff and said go ahead, get out. To speed her on her way, Blanche borrowed money from friends to give to Mallie as down payment on the first month's rent in an apartment of her own. Mallie demurred.

At a neighborhood card party one night, Mrs. Dunkel spied Ervin squeezing Mallie's hand. "Something came over me, something I don't understand," she later recalled. "I jumped up from the table and ran over to him and smothered him with kisses. I was sorry then, she was already ill. And at the same time I wanted her to suffer because she made me suffer—making me jealous."

Ervin Lang eventually succumbed to his mother-in-law's game of seduction, and was locked in her embrace nearly every waking moment that Mallie's head

LOVE	DEATH	HATE

JOSEPHINE MCKINLEY . . . SHE LOVED VICTIM OF BRUTAL TORSO MURDER AND WAS TO MARRY HIM.

ERVIN J. LANG . . . HE WAS DOPED AT "MIDDLE WOMAN'S" APARTMENT, SLAIN BY HIRED KILLERS.

MRS. BLANCHE DUNKEL . . . HER "MAD LOVE" TURNED TO HATE, SHE PAID FOR TORTURE SLAYING.

was turned. It went on like this for months.

In delicate health from the start, Mallie died of a broken heart on December 20, 1934.

Blanche blamed herself, and began to hate her son-in-law, who wasted no time finding a lover. He started keeping company with a woman closer to his own age, twenty-one-year-old Josephine McKinley. His failure to remain constant to the memory of his late wife drove the delusional Blanche to madness and desperation. She imagined that Ervin had "done away" with Mallie in order for him to be close to Josephine. It was a lie of course. Blanche wanted Ervin all to herself, but he was rapidly losing interest.

Fueled by jealousy, Blanche confided her suspicions to her sister, Mrs. Jessie Langdon, who put her in touch with a laundry-room worker at the Belmont Hotel (3156 Sheridan Road) named Evelyn Smith, a retired West Side striptease queen and a woman of the road who led a curious life.

Born in Berlin, Germany, to a man named Vackicko, Evelyn Smith told investigators she had been brought to the prairie of North Dakota at a young age. Not long after, her father died of pneumonia. A younger sister burned to death in a bonfire accident, and the mother expired from grief and emotional torment.

Beginning at age ten when she ran away from her foster family, Evelyn traveled the boxcars and rails of backroads America, living the life of a hobo and moving from place to place. In the big cities and rural villages she gravitated to wherever there happened to be a Chinatown district, because the ethnic Chinese were always willing to provide shelter and food.

In 1929 Smith and another wandering woman settled in Minneapolis where they learned the laundry trade. Three years later, Evelyn drifted into Chicago where she crossed paths with Harry Jung. After a short acquaintance they were married.

Jung and his brothers had established a chain of successful laundries and were "flush," but apparently none of his money fell into the hands of his embattled, man-hating wife, who was forced to fend for herself by taking irregular jobs following a miscarriage. Smith danced in a burlesque house under the stage name "Trixie."

Evelyn was a plain-looking four-letter-word woman of the streets. She wore wire spectacles and kept her auburn-colored hair close-cropped. She was living at 731 West Barry and was employed as a laundress at the Medinah Club at the time of her first meeting with Blanche Dunkel.

Smith claimed to have fallen "under the spell" of Dunkel, and was eager to ease her out of her present sufferings. The likelihood of Smith being a lesbian was alluded to in the case file. The "spell" she was under was undoubtedly one of romantic attraction.

"Why doesn't your sister have this fellow bumped off?" she whispered to Mrs. Langdon one day. "I could get it done for $500." By now Smith was intimately familiar with the customs of the insulated world of Chicago's South Side Chinatown. She offered the services of her husband and his associates for a sum of money that she knew was easy for Blanche Dunkel to obtain.

Blanche approached Lang's naive little brother William for the key to a safety-deposit box at the Lake View Trust and Savings. There, she withdrew $100 of Ervin's own money for the down payment on his murder. The money was handed to Smith in a plain brown envelope at the corner of Belmont and Lincoln. "Bring 'im over to the house," said Smith with a grin. The milk of human kindness had evaporated in the soul of this cold-blooded harridan.

Not long afterward, Lang was lured to Smith's flat on Barry Avenue where he was served four whiskey highballs laced with knockout drops during a night of drinking and card playing. The women waited until four-thirty in the morning for him to pass out. Finally, Mrs. Smith slapped his face to see if he was really out or had just nodded off. Satisfied with her work, she winked at Dunkel. "You might as well go home. I got him now!"

Full of misgivings and mounting terror, Blanche fled the apartment while Evelyn administered ether, tied Ervin up, and rolled him into the closet where she strangled him with a cord. The next morning, according to the grizzly story told to Captain Dan "Tubbo" Gilbert of the Cook County state's attorney's office, Harry Jung arrived in a green car with saw in hand.

Evelyn hacked off Lang's legs at the hip, carrying out this morbid task with fiendish delight. She bragged to Jung about what a woman could do once she set her mind to it. The remains were wrapped inside a trunk purchased from a Salvation Army store and transported to a remote swamp outside Hammond, Indiana, where the torso was left. The legs were carefully laid out in a roadside ditch near Munster and the torso near the marshy areas of Wolf Lake at Hammond. While all this was going on, Mrs. Dunkel decided that now was as good a time as any to have her tonsils removed.

The gruesome discovery of the severed corpse was made four days later. The trunk was recovered in a Chinatown warehouse at 231 West Twenty-second Street.

The first break in the case came within twenty-four hours, when the sister, Jessie Langdon, told Chief Investigator Thomas Kelly of the state's attorney's police about Dunkel's solicitation of murder with the Smith woman. The unmistakable smell of lye and laundry soap on Lang's clothing provided another clue, leading police to the Jung laundry rooms. Josephine McKinley supplied the motive. Smith was picked up in New York within forty-eight hours.

Speaking in a barely audible rasp, Mrs. Dunkel freely confessed to her role in the death plot after being taken to the Hammond swamp to view the remains. "I am his common-law wife," she said, murmuring tender words of endearment for the deceased. Grand jury indictments were drawn up.

In the belief that the electric chair was far too generous a fate for these "Women from Hell" (as the police dubbed them), Judge Cornelius J. Harrington imposed a 180-year sentence to be served at the Dwight Reformatory for women. He added a grim proviso after passing sentence. Beginning on July 6, 1936, and for every year thereafter, they were ordered to spend the anniversary day in solitary confinement.

The Dunkel-Lang case climaxed a spectacular wave of brutally savage mutilation murders in Chicago. It was the third crime of passion involving dismemberment in less than a month. All in all, 1935 was a tough crime year in Chicago.

In 1955, on the twentieth anniversary of the killings, a *Chicago American* reporter visited the two women at Dwight, Illinois. Dunkel, now sixty-three, clutched her prayer book and praised Jesus, saying how she had devoted her life to religion and the Episcopal faith. She bowed with remorse for the savage act she had committed and wept openly upon learning that the State refused to relent concerning her request to waive the annual day of atonement in solitary.

Remorse slid off Evelyn Smith like raindrops. Sorrow was never a part of her vocabulary. She said her conscience was clear, and her only interest in life these days was raising flowers. "I never abused my life—I never had any use for men or drink," she added.

In twenty years, the only other visitor to Evelyn Smith's cell besides the reporter was a Catholic priest. He was turned away.

Blanche Dunkel was paroled from Dwight on March 6, 1961, with a final discharge granted by Governor Otto Kerner three years later. Evelyn Smith, prisoner #1037, was granted parole on December 12, 1962, after promising to lead a frugal and industrious life. She was by then seventy-three years old.

New Town

3422

North

Broadway

THE SECRET LIFE OF A MARRIED MAN, MONTEREY RESTAURANT
April 28, 1953

The crime scene is remarkably preserved. The Monterey Restaurant, where a wealthy Park Ridge building contractor was slain in 1953, served over-the-counter short-order fare until it closed its doors in 2001. Enter through the front door and step back in time; it is doubtful that much has changed here since 1953. Late at night when the street outside is quiet, it is easy for the mind's eye to reconstruct the chain of events leading up to this crime, and visualize the image of a tall, woebegone suburban businessman in a topcoat leaning over the counter. Located a half-block north of Roscoe and just south of Hawthorne Place, the restaurant is adjacent to the Best Western Hawthorne Terrace, where the "other woman" in this one-act melodrama kept her clandestine appointments with the murder victim. The restaurant and the vintage four-story hotel once known as the Hawthorne Arms are situated in the heart of Chicago's bustling New Town neighborhood, a collage of Starbucks coffeeshops, restaurants, bars, all-night copying centers, and storefront theaters catering to young singles and those who choose to lead alternative lifestyles.

Far away from the deadening quiet of suburbia, the tedium of backyard cookouts, Little League games on Saturday, and the drone of gas lawn mowers disturbing the early morning tranquillity, there exists, for some men, a carefully hidden and secret world. Rising out of the scar tissue of an unhappy marriage, squandered dreams, and ungrateful children, or just out of the sheer frustration and boredom of it all, the restless middle-aged Lothario finds rejuvenation in the arms of a much younger woman; rekindling memories of summer flings and lost loves.

Arnold L. Spietz, a gaunt, sad-looking man of fifty-three, was the president of Interstate General Contractors, Inc., and a copartner with his uncle in a painting and decorating firm. The business was prosperous, and Spietz's station in life was well defined. That is, until he met up with Doris Mahal, a buxom brunette waitress from Duluth, Minnesota, who was only fourteen when a girlfriend introduced her to the contractor. For the next nine years the pair kept steady company. Mahal waitressed at a country club in Rochelle, Illinois, a small town located sixty-five miles outside Chicago. She cared for two young daughters—the result of a brief but failed marriage that had momentarily interrupted her love affair with Spietz.

An intensely private person, Spietz lived with wife Dolores, who had been with him for twenty-four years, in a beautiful home on a corner lot with an adjoining two-car garage at 900 South Delphia in Park Ridge, a tree-lined bedroom suburb for the postwar nouveau riche. The house on a quiet residential side street stood a world apart from the after-hours love nest Spietz set up for Mahal at the Hawthorne Arms Hotel, 3434 West Broadway.

In the obdurate moral climate of the 1950s, when adulterous affairs were punishable (in some states) by imprisonment, and the titillating bedtime disclosures were a matter of public record in the legal notices section of the daily newspaper, extra precautions to ensure one's privacy had to be taken. Under these circumstances, many married men of the Eisenhower era who feared financial ruin, public humiliation, and the threat of jail would pool resources and rent a flat in an out-of-the-way corner of the city in order to carry on with the opposite sex like college boys executing a successful panty raid.

Spietz, however, was genuinely devoted to Mahal and looked out for her well-being. He could afford to keep a private flat for Doris, and he lavished her twin daughters with presents.

The lovers had their little routines, their places to go, and no one, outside of a small circle of acquaintances, knew of Spietz's double life or bothered to check up on his whereabouts at night. Twenty-four years of marriage breeds complacency and indifference among some women. Dolores could reasonably convince herself that her husband was an important man of affairs, and building contractors were known to keep odd hours.

Arnold Spietz and Doris Mahal spent their last happy hours at Sportsman's Park in Cicero. "Arnold lost $130 on the races," Mahal would always remember. "We had dinner at the Old Prague, Cermak Road and Cicero Avenue." (*Author's Note:* This landmark Bohemian restaurant was destroyed by a fire of suspicious origin in May 1993, less than a day after health inspectors cited the owner with sanitation violations.)

AN ALTERCATION WITH A NEIGHBORHOOD BULLY COST ARNOLD SPIETZ HIS LIFE ON THE SIDEWALK OUTSIDE THE MONTEREY RESTAURANT (NOW CLOSED). THE AFTERHOURS HAWTHORNE ARMS LOVE NEST IS NOW A BEST WESTERN MOTEL (BELOW).

"We saw a show at the L&L Lounge on West Madison Street, then went to Barney's Market Club at Halsted and Randolph."

A heavy spender when he was out on the town with his sweetheart, Spietz ordered round after round, and was pretty well juiced by the time the couple made their way back to the Hawthorne Arms apartment after their carefree afternoon and evening of entertainment to spend the remainder of the night. They stopped at the Monterey Restaurant for coffee and rolls to take back to the room, when Spietz noticed three surly looking neighborhood hangers-on giving him the big eye.

The trouble started when Doris reached inside her purse for some loose change to pay the cashier. Spietz had run out of money and was embarrassed by his social faux pas. "Whatsa' matter, Bud, ain't you got enough dough to pay for your lady friend?" The three men looked at one another and chuckled. It was barroom provocation, nothing more, nothing less.

Emboldened by an afternoon of drinking, Spietz turned to the roughneck known as "Big Sam" and told him to shut his yap. Muttering contemptuous words under his breath, Spietz walked toward the door with a milk bottle filled with fresh ground coffee under his arm. He was rudely shoved out of the cafe by Andrew Kish, a downtown theater manager who had dropped in for a quick bite.

That started the terrible row that was finished by Big Sam.

Sam Ciro, a bartender when he was gainfully employed, grabbed Spietz by the shoulder and spun him around. The altercation spilled out onto the street. Ciro seized the milk bottle and crashed it over Spietz's head, fracturing his skull.

Doris Mahal stood over her suitor, who was covered with blood, broken glass, and coffee grounds. Her screams were piercing. Within moments, Police Officer Harry Moore hastened to the murder scene. Meanwhile, Big Sam and his pals had fled the crime scene. Rushed to Illinois Masonic Hospital in a fire department ambulance, Arnold Spietz was pronounced dead on arrival.

The widow, who was completely oblivious to the nine-year intrigue or the identity of the "other woman," was rousted from her Park Ridge bedroom in the middle of the night and dragged down to the Town Hall Police Station at Halsted and Addison to ID her husband, beaten to death in a street brawl. She said she had no knowledge of the affair, and appeared to be dazed and on the verge of nervous collapse from the aftershocks of the murder and learning about the affair. Having no desire to confront Mahal, and prostrate from grief and shock, Dolores Spietz did not bother to show up at the inquest.

Acting on the tip of an eyewitness, police arrested Sam Ciro, alias "Big Sam" Cannatta, a burly, 200-pound street-tough with a record for criminal pandering and assault. Figuring that Doris Mahal should not be let off the hook quite so easily, the cops booked her on a charge of disorderly conduct. "You have to live with your-self," sermonized Coroner Walter McCarron.

Whatever happened to the widow and the "other woman" after the fatal affray is not known. The streets of Chicago were no place for this meek, inoffensive man to play a cheating game.

Were his parting thoughts with Doris or Dolores in those last fateful moments?

Lake Michigan Tidal Wave, June 26, 1954
Montrose Beach Pier on Lake Michigan

S I D E T R I P

Without warning, a wall of water swept over the Lake Michigan shoreline stretching from Wilmette on the north to Jackson Park on the south end. The mighty wave, known as a seiche, struck with its greatest fury at Montrose Beach and North Avenue Beach at nine-thirty in the morning, June 26, 1954. Fishermen perched on a rock jetty at Montrose Avenue already had their lines in the water, and children were frolicking innocently on the sandy beach when the huge swell, measuring thirty-five feet in some places, rolled over them. The seiche accompanied an early morning squall line moving swiftly across the lake. The U.S. Weather Bureau explained that the phenomenon was caused by heavy air pressing down on the lake with squalls, or storms, following behind. Before the wave hit, sections of beach extended fifty to one hundred feet into the lake, indicating that the water level had dropped six feet or more. But only the trained eye of a meteorologist or member of the Coast Guard would have recognized the approaching danger. Eight people were swept away and drowned at Montrose and North Avenue beaches, but a hundred more were saved in Rogers Park thanks to the alert reaction of lifeguard chief Sam Leone, who shouted warnings to the bathers, who ran up the shoreline to safety. Oddly enough, on that same morning, the captured Nazi submarine, the U-505, was navigating the strong Lake Michigan current en route to its Chicago berth at the Museum of Science and Industry. Seized off the coast of North Africa on June 4, 1944, the famous prize of war was to be met by Rear Admiral Daniel V. Gallery and a party of Chicago dignitaries, but the seiche delayed the welcoming ceremonies and forced the U.S. Naval Reserve ships to steam out to the Gross Point lighthouse in Evanston, to bring the sub in safely. A seiche of this size and strength occurs maybe once every five hundred years, or about as often as an enemy submarine turns up in the waters of Lake Michigan.

Uptown

"YELLOW KID" WEIL NABBED
IN HIS UPTOWN HOTEL
May 12, 1925

Uptown is a place of remarkable contradictions. The strik-
ing feature of this North Side lakefront community is its amaz-
ing ethnic diversity and extremes of wealth and poverty.
Coalitions of street people and the dislocated, the ragged street
urchins hovering outside the homeless shelters, and the pull-
down grates protecting the storefronts at Lawrence and
Broadway wage continuous guerrilla warfare against civic-minded residents
desiring to plant grass, raise children, and restore the luster to the once glim-
mering façades of the Uptown of legend—the Uptown of Charlie Chaplin,
Gloria Swanson, and the other stars of the Essanay Studio on Argyle Street.
Uptown in the 1920s and 1930s was a North Side "Mecca" of gaudy show
lounges, the Aragon Ballroom, elegant residential hotels, and fabulous after-
hours hideaways. Uptown had it all, but then, almost overnight, the commu-
nity was plunged into an economic abyss from which it has been slow to
recover. The six-story "mid-rise" building at 4526 Sheridan Road, just south of
Wilson Avenue on the south side of the street, was originally the Hotel
Huntington, and was quite a fashionable address catering to a respectable
clientele. In 1924, "Yellow Kid Weil" and the missus bought the place and
changed the name to the Hotel Shenandoah. Word got around that the master
of the short con had gone legit, and soon his hostelry was full-up with grifters,
safecrackers, and bank robbers. The Shenandoah became a haven for "people
on the run." Now a businessman just trying to scrape by and earn a buck the
old-fashioned way, Weil complained bitterly about overnight guests "laying
stiffs," that is, paying him with worthless checks. Today, nearly seventy-six years
after the Kid squandered his one chance at legitimacy, the famous hotel still
stands, but now is called the Sheridan View Apartments and is located in a
part of Uptown where the streets are lined with low-income SRO's (single-room
occupancy apartments), Chicago Housing Authority high-rise units, Salvation
Army "thrift" stores, and storefront missions attending to the needs of the indi-
gent and displaced. With poverty, there are always criminal victimization,
homelessness, and a sense of abandonment. These are the modern-day realities.

"You can't cheat an honest man," or so the story goes. If "Yellow Kid" Weil were around today to challenge the credulity of W. C. Fields, who coined the famous phrase, he would respond by saying, "There's nothing to it, but if I had my choice I would rather clip a scoundrel than a sucker."

Born Joseph Weil in 1875 to a French mother and a German-American grocer named Otto Weil, the "Yellow Kid" fancied the exploits of the mischievous comic strip character of the same name popularized in the Hearst newspapers around the turn of the last century.

In his autobiography, Weil attributes the blustering alderman of the First Ward, "Bathhouse" John Coughlin, as the source of the famous nickname—one that would follow Weil all his days.

While in his teens, the Kid pitched "Doc Meriwether's Elixir" to the hayseeds as a cure for tapeworms. The worthless potion earned Weil a tidy sum in the days when the American public was often gulled into purchasing medicines from street-corner barkers and shills.

"Yellow Kid" Weil refined his techniques, and by the 1920s he was the reigning "king of the con men" and America's foremost swindler. The "Kid" lived to the ripe old age of 101. During his extended stay on earth, he boasted of fleecing thousands of victims, to the tune of $12 million, through an ingenious array of bogus stock sales, worthless land schemes, racetrack "wireroom" scams, and the famous short and long cons, which were to become his stock and trade.

Weil trained his apprentices well. One of them, a portly Chicago police officer named Fred "the Deacon" Buckminster, gave up chasing criminals to become a con man himself, after spying the Kid's bankroll.

Crime writers and reporters who fancy clever exploits and bestow glory upon cunning tricksters like Weil will continue to do so, just as long as *they* do not become the victim of the scam. In truth, there was nothing very romantic about "Yellow Kid" Weil, and he undoubtedly played to the suckers when he announced that he had never used a gun or cheated an honest man.

Between January 1, 1924, and May 12, 1925, when Sergeants Roche and Burke of the Town Hall Police District stormed into the Shenandoah Hotel in Uptown and grabbed Weil by the collar, there had been a rash of fifty unsolved bank robberies throughout Illinois. Federal authorities pieced together an intricate chain of evidence, revealing the unmistakable mark of "Yellow Kid" Weil written all over the recent spate of bank heists.

His peculiar genius was evident in the Farmers State Bank robbery in

Chenoa, Illinois. Posing as bank examiners "reporting directly" to state auditor Oscar Nelson, the Kid and an accomplice many believed to be safe-blower Jimmy Head waited until the end of the day when the employees of the bank departed their teller cages and went home to dinner. Left alone with bank president William Kelley, the robbers emptied the contents of the vault, bound and gagged Kelley, and made off with $184,000 in hard currency belonging to average work-a-day men and women.

The Weil & Head gang recruited William H. Suchier, a professional bondsman with a shady past, and Anthony Barosso, a henchman of Suchier. These men maintained offices at 27 North Dearborn, and were busily disposing of the gang's stolen securities and counterfeit Liberty Bonds when Secret Service Agent Peter

CON MAN JOSEPH "YELLOW KID" WEIL JOINED THE STRAIGHT WORLD WHEN HE PURCHASED THIS APARTMENT HOTEL ON SHERIDAN ROAD IN 1924.

(Photo by author)

Drautzberg arrested Head in a Loop brokerage office while he was attempting to pass $10,000 in "hot" bonds. With the arrests of Suchier and Barosso hours later, the recent adventures of the "Yellow Kid" came into sharper focus.

Armed with warrants, the Chicago cops seized nearly $750,000 in stolen bonds and delivered the pink-bearded Weil into the hands of the U.S. marshals. "It's all bunk!" the Kid snorted, outraged by the great indignity of being arrested with bank robbers. But the Feds had planned their own little caper with precision and the expert attention worthy of the practitioners of the "pigeon drop." Agent George H. Harris of Cleveland had doggedly shadowed Weil from place to place, through a maze of confidence game whimsies, which had to be ignored in order to trap the Kid while he was fishing for much bigger prey.

"Yellow Kid" Weil served five years in Leavenworth. No stranger to the inside of a prison cell, he had been there before and would return many more times before cashing in his chips in a North Side nursing home in 1976. In his last years, Weil complained bitterly about the lack of panache among the modern-day criminal fraternity. "There are no good confidence men anymore because they do not have the necessary knowledge of foreign affairs, domestic problems, and human nature."

922

West

Eastwood

"THE ANGEL OF DEATH WILL CALL ON YOU!" THE LAST DAYS OF "TWO-GUN" LOUIE

July 19, 1935

In July 1935, there was no finer place to live in all of Uptown than the swanky Eastwood Towers, located at 922 Eastwood, a few doors east of Sheridan Road and a block north of Joseph "Yellow Kid" Weil's hotel. It was here that "Two-Gun" Louie lived . . . and died. The Eastwood Towers is now a rather dismal-looking art-deco apartment house on a street pockmarked by sinister decay, empty weed lots, and young men loitering on the stoops of run-down buildings. Eastwood dead-ends in a cul-de-sac, which speaks volumes about the decades of urban neglect, fear of gangs, and dope peddling. But across from the Eastwood Towers, Rita Semo's newly constructed People's Music School provides a slice of culture to all who aspire to a better way of living than the attending miseries of poverty, drugs, and alcohol. Amid economic want, there is a richness of the human spirit that is continuously reaffirmed in this multidimensional neighborhood. It is Uptown's most priceless treasure.

Threaded T — **T**he labor racketeer and former rumrunner known in gangland circles as "Two-Gun" Louie Alterie earned his famous moniker during the gaudy 1924 funeral of bootlegger Dion O'Banion, leader of the North Side mob who was slain inside his flower shop in November of that year.

While other men wept openly in front of Deanie's $25,000 funeral bier, Alterie paraded in front of the Sbarbaro funeral home on Wells Street, flashing a pair of fancy six-shooters and vowing to "shoot it out" with O'Banion's killers in broad daylight at State and Madison. No one took him up on the offer. He must have been either the most ridiculous-looking gangster the Capone boys had ever seen, or the deadliest.

"Two-Gun" Louie, whose real name was Leland Verain, was a suave, ambidextrous cowpoke from the California flats who drifted into Chicago sometime in the early 1920s. A jaunty man of the wide-open spaces, Alterie cultivated a false reputation as a back-alley fighter, and he made everyone believe that he appreciated a good scrap. He fell in with O'Banion, Samuel "Nails" Morton, George "Bugs" Moran, and Hymie Weiss. They were a bad lot, but relentless in their defense of the North Side rum rackets against the overwhelming firepower of Al Capone.

To the unflinching Alterie, Chicago was even more "rootin'-tootin'" than the Old West he so dearly loved.

Alterie specialized in labor racketeering, generally regarded as a side business of only passing interest to the overlords of gangland during Prohibition. Following repeal in 1933, the major funding source for gangster income permanently dried up. Jobs had to be found for the vast army of unemployed musclemen, hijackers, and rumrunners. Honest union officials, desirous of open elections and the integrity of the collective bargaining process, began to feel squeezed.

The control of the locals, with access to millions of dollars of dues and pension money, proved an easy and inviting target for Chicago racketeers in the early 1930s. As the Great Depression wore on, the body count in gangland steadily rose.

In February 1935, Tommy Maloy, czar of the moving picture operator's union, was mowed down as Chicago police nervously braced for a renewal of the gang wars. They only had to wait until the morning of July 19 for the imprisoned Al Capone to turn loose the syndicate armor.

Louie Alterie was the titular head of the Theatrical Janitors Union Local 25— a job for life because of his connections to the North Side mob. But he did not enjoy the same fearsome reputation as O'Banion, Bugs Moran, or lesser-known gunsels. Despite his "two-gun" escapades, his penchant for slapping around chorus girls who rebuffed his advances, and his false swagger, Louie was mostly bluff and hardly respected.

Then came a particularly humiliating incident involving Alterie and Chief of Detectives John Stege at the Midnight Frolics Café. (*Author's Note:* The notorious Levee sin spot located at Wabash and Twenty-second Street was known as Freiberg's Dance Hall until 1919.)

Stege, a bold and fearless crime fighter but well up in years, slapped Louie in the face in front of the usual gangster gathering of Levee barflies and dime-a-dance girls. The shame-faced hood, who had been shown up by a man old enough to be his father, turned and stormed out. Alterie kept running, all the way to Glenwood Springs, Colorado, where he opened a six-hundred-acre dude ranch and married the local beauty, Erma Rossi.

Lost in the Wild West, Alterie rode his horse across the range with his holstered six-shooters snug at his side and managed to stay out of trouble until 1932, when he got into a barroom scuffle with two traveling salesmen in a Denver hotel and was ordered to the penitentiary. The State of Colorado suspended his sentence in return for his promise to leave and not come back. Louie obliged. He loved the range, but not enough to dream of it from behind bars.

"Two-Gun" Louie's weapon was holstered when he was shot dead in the street in front of this address at 922 West Eastwood in Uptown.

Alterie and his wife of nine years returned to Chicago where they lived in hotels, ran the union, and otherwise shunned the nightlife. Why, then, with the O'Banion-Moran gang vanquished, was this oddball ex-hood targeted for murder? The cops had their theories.

Louie and Erma moved their suitcases into the Eastwood Towers on April 1, 1935. The graystone apartment house was tucked into a quiet residential side street, but the surrounding buildings afforded a perfect cover for surveillance sharpshooters renting by the week. The gunmen, skilled in the technique from many long years of practice, watched and waited.

At around 10:20 A.M., the morning of July 19, Louie stepped out his front door and was in the middle of the street, when eleven slugs fired from an open window at 927 Eastwood tore into his chest and head. As he lay dying in the street, Erma rushed to his side. "They shot you, Louie!" she screamed. "Honey, I guess I'm through!" came the reply.

Erma Alterie remembered a recent phone call to the home. The stranger on the other end had warned Louie that "the Angel of Death will call on you unless you get out. The syndicate wants that union."

Alterie died on the operating table at Lake View Hospital less than a half-hour later, as the prophetic warning flashed through Erma's mind.

"It's labor trouble," theorized Captain Dan "Tubbo" Gilbert, himself a hinky, vainglorious cop thriving on the ragged edge of gangland. "He was a bigshot of the union, and they were trying to push him out."

Questioned later by detectives, the widow described her late husband as a "homebody." She said they were going back to Colorado in a few days to attend to the two horses, "King" and "Lady." Now she had the solemn task of transporting Louie to a California cemetery inside a box.

"I can't think why anyone would want to kill him," she said. "He was the kindest, most gentle man in the world."

The Uptown Theatre

SIDETRIP

4816 North Broadway (Broadway just north of Lawrence)
This story was first told to Andy Pierce, lately of the Lerner Newspapers, by a Chicago police officer, and it has gained currency among the true believers in the supernatural. But first, a bit of history. The beautiful Uptown Theatre was built by the Balaban & Katz chain in 1925 on a parcel of land formerly occupied by the Green Mill Gardens, a wonderfully lavish dancehall, nightclub, and restaurant. (Though diminished in size, the Green Mill Lounge has survived all these years as a popular venue for live jazz and poetry slams.)

The Uptown Theatre was a master production costing investors four million pre-inflation dollars to build. With 4,381 seats, it is one of the world's largest indoor movie theaters. The Moorish architecture of Spain complements the interior of the old Aragon Ballroom, a half-

OCTOBER 28, 2000. UPTOWN NEIGHBORS GATHER IN A SHOW OF SUPPORT FOR THE RESTORATION OF THE SHUTTERED UPTOWN THEATRE, A HISTORIC LANDMARK.

(Photo by Mark Montgomery and courtesy of the Friends of Uptown)

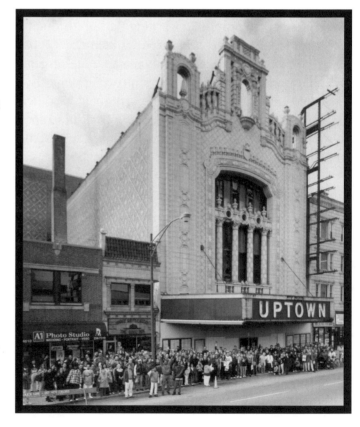

block east on Lawrence Avenue, and the Uptown façade rises like a phoenix over Broadway. In every respect, it is a show palace unrivaled anywhere in the Midwest, perhaps even the entire county. Rome in all its glory could never have built such an ornate temple to the performing arts as the Uptown Theatre.

In order to sustain an operating profit, all 4,381 seats had to be filled at least a couple of times a week. This was certainly possible during the Great Depression and throughout the war years when tickets were cheap and television was still a laboratory experiment in the design studios of RCA. Local residents loved the Uptown, until TV, rock 'n' roll, and other diversions came along and attendance dwindled. The Uptown was a relic—the casualty of a lost age when Gary Cooper, Wallace Beery, and Greta Garbo were the reigning matinee idols.

The Uptown was closed in 1981, and the succeeding years have not been kind. Chunks of plaster have fallen from the ceiling. The woodwork has deteriorated, and the massive turbine engines, heating units, and stage equipment needed to power the theater are rusted and falling apart. The dripping water, the gloomy silence, the darkened shadows of the place, give you pause. You begin to wonder if ghosts dwell in this place that gave so much joy to so many, but is now so decayed, creepy, and old.

One night a Chicago police officer, assigned to patrol the interior of the darkened theater to keep scavengers, souvenir hunters, and homeless people out, was standing at the foot of the stage in the massive auditorium absorbed in the eerie silence and darkness when he thought he heard something rustle up in the balcony. Convinced that he had roused a stew bum from one of the cobwebbed seats, the cop trained a flashlight on the deserted balcony. A figure glided silently across the balcony aisle. The police officer ordered the person to halt. A moment later the figure vanished. The cop raced up to the balcony, knowing that it would have been impossible for the homeless wretch to get to the first floor without running into him, but there was no one there, only the unearthly silence of an empty theater engulfed in shadows that had seen its better days.

<table>
<tr><td>

5116

North

Kenmore

Avenue

</td>
<td>

J. EDGAR HOOVER IN UPTOWN:
ROGER "THE TERRIBLE" TOUHY CAPTURED
December 29, 1942

</td></tr>
</table>

Roger Touhy's hideout is located a few doors south of Foster Avenue on the north side of Kenmore Avenue. The classic three-story, graystone apartment building is common in the Uptown-Andersonville community, but what happened here on a cold December night in 1942 lives on in the crime annals of Chicago.

Roger Touhy's career as a beer supplier to Northwest Suburban roadhouses and speakeasies was abruptly cut short by Al Capone in 1933. Failing in his attempt to absorb Touhy's beer-running operation through coercion and intimidation, old "Scarface" staged a phony kidnapping, with the connivance of a corrupt state's attorney named Thomas Courtney, and his henchman Dan "Tubbo" Gilbert. It was the perfect setup. The staged abduction of international con man Jake "the Barber" Factor, and the immediate arrest and imprisonment of Roger Touhy, was a colossal travesty of justice—even for the loose standards of Chicago. One could hardly blame the piteous Touhy for deciding to make a run for it. He certainly could not expect justice from the crooked Chicago politicians or the cops assigned to the state's attorney's office. We can only hope that the unlucky bootlegger enjoyed a few good nights out on the town before J. Edgar Hoover arrived in Chicago to personally supervise a predawn FBI raid on the hideout, leading to Touhy's final capture. The powers that be dragged Roger Touhy in his red silk pajamas back to Joliet for a crime he did not commit.

Languishing in his prison cell at the Stateville Penitentiary, Roger Touhy weighed his options. "I was without hope. I was buried alive in prison and I would die there. I couldn't see a light anywhere. Nothing but darkness, loneliness, and desperation. The world had forgotten me after eight years."

The image of "Tubbo" Gilbert, and his dapper-looking boss, Tom Courtney (the two of them blinded by greed and ambition), festered in Touhy's mind, day after day.

No one believed him. No one cared. In gangland, it was common knowledge that Touhy was framed by a power-hungry office seeker who was on friendly terms with the Al Capone mob. The confidential report on Tom Courtney was filed by "Secret Six" investigator Shirley Kub on December 6, 1932. The file remained locked away in a rusty safe inside the state's attorney's office until 1960, when Chief Investigator Paul Newey discovered the contents.

At the time of Courtney's election, Kub had interviewed Joe Grabiner, a fringe player in the Capone organization, but a clever little thief and panderer who had survived in the rackets for close to thirty years. Here's what Grabiner had to say about the alleged integrity of Tom Courtney:

> This fellow Courtney is right for us. Other years when a new State's Attorney took office everyone closed their gambling houses as soon as he took office. This fellow says, "It is okay with me, as I am not a reform man." The word is out that they will be able to control Courtney after he has had a chance to make a showing. They [the gangsters] are the men who put Courtney in, and they are not going to let Courtney go back on his word. Of course the dagoes [sic] will have to lay low for a while, but Snorky [Al Capone] is still the king.

The "showing," of course, was the perfectly choreographed frame-up of Roger Touhy, who instinctively understood that he was not only up against "King maker" Capone but the entire apparatus of the Democratic machine that Courtney desired to one day control from the mayor's fifth-floor office in City Hall.

Knowing that he was likely to rot in prison unless some decisive action was taken, Touhy, joined by two cop killers named Eddie Darlak and Gene O'Connor, Midwestern bank robber Basil "the Owl" Banghart, and three other men, busted out of Stateville on October 9, 1942. They made a clean getaway out of the prison yard in a laundry truck and headed back to Chicago after bribing the tower guards at the heavily armed compound.

With $2,500 in cash given to him by his brother, Roger Touhy lay low in Chicago. Using a forged draft card identifying him as "Robert Jackson," an exempt 4-F worker, he was able to navigate from the West Side to the North Side undetected and enjoyed a few bittersweet months of freedom before the headline-hunting J. Edgar Hoover closed in.

The Touhy gang moved from place to place, winding up at the Doversun Apartments at Sunnyside and Dover Street in Uptown. There, Touhy and Banghart quarreled with fellow fugitives Matthew Nelson and William Stewart, who refused to follow orders and lay low. When the pair returned home drunk after a raucous night of prowling the Uptown bars, the "Owl" pistol-whipped them both to unconsciousness for their insubordination.

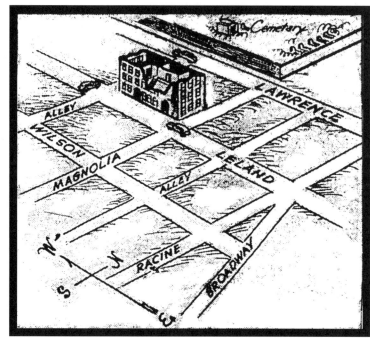

DIAGRAM OF THE LOCATION OF BUILDING AT 1254-56 LELAND AVE., WHERE TWO MEMBERS OF THE TOUHY GANG WERE KILLED.

ROGER TOUHY'S HIDEOUT AT 5116 NORTH KENMORE (CENTER BUILDING) WAS THE PERFECT PLACE TO CRASH UNTIL J. EDGAR HOOVER SHOWED UP.

Tired of being "cramped," Nelson fled to Minneapolis, where he was picked up by police in a pay-as-you-go hotel and turned over to the FBI on December 16. Nelson put the Feds on the trail. Stewart, a stickup man with his own gang, was arrested outside an Oak Park bank three days later. He supplied the G-men with the rest of the details.

Because of the unexpected rift that had developed in the gang, the FBI had a continuous line on the movement of the Touhy gang, even as Banghart, O'Connor, Roger Touhy, and the recently paroled safe-blower St. Clair McInerney sought refuge inside the Norwood Apartments at 1254–1256 Leland. (*Author's Note:* The building was situated off the alley between Wilson and Lawrence Avenues, but was razed some years ago to make way for a public housing unit.)

On December 26, Touhy, Darlak, and Banghart left O'Connor and McInerney for a street-level apartment on Kenmore Avenue. Within hours of their arrival, a detail of FBI men had the entire block covered. They rented rooms at the 5120 and 5124 addresses and across the street from Touhy's hideout. One of the G-men told the landlady at 5120, Mrs. Mary Macardo, that he was a "traveling man." He signed the register "Mr. Tierney" and set up a machine-gun nest over the alley to prevent an escape attempt.

Late in the evening of December 29, Special Agent S. K. McKee, dispatched from Washington, D.C., three days earlier, put the plan into operation.

With all the earmarks of a looming disaster, McKee led a sortie of heavily armed G-men in a risky midnight raid on the Leland Avenue building where McInerney and O'Connor were holed up. The tenants were cleared out, and the Chicago homicide detectives were warned that they should also stay away. "Come to our office in the morning, and you will be given a statement." The Chicago cops could not be trusted.

Director Hoover, who was in town to personally "supervise" the roundup of the Stateville fugitives, remained safely out of harm's way near the Kenmore address.

The exchange of gunfire began shortly after 11:30 P.M., when the two men entered the building. Sensing trouble, O'Connor, gun in hand, had begun firing wildly after realizing there were agents lurking about his third-floor apartment. A barrage of shotgun and pistol fire coming from McKee's agents positioned on the second- and third-floor landings tore through the escaped cons.

Neither man had much of a chance. Armor-piercing bullets struck them from all directions as they tumbled over the railing and landed on top of each other, two floors down.

Five hours after the bullet-riddled remains were toe-tagged at the morgue, and long after Touhy, Darlak, and Banghart had drifted off to sleep, Hoover's men cordoned off a four-block radius around the Kenmore address extending from Foster Avenue on the north to Winona on the south, Sheridan on the east and Winthrop to the west. Large skylights were affixed to the rooftops of the nearby buildings, and canisters of tear gas were loaded and trained on the building. The press had been put on full alert. Hoover had seen to it.

From the loudspeaker of a car parked in front of the house, an FBI man demanded immediate surrender of the trapped outlaws. "Touhy and Banghart— we are the FBI! Surrender and come out with your hands up! There is no hope of escape! You are surrounded!"

It was an unforgettable scene straight from the movies. Jimmy Cagney could not have carried it off with greater flourish or better timing. The carefully scripted scene on Kenmore Avenue that cold dark morning would be replayed by dozens of actors in scores of B-grade gangster yarns (including the 1944 classic *Roger Touhy: Gangster*) churned out by Warner Brothers in the back lots of Hollywood. Whatever else one may say about J. Edgar Hoover, he always played to the masses.

Not a shot was fired. Banghart, Touhy, and Darlak staggered through the door in a haze of disbelief. Hoover, surrounded by a dozen agents and reporters, approached the prisoners and said, "Well, Banghart, you're a trapped rat!"

"The Owl" chuckled. "You're J. Edgar Hoover, aren't you?"

"Yes," Hoover said, beaming. "I am he!"

"Well, you're a lot fatter in person than on the radio!"

The trio of escaped convicts were hustled back to Warden Joseph Ragen at Stateville, who patiently awaited their arrival, his two large attack dogs poised at his side.

Roger Touhy, innocent of kidnapping but guilty of poor planning, was sentenced to "life plus 99." Director Hoover called Touhy "more dangerous than John Dillinger, or the Clyde Barrow–Bonnie Parker mob."

From his plush apartment in the Belden-Stratford Hotel on Lincoln Park West, cosmetics heir and international swindler John "Jake" Factor was exultant upon hearing the news. He kissed his wife, Rella, and gushed, "How I am going to sleep tonight! Oh, the dreams I have had . . . such terrible dreams . . . nightmares," he said, his hands shaking from the awful anxiety of it all. "Now I can sleep. Now I can eat. Now I can go places. I can't say too much in praise of J. Edgar Hoover and his men. When they get into a case you may rest assured they won't stop until they get their man."

Indeed.

(Author's Note: The final outcome of the Roger Touhy saga is covered at length in my first volume, *Return to the Scene of the Crime: A Guide to Infamous Places in Chicago.)*

Ravenswood—Uptown

THE SAGA OF JOHN DILLINGER: A CLOSING CHAPTER
July 28, 1946

4957 North

Wolcott

Avenue

(Wolcott and

Winnemac)

A sprawling postwar apartment complex with art-deco overhangs defines the landscape of an entire city block of Ravenswood, once a remote German farming community but now an ethnically diverse residential neighborhood. According to legend, the cawing of crows gave Ravenswood its name. The housing development at Wolcott and Winnemac marks the spot where Dr. Harold Cassidy, one of John Dillinger's private physicians, committed suicide in a moment of despondency. Cassidy maintained his practice in two separate locations in Uptown. The run-down, three-story building at 1123 West Argyle Street leaning up against the CTA Red Line station is now the Moa My Chinese Herb Market and Hep Loi Gift Company. Following his graduation from the University of Illinois Medical School in 1927, Cassidy opened his practice in this building. Argyle Street, once a slum neighborhood of boarded-up buildings inhabited by winos, panhandlers, and dope peddlers, is today the "Main Street" of the busy North Side Chinatown. Dr. Cassidy also rented office space on the second floor of the famous 1920s nightclub, the Green Mill Gardens, at Lawrence and Broadway. (Author's Note: *See* Return to the Scene of the Crime *for additional details about this famous nightspot.)*

Dr. Harold Bernard Cassidy, a handsome thirty-two-year-old physician making a choice in life he would live to regret, was paid the sum of $500 to assist Wilhelm Loeser in an operation to alter the appearance of FBI poster boy John Dillinger.

Loeser's medical practice bordered on quackery, but he happened to be a good friend of Louis Piquett, the faithful attorney serving the outlaw brigand Dillinger. In May 1934, when Dillinger's mug shot appeared in nearly every U.S. post office and police station from Albuquerque to New York, desperate measures had to be taken to alter the appearance of the too-famous face.

Dr. Loeser, convicted on a narcotics rap under the Harrison Act and sentenced to the Leavenworth Penitentiary in 1931, was granted an early parole by the government and made his way back to Chicago just in time to perform plastic surgery, first on Dillinger, then later on his sidekick, Homer Van Meter.

In a two-story frame building at 2509 Crawford Avenue on May 28, 1934, Cassidy and Loeser hacked apart Dillinger's face. Cassidy injected a near-fatal dose of anesthetic, and for a hot second there were grave fears that the young doctor had succeeded where the FBI and hundreds of local police had failed, that is, sending Dillinger to the great beyond.

Luckily for John Dillinger, he came out of a coma-like state with his mental faculties still intact. Pleased with the results, Dillinger met up with Cassidy two months later at Kedzie and North Avenue. Huddled in a parked car with girlfriend Polly Hamilton, Dillinger handed over five crisp C-notes (one-hundred-dollar bills)

JOHN DILLINGER'S SUICIDAL PLASTIC SURGEON, DR. HAROLD CASSIDY, OPENED AN OFFICE AT 1123 WEST ARGYLE (BUILDING SHOWN AT THE LEFT) ADJACENT TO THE NORTH-SOUTH ELEVATED LINE. THE ARGYLE STREET COMMUNITY IS ALMOST EXCLUSIVELY SOUTHEAST ASIAN TODAY.

and thanked him for his services. Cassidy celebrated by buying himself a new roadster, enjoying the last moments of an otherwise unhappy and bleak existence.

In December 1933, the two doctors who performed the plastic surgery were indicted on charges of harboring a fugitive. In exchange for their testimony, Cassidy and Loeser were handed suspended sentences, but Cassidy's troubles were far from over. Divorced for nearly two decades, Dr. Cassidy was hit hard with writs of attachment by his ex-wife Freida for nonpayment of child support.

Before America's entry into World War II, Cassidy worked as a government physician at an Indian reservation in South Dakota. During the war he served with distinction in the Medical Corps in the Pacific theater, rising to the rank of major. But coping with a skeleton in his closet known as John Dillinger was another matter.

Cassidy resumed his practice at the Coleville Reservation in Washington State after the war had ended, then returned to the homestead of his sister, Mrs. Georgia Claypool, at 4957 North Wolcott on July 27, 1946, announcing that his prospects were good for reassignment to a tribal health-care clinic in Wisconsin. His pleasant demeanor masked a deeper and more profound sorrow.

In the presence of his mother and sister, Dr. Cassidy pulled out a gun and fired a bullet into his temple seconds before they could pull the weapon from his grasp. They told police that he had been suffering from nervous exhaustion and was on the verge of emotional and mental collapse.

East Rogers Park

Devon Avenue and Newgard Street

MIDGET DESPERADO SEIZED!
JAIL SCANDAL PROBED
October 28, 1935

A lesser-known criminal malefactor of Depression-era Chicago was seized at Devon and Newgard, east of Clark Street, on October 28, 1935. Newgard is a one-way, southbound side street dead-ending at Devon in East Rogers Park. The brownstone commercial building located at the northeast corner is where the "collar" of "Midget" Fernekes likely occurred.

On the very same day the corpse of the notorious gangster "Dutch" Schultz was carried out of New York for burial in the family plot, the Cook County state's attorney's police made short work of one of Chicago's most persistent gunmen, a pint-sized social misfit named Henry "the Midget" Fernekes, who had made a mockery of the state penal system until events conspired against him. Fernekes robbed banks. Granted, it was not with the same panache as John Dillinger, Ma Barker, or even Bonnie and Clyde, but his periodic spurts of bloodletting earned him top billing alongside the mug shots of these more famous desperadoes on the walls of U.S. postal facilities.

Fernekes, though standing less than five feet tall in his stocking feet, was blamed for at least five murders. He was married to the owner of a local nursery that had been attended by the babies of several Chicago police officers. At a time when the combined resources of city, county, and state law enforcement were combing all the known criminal haunts, Fernekes was hidden among the cribs and bassinets at his wife Jennie's daycare center.

Fernekes' criminal career dated back to 1918. Already a full-fledged gunman, he and his gang robbed the Argo State Bank of $105,000.

In succeeding years, Fernekes pulled off a string of successful bank heists, including the September 20, 1935, robbery of the University State Bank at 1345 East Fifty-fifth Street on the South Side. Five persons were shot after tear gas canisters seared the interior of the building. Only a month earlier, Fernekes, clad in civilian clothes, walked out of the prison yard of the old Joliet penitentiary unmolested. His flight from custody was aided and abetted by guard George F. Friend and Captain A. L. Anderson, who had signed Fernekes last will and testament. The two security men must have expected to receive a cut of Fernekes' estate, valued at $100,000. How else can this unbelievable lapse in prison security be explained?

After the University State Bank robbery, Chicago police redoubled their efforts to locate Fernekes and wipe away the egg on the face of Illinois law enforcement.

Three weeks of sleuthing ended on October 28, when Captain Dan "Tubbo" Gilbert of State's Attorney Thomas Courtney's investigating staff curbed Fernekes' automobile at the intersection of Newgard and Devon up in Rogers Park. Unarmed, Fernekes docilely submitted. He insisted his name was "Kuklinski," but fingerprint records at the Bureau of Identification refuted his claim. Gilbert, Chicago's erstwhile "millionaire cop," failed to conduct a proper pat-down of the suspect, however, and missed a tiny vial containing potassium cyanide hidden away in Fernekes' coat pocket for just such a moment.

Handed a cup of coffee by one of the guards, Fernekes grumbled that he "wasn't going to no more showups." He slipped the poison into his coffee, smirked at the cops, then collapsed to the floor. Death came minutes later inside a patrol wagon bound for County Hospital. Fernekes' last will and testament was filed in probate court with the entire estate going to his wife and two kids. Officer Friend and Captain Anderson were not mentioned—except as possible codefendants in a criminal indictment for conspiracy.

West Rogers Park

2525

West

Morse

Avenue

"VOTE FOR TIM MURPHY, HE'S A COUSIN OF MINE!" THE DEATH OF A LABOR RACKETEER
June 25, 1928

Bullet holes from shots fired at "Big Tim" Murphy in a gangland drive-by shooting late one summer night in 1928 are still visible in the yellow brickwork of this common Chicago bungalow located in the West Rogers Park section on the city's Far North Side. Gunmen in a passing car raked Murphy with .45-caliber slugs as he ran for cover across the front lawn, and the grisly reminders of their handiwork mark the spot of one of the most famous gangland executions of Chicago's bloody labor wars of the 1920s. With the exception of the striped awnings that disappeared long ago, Tim Murphy's residence on the south side of this quiet residential street sandwiched between Campbell (on the east) and Rockwell (on the west) looks much the same as it did in Big Tim's day.

A towering bully, born and raised in the "Back of the Yards" neighborhood on Chicago's South Side, Timothy Murphy scraped and clawed his way up the money ladder. He was a plucky Irish lad who later boasted about selling newspapers to the famous meatpacker J. Ogden Armour outside the main offices of Armour & Company at Forty-third Street and Racine. When he was older, Murphy obtained a job as a railroad switchman for the Chicago Junction line. He worked in the yards and came to know the hardships of the grueling and dangerous conditions the section hands faced every day.

Big Tim's sympathies were with the workingmen, and he always looked out for their interests in the days when union organizers were often met outside the factory gates by hired goons wielding baseball bats and lead pipes.

Murphy was a devoted family man, but he possessed a contradictory nature and was dangerous when provoked. All the good he might have accomplished as

GRAVESITE OF

"BIG TIM" MURPHY.

THIS IS NOT A NORTH SIDE LOCATION, BUT IT IS IMPORTANT TO THE STORY OF
"BIG TIM" MURPHY. IN 1929, THE CORNER BUILDING AT 1725 WEST 47TH
STREET ON THE SOUTH SIDE WAS A FLOWER SHOP BELONGING TO "DINGBAT"
O'BERTA. HE MARRIED FLORENCE DIGGS MURPHY, WIDOW OF BIG TIM THAT
SAME YEAR.

(Photo by Lawrence Raeder)

a leader of workingmen was negated by his associations with criminals and thugs throughout much of his career.

In 1909 he sided with Mont Tennes, boss of the North Side racing wire. Tennes operated an illegal monopoly distributing fast results direct from race-tracks all over the country to the city "poolrooms" and off-track parlors via Western Union and other telegraph services. Murphy forged an expedient alliance with Tennes before selling him out to the grand jury in 1911 by baring secrets of the "gambling trust."

As a result of his profitable association with the influential Tennes, who bribed many officeholders during his twenty-year reign over the North Side handbooks, Murphy decided to take a stab at politics. In 1915, he ran a highly suc-cessful campaign and was voted in as the Fourth District state representative, on the punchy slogan "Elect Big Tim Murphy, He's a Cousin of Mine!" After just one term in Springfield, Murphy returned to Chicago where he devoted his time to building a name in the trades.

His closest friend in those days was Maurice "Mossie" Enright, veteran labor slugger, convicted murderer, and secretary of the Pipe's Trades Council. Inside "Old Quincy No. 9," a famous watering hole at Randolph and LaSalle Street, Tim Murphy and Mossie Enright were, for a very short period of time, inseparable companions. It was through Enright that Murphy was delegated to organize the Gas Workers union, but the two had a falling-out over the division of proceeds from the settlement of a labor strike.

Enright should have been more careful. He was blind-sided by the eternally ambitious Murphy, in the same manner as the gambler king Mont Tennes had been duped years earlier. There was little doubt as to the identity of the men who shotgunned Enright to death outside his home at 1110 Garfield Boulevard on February 3, 1920. Murphy and three cohorts were jailed on suspicion, but they were never tried or convicted, Chicago justice being what it is.

A free man, Big Tim returned to his control of three local trade unions, but he was arrested on suspicion so many times that it became something of a stand-ing joke in labor circles. "I never carry a rod, so why do you fellas want to both-er me?" he asked innocently enough.

Murphy served a prison term in Leavenworth for a 1921 mail robbery at the Polk and Dearborn Street Train Station that netted his gang $125,000 in stolen securities. For the crime of armed robbery he was sentenced to four years. Murphy accused postal inspectors of framing him, but he had bigger problems back home. His power base in union circles was slowly being usurped by rival factions of racketeers.

By the time of his parole, Big Tim was washed up. Everyone knew it, but

Murphy pressed on with his schemes nevertheless, while his long-suffering wife, Florence, nagged him to find a more suitable line of work. Florence was a church-going woman doing her best to care for their adopted daughter, Doris, in a pretty little bungalow tucked away on the peaceful side of town.

Murphy tried to lure investors into a harebrained business venture in Texas promoting the "culture of bananas." The cockeyed scheme did little to enhance his reputation. Next he came up with a plan to manufacture stop-and-go traffic lights—an idea well ahead of its time, but no one was paying him any mind.

Murphy realized rather late in life that it was the union dues of the rank and file, and not the "get-rich-quick" schemes, that kept him in silk pajamas. To not be included in that action in his productive middle years was to die by inches. Murphy's fertile mind hatched a plot to take over the Master Cleaning and Dyers Association, a ten-thousand-member, mob-fronted union controlled by Al Capone. (*Author's Note:* The union was actually one of four separate entities under the thumb of the Laundry and Dye House, Chauffeurs, Drivers, and Helpers Union.)

Storming into the business offices of the union at 629 South Ashland Avenue with his gun-toting flunky Abe Schaffner at his side, Murphy announced a "hostile takeover."

"From now on we're in and you guys are out—understand that? From now on we get the cut, and if there's any left, we may give you a little break!"

It was his incurable desire to break in on Capone's racket, against the sobering advice of his wife, that led to Murphy's fall. Florence was away at a nearby church festival the night of June 25, 1928, when the gunmen came calling.

Big Tim was spending a quiet evening at home listening to the 1928 Democratic National Convention on the radio with brothers-in-law Harry and William Diggs, when a knock at the door was heard around 11:00 P.M. One of Murphy's many "cousins," in this case a fourteen-year-old lad named Earl Glynn, raced upstairs to investigate.

Murphy and his guests bolted down the front stairs and turned into the backyard, concerned about lurking prowlers.

The evening was quiet. Ever vigilant, Murphy was standing in front of his bungalow surveying the street when the death car rolled past. Big Tim vaulted across the front yard like a scared rabbit, but was caught in a spray of .45-caliber bullets fired from handguns. There were four gunmen—but none of them could be identified by the Diggs Brothers or the boy.

The Diggs brothers carried the fallen Murphy into the living room, but he was already dead by the time Florence arrived.

Tim's sudden demise canceled the widow's plan to retire to a dairy farm in Woodstock, Illinois. "He was to have closed the deal tomorrow," she sighed. "We were going to live out there and be happy."

Chief of Detectives Michael Grady rounded up ten suspects linked to the recent labor wars, but none of them were ever indicted for this latest gangland homicide.

Florence Diggs Murphy promised reprisals. "If I knew who killed Tim Murphy I wouldn't tell anybody—I wouldn't wait for anybody. I'd take a gun and kill them as they killed him!"

In contrast to the gaudy gangster funerals characterizing the crazy 1920s, only twenty cars trailed the Murphy bier. None were driven by friends or admirers of the late Mossie Enright, who was finally avenged in death.

Big Tim was laid to rest in a modest silver gray coffin at Holy Sepulchre Cemetery in Worth, Illinois, in the same plot as John "Dingbat" O'Berta, one of Murphy's closest friends in life and a gangster associate of the Joe Saltis–Frankie McErlane bootlegging gang until the inevitable falling-out occurred early in 1930.

O'Berta, like Murphy, was a character from the half-world trading upon his minor political connections. He owned a floral shop at 1725 West Forty-seventh Street, was elected committeeman of the 13th Ward on the Republican ticket, and bootlegged intoxicants in open defiance of the Capone mob.

The "Dingbat" squired Florence Diggs Murphy down the altar in April 1929. O'Berta gained a wife and an entrée into the labor unions. Florence hoped to groom her new husband in Murphy's shadow. Neither of them got what they wanted.

Florence prodded O'Berta into the labor rackets against his better judgment. To her eternal dismay, she quickly realized that he was no Tim Murphy in either physical stature or mental toughness, and his feeble attempt to organize the downtown theater janitors and ushers into a union local under his control was met with fierce resistance.

Florence became a widow for the second time on March 6, 1930, after O'Berta was found slumped over the steering wheel of his abandoned car, parked in a ditch near Roberts Road and 103rd Street in Chicago Ridge. (*Author's Note:* The name of this Southwest Side community was eventually changed to Palos Hills. A branch of the LaSalle Bank occupies the site today.) The "Dingbat" and bodyguard Sam Malaga were riddled with shotgun pellets. Frankie McErlane, a berserk gunman from the Stockyards District, was blamed but never indicted. (*Author's Note:* McErlane, the first gangster to employ a machine gun on the streets of Chicago, and his brother Vincent are buried less than a hundred feet from the gravesite of Tim Murphy.)

In preparation for the funeral, Florence Diggs Murphy O'Berta took her widow's weeds out of mothballs; the same gown she had worn for Big Tim nearly two years earlier.

"Neither one of my husbands could be beat for goodheartedness and fineness," she said, sobbing. "I never suspected for a moment that this would happen to either Tim or Johnny."

A MAN OF REGULAR HABITS: THE MURDER OF DR. SILBER PEACOCK

January 2, 1936

6438 North Whipple Street and 6358 North Francisco

Devon Avenue, from Lincoln east to Damen, is a fascinating kaleidoscope of ethnic culture, clogged with exotic restaurants, Kosher delicatessens, Indian bakeries, sari shops, and wholesale electronics stores. Automobile traffic from the west, already a slow caravan, grinds to a halt east of California Avenue on market days when Indians, Assyrians, Croats, and Asians dart from one store to another in search of bargains. Once a cohesive Jewish enclave populated by Hasidic Jews who made the big push out of Lawndale after World War II, the neighborhood and the central shopping district have undergone profound changes since the early 1970s when a burgeoning Indian population began moving westward from Damen Avenue. The curious spectacle of so many divergent people coexisting in one place suggests that harmony among cultures is an attainable dream. But like any other Chicago neighborhood, the Devon Avenue corridor has its own famous and forgotten crimes to live down. The Peacock case was a notorious Depression-era murder. The victim was accosted in the gangway next to a four-story low-rise apartment building at 6438 North Whipple Street (one-half block north of Devon, between Devon and Arthur Avenue). The structure still stands, but it is curiously out of place on this residential side street lined with post–World War II, single-family ranch houses owned mostly by Orthodox Jews. At the time of the Peacock murder, the entire block and the surrounding area was vacant prairie land on the verge of being developed. It was an odd murder mystery occurring in a most unlikely location. The killers removed the bludgeoned remains of the good doctor two blocks east, at 6358 North Francisco, the southwest corner of Francisco and Devon, which was also a vacant parcel of land at the time. A package-liquor store stands on the lot today. The rough handling by Chicago police of one of the suspects—a retarded youth who was beaten and tortured into signing a confession—once again exposed the reputation for raw brutality that the department has never been able to dispel. It is a perception that lingers to this day.

At the age of forty, Dr. Silber Charles Peacock was a respected and admired physician, well liked by his colleagues in the medical profession. There was not a hint of scandal or impropriety to his name, and by slow degrees he was becoming socially prominent.

Before graduating from the Rush Medical College, Peacock had practiced in Chicago for ten years, and was researching the deadly childhood diseases of scarlet fever and diphtheria. He maintained a suite of offices in the Uptown National Bank Building at 4753 Broadway with two associates, and was attached to the staff of Children's Memorial Hospital. Peacock resided comfortably with his wife, Ruth Pearce, at the fashionable Edgewater Apartments (5555 North Sheridan at Bryn Mawr), among other influential Chicagoans doing important things.

Dr. Silber Peacock was a man of regular habits, on call twenty-four hours a day. Physicians routinely visited their patients at home in those days, and pediatricians were often summoned to the bedside of a sick child at odd hours.

On the evening of January 2, Peacock had picked up his wife and daughter from Union Station. They had returned home from a family funeral in Bowen, Illinois, and were anxious to settle in for the evening. Dr. Peacock was already in his pajamas preparing for bed when the phone rang at his apartment. It was 10:05, and a mysterious woman was on the other end of the line.

Ruth Peacock, pregnant with her second child, turned the phone over to husband and watched him scribble an address and a name on the notepad: "G.W. Smale, 6438 N. Whipple." The woman caller had not left a telephone number, which seemed rather curious to Mrs. Peacock, who was told by the switchboard operator that this same person had called earlier in the day but refused to leave a message.

Appearing to be in a great hurry, Dr. Peacock called for his car, raced down to the garage, then paused to make a five-minute telephone call to some unknown person. The garage attendant thought it to be strange, and so did the cops, in hindsight.

When he still had not returned home at 1:30 A.M., Ruth placed a frantic call to Cook County State's Attorney Thomas Courtney, a personal friend. The police were notified, and a missing person's report was filed. Detectives from the Summerdale Police District tracked down G. W. Smale, but at 6438 *South*

IN THE 1930S, THE CHICAGO *DAILY TIMES* PROVIDED THE BEST NEWSPAPER CRIME COVERAGE IN THE CITY, MINUS THE SENSATIONALISM (AND OCCASIONAL FABRICATION) OF STORIES AT WILLIAM RANDOLPH HEARST'S *HERALD & EXAMINER*.

Washtenaw Avenue—virtually at the opposite end of the city. Neither Smale nor the seven families residing at the Whipple address knew Peacock.

Police puzzled over another bit of information, something Peacock's private secretary had shared with them. The doctor made it his standing policy to refuse house calls, and he was not taking on any new patients at the moment.

Twenty-one hours passed. A teenage youth named Jack Dieterich observed a parked car with the headlights on north of a three-story building at 6236 North Francisco. Dieterich went to investigate and found the lifeless form of Dr. Peacock hunched over in the rear of his 1931 sedan. The contents of his instrument bag were spread across the front seat. It was determined that he was killed by two gunshots to the head and seven knife wounds to the skull. The savagery of the crime suggested the killer had a personal motive.

Found outside the Whipple Street apartment on the sidewalk were six crushed cigarette butts and a discarded matchbook. Police surmised that the killer was an impatient, nervous sort of man, who had been lying in wait for Doc Peacock's arrival.

The mystery deepened when the Reverend Dr. Kenneth A. Hurst told police that he was told Peacock had two very influential "enemies" who wished him dead. Hurst's wife was a cousin of Peacock's widow. One of the two deadly enemies, an angry husband named Arthur St. George, allegedly accused Peacock of performing an illegal abortion on his wife, Arlene Johnson Thompson. But when the cops brought St. George in for questioning, he revealed that that wasn't the case at all. Dr. Peacock had been paying attention to his wife, and she walked out on her marriage as a result. Mrs. Thompson denied it all, and the police found very little in her story to suggest adultery as a possible motive for murder. The compelling lead turned out to be a red herring.

The real killers turned out to be four teenage street urchins who confessed to killing a sixty-three-year-old tailor named Peter Payor three weeks before the Peacock slaying. The four young desperadoes, Robert Goethe, Durland "Jimmy" Nash, Michael Livingston, and Emil Reck, ended up in the hot seat and confessed to the murder of Dr. Peacock—a crime that netted them the grand sum of $20 in change. It was all the money that Peacock carried in his pocket, and according to Nash, who was the first to confess following his arrest on March 25, the boys used it to gorge on beefsteak dinners and beer.

Driving a stolen car, the gang of four had stopped at Mary Pybas's candy store at 2244 Cortez Street, where they picked Dr. Peacock's name in a random

DR. SILBER PEACOCK WAS LURED TO THIS APARTMENT HOUSE AT 6438 NORTH

WHIPPLE AND MURDERED ON THE SIDEWALK. THE CRIME WAS SENSELESS, AND THE

AFTERMATH TRAGIC.

search of a telephone directory, nothing more sinister than that. Lured out of his residence, the unwitting Peacock was beaten to a pulp and shot to death on Whipple Street after putting up a terrible struggle against his youthful assailants. In every respect, this was as much a "thrill killing" as the Loeb-Leopold murder case had been a decade earlier—except for one interesting and important detail.

Robert Goethe was the son of Mrs. Rose Kasallis, a dowdy brothel madame who lured runaway girls into a life of shame in her rented flat at 1336 North Maplewood. The Kasallis woman was serving a two-year sentence in the Bridewell on a morals charge at the time of her son's arrest. It came out in the trial that she plied her own son, and his companions, with booze and women. She was a cunning, real-life Fagin, running a crime school for vandals, thieves, and murderers. Twenty-five girls were loaded into a paddy wagon, climaxing a sensational police raid that exposed her entire operation.

"Oh, if only they could bring him to me so I could put my arms around him!" Between hysterical sobs, Mrs. Kasallis said her "Bobbie" was a "regular churchgoer," and had never been in trouble.

It was established in Judge Joseph Burke's courtroom that Goethe fired the fatal shots after grappling with Dr. Peacock. According to testimony, either Reck or Livingston struck him repeatedly with a club after the shots were fired. Amid growing doubt, the court held to the belief that Reck administered the beating.

Goethe and Nash both pleaded guilty and accepted the judgment of the court, which was fixed at 199 years.

With the boys' guilt a foregone conclusion and a ringing demand for the death penalty coming from Assistant State's Attorney John Boyle, defense attorneys shifted their argument away from the crime itself in order to focus on the illegal extortion of confessions by Chicago police detectives—otherwise known as the "third-degree sweat."

During an all-night interrogation of suspects, Emil Reck was shuttled back and forth from the Shakespeare Station to Warren Avenue and finally the West North Avenue Police Station. The mentally retarded youth (he was found to have the intelligence of a child between ten and eleven) at one point had become violently ill and was vomiting up blood after receiving repeated blows to the abdomen and chest.

The cops had forced him into signing a confession of guilt after he was kept incommunicado and without benefit of legal counsel for nearly eighty hours by Captain Harry O'Connell and Officer George Youhn.

Reck and Livingston were convicted on May 20, 1936, narrowly escaping the electric chair. Having taken no part in the actual killings, Livingston was let off with thirty years. Reck's punishment was fixed at 199 years.

In 1961, the American Civil Liberties Union (ACLU) presented oral arguments before the high court in the case of Reck vs. Pate. In a 7–2 decision the U.S. Supreme Court threw out the illegally obtained confession and sent the case back for retrial. The new charges filed against Reck were dismissed for lack of evidence.

TOUR 4

Crimes in High Places:

The North Shore and Beyond

North of Rogers Park, some of the oldest, wealthiest, and most exclusive suburbs hug the windswept shoreline of Lake Michigan. The North Shore is, in the main, an impressive vista of landed estates and secluded mansions, many of them dating back to the late nineteenth century.

Life moves along at a slow, plodding pace, and crime is of no serious concern to the wealthy country squires that inhabit this area. That is, until a jarring tragedy occurs, such as the 1966 murder of Valerie Jeanne Percy, daughter of U.S. Senator Charles Percy, or the May 20, 1988, shooting rampage inside the Hubbard Woods Elementary School in Winnetka, carried out with manic efficiency by a mentally disturbed young woman named Laurie Wasserman Dann. Such crimes draw national attention and focus an awkward spotlight on the lifestyles of Chicago's powerful "old-money" aristocrats whose families have lived up this way for generations.

There is always an air of disbelief in the aftermath of such heinous crimes like the shooting of six children by Dann, the heretofore unsolved murder of Valerie Percy, or the poisoning death of the "Millionaire Orphan" of Kenilworth. The members of the community band together and put on brave faces, but explanations from public officials and social psychologists are slow in coming. "If it can happen in an idyllic community like Winnetka, which really does believe in Camelot," sighed Police Chief Herbert Timm following the Dann incident, "then it can happen anywhere."

These crimes serve as a wake-up call illustrating the inescapable fact that crime transcends race, economic station, and tightly drawn suburban boundaries.

The Edens Expressway (I-94) insulates the provincial North Shore estates from modern bedroom suburbs and executive communities like Northbrook and Glenview, former home of candy heiress Helen Vorhees Brach before she vanished off of the face of the earth in 1977.

Beginning with the building frenzy after World War II, once-rural villages like

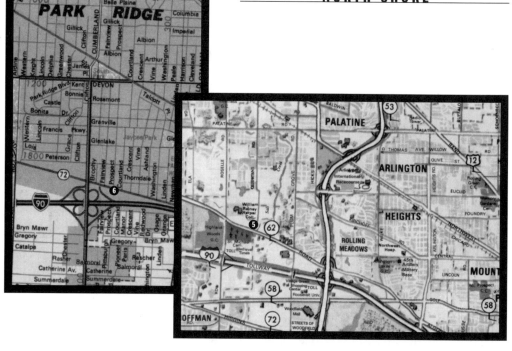

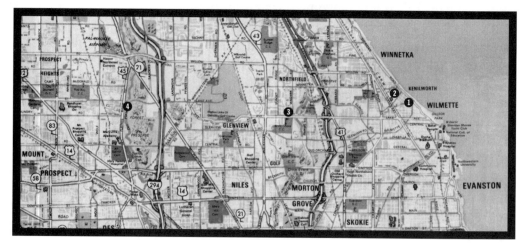

1. No Man's Land, Wilmette-Kenilworth border.
2. 341 Melrose St., home of the "Millionaire Orphan."
3. Helen Brach residence on Wagner Rd. between Lake St. and Glenview Rd.
4. German POW Camp in the woods.
5. Tri-Color Stables, Palatine.
6. The "Elevator Murders," 216 West Higgins Rd.

Palatine, lying straight west of the expressway, evolved into densely populated suburbs with extended office parks, town-home developments, strip malls, and single-family residences. The line of demarcation between town and country has mostly disappeared, and with it the sense of security cloaking circles of friends and neighbors who assumed that crime was a Chicago problem.

Wilmette

FIRE IN NO MAN'S LAND
March 8, 1932

Sheridan Road between Chestnut Street in Wilmette and the Kenilworth border (currently the Plaza del Lago Shopping Center)

The scenic tour of Chicago's beautiful North Shore rightfully begins on Sheridan Road where Evanston abuts Chicago's northernmost border. On a clear autumn afternoon when the leaves are starting to turn, drive north in a leisurely fashion and rediscover the beauty of nature as well as how the other half lives. Sheridan Road, a nineteenth-century access route laid down by architect Daniel Burnham for U.S. Army troops bivouacked at the fort of the same name, twists and turns past breathtaking panoramas overlooking Lake Michigan, wooded estates, and patrician mansions belonging to the area's blue-book elite. Just past Evanston and fifteen miles north of the Chicago Loop lie the Village of Wilmette and its Plaza del Lago (Plaza on the Lake, formerly known as Spanish Court) shopping center. The Plaza achieves a European look and feel with an aesthetically pleasing Moorish architectural motif. With thirty-five retail stores targeting the affluent Doc Martin–wearing, Starbucks-sipping, whale-watching crowd, Plaza del Lago is one of the oldest open-air malls in the country. The history of this area is curious. The shopping center was built on an infamous disputed property known in the 1920s and 1930s as "No Man's Land." The patrons of this tiny sliver of land, sandwiched between Wilmette on the south and Kenilworth to the north, fended off repeated attempts at annexation in order to maintain the district as a racy, "honky-tonk" attraction luring gamblers and thrill seekers from all over Chicagoland, until an act of God akin to the destruction of Sodom and Gomorrah forced them to capitulate.

Brushing up against the Lake Michigan shoreline in the middle of "No Man's Land," the Miralago dancehall and retail complex was a superb example of early art-deco architecture until the Kenilworth bluenoses allowed it to burn down one night because its presence offended community standards.

Miralago architect George Fred Keck had in mind a shopping arcade and dancehall reminiscent of the early Spanish missions in California, accenting the pre-existing Teatro del Lago movie theater, the Vista del Lago club, the Breaker's Beach Club, and a collection of residential apartments. The entire complex, when completed in the late 1920s, was named Spanish Court. Several of the buildings in the current Plaza del Lago date back to that time.

The entertainment complex, owing to its proximity to a major highway, soon attracted an unsavory crowd of gin-soaked flappers and their mobile male consorts. Chicago's "Flaming Youth" of the Roaring '20s, with their fast cars, objectionable dancing, and loud, raucous behavior, made the sedate oldsters living in Wilmette and Kenilworth very uneasy.

There were rules against unescorted women entering Miralago. Dime-a-dance girls were not allowed on the premises, but illegal gambling, although not *officially* sanctioned, went on nonetheless. In July 1931, a spectacular police raid closed down an illegal game on the second floor of Miralago.

The proprietors did their best to keep things on the up and up, but as the decade of the twenties wore on there were reports of drunken brawls and harassment of the locals. Neither of the two adjoining suburbs allowed their police to get involved. They had no jurisdiction in the matter, nor were they invited. According to author Robert Shea, a community banner inscribed "No Man's Land of the Free" proclaimed their independence from the other towns.

In 1931, after the property owners voted down a proposition to be annexed to Wilmette, local officials there responded by withdrawing fire protection and shutting off the water supply. No Man's Land property owners thumbed their noses at their strait-laced neighbors and sank their own wells.

They had not counted on the cataclysmic fire that erupted inside the two-story, stucco dancehall in the late afternoon on March 8, 1932. High winds in sub-zero temperatures fanned the flames as firefighters from Evanston answered the urgent call for help.

The Kenilworth police, however, refused to allow Evanston firefighters access to the village water mains. "This dancehall hasn't paid for the use of the water!" snorted one indignant official on the scene.

"But the building is burning down!"

"Rules are rules!" came the reply.

At six o'clock that evening, Wendell H. Clark, the Kenilworth village clerk, finally relented and ordered the water turned on when a gas station on the east side of Sheridan Road and a restaurant were threatened. By that time, the beautiful Miralago Building, valued at approximately $150,000, was a total loss. The owners of the ruined dancehall filed suit, but their claims were all dismissed.

The adjoining Vista del Lago beach club (opened on the palisades of Lake Michigan in 1926) was sold to a gambling syndicate. It operated on the fringes for a few years, then went into decline. By the late 1950s, all that was left was an abandoned ruin that had become a popular location for moonlit beach parties.

On January 6, 1942, No Man's Land was officially annexed to the Village of Wilmette over the objections of the seventy-five or so people living there. The measure was put through without a vote.

In the early 1960s, a high-rise development known as Vista del Lago (1630 Sheridan Road) replaced the crumbling ruins of the beach club and drove out a row of hot dog stands and small retail shops gracing the roadway. All 104 apartments were sold out before construction, sparking redevelopment of the Spanish Court shopping center and the entire stretch of Sheridan Road once known as No Man's Land—a name that is now all but lost to history.

```
Kenilworth
```

THE CURIOUS DEATH OF THE MILLIONAIRE ORPHAN
December 4, 1925

341 Melrose Avenue (east of Green Bay Road between Essex Road and Cumnor Road)

With Prohibition in full swing, public fascination over bootlegging wars and the ritual of gangland rubouts was temporarily suspended with newspaper accounts describing a vexing mystery surrounding one of the handsome young men of Chicago society. There occurred in one of the wealthiest sections of the North Shore, on a bitterly cold winter evening, the sudden passing of William Nelson McClintock, the sickly heir to a vast fortune. McClintock's pending nuptials to a local golddigger were thus interrupted. McClintock's fiancée was determined to marry him on his deathbed, if necessary, lest she be cut out of the sizable fortune. His legal guardians were opposed to any arrangement of the sort. That would deprive them of what they perceived to be their rightful inheritance. By terms of the will, if McClintock succeeded in slipping a wedding ring around the dainty finger of the girl before his ticker gave out, they stood to lose everything. 'Twas murder most foul, or so it seemed to State's Attorney Robert Emmet Crowe and his bumbling army of political hacks masquerading as homicide investigators. But nothing was as it really seemed, except for the stolid English country house basking in the shade of the surrounding trees after witnessing more than seventy-five years of old secrets, passions, jealousies, and murder . . . indeed, most foul.

As he lay dying, William "Billy" McClintock expressed a solemn wish. He wanted to be joined in matrimony to Miss Isabelle Pope, his most devoted admirer and intimate friend ever since their days together at New Trier High School. Fearing the inevitable, Miss Pope raced down to the marriage license bureau to obtain the necessary document over the stern admonishments of McClintock's legal guardians, Attorney William Darling Shepherd and his wife, Julia, who had looked after the young man's interests since he was orphaned at age six.

Shepherd was named chief heir of the $1 million McClintock fortune in a will that had only recently been revised at Master William's request. Had a marriage actually occurred, Miss Pope, and not the Shepherds, stood to inherit all personal property, one-half of the real estate, and $200,000 in cash and bonds. The remainder of the estate would have gone to seven of the cousins with Shepherd receiving nothing.

It was with greatest urgency that the girl be stopped.

The foster father would later deny standing in the way of true love, but Miss Pope was quite adamant on that point after William lapsed into a coma seconds before the bedside wedding ceremony was scheduled to begin.

The vast McClintock fortune was inherited money, earned by a nineteenth-century man named Hickling, who left it all to Sara, his widow, upon death. Sara, in turn, married William McClintock Sr., then died shortly thereafter. McClintock, who had the good fortune of falling into a money pit not of his own making, married Emma Nelson of Salina, Kansas, and they had a son—William McClintock Jr., soon to become "the Millionaire Orphan."

The boy's natural father was killed in a freak automobile mishap with a horse wagon in 1906. A wagon shaft was driven into McClintock Sr.'s side when the frightened horse reared up. Emma Nelson McClintock died in 1909 from

THE KENILWORTH HOME OF "THE MILLIONAIRE ORPHAN" IN 1924 (ABOVE) AND AS IT LOOKS TODAY.

(Photo by Albert Schafer)

what doctors termed rheumatic heart disease. She had battled her illness for quite some time and had even traveled to Hot Springs to revitalize in the mineral waters. When there was no immediate improvement, however, she was forced to weigh her options with respect to the future care of young William.

The upbringing of the orphan boy was left to the Shepherds, a pair of Kansas fortune hunters who drifted through Indianapolis, Indiana; Texas; and finally into Chicago to (ostensibly) assist the McClintocks in their hour of crisis. Emma McClintock and Julia Shepherd had attended classes together at Bethany College in Topeka, Kansas, and were especially fond of each other. William assured Mrs. McClintock that he would "look after the estate" until she was back on her feet. He said he was good at that kind of thing, and the dying woman was most grateful.

It was whispered at the time that William Shepherd came from "traveling people." His mother was a fortuneteller and his father an instructor in "physical culture." While in Salina, Kansas, the father and son opened a pharmacy. Young William Shepherd aspired to the law, but his chances of success were not good. Instead he became quite adept at mixing potions, perhaps even deadly poisons.

The pharmacy turned out to be a bust, and the Shepherds moved on, seeking opportunity here and there—wherever the four winds led them. In his later statements, Shepherd claimed to have traveled overseas and fought bravely in the Boer War in South Africa. He proudly boasted of suffering wounds in the Battle of Spion Kop, when in fact he had never once left the country of his birth.

For the conniving pair, who applied form and subtlety to their tricks, a spate of bad luck was about to end. On her deathbed, Mrs. McClintock beckoned them to assume the guardianship of her son and manage the household duties.

By dint of a girlhood friendship in Kansas so many years ago, the Shepherds were soon rolling in dough. William resumed his law studies, graduated, found a partner, and hung out his shingle. Julia hired cooks and maids and was cautiously welcomed into Kenilworth society.

Trouble began to brew when the young ward made overtures to Henry Pope's pretty young daughter Isabelle. Against the wishes of the Shepherds, he had returned home from Dartmouth to plan a large wedding that was to include many of Isabelle's college friends from Northwestern University and a bevy of society folk who remembered McClintock's parents with fond admiration.

On November 22, 1925, as the young couple forged ahead with their plans, William took sick. His fever rose to 102 degrees, and with the sudden downturn in the boy's health, the Shepherds' outwardly polite manner vanished. "I noticed Mr. Shepherd was rather cold to me, but I also knew that many real parents feel that way when their only son chooses a wife, so I tried to understand," Isabelle sighed.

The young man possessed a delicate constitution, the doctor explained. "Too many late-night social affairs," groused Shepherd, who shared a bedroom over the kitchen with Billy (a very peculiar arrangement, indeed). "It was a dance or a card party, or something every night!"

William had been ill for about a week when Shepherd was informed by Isabelle that they planned to marry right away and she would procure the license. "By thunder, you can't do that!" raged the foster father to his ward. "The Illinois law requires that both parties make application for the license!"

It was at this time that the Shepherds issued strict orders to family physician Dr. Rufus Stolp and the domestic help to turn away Isabelle, her father, Henry Pope, or anyone else who came to call.

On December 1, Isabelle secured the marriage license against the wishes of Billy's guardians.

Dr. Stolp's diagnosis was typhoid fever. The boy had not long to live, and preparations needed to be made. With McClintock's life hanging in the balance, Isabelle was at last permitted to enter the bedchamber with license in hand and a minister trailing close behind. The Shepherds glanced nervously at each other, but they could hardly refuse a dying man's last request.

Billy was pale and delirious. He drifted in and out of consciousness. When he closed his eyes the ceremony was halted and Isabelle was asked to leave. The Millionaire Orphan lapsed into a coma and died before he could say, "I do." Death came at three o'clock the following morning.

In a barely audible whisper, moments before he faded away, he said to Julia Shepherd, "Mother, I love you."

The last will and testament, originally drafted by Sara McClintock in September 1897, but amended by Billy McClintock and William Shepherd days before his death, revealed that Shepherd stood to inherit $1 million. "He wished Mrs. Shepherd to have the estate in the event of his death," said the foster father. "But wishing to avoid that the burden of administration fall on Mrs. Shepherd's shoulders he directed that I should be included in the will."

Prostrated by grief, the couple decamped to Albuquerque, New Mexico, aboard the California Limited, leaving the lawyers to sort out the sticky matter of probate.

Cook County State's Attorney Robert Emmet Crowe was naturally suspicious about the issuance of a revised will and pondered the notion that the boy had died of unnatural causes. Conferring with Coroner Oscar Wolff, it was decided to conduct an autopsy and bring forth witnesses.

Crowe ordered Shepherd back from the desert, then proceeded to question the domestic help. Maria Gartner, a maid in the Kenilworth home who had wit-

MARIA GARTNER WAS

EMPLOYED AS A MAID

IN THE MCCLINTOCK

HOUSEHOLD AND

ALWAYS BELIEVED HER

EMPLOYER TO BE

INNOCENT.

(Photo courtesy of Albert Schafer)

nessed the signing of the will and appended her signature to the document, was among the people who appeared before state's attorney investigators.

Gartner's son, longtime Chicago resident Albert L. Schafer, remembers his mother talking about her employers with measured fondness. Schafer has kept a collection of brittle newspaper copy with pictures of Maria on the day she took the stand as a defense witness. "She always believed they were innocent of any crime," Schafer said of the woman, who had immigrated to America from the former Yugoslavia. "Mother never believed for a moment they had murdered that young man."

Others were not so sure. Within days of McClintock's death, Dr. F. T. Breidgan of the Kellogg Sanatorium in Battle Creek, Michigan, volunteered information to Assistant State's Attorney George Gorman that Shepherd experimented with guinea pigs and had a keen interest in bacteria cultures and typhoid germs when the two men first became acquainted in Chicago in 1919.

The statements were corroborated by Dr. George E. Fosberg, who worked as a sales agent for Norwood Pharmaceutical, one of the local patent-medicine supply houses. (*Author's Note:* Dr. Fosberg offered his services to Clarence Darrow as a professional witness for the defense during the 1924 Loeb and Leopold trial. The offer was refused.)

In 1924 the average person could purchase typhoid germs and other deadly bacteria directly from research chemists for experimental purposes. In Chicago, the Accuracy Laboratories at 1734 West Madison Street sold such items directly to the public. It was scandalously easy for the man on the street to purchase death in a test tube for only a few dollars. The suspicion grew that McClintock had been injected with the fatal germs purchased over the counter at a drug supply house. Crowe produced eyewitnesses who placed McClintock at the laboratory in February 1924.

A trail of circumstantial evidence tilted ever so slightly toward the existence of a fiendish murder plot. Letters were produced showing that Shepherd was not the devoted family man he pretended to be. For seven years, he had been carrying on with a pretty young nurse named Estelle Gehling, his "Precious Sunshine." The day turned gloomy for Shepherd when the woman testified that during the months leading up to Billy's death, her paramour would disappear for days on end, suggesting that he was using his time alone to hatch a murder scheme.

The inquest into the death of young McClintock brought forward an astonishing array of witnesses, not all of them nearly as supportive to the man under suspicion as Maria Gartner had been. Former maid Signe Gustafson testified that Shepherd poisoned his young charge with contaminated oysters.

The strange death of Dr. Oscar G. Olson, brother of Chief Justice Harry Olson of the Cook County Municipal Court, was ascribed to prussic acid poisoning. Olson had treated Shepherd for nosebleeds some years earlier and had dined with him only a few hours before his death. The judge, of course, had more than a passing interest in the final outcome of the McClintock investigations. He firmly believed Shepherd guilty of murdering his brother and built a strong case in the press to that effect.

The telling piece of evidence against Shepherd was produced by Coroner Wolff, who ordered the remains of McClintock's mother, Emma Nelson McClintock, exhumed from the family grave in Oakwoods Cemetery. Wolff supervised the inquiry and announced to the press that his staff of toxicologists and pathologists had proved that the mother did not die from heart disease, as was reported back in 1909, but was the victim of a poisoner. Mercury, sufficient to have killed two people, was found in the remains.

"It is very evident that the poison was administered to Mrs. McClintock in small doses," said Wolff, "showing that the murderer not once, but several—maybe six or seven—times gave Mrs. McClintock deadly poisons."

The conclusion seemed inescapable. The murder plot dated back sixteen years.

By now, William Shepherd was under arrest and charged with the murder of his twenty-one-year-old ward by means of inoculating the young man with a fatal dose of germs. A second indictment charged his wife as an accessory to murder. Sounding like Lady Macbeth, she indignantly snorted: "I hope there will be a fitting punishment for the fiendishness of Judge Olson, that filthy beast!"

As the opposing sides prepared to do battle, State's Attorney Crowe and Judge Olson vented their political differences in the press. The two men were combative and surly, and Crowe was particularly miffed at Olson for allowing the coroner's jury to carry on as a grand jury. It was yet another monotonous example of Chicago's backroom politicking intruding upon the solemn proceedings of the judicial system, and it compromised the State's case against the Shepherds on the eve of trial in May 1925.

John Sbarbaro, erstwhile assistant Cook County state's attorney, whose funeral home was patronized by the bereaved wives and family members of slain Prohibition gangsters, led for the prosecution.

Representing the Shepherds in the proceedings were Attorneys William Scott Stewart, and William W. O'Brien, infamously known in his prosecutorial days as "Ropes" for the score of cons he had dispatched to the gallows. Now he was a member of the defense bar, but he had the unenviable task of having to plead his client's case before a judge with the last name of . . . Lynch.

The State managed to produce a less than creditable witness in one Charles C. Faiman, who told the court that he had sold the germs to Shepherd for a promise of $100,000. The state, however, refused to vouch for his testimony, nor would they agree to a grant of immunity. Faiman was the proprietor of the "National University of Sciences," a correspondence school and diploma mill termed a "colossal fraud" by the defense. The entire case rested on his feeble statements, easily punctured during O'Brien's blistering cross-examination.

On June 27, 1925, a verdict of not guilty was returned by the jury. The Shepherds were freed amid heated denunciations leveled against State's Attorney Crowe by Judge Olson, who accused Crowe of botching the entire case by failing to call credible witnesses like Dr. Fosberg to the stand.

Out of spite, Crowe deliberately set out to prove that he could win this case on its own merit without Judge Olson's meddling, which meant bypassing

Olson's list of prospective prosecution witnesses.

William D. Shepherd's three-month prison ordeal was over. With a smile he answered the reporters' questions straightaway. "I think Billy our boy is looking down upon us with a happy smile," he gloated. "Yes, God is good. It is good to be back, good to be free, to be vindicated, to be released from that stifling atmosphere of lies and hate. It's good to forget all that and love."

It was especially good to divide up the loot and embark on a merry course. After all, the nouveau riche Shepherds had waited sixteen long years to experience the joyous blessings bestowed upon them at this "precious" moment.

Glenview

THE DISAPPEARANCE OF THE CANDY LADY: HELEN BRACH GOES MISSING

February 17, 1977

Opposite the North Shore Country Club on the east side of Wagner Road between Lake Street (north) and Glenview Road (south)

The disappearance of candy heiress Helen Vorhees Brach is a story without an end. Maybe we will never find out the fate that befell the unfortunate widow after she checked out of the Mayo Clinic in Rochester, Minnesota. She seemingly vanished into thin air while preparing to head back to her two-story, eighteen-room house nestled in a sprawling seven-acre estate in Glenview, a modestly affluent suburb buffering the palatial North Shore mansions along the lakefront from the hoi polloi residing directly west. Over a period of years, the Brach disappearance has evolved into something far more significant than the usual missing person's case. It has become a complicated murder mystery and horse swindle that has caught the eye of the national media and documentary filmmakers. Richard Bailey, a prime suspect in the Brach murder, stands convicted of conspiracy and is presently incarcerated in a federal prison, but prosecutors are unsure as to whether he merely solicited murder or actually carried out the bloody deed with his own hands. A forty-six-year-old unsolved murder involving three young boys was finally cracked as a result of expert sleuthing, and a ring of insurance swindlers suffered the consequences of their treachery. But when all these crimes (both old and new) were cleared, frustrated investigators found themselves back to square one with respect to shedding light on the where-abouts of Helen Brach. Brach's remains have never been found. How she died remains a mystery, though rumors and innuendo surrounding the case still circulate. The Brach home on Wagner Road was sold, and the family fortune has been dispersed. The candy company her father-in-law founded in the horse-and-buggy days recently abandoned Chicago, its home base of operations for nearly a century. Thousands of confectionery workers, who earned their liveli-hood in the big West Side plant, have been left to fend for themselves. To say it has been a daunting fifty years for the embattled Brach company and the fam-ily that built it to greatness is an understatement.

Helen Vorhees was raised in the Appalachian hills of southeast Ohio in mod-est circumstances. In her younger years, she was an arresting beauty with flow-ing red hair.

A divorcée at age twenty-one, Vorhees blamed herself for the breakup of her marriage to a philandering, feckless playboy. Fueled by a rugged ambition instilled in her by her Yankee forebears, Helen Vorhees picked up the broken shards of her life and went to work in a pottery factory before setting out for the gaudy decadence of Miami to strike her fortune or marry a millionaire—whichever happened to come first.

Helen's lucky break came when fifty-four-year-old Frank V. Brach, the candy king of Chicago whose marketing genius spearheaded a rapid expansion of the family business, wandered into her life. Helen was earning a living collecting tips as a hatcheck girl at Miami's Indian Creek Country Club, one of many play-grounds for wealthy *bon vivants* in an era of sumptuous and extravagant living.

In Miami and elsewhere, there were scores of live-performance supper clubs where scantily attired women dreamed of snagging a millionaire as they cavorted about the dining room hawking cigarettes, chewing gum, and souvenir program books.

Some were more lucky than others and in 1950 Helen Vorhees reeled in a big prize. The hatcheck girl from Unionport, Ohio, bewitched Frank Brach, whose marriage to wife June was no longer on solid ground. On that fortuitous night, he invited the shy and withdrawing woman to dine with him at his table. She was a charming conversationalist, an accomplished dancer, and a peach of a woman. The older man was enchanted.

Within a few months, Brach was actively courting Helen while divorce lawyers wrangled over the particulars of the settlement back in Chicago. Among

other bitter accusations leveled against Vorhees by the injured ex-wife was "man stealer." The following year the newlyweds began their married life together at Frank's home in the wooded seven-acre estate in Glenview. Another house in Ohio and a penthouse apartment in Ft. Lauderdale, Florida, were soon added to the list of marital assets.

The Brach name is noticeably absent all those years from Chicago's blue-book social register. Helen was no first-nighter or art gallery maven. (Her birthright and marital history may have also had something to do with the snub.) Instead, she preferred to maintain her veiled privacy behind the walls of Frank's spacious but rather drab-looking suburban country house.

With the passing of his brother Edwin Brach, control of the candy company fell to Frank, but Frank Brach was getting on in years and losing steam. He divested his interests in the company in order to live at home and shower Helen with expensive gifts like a lavender Rolls-Royce convertible, a coral-colored Cadillac sedan, and a white-over-pink Lincoln Continental. Then, on January 29, 1970, Frank passed away, leaving Helen with the house, the cars, and about $30 million in assets. The widow interred her late husband in the family plot back in Unionport, Ohio, under three solemn arches soaring skyward. The $500,000 monument was the result of a four-year project. Helen traveled to a Vermont quarry to personally select the grade of marble.

Mrs. Brach was now effectively cutoff from the world outside that rambling house, alone except for the yardman, Jack Matlick, who had toiled in the garden for Frank since 1959, and her own sad memories of her late husband. Helen's interests and ambitions during these years were closely tied to the cause of animal welfare. She established the Helen Brach Foundation, and donated vast sums of money to animal rights causes. Brach showered all her love on an extended family of stray cats, horses, and two poodles named "Candy" and "Sugar." The two dogs now rest comfortably alongside Frank.

Helen Brach seemed less interested in men than in animals, so for the next three years she remained devoted to her causes and Frank's memory, until, by chance, her Florida landlord introduced her to a dapper middle-aged con man named Richard Bailey, owner of Bailey's Stables and Country Club Stables.

The eventful meeting occurred inside the Morton House, a once famous Morton Grove restaurant located on the edge of the Cook County Forest Preserve at Lehigh and Lincoln. Up until its closing some years back, the Morton House was a favorite luncheon destination for two-cocktail-a-day businessmen, their admiring secretaries, and men like Richard Bailey who ate fast and traveled light.

A mordantly funny horseman tagged Bailey "the Golden Tongue," an aptly applied sobriquet for a parasitic gigolo whose professional game was seduction. According to author Ken Englade, men quickly saw through Bailey—the gold chain and suntanned façade masking a basic dishonesty and shallowness of character. They recognized Bailey as a sleazy hanger-on in the world of show horses and society parties where wealthy widows and divorcées craving male attention congregated around the punch bowl.

Though Bailey was already married, women found him to be sensitive and caring. He flashed a feminine side of his nature that belied the cruel and arrogant temperament he exhibited when among stable hands, fellow con men, or male acquaintances.

Bailey incessantly boasted of his conquests of older women, commenting on his sexual encounters with them in low, vulgar ways. When asked about Helen Brach, he chuckled and called her "the Candy Lady" and a "bad biff." How was it possible, then, for him to sustain such robust sexual energy? Bailey confided to a cohort that he closed his eyes and dreamed of all that money.

Helen Brach could not have been so blind or naive to believe that Bailey was out to steal her heart and not her bank account. Federal prosecutors suspected that Richard Bailey had swindled between twenty and one hundred wealthy North Shore women with promises of romance and sex before implementing various schemes to get them to purchase overvalued horses. When he had swindled as much money as he was able, Bailey broke off the relationship or passed the hapless women on to his coconspirators to further defraud. Many were left broken and destitute.

Maybe at this point in her life Helen Brach was beyond caring and appreciated whatever flattering attention was offered to her by the opposite sex after years of consulting with psychics and fortunetellers and living a celibate life. Bailey was forty-four years of age when he was introduced to the candy heiress. Brach was sixty-two and playing it for laughs.

In 1974 she confided to Bailey that she wouldn't mind coming into possession of a few good racehorses. Her late husband was a fan of the equine world, and she thought it might be fun. Accordingly, Bailey arranged, through his brother Paul J. Bailey, the sale of three horses, each with one hoof in the glue factory: "Brach's Sweet Tooth," "Vorhees Luv," and "Pontenciado." Helen Brach paid Bailey $95,000 for her investment. The horses cost Bailey a measly $17,500. In addition, Brach was also persuaded to buy a group of broodmares.

On New Year's Eve, 1977, just six weeks before she vanished into thin air, Brach and Bailey celebrated good times at the Waldorf-Astoria Hotel in New York. They danced to the sweet sounds of Guy Lombardo and his Royal Canadians, before Brach repaired to her vacation home on Tappan Lake in Scio, Ohio, where she caught up with old friends from Florida and Ohio.

It was around this time that Bailey arranged an extensive horse showing for Brach, hoping to coax her into parting with $150,000 for more worthless horses. The candy heiress became suspicious, however. She hired an appraiser, who recommended that she invest nothing more in the first three horses, let alone in new additions to her stable.

Furious at the obvious duplicity, Brach screamed her displeasure at Bailey and his henchmen. She threatened to go the State's Attorney and confided her intent to a friend, who promised to introduce her to prosecutors who would be willing to investigate the matter.

After that, the chain of events is less distinct.

On Thursday, February 17, 1977, Brach left the Mayo Clinic in Rochester, Minnesota, where physicians had pronounced her fit and in good health following her yearly checkup. At a local boutique, Brach charged $41 worth of cosmetics before proceeding to the airport to fly back to Chicago. Though registered for the flight, she apparently never boarded the jetliner.

Jack Matlick, however, told investigators that he had picked Brach up from

O'Hare Airport on Thursday and escorted her safely back to the house where she remained secluded all weekend, except for a brief meeting with a man he had never seen before.

The faithful gardener, chauffeur, and houseman insisted that he was with Brach thereafter, from the moment she was packing her trunks until the time he dropped her off at O'Hare the following Monday morning.

According to Matlick, she was bound for Florida to attend to the details surrounding the recent purchase of a condominium. But no one other than Matlick had so much as talked to Helen over the course of the weekend, which was highly unusual. Mrs. Brach was a telephone chatterbox, but none of the dozen or so calls taken by Matlick were given to Brach. Those who inquired were told that she would call them back when she was up to it.

Helen Brach's vanishing act was as vexing to investigators as the now infamous disappearance of New York State Supreme Court Judge Joseph Crater on August 6, 1930. Crater hailed a cab on a busy New York thoroughfare and was never seen again. Brach was observed at a cosmetics counter in a Minnesota boutique, then faded without a trace.

Matlick waited two weeks to report her missing, and when he did, his story was laden with inconsistencies. Brach was a late riser. She would not have gone to the airport at 6:50 A.M., as the gardener asserted.

"There was no flight to Florida until 9:00 A.M.," said Glenview Police Chief William Bartlett. "And friends say that she never went to the airport that early or even flew in the morning." It was customary for Brach to notify her Ft. Lauderdale friend, Douglas Stevens, to come and pick her up, but he did not even know she was coming.

Matlick had jealously guarded Helen Brach's privacy, and despite rumors to the effect that he was to inherit $50,000 upon her death, there was no immediate evidence to corroborate the claim. At this stage of the investigation, police concentrated their efforts on Matlick, who cashed three allegedly forged checks after Brach's disappearance and continued to live on a Schaumburg farm owned by Brach until the estate accountant, Everett H. Moore, intervened and fired him. Brach's brother Charles Vorhees personally believed Matlick innocent of any wrongdoing.

Jack Matlick flatly asserted his innocence. He remained a suspect though he was never formally charged with a crime.

Days and weeks dragged by with no new leads. "Without a body, you don't have a case. You don't have anything," said Chief Bartlett.

One year after Brach disappeared, a spray-painted message mysteriously appeared on the sidewalk near her eighteen-room Glenview residence. It read:

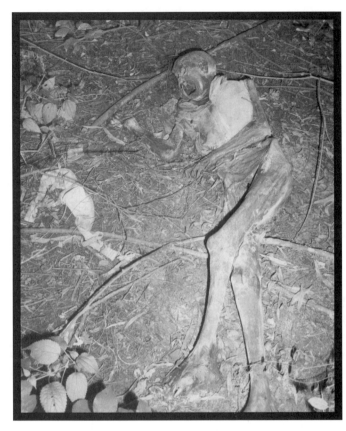

HELEN BRACH OR

"HELEN DOE?"

THE REMAINS OF THIS

UNIDENTIFIED FEMALE

MURDER VICTIM WERE

FOUND OFF 159TH

STREET ABOUT TEN

MONTHS AFTER HELEN

BRACH VANISHED.

(Photo courtesy of

James Dilorto)

"Richard Bailey knows where Mrs. Brach's body is! Stop him!" Bailey was questioned and released. By May 1984, the case was cold and Helen Brach was declared legally dead by Probate Judge Henry A. Budzinski.

Leads once thought promising dried up and were easily discounted. The body of an unidentified woman, a "Jane Doe," was found in a forest preserve near 159th Street and Wentworth Avenue in Calumet City in October 1978 and reburied in a potter's field. Not long afterward the skull was lost or stolen, and the lead was temporarily abandoned.

With renewed interest in the case, the Cook County medical examiner ordered the "Jane Doe" remains exhumed in 1990, but it was not the reclusive widow Helen Brach.

In 1987 a Mississippi convict named Maurice Ferguson spun an interesting tale to local investigators. He claimed that millionaire horseman Silas Jayne (discussed elsewhere in the chapter) hired him to remove the remains of Helen Brach from a Morton Grove gravesite and transport them to Minneapolis.

Jayne, who was in prison when Mrs. Brach disappeared, partnered with Richard Bailey in Bailey's Grand Champion Stables in Northbrook, Illinois. But when Ferguson was escorted to Minnesota by Illinois state police to help locate the grave, he could not find it after hours of fruitless searching.

There was a mounting suspicion among investigators that the gnarled horseman Jayne had something to do with the skull of the missing "Jane Doe." Investigators captured Jayne on tape ordering one of his stable hands to "Give them the head!" The theory was advanced that Silas Jayne was angling to collect the Brach reward money.

The first big break in the mystery came in July 1989 when federal prosecutors in Chicago announced a twenty-nine-count indictment charging Bailey with conspiring, soliciting, and causing the death of Helen Brach. He was one of twenty-three persons indicted in a far-reaching criminal fraud scheme aimed at bilking insurance carriers into paying off policies on overvalued horses destroyed by unscrupulous owners. Richard Bailey and his personal involvement with Brach formed the centerpiece of the government case.

No one was actually charged with carrying out the murder of the candy heiress, but U.S. Attorney James R. Burns outlined a likely scenario. Prosecutors verified that shortly before her disappearance, Helen Brach had come to the realization that she had been swindled by Bailey. She was about to blow the whistle on his entire questionable operation, bringing to the fore dozens of questionable transactions going back years. In desperation, Bailey allegedly plotted her death.

Gambling that the case against him was weak, Bailey avoided trial by pleading guilty to racketeering charges, mail fraud, money laundering, and unlawful money transactions. He begged for mercy from the court and counted on the judge to give him a break. He said that his feelings of inferiority stemming from a debilitating physical condition caused him to take a devil-may-care attitude toward life. Bailey told the judge that he only "wanted to feel good about himself." Bailey's courtroom gambit failed miserably.

With a preponderance of evidence pointing toward the existence of a murder conspiracy, U.S. District Judge Milton Shadur sentenced Bailey to a mandatory term of life imprisonment. The verdict of the court was affirmed on appeal.

After all the negative publicity, Richard Bailey still maintained a coterie of female admirers. In a weak moment, Chicago cosmetic surgeon Dr. Annette Hoffman married the creditless con man. Hoffman later told *Time* magazine that she didn't think Bailey had the intellectual wattage to carry out a diabolical murder plot such as this one.

The union with Bailey was annulled after nine days. Incredibly, Hoffman remarried him while he languished behind bars at the Metropolitan Correctional

Center under federal indictment. "He's the most charming man I ever met," she sighed.

The final outcome of the wacky and bizarre soap opera brought only partial closure. Retired Illinois State Police Investigator David Hamm has worked relentlessly on the Brach investigation, tying together loose ends. In an interview with the *Chicago Tribune*, he said that it is far from being over. "Bailey is obviously an integral part of the story but you don't get satisfaction with part of the story. My quest for completion is ongoing."

Thus far Richard Bailey has not volunteered any new information.

The mysterious disappearance of the candy heiress has seeped into the mainstream of popular culture in strange and startling ways. During the 1988–89 theatrical season, the Live Bait performance theater at 3914 North Clark Street in Chicago debuted *Candyland: The Saga of Helen Brach and Her Pet Poodle Sugar*, a play written and directed by Sharon Evans.

Des Plaines

Cook County Forest Preserve, half a mile south of Lake Street and due east of River Road near the Des Plaines River (entrance off Lake Street)

CAMP PINE: A GERMAN POW CAMP IN THE WOODS
April 25, 1945–April 1946

Nestled deep in the forest preserves adjoining Des Plaines, crumbling concrete foundations, which once supported a collection of austere wooden barracks housing 215 well-fed and contented German POWs, and a rusty flagpole are all that remain of Camp Pine and a fascinating but almost forgotten episode of wartime history. Camp Pine was constructed in 1934 by the Civilian Conservation Corps (CCC) to provide rural employment for desperate young men savaged by the Great Depression. The camp fell into disuse after the U.S. entered World War II in December 1941 and was phased out along with all other CCC programs in June 1942. Rather than tear down the discarded CCC barracks, the provost marshal general convinced Congress to convert these camps into prisoner housing to accommodate the tens of thousands of German soldiers captured in the deserts of North Africa and the campaigns through Sicily and the

Italian boot. The logistics of shipping food to Europe to feed captured POWs drove the decision to relocate them to remote locations in the U.S. Fort Sheridan was designated the base camp for northeast Illinois, but the overflow of prisoners forced the opening of fifty branch camps in Wisconsin, Illinois, and Michigan. Besides Camp Pine, three other POW centers were opened in the Chicagoland area: Skokie Valley in Glenview, and in Arlington Heights and Thornton. All of them were located in secluded areas far removed from population centers. The growth of suburbia was still a few years off, and there was little fear that the POWs would stage an uprising. Where could they run to?

Two hundred fifteen ragged German prisoners, baked by the blistering sun of North Africa and hardened by the lessons of war, were issued dark blue fatigues by their American captors with the letters "PW" stenciled on the backs of the shirts.

Two officers and thirty-eight enlisted men were assigned to guard the barracks buildings at Camp Pine, modestly furnished with beds and stoves but with very little else to kindle memories of the Fatherland. There was no central heating, and a separate facility provided for bathroom and bathing functions. For 215 prisoners, the government provided only thirty functioning toilets. Church services were held on Sundays, and the Red Cross delivered supplies to the camp for distribution.

Morale remained high among the men. The tedium of captivity was interrupted by a daily regimen of sports and games. There were soccer tournaments, games of Ping-Pong, and card playing. One prisoner remembered the collegiality of the guards who treated him well and provided extra rations. Nearby, the Pesche Greenhouse on River Road hired several of the men to pick flowers. (*Author's Note:* Pesche's is still open for business, just north of Rand Road.) Fred Pesche spoke German and treated the men just like his regular employees.

Other POWs were engaged in food processing and general farm work; picking onions, carrots, and sugar beets on nearby truck farms at the rate of eighty cents a day. In an undated letter from former Camp Pine inmate Hans Reinhold to Des Plaines farmer Arthur G. Schroeder years after the war ended, Reinhold remembered his time in America with a degree of fondness. "Often I remind [sic] of the good time when I was working for you. There was the best time of my prisoner life. Never I forget the dinner in your cellar. Full of thanks."

The internment of 375,000 German prisoners of war in the U.S. officially ended on July 23, 1946, but Reinhold had already been shipped out of Camp Pine in September 1945. Expecting to be home for Christmas, he was instead sent to Colorado to pick sugar beets and potatoes for the fall harvest. The following August he was transferred to Los Angeles, and after a grinding ocean voyage of twenty-eight days, he wound up in Liverpool, England. "We got the news that we're now English prisoners," Reinhold wrote, "and we must work for England. There was not a good time [sic] for us, we had to do a hard work for much less pay than in America. In England we got one shilling for one day work, just no more to buy only eight cigarettes."

When Reinhold finally was allowed to return to his home in Naumburg, he discovered that his building had been obliterated in the air raids and his father killed in an automobile accident. "Nothing to eat, nothing to smoke, no clothes, shoes. But I hope the bad time goes over and a few years we can live as a men again."

Despite hardships, the prisoners were nearly unanimous in their praise of American wartime hospitality. The most interesting POW story coming out of Chicago during those years involved German Infantry Sergeant Reinhold Pabel, who escaped from a branch camp in Washington, Illinois, on September 9, 1945. He hitchhiked to Peoria, then jumped a train back to Chicago where he changed his name to "Phillip Brick."

"Brick" found a job as a bookstore clerk. He filed an income tax return for 1946, married an American girl and sired a child with her in 1952, by which time he *owned* the bookstore. It wasn't until March 9, 1953, that his true identity was exposed by FBI agents who came to arrest him at his shop.

Pabel was granted a "voluntary departure" by the U.S. government in 1953, but was allowed back into the country six months later after his story aroused a hue and cry to give the poor devil a break. Reinhold Pabel lived in the U.S. for another ten years before emigrating back to Germany.

Palatine and Park Ridge

1200 Algonquin Road

(between Quentin

and Roselle Roads),

Palatine (former site

of the Tri-Color

Riding Stables, now

the parking lot of

William Rainey

Harper College)

THE JAYNE GANG RIDES AGAIN
June 14, 1965

Also: 8600 Higgins Road (east of Dee Road), Park Ridge (former site of the Idle Hour Stable, now the parking lot of the Marriott Hotel)

Only in recent years has the public become fully aware of the extent of treachery and violence perpetrated by millionaire horseman Silas Jayne. Old murders, once thought unsolvable and relegated to the cold case files by frustrated homicide investigators, are now attributed to Silas, a wild-eyed roughneck from the Chicago "horse mafia," whose charter members cloaked their ruthless nature with a veneer of gentility. The buying and selling of show horses is often an unseemly and disreputable business. James Dilorto, a retired supervisor in the Bureau of Alcohol, Tobacco, and Firearms (BATF), penetrated the insular world of Silas Jayne, his brother George, and other unscrupulous peddlers of horseflesh and got to know their ways. "You can't make any money in that business unless you are a swindler," Dilorto said. "You buy a horse for $1,500 and turn around and sell it for $75,000. Otherwise, there is simply no profit margin." The Jayne Gang (so named by the residents of Woodstock, Illinois, who remembered the wild-west shenanigans of the fast-living and hard-drinking family who drove their horses through the town square) owned stables in three counties. Most of these places, where horses were bought and sold, are long gone. George Jayne's Tri-Color Stables, where pretty Cherie L. Rude was blown up by a car bomb intended for George, is an immense asphalt parking lot situated on the campus of Harper College in Palatine overlooking the Plum Grove Reservoir. Paved walkways adjacent to the serene little reservoir lined with picnic tables were undoubtedly bridle paths in George's day, when a sprawling stable and three barns covered one hundred acres of ground. A parking lot is not an altogether unexpected fate awaiting places of infamy and murder, as we have witnessed time and time again in our underworld explorations. Similarly, brother Silas's Idle Hour Stable in Park Ridge, where even more unspeakable crimes were perpetrated,

CHERLE RUDE

is a parking lot fronting the Marriott Hotel. The O'Hare Plaza office towers next door to the hotel obliterate much of the forest preserve land where Jayne quartered his horses, and where the screams of the Schuessler and Peterson boys were likely to have been heard that night in October 1955 when they were abducted and murdered, allegedly by a Jayne stable hand. The evil nature of Silas Jayne, as well as his bloody legacy of fraud, deceit, and murder, haunted these woods for many years. Drive west from Chicago on Higgins (between Dee and River Roads) and gaze off to your left into the last remaining Cook County Forest Preserve acreage where Si and his clients were likely to have ridden their mares in years past. The underbrush obscures the old bridle paths. No one comes here any longer. In the winter months before the foliage turns *green, one senses the great desolation and feeling of abandonment so typical of infamous places, crime scenes, and haunted woods.*

At twenty-two, Cherle Lynn Rude (pronounced RUDY) was praised as one of the most accomplished horsewomen in Illinois. She savored the thrill of riding and hunting, and had for the past three years been employed by George Jayne (a top-rated Illinois horseman and show judge) as both trainer and exhibitor of prizewinning steeds.

Born and raised in West Suburban Hinsdale, and well admired by her friends in the horsey set, Cherle Rude was fearless of heart but naive about the character of the men who inhabited the circle in which she traveled.

In July 1962, a horse Cherle was riding fell over a three-foot jump, crashed on top of her, broke all of her ribs, and crushed both lungs. The star equestrian hovered near death for several weeks, but made a valiant comeback and resumed jumping.

Cherle had to be aware of the murderous feud existing between her employer and his psychotic brother, Silas Jayne, and she might have even caught an earful of Si's threats after George's daughter, Linda Wright, won a prestigious event at the Oakbrook Horse Show in 1961. "I'll never talk to you again, you SOB!" snarled Si.

Two years later George's bay mare won top honors at the plush Onwentsia Country Club in Lake Forest. "I'll kill you, you son of a bitch!" screamed the coarse and vulgar Si to his better-educated and socially more refined sibling. "I'll get you! You're as good as dead!" Over the next few years, the threats intensified and were repeated in the presence of witnesses many times.

George and Si frequently clashed over business deals gone bad. In a moment of pique, George provided the Internal Revenue Service with sensitive information about Si's income. For years this kind of petty sniping went back and forth, and undoubtedly the great difference in age between the two men (Silas was sixteen years older than his half-brother), and Si's perception that George was a "pampered child" were contributing factors to this blood feud that dragged on and on.

George Jayne's widow described her brother-in-law as "unbalanced," which was no mean exaggeration. As a boy growing up in Lake County, Silas was bitten by a goose. According to a family legend that has gained currency, he retaliated by killing the entire flock.

In 1952, George Jayne's house in Morton Grove burned down while he was vacationing in Florida. Si was blamed, though arson could not be proved at the time.

In 1963, twenty-eight bullet slugs tore into the wall of George's Tri-Color Stables.

Fires of mysterious origin continued to plague stables belonging to business rivals around the Midwest. Dozens of horses were killed for the insurance money. The deaths of George Jayne's horse "Schottzie" in 1964 from a fatal injection of turpentine and another horse named "Wildcat" (valued at $35,000), who was killed in a similar manner, were ascribed to Silas, though one investigator close to the case believes that George (far from being an innocent, wealthy country squire) was also not averse to employing such tactics if he was stuck with a worthless animal. It was a matter of dollars and cents, and many others in the horse world were complicitous in destroying animals in hideous and vile ways.

George Jayne harbored private fears that his life was endangered the afternoon of June 14, 1965, when he asked Cherle Rude to pull his late-model Cadillac up to the door of the office. It was common practice around the ranch for the eight employees to share one another's vehicles to run minor errands.

Earlier in the day, Jayne had received a call telling him that there was a horse out in Hinsdale to be picked up. He turned and went to the bathroom, telling Cherle that he would be with her in a moment.

The blast that followed rocked the building. "From the window I saw a big black cloud around where my car had been," George Jayne told the Cook County sheriff's police.

Cherle Rude was killed instantly. The blast nearly amputated her right leg, and pieces of automobile debris severed her jugular vein. The dynamite bomb had been clamped to the ignition wire under the hood.

Without hesitation, George reported his suspicions to the police.

"He is making a mountain out of a molehill," Silas shot back. "We've had disagreements for years. We have nothing in common." (*Author's Note:* George Jayne was shot through the heart by a marksman with a rifle while seated in his basement recreation room at his Inverness home on October 28, 1970. Silas was convicted on a lesser charge of conspiring to murder George, but served only six years and two days before being paroled from the Vienna Correctional Center. The flamboyant criminal defense attorney F. Lee Bailey acted as his defense counsel and was paid more than $200,000.)

There were reports of suspicious men hovering near the Cadillac moments before the bomb that killed Rude was detonated. Two men nominally connected to the show-horse world testified that they were hired by Silas to kill George. But when Silas was brought to trial in March 1966, the star witness suffered a terrible case of amnesia and could barely remember his own name, let alone the $15,000 bounty placed on George Jayne's head.

The case against Si collapsed, and the investigation remained closed until

1995 when BATF prosecutors working under the direction of Cook County State's Attorney Dick Devine questioned former stable hand James Blottiaux about the bombing. Investigators believed that Blottiaux was offered $10,000 to kill George, and had enlisted the help of a bomb maker to construct the infernal device.

George Jayne's daughter Linda testified that she had seen two men drive a Buick LeSabre onto the grounds the day Cherle was killed. Blottiaux drove such a car.

The investigation was a spinoff of the probe into the disappearance of candy heiress Helen Brach. Every clue in the Brach case, the 1955 murders of Craig and Anton Schuessler and their friend Bobby Peterson, and Cherle Rude's death pointed in the direction of Silas Jayne, who died of leukemia on July 13, 1987, thereby depriving the state's willing executioners of the opportunity to pull the switch on a man who, by all accounts, lacked a moral compass and was devoid of conscience.

In July 1999, Blottiaux was convicted of murder. Investigators had determined that he was personally responsible for eleven bombings over a four-year period between 1962 and 1966. Cherle Rude's family no longer resided in Cook County. Her sole surviving relative, a sister living out of the state, expressed profound gratitude for the efforts of law enforcement to bring an end to the case.

At the same time, BATF Agent James Dilorto brought closure to a another decades-old mystery, the 1955 abduction-murders of the Schuessler-Peterson boys. (*Author's Note:* See *Return to the Scene of the Crime* for complete coverage of that story.)

In the early 1990s, a series of insurance swindles involving forty sportsmen and investors in the Northwest suburbs led Dilorto to a federal informant named William "Red" Wemette, who fingered Silas Jayne's stable hand Kenneth Hansen as the kidnapper. Hansen allegedly picked up the boys at Lawrence and Milwaukee Avenues in the Jefferson Park neighborhood on the city's far Northwest Side, drove them to Silas Jayne's Idle Hour Stable in Park Ridge, and molested them.

The boys were slain in the tack room when they tried to fight off their attacker, and their trussed-up bodies were dumped in the nearby forest preserve near Lawrence Avenue. Incompetent police work on the part of Cook County Sheriff Joseph Lohman and jurisdictional rivalries with the Chicago police compromised the investigation from the very beginning. As the years passed, hope of ever solving the case had evaporated. But in the early 1990s, Wemette filled in enough missing details to incriminate Hansen, a homosexual hustler who admitted molesting as many as a thousand boys.

In the spring of 1956, arson destroyed a barn at Idle Hour. "We had information from different witnesses that this was the barn where the screams of the boys were heard," recalled Dilorto, who formed a private company, Dilorto & Mazzola & Associates, following his 1995 retirement.

"The week prior to the barn burning, the Cook County medical examiner announced to the press that he wanted to exhume the bodies of the Schuessler-Peterson boys for trace material. What was found would have been consistent with material you see in a milling shop, an auto repair place, or a stable. If someone put it all together, Jayne knew he would be in big trouble, so he had the barn torched. There were no horses involved—no insurance money."

It was an ingenious cover-up to a murder. Jayne supposedly read the item in the newspaper, and out of fear torched the barn to destroy any incriminating materials. The sheriff and the Chicago police were oblivious. The stable was eventually closed, and once again Si Jayne managed to wiggle free of the clutches of the law.

Kenneth Hansen was convicted of the forty-year-old crime, but the verdict was reversed by the appellate court. At present, he is being held on a $3.5 million bond, awaiting trial.

Park Ridge

216 W. Higgins Avenue (the frontage road overlooking the John F. Kennedy Expressway), between Linden Avenue and Washington Street

FOUR MEN DEAD IN AN ELEVATOR
July 22, 1977

The modern two-story office building facing the bustling I-90 expressway linking O'Hare Airport to downtown Chicago attracts scant attention these days. The nondescript red-brick façade is virtually indistinguishable among the freeway traffic, nearby residential homes, and places of business lining Higgins Avenue. Less than a mile away, however, at 8550 West Bryn Mawr in Chicago, stands a high-rise office tower of more than passing interest. Back in the 1970s, Allen Dorfman, a millionaire insurance broker aligned to top-ranking Chicago hoodlums, maintained a suite on one of the upper floors. Here, over a period of years, mob-engineered loans from the Teamsters Union Central States Pension Fund, which Dorfman administered with the blessing of Jimmy Hoffa, were dispersed to a score of Nevada casino hotels with ties to organized crime. Until Dorfman was gunned down in the parking lot of the Lincolnwood Hyatt Hotel in 1983, he was the sole agent for the union's health and welfare insurance fund. The rape of the Teamster pension funds and the organized crime buildup in Las Vegas in the 1970s was the story line of the 1995 Hollywood motion picture Casino. *Is it just a mere coincidence that Dorfman's office, where the mob heavyweights congregated, stands in close proximity to another crime scene? The latter is the sight of a baffling murder mystery and one only can wonder if there is a connection.*

A secretary arriving for work at her office on a warm, sunlit Friday morning made a ghastly discovery upon opening the elevator doors in the two-story, brick office building at 216 West Higgins Avenue. The horrified woman ran out the front door screaming, toward a nearby Shell service station at Higgins and Washington. Owner John Lucas tried to make sense of what she was saying, then went over to see for himself what all the commotion was about.

He found four men sprawled dead on the floor of the elevator. The victims had been shot twenty-five to thirty times at very close range. At 7:56 A.M., the Park Ridge police were notified and a score of officers descended on the scene.

The Park Ridge public safety director ID'ed the victims as Joseph LaRose, 35; John F. Vische, 32 and a brother-in-law of LaRose; Donald Marchbanks, 53; and Malcolm Russell, 36, supposedly on the verge of a federal indictment for operating a confidence game and committing mail fraud, interstate transport of stolen property, and telephone fraud.

Russell was in partnership with LaRose in U.S. Universal, Inc., a security alarm company maintaining offices on the second floor of the building. They had incorporated the firm in February 1977 to sell electronic security products and burglary alarms, but police investigators charged that it was a "smoke-and-mirrors" operation. LaRose and Russell were described as "high rollers" who had set out to dupe employees and job applicants into peddling "distributorships" in a fashion not unlike a classic pyramid scam.

"The pyramid concept is like a chain letter," explained Assistant Cook County State's Attorney Terry Sullivan. "They can get money for bringing more people in. Each salesman would get a title like 'field supervisor,' but then he would find out that he was supervising only the person he brought in, or there would be no such job."

Every Tuesday and Thursday evening, the office staff interviewed prospec-

FOUR PARK RIDGE

BUSINESSMEN

NEVER MADE IT

OUT OF THIS

UNDERGROUND

GARAGE ALIVE.

tive "salesmen" during raucous "motivational" sessions where large-denomination bills were held aloft to whip the newcomers into a state of frenzy; convincing them that the proverbial pot of gold waited at the end of the rainbow if they agreed to pony up $1,750. The "investment" was for the purchase of opening inventory—four burglary alarms (worth only $400 apiece).

The dappled salesmen were mostly poor down-and-outers wandering in off the street in answer to newspaper advertisements placed by these sharpers. Their gullibility was their downfall.

Ginny Lescek, the secretary who discovered the dead men on the floor of the elevator, told a *Chicago Sun-Times* reporter that "they [the victims] used to carry a lot of cash on them. Russell used to have at least, oh, a couple of hundred dollars on him always." She said that the men always flashed diamond rings in the office.

"It was always big bucks all the time," said another.

At first blush, it appeared to veteran homicide detectives from Park Ridge and Area Five in Chicago that the four men were shot dead in a robbery-gone-bad scenario by one of the mulcted salesmen who might have been present in the room that night.

The robbery motive seemed out of the question, however, because the gunman left behind an undisturbed cache of gold watches, wallets, and expensive items of jewelry belonging to the victims. The murderer had carefully removed all but four of the spent shell casings.

This was no smalltime stickup of a Seven Eleven on a Saturday night carried out by a thug in a stocking hat, but rather a chilling execution with the unmistakable markings of organized crime.

The four men were facing their assailant as they were shot, suggesting that the assassin was known to them or that they felt they had no cause for fear at that particular moment. The killer, after completing his work, sent a resonant message to police by tearing out a pocket from the pants of LaRose, Russell, and Marchbanks. In the criminal underworld, the very act symbolizes a serious breach of trust—a double-cross. Whoever wanted them dead must have had old scores to settle.

It was a quick walk down a short flight of stairs to the underground garage, but on the night in question they elected to ride. Investigators were at first puzzled by this, but the only reason LaRose and company were occupying an elevator in the first place was because of Donald Marchbanks's physical impairment. He could not walk without a cane. The cane was found lying alongside his body the next morning.

The FBI probed deeper into the personal and financial affairs of each of these men. It was ascertained that the government had placed a tax lien against Marchbanks in 1971. Three years later he defaulted on a $66,000 loan from the Bank of Clarendon Hills.

LaRose, reportedly dying of cancer at the time of his murder, was the subject of an FBI inquiry into his dealings with a cosmetics pyramid scheme known as Holiday Magic.

The Feds were also busily investigating Russell for allegedly setting up a boiler-room business called Steel Liquidation Services, aimed at buying excess steel using false references and credit, then reselling it to scrap yards.

The execution-style murders in Park Ridge were so clearly the handiwork of the Chicago "outfit" that on the surface of things, the motive for the killings and the perpetrator should have been a slam dunk (or so one would think). At this late date, law enforcement is still no closer to cracking the mystery or establishing a motive than it was in 1977.

Revisiting a Massacre: Machine Guns Rake a Fox Lake Summer Resort Hotel, June 2, 1930
Along the shore of Pistakee Lake on the western edge of Lake County in the town of Fox Lake.

S I D E T R I P

A distance of fifty miles separates downtown Chicago from the rustic Chain-O-Lakes region, where, on any given summer weekend, thousands of speedboaters, picnickers, and outdoors enthusiasts descend to guzzle beer, commune with nature, drop a fishing line into the water, or otherwise act in an unbridled and uproarious manner until it is time to head back home and resume normalcy.

The advent of the automobile and the paving of Routes 12 and 14 (Rand Road and Northwest Highway, respectively) made it possible for caravans of fun-seeking weekenders to trek from the city out to the country in only a few hours. With minimal interference from the local police, the Prohibition bootlegging gangs of Chicago recognized a golden opportunity to make inroads into the "northwest territory" and ply the tourists with enough illegal intoxicants to make their trek to the beaches and return trip home a truly memorable occasion. The resort town of Fox Lake and the adjoining communities forming the "Chain" were overrun by gangsters in the 1920s and 1930s. Even today, throngs of curious visitors to the area (without knowing much of the local history) routinely inquire about the places that Al Capone and his minions were known to frequent during the wild and reckless days of the Roaring '20s and the one-way ride. Sadly, there is not much left of these old attractions, but the stories can still be told.

In 1930, a little more than a year after the St. Valentine's Day Massacre, the Capone gang desired to further consolidate their holdings by laying claim to the Chain-O-Lakes region. To do so, they had to first neutralize the stiff competition coming from the smaller, independent bootlegging gangs from Chicago's West Side "Valley" District, a Lake County rumrunner named Ray Pregenzer, and the remnants of George "Bugs" Moran's North Side mob.

(*Author's Note:* Contrary to the conventional wisdom espoused by crime writers, the Moran gang was not nearly as decimated by the St. Valentine's Day Massacre as one might think. Not every hoodlum aligned to the North Side mob perished inside the Clark Street garage that day.)

"Bugs" Moran had long had an interest in the summer beer trade in Fox Lake. (*Author's Note:* The resort season traditionally commenced on Memorial Day.) Moran's suburban Chicago "branch office" was headquartered at Cassidy's Resort, located on Grass Lake, a distance of five miles from the "Chain." For several years, the owners of the Lake and McHenry County roadhouses were Moran's most steady and dependable customers.

In the waning years of National Prohibition, the deposed North Side boss forged expedient alliances with Ray Pregenzer and Chicago gangsters Jack Zuta and Joe Aiello in order to remain active in the beer rackets. These men provided Moran with enough "muscle" to hold lesser competitors at bay. Business was booming, and the gunplay that characterized Chicago during this time was strangely absent out in the country, partly because the Capone gang was more concerned with maintaining profitable operations in the southern end of Cook County.

Existing territorial boundaries began to shift in 1930, when the Capones, emboldened by their rout of the Moran forces in Chicago, descended on Fox Lake like a plague of hungry locusts. They intimidated local barkeeps into buying Capone beer to the exclusion of all others. But Al Capone was not alone in his Lake County foray.

George Druggan, brother of Terry Druggan, who, with Frankie Lake, ruled the West Side "Valley" District in the early years of Prohibition, also had designs on the lucrative beer business controlled by Moran. George Druggan was active in DuPage County at this time, but had shown no fear in aggressively targeting establishments controlled by Al's brother Ralph Capone in Cicero and the Moran roadhouses in Fox Lake.

Druggan's intention to undercut the price of beer charged by the Moran forces in Lake and McHenry Counties triggered the episode that has come to be known as "the Fox Lake Massacre."

A Fox Lake alderman named James L. Manning owned and operated a two-story resort hotel on the edge of town overlooking the water. Only two years earlier, Manning listed his occupation as barkeep, serving liquor at a West Side saloon belonging to Vivian Ponsic McGinnis, wife of Chicago attorney Arthur McGinnis.

McGinnis and his mother-in-law, Mary Ponsic, had a stake in a nearby Fox Lake summer resort.

Vivian was "running with a bad crowd," according to published statements made by her father, Vincent Ponsic, an attorney estranged from both his wife and daughter. The presence of "unsavory West Side characters" congregating inside Vivian's Fox Lake resort was a major cause of his concern. Ponsic deflected blame to his ex-wife for contributing to Vivian's delinquency by introducing her to case-hardened West Side hoodlums at a tender age.

It was Vivian's great misfortune to be seated inside an enclosed porch at the Manning Hotel when the fatal affray occurred the night of June 2, 1930.

That night, Mrs. McGinnis was joined at her table by George Druggan; Joseph Bertsche, a henchman of the Druggan–Lake County gang with a long criminal record; Michael Quirk, aligned with the West Side "Klondike" O'Donnell mob and active in the takeover of the Teamsters Union locals in Chicago; and Sam Pellar, a 20th Ward election terrorist who had had a falling-out with the North Side Moran gang before defecting to the Capone interests. Also present to share in the victuals was gunman Leo Mongoven, a "Bugs" Moran henchman who had survived a botched kidnapping attempt a week earlier, and several other men whose identities were never proved.

The party entered the hotel in a light-hearted mood at around 9:00 P.M. They drank heavily for several more hours before Manning repaired to bed, leaving his bartender, Louis Capella, in charge. Another round of drinks was ordered. Pellar asked Capella for a sandwich and some beer, then leaned back in his chair to pass the time.

George Druggan had gone to the lake region earlier that day to check up on his shipments of beer to the resorts. He had just concluded an agreement to sell his suds inside the Manning Hotel, where the Moran gang had only recently held the concession.

SKETCH OF JAMES L. MANNING'S FOX LAKE RESORT HOTEL THE MORNING AFTER THE "MASSACRE."

"They were having a good time all evening," recalled Capella, who was sweeping the floor when he heard what sounded like gunfire. It was nearly 1:40 in the morning, and after Capella determined the sound wasn't a firecracker or some vacationer's prank, he dived behind the bar for cover.

From her upstairs bedroom, Mrs. Manning said she observed five gunmen entering her establishment but could not identify any of them. They had parked their car in a copse of trees, fifty feet from the entrance to the hotel.

Quirk, Pellar, and Bertsche scrambled for the exit, but each died instantly in the hail of machine-gun fire. Mongoven and several others in the party escaped into the woods. Druggan and Mrs. McGinnis were peppered with four shots apiece, but they survived the attack and were dragged back to a West Side Chicago hospital—then a two-and-a-half-hour drive from Fox Lake.

Efforts to pry information from the dark-haired woman failed. "Please go away and leave me alone!" she stammered.

As usual the police were stymied, and running at wit's end to solve this second "massacre," as well as a spate of eight other gangland shootings involving immigrant Sicilians killed within a forty-eight-hour period. The streets of Chicago came to resemble a shooting arcade at a county carnival, as the ducks fell, one by one.

It can be said without fear of exaggeration that this was the most violent week of the Prohibition Era.

The year 1930 also ranks as one of the bloodiest of the Volstead years. Sixty-four men (excluding the victims of the Fox Lake Massacre, who didn't count because the shootings occurred well outside the city limits of Chicago) connected in some way to organized crime died by the gun during that year.

The Moran gang was strongly suspected of reprising the St. Valentine's Day Massacre, but when the brother of Michael Quirk turned up inside Moran's Cassidy's Resort, that theory was quashed.

Over the next twenty-four hours, Chicago police rousted two hundred randomly selected Italians. They were locked up overnight, while the cops prepared to file deportation papers against any man who could not establish proof of citizenship. Not one of them was linked to the Fox Lake Massacre or the seven days of mayhem.

George "Machine Gun" Kelly would later confess to FBI agents that fellow bank robber Verne Miller carried out the Fox Lake executions for purely "personal" reasons. Supposedly it was in retaliation for the death of his hoodlum pal Eugene "Red" McLaughlin, the truculent younger brother of Robert McLaughlin, boss of the Checker Cab Company and an associate of known organized crime figures.

Chicago police attached no special significance to Kelly's suspicious jailhouse confession. McLaughlin, who had been spending a lot of time in Miami, Florida, went missing ten days *before* the Fox Lake Massacre. On the night in question, his brother Robert was observed in the company of the Druggan party at the Manning Hotel. The theory was that plans were being hatched for the formation of a new beer syndicate backed by cab company money. Moments after the gunfire erupted, Robert McLaughlin crawled to safety.

The bloated and waterlogged remains of his kid brother Red McLaughlin were pulled out of the polluted waters of the drainage canal in south suburban Summit five days later. The victim had been shot twice through the head. Prior to its disposal, the executioners had weighted the body down with seventy-five pounds of iron chain.

"How could he organize a beer syndicate?" demanded brother Robert, shaking his head in bewilderment. "He'd only been back in town four days when they took him. He was friendly with them all, the West Side outfit, the North Side boys, and the bunch on the South Side. Yes, he knew Al Capone and was friendly with him, too."

Hair-triggered "Red" McLaughlin was best remembered for shooting Harry Morley, general superintendent of the Checker Cab Company, through the temple in front of horrified company executives on Jackson Boulevard back in 1924.

Seven decades have elapsed since the bloody carnage in Lake County, and to this day no one can say with any degree of certainty just what this crazy affair was all about. Was it a union squabble? Did "Bugs" Moran exact his revenge for the St. Valentine's Day Massacre?

The shootings at Fox Lake are a puzzling footnote to the gangland saga. They are remembered by devoted, hard-core Capone-era aficionados and forgotten by everyone else. In any other city but Chicago, a slaughter of this magnitude would have been discussed for years and probably turned into a screenplay with Jimmy Cagney or George Raft cast in a leading role. Here in Chicago during that first full year of the Great Depression, life returned to its normal paces, with so much more of the same yet to come.

I am told that Manning's Resort Hotel was knocked down many years ago. The exact spot of the hotel is nearly impossible to trace, though a boat pier once connected to the guesthouse is said to remain. It would require a considerable expenditure of time and effort to find this old wooden pier, for such reminders of infamous acts are never marked by plaques or statuary.

TOUR 5

Stockyard Society:

The Great South Side of Chicago
(Roosevelt Road to Wolf Lake)

The history of Chicago south of Madison Street is written in the blood, toil, and sacrifice of various tribes of people who ventured into the stockyards, planing mills, and great steel foundries dotting the lakefront.

According to Jack Lait and Lee Mortimer in *Chicago Confidential*, a rollicking examination of the city inside-out, European social climbers from the eastern seaboard—the distinguished "400"—were most unflattering in their pronouncements of Chicago during a time far back, when their stodgy opinions had the power to offend. The Potter Palmers, the Marshall Fields, and local cattle barons were narrowly viewed by the aristocrats of the eastern establishment as "Stockyard Society," a reflection of the South Side's most viable industry and potent legacy.

The implications were very clear. Chicago *was* a rough-and-tumble place. Maybe it still is. Just ask the baseball fans who were thrown to the ground and kicked and beaten in the summer of 2000 in Armour Square Park, a section of Bridgeport located north of Comiskey Park and see what they have to say. The mean streets of the South Side speak to a cycle of violence that has persisted since the potato famine Irish settled in Bridgeport to dig the Illinois and Michigan Canal in the 1840s.

From the bitter labor disputes in the steel mill districts of South Chicago to the lockouts in packing town, no South Side community was immune. The road map of crime stretched from Eighteenth and Prairie Avenue where a wagonload of white settlers were massacred while escaping old Fort Dearborn during the War of 1812, down to the notorious Calumet City "sin" strip bordering the Indiana state line.

Al Capone, Johnny Torrio, the Everleigh sisters, and legions of underworld gangsters visited their sins upon the South Side, which includes both the city and its suburbs.

In modern times the pillage of street gangs has destroyed once stable

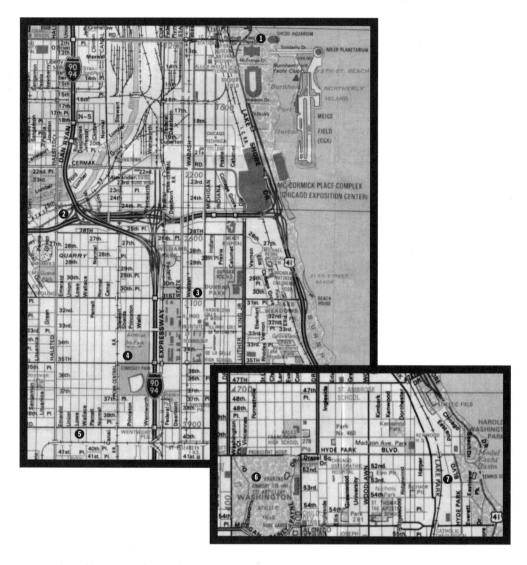

1. The Field Museum of Natural History (Man-eating lions on display).
2. The "Violent Vincis" (2505 South Halsted St.).
3. Site of Jack Johnson's "Café de Champion," 41 West 31st St.
4. Armour Square Park/Bridgeport (31st and Shields).
5. 1921 Stockyards Strike (Mob action, 40th and Wallace).
6. Kozlarek-Van Der Molen murder site, Washington Park.
7. Del Prado Hotel, 5307 Hyde Park Blvd.
8. Mossie Enright's home, 1110 West Garfield Blvd.
9. James D. Crowley residence, 7225 South Merrill.
10. Southmoor Bank, 6760 Stony Island Ave.
11. Leon Marcus murder site, 50th St. and Campbell.
12. Former home of State's Attorney John Wayman, 6834 South Constance.
13. The case of the castrated professor, 71st and Stony Island Ave.
14. Johnny Torrio residence, 7011 South Clyde Ave.
15. Marty Durkin residence, 508 East 75th St.
16. The Memorial Day Massacre, 116th and Burley Ave.
17. Wolf Lake/Powers Conservation area.

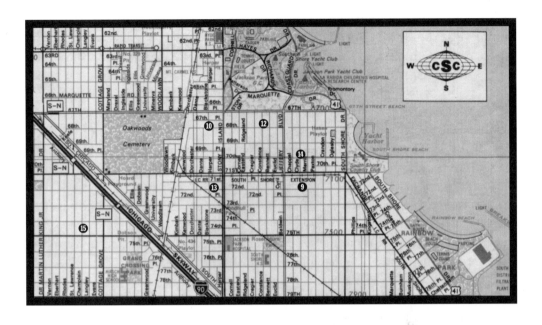

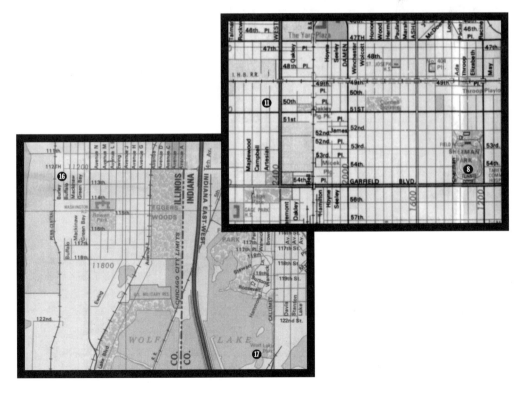

African-American neighborhoods up and down the South Side's lakefront. The Robert Taylor homes are a Chicago Housing Authority (CHA) project symbolizing urban decay, poverty, and crime. The Taylor homes, bordered by the Dan Ryan Expressway to the west, formed an impenetrable wall intended to segregate the haves from the have-nots, the poor from the middle class, and white from black.

The city claims to have figured out a better way to house the poor, without the strain of racism and class division symbolized by the rodent-infested row of projects that will soon vanish from the landscape as twenty-first-century Chicago rebuilds and reinvents itself.

The South Side is recognizable by place names on numbered streets running east and west. If a stranger wandered into an Irish pub in Canaryville, Bridgeport, or some distant place out on 111th Street in Mount Greenwood and was asked by a local where he lived, the stranger would identify the parish. And if that parish was situated on the great South Side of Chicago, the newcomer would have revealed much about his circumstances, the ethnic composition of his ward, and the company he kept. South Side living is all about the migratory habits of people as they moved from one place to another.

Visit the South Side and get to know Chicago. The crime tour we embark upon speaks to old and new villainies with the one consolation of knowing that the malefactors of evil are either dead, in jail or, in this first episode, on permanent display at the Field Museum.

THE ROBERT TAYLOR HOMES; A FORTRESS-LIKE PUBLIC HOUSING PROJECT DESTINED FOR THE WRECKING BALL.

Field Museum of Natural History. "The Man-Eating Lions of Tsavo."

1400 South Lake Shore Drive

S
I
D
E
T
R
I
P

In 1924, the Field Museum came into possession of a morbid curiosity—the skulls and skins of two large man-eating lions responsible for the deaths of 130 workmen constructing a railway from Mombasa through Kenya to Uganda in East Africa. In 1898, a thousand workers were camped out in Tsavo (now a sprawling national park), 130 miles from the coastal city of Mombasa, an old Arab settlement that was the starting point of the Uganda Railway.

The laborers were mostly Indian "coolies" (as society dubbed them), recruited to build a bridge over a stream of water fed by the eternal snows of Mount Kilimanjaro. For a period of nine months, a pair of lions attacked the workers' tents, dragging them off to a remote location and devouring them in the dead of night. It is highly unusual for lions to prey upon humans in such a fashion. Though they have been known to attack human quarry, a lion's normal food stock consists of zebras, gazelles, and antelope.

The arrival of European settlers in the 1890s triggered a deadly outbreak of rinderpest, a fatal disease found in the domesticated livestock imported from the Continent. The shortage of food may have had something to do with the outbreak of lion attacks. Fear was rampant. Superstitious Indian coolies called the nocturnal killers "devils" and were fleeing the campsite in greater numbers with each passing day, forcing delays in the construction schedule. A fearless "devil killer" was needed, and for that purpose the British Railway sent in Lt. Colonel John Henry Patterson to track down the lions and dispose of them so the work could resume.

The English adventurer laid several traps and nearly became the next human casualty before taking dead aim at the beasts from a strategic tree limb. A peculiar oddity was noted upon closer examination of the twin carcasses. Neither lion had a mane, and one of them measured nine feet eight inches from nose to tail. Lions generally live in family groups, but these two traveled alone. Scientists pondered the question of whether or not the absence of a mane influenced their predatory behavior, but the depletion of the food stock was a more likely explanation.

In 1924, Colonel Patterson was a guest lecturer at the Field Museum. At the suggestion of museum president Stanley Field, the remains of the "Man-eaters of Tsavo" were sold to the museum where they were reconstructed and placed on permanent display. They can still be seen in the Field Museum's Rice

Wildlife Research Station off the main hall.

The 1996 adventure saga The Ghost and the Darkness, *starring Val Kilmer and Michael Douglas, depicts the hunt for the Tsavo lions. There is one interesting footnote to this story. In 1997, Dr. Kerbis Peterhans and a staff of researchers from the Field Museum and the Kenya Wildlife Service rediscovered the lost cave where Patterson reported finding the human remains in January 1899. No bones were found this time, human or otherwise.*

The scientists deduced that if this were the actual spot where the lions devoured their prey, the spring rains had probably washed them all away four months after Colonel Patterson made the initial discovery.

Chinatown

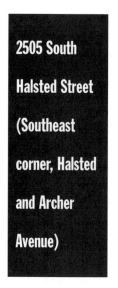

2505 South

Halsted Street

(Southeast

corner, Halsted

and Archer

Avenue)

THE VIOLENT VINCIS AND THE FIGHTING SULLIVANS: CONTRASTING WORLD WAR II FAMILIES
December 3, 1942

The Violent Vincis of the Eleventh Ward and the Fighting Sullivans of World War II were two memorable American families making news for altogether different reasons in 1942. One set of brothers hailed from the South Side of Chicago, the other from Waterloo, Iowa. The five Sullivan brothers died in the South Pacific defending their country's honor against the military might of Imperial Japan. Three of the four Vincis (Charley, Mike, and James) fought and died to protect their bankroll against the deadly subterfuge of Chicago gangsters and politicians who might want to steal it. The Sullivans (George, Francis, Joseph, Madison, and Albert) went down with the USS Juneau *in the Battle of Guadalcanal on November 13, 1942. They were heroes in the time of war. As for the Vincis? Well, what else could their poor Italian mother say, except that when the cops rolled her boy over to ID him less than three weeks after the entire nation mourned the sacrifice of the Sullivans, Charley Vinci proudly carried to his death an honorary deputy sheriff's star, #160—issued by Congressman Thomas "Blind Tom" O'Brien. Charley was the third Vinci brother to go down in a hail of gangland bullets, though no one really understood the whys and wherefores or the special significance, except that something like this was destined to happen to a Vinci brother every few years or so. Charley Vinci expired in the Point Tavern, a famous saloon of yesteryear that stood on the southeast corner of Halsted and Archer (on Halsted). This is the western edge of Chinatown, a grim-looking industrial area speckled with decayed and abandoned factories, warehouses rented by the Chinese merchants on Wentworth Avenue. Off in the distance, one can hear the deafening clamor of the CTA Orange Line elevated cars rumbling past, en route to Midway Airport. Nearby, we find signs of life at Connie's world-famous pizzeria, but not much else goes on around here, not anymore. The Point Tavern was torn down. In its place stands a building that must have been a gas station at one time or another. The sign outside reads:"Benedict's Delicatezzi Italiano." There, on the exact spot where the third "Fighting Vinci" fell in the line of duty, you may wish to hoist a stein to the wartime memory of one Chicago family and its sacrifice to gangland.*

T he "Violent Vincis" were notorious all over the South Side, but why anyone wanted to do away with little Charley was a mystery to the most grizzled veterans of the Detective Bureau. No one ever accused Charles Vinci of being a choirboy—his siblings undoubtedly drew him into the half-world, particularly his big brother Jimmy, who cheated the hangman in the 1920 murder of labor racketeer Maurice "Mossie" Enright (discussed elsewhere in this chapter).

Charley was never involved with the police, as far as anyone could remember. He lived with his wife at 718 West Twenty-fifth Place and traded on political connections harvested by brother Mike, who was shot to death in 1925 in a dispute over money with the patron of a gambling house. Brother Jimmy died in a pistol duel with "Machine Gun" Joe Granata on Wells Street in the Bridgeport neighborhood that same year.

Then things were quiet for a while. The family that lived by the gun managed to avoid trouble until the bullet-riddled corpse of Charles Vinci was found inside the Point Tavern at 3:15 in the morning by three happy wanderers who staggered into the place for a snort. They found only one occupant inside, and he wasn't talking.

There were bloodstains behind the bar and bullet holes in the wall. Police counted five slugs in Vinci, but it wasn't exactly clear to them whether there was a gun battle or Charley was ambushed while polishing off a cool one. The bartender, John Spoto, said he went outside to take in an electric sign when he heard four or five shots. "I got scared and ran to my sister's home," he told the cops the next morning.

Millie DeMarco, the plump Italian chanteuse who lit up the bleary, early morning hours with torch songs, went home at 2:30. Two dice girls and a three-piece orchestra were given the heave-ho minutes before Spoto took down the sign. It was bad luck all around for Vinci.

A search of the dead man's pockets revealed the "courtesy" badge, given out to "honorary" Cook County sheriff's deputies. In this case the presenter was Congressman Thomas O'Brien, a silver-tongued old grafter who supported term limits for the sheriff on the grounds that "if they weren't smart enough to make their dough in the first four years, they shouldn't be given a second chance."

In those days, anyone who chipped in twenty-five bucks to the political war chest of one of the Cook County bigwigs was likely to be awarded a deputy sheriff's badge, entitling the bearer to carry a concealed gun and save himself from the time and expense of speeding tickets should he be pulled over one night by an overly enthusiastic cop.

Vinci was drawing a salary from City Hall as an assistant sergeant at arms in the City Council chambers. That was a breach of etiquette even Mayor Ed Kelly found hard to explain. Since when was the city in the habit of finding work for unemployed gunmen and their family members? Mimicking the bemused Inspector Louie Renault in the movie *Casablanca*, Mayor Kelly raised his furrowed eyebrows and expressed outrage. "I am shocked! Shocked I tell you!"

Everyone else on the street seemed to remember that Jimmy Vinci was a real "straight shooter," especially when he drew down on "Moss" Enright, and that another brother, Salvatore "Sam" Vinci, spoiled the coroner's inquest by killing John Minatti, the state's star witness in Mike's death.

Piecing events together, the police concluded that the Point Tavern was maintained by a fourth brother, Joe Vinci, a Democratic precinct captain arrested for stuffing ballot boxes in the 1938 judicial election. Joe was acquitted, but State's Attorney Thomas Courtney charged that jurors had been bribed. The case was eventually stricken from the criminal court docket.

Charles, they surmised after days of fruitless investigation, was an unlucky hanger-on. But Joe wasn't talking either, other than to say that he had attended a charity ball sponsored by 11th Ward Alderman Hugh Connelly earlier in the evening, and that his brother was at the same affair flashing a big bankroll.

There was no one else alive to add anything to the life-and-death saga of the "Violent Vincis." They had all gone down with the ship.

Douglas

REQUIEM FOR A HEAVYWEIGHT'S WIFE
September 11, 1912

41 West 31st

Street

(between State

Street on the

east, and

Dearborn on

the west)

Named after Senator Stephen A. Douglas, who took up residence at 34 East Thirty-fifth Street in 1854, this historic South Side community stretches along the lakefront from Twenty-sixth Street on the north down to Thirty-fifth Street. Douglas, with its many high-rise apartments and subsidized public housing, cuts through the heart of "Bronzeville," where efforts are under way to re-create the vitality of African-American community life as it existed in the 1930s and 1940s. To earlier generations of whites living outside the district, this area was known far and wide as the "Black Belt" of Chicago. State Street was the place to go for jazz, and the "Black and Tan" resorts (where the two races comingled) were filled each night with party revelers enjoying the music and South Side hospitality. In recent years, Thirty-first Street has been designated "Sammy Davis, Jr. Way," for the entertainer's contributions to the show business world. The street was a thriving east-west thoroughfare, and one of the meccas for live performance, showcasing musical talent from around the country. Some years before, there existed along Thirty-first Street a collection of disreputable places drawing the ire of Chicago police and ecumenical reformers. The district was peppered with notorious concert hall saloons, poolrooms, and low dives for late-night assignations spilling over into the Black Belt from the Twenty-second Street Levee. Then in July 1912, Jack Johnson, heavyweight champion of the world and the first African-American titleholder, opened Cafe de Champion at 41 West Thirty-first Street. As word of mouth spread, a more upscale gathering of bon vivants *eager to rub elbows with the celebrity host began dropping in to pay their respects. The first-nighters made Cafe de Champion a very chic after-hours rendezvous. Jack Johnson, who could not have succeeded as a restaurateur without the guiding hand of his wife, Etta, was a man who lived riotously but not always wisely. He won seventy-eight heavyweight bouts, lost only eight, and was celebrated on stage and screen. The 1970 motion picture* The Great White Hope, *starring James Earl Jones, was based on his life. Jack Johnson drove flashy yellow sports cars, had a set of gold teeth to match, and owned a pet leopard. He was a supreme egotist, confident that he could succeed in any field of human endeavor. There was another side to the champ, however, a vicious, mean-spirited attitude he exhibited toward his women, manifest in the suicide of his first wife, the society divorcée Etta Duryea, who took a gun to her head inside the café while her husband was rollicking with friends downtown. Cafe de Champion stood at Thirty-first Street and Dearborn, but with the rapid expansion of the Illinois Institute of Technology campus in the 1960s, both the restaurant and Johnson's private residence at 3344 South Wabash were obliterated. In fact, the entire block is cut off to motor vehicle traffic. Things are very quiet now on Bronzeville's western exposure. A classroom building with a façade of glass and metal and the howling winter winds tearing off the lake serve to remind us that infamous places, with their evil pasts, often leave behind a sterile mosaic.*

One fateful day in the spring of 1910, Etta Terry Duryea answered the fluttering of her heart and ran off with the champion prizefighter Jack Johnson.

In the prime of life but childless, Etta was married to Clarence Duryea, the wealthy son of Wall Street's John Duryea, who controlled a brokerage house that gained the family entrance into the Long Island country club set. She lived in a staid world and tried to keep alive her sense of life's promise.

Though horse breeding out on Hempstead, Long Island, and charity balls in the city were more to her husband's liking, Etta was desperately bored by her life of protocol and convention. In the vernacular of the day, Etta Duryea ran with a "sporting crowd." She loved the races, clocking bets with bookies, and the ribald joshing of the touts and railbirds she met along the way. On one fateful afternoon while wagering at the Coney Island track, she met Jack Johnson and fell in love.

In his usual custom, Johnson was accompanied by two Chicago prostitutes, but their presence did not seem to matter one way or the other to Mrs. Duryea.

(*Author's Note:* One of the two female traveling companions was Belle Schreiber, a former stenographer at Milwaukee's Plankinton Hotel. At Johnson's 1912 trial for Mann Act violations, she said she was "swept away" by Johnson's easygoing charm after meeting him at a vaudeville show early in 1910 while the champ was on a celebrity goodwill tour. Belle was the daughter of Philip Schreiber, magistrate at the Milwaukee Central Police Station. Only eighteen at the time, Belle ran off with Johnson and remained his "kept" woman until society matron Etta Duryea entered the picture. That Schreiber was a seasoned prostitute, as Johnson biographers assert, seems highly doubtful. The evidence suggests that she entered the "immoral life" only after being cast adrift by Johnson and forced to confront a prejudicial society intolerant of white women who consorted with African-American men.)

With Clarence Duryea away in the Adirondacks recovering from a malady many believed to be tuberculosis, Etta packed together her belongings and informed the servants that she was "going west" to accompany the champion during his celebrity appearances.

If Etta were to become Johnson's legal wife, and not just a part of his harem, she had to first obtain a legal divorce, which was an easy enough thing to do once the cuckolded husband had learned the awful truth of the matter. To save his family name from further disgrace and embarrassment, Duryea did not contest. The decree ending the six-year marriage was signed in Chicago by Judge Cooper. The gay divorcée continued west to Reno, Nevada, to embrace Johnson, who was in training for his legendary July 4 title bout with Jim Jeffries—"the Great White Hope."

America was not yet ready for a man of color to hold a major boxing title, let alone take up with a divorced society woman whose name was prominent in the newspapers. The search for a "Great White Hope" to wrest the crown away from the proud and arrogant Johnson was already on. Fight promoter "Tex" Rickard scoured the country with little success, until he managed to coax Jim Jeffries out of retirement to do battle against the knuckle-pounding brawler. The punch-drunk Jeffries proved no match for Johnson.

The "Fight of the Century" was called off in the fifteenth round when it was evident to the referee that the challenger was about to collapse from the beating he had absorbed. "I could never have whipped Jack Johnson at my best. No, I couldn't have reached him in 1,000 years," Jeffries conceded. When the news of Jeffries' defeat flashed across the sporting wire, race riots erupted in the streets of several American cities.

With $117,000 in earnings, the champion and his lady friend traveled in grand style all that year. In November, Johnson raced Barney Oldfield at Coney Island for the publicity value, but he lost both times and returned to Chicago to open his restaurant and find a place to settle in for the winter. The following January, Etta and Jack were joined in marriage.

The couple bought a residence at 3344 South Wabash Avenue. Johnson moved his mother, brothers, and sisters into the place, but upon hearing the news of his intention to have them all live under one roof with the white wife, they balked. The African-American community was incensed over the whole affair.

The bitter fruits of interracial marriage in 1911 came home to roost for Etta when her own family and former society matrons shunned her. She was becoming increasingly despondent and isolated.

Etta turned inward and was naturally suspicious of Johnson's carrying on. The champ was a late-night ladies' man—he could not help himself in the company of the opposite sex, and was said to have been a frequenter of the South Side Levee District whorehouses. His first manager was George Little, the operator of a dozen shabby brothels up and down Dearborn Street and south Federal.

Little was a notorious white-slave trafficker, pimp, and erstwhile "sportsman" who looked after the champ and booked all his fights. But when Little confessed his love to Etta and presented her with a three-karat diamond ring as a symbol of his affection, the wife ran to her husband and told him the whole story. Johnson dismissed Little only a few weeks before the Jeffries bout and hired Sig Hart to run his affairs.

In a huff over losing his job and forced to endure the humiliation of seeing the diamond ring on Johnson's pinky finger, Little made a slanderous accusation. He said that Etta was suffering from the "Black Pox," a form of syphilis.

The marriage suffered one crisis after another. Etta Duryea, porcelain, distant, and unsmiling, lapsed into a deep depression and had no one to turn to. She was a social outcast unwelcome on both sides of the racial divide, and Jack had become indifferent to her needs. He was too busy carrying on.

When called to account for his many marital indiscretions, Johnson seized Etta by the throat one night and savagely beat her face until she lost consciousness. Trainer Bob Mott had to pry loose Johnson's hands from her throat, otherwise she might have died on the spot. The woman was taken to Washington Park Hospital for treatment.

Jack Johnson was sorry for what he had done and presented Etta with a costly pearl necklace valued at $6,000, but she was frightened and out of her mind with fear when customs officials indicted Johnson on smuggling charges, naming her as a correspondent. On board a train bound for Las Vegas, the woman suffered a nervous breakdown and had to be returned to Chicago after attempting to jump out the window of her sleeping car.

Back home, Etta set aside her desperate loneliness and alienation and volunteered to run the café for Jack. She was kept busy hiring waiters, interviewing chefs, and selecting menu items. Everyone agreed that Mrs. Johnson, and not her husband, was the main reason why the restaurant was such a hit in Chicago after its grand opening in July 1912.

The dining room was always noisy and crowded. "Toots" Marshall, majordomo of the café, entertained lavishly. He hired a ragtime band to regale patrons, while the help scurried to and from the dumbwaiter fetching serving plates and bottles of wine. In a circus atmosphere such as this, it is easy to see why Etta was unable to soothe her jangled nerves and sleep through the night.

BELLE SCHREIBER—

DRIVEN TO A LIFE OF

PROSTITUTION.

From her bedroom above the saloon on the night of September 11, 1912, she bid the two maids, Helga Simmons and Mabel Bolden, good night. Before they closed the door behind them, Etta gazed up at them with a forlorn, distant look. In a near whisper she said, "Pray for me." A moment later, she produced a pistol and shot herself through the head.

The crack of the gun and the screams of the servant girls caused a momentary lull in the gaiety and celebration going on downstairs. Henry Johnson, the champion's brother, was informed of what had happened upstairs, but he shoved the two girls aside. "I ain't got time! I'm too busy!"

The injured woman was carried down the stairs by an ambulance team answering the call, while "Toots" Marshall ordered the café orchestra to strike up something speedy. The show had to go on, of course.

JACK JOHNSON EXCHANGING MARITAL VOWS WITH THE IMPRESSIONABLE LUCILLE CAMERON.

Etta Duryea expired at Provident Hospital at three o'clock the following morning. (*Author's Note:* So many authors and journalists who write about this lamentable incident in Johnson's life get the date wrong. Etta Terry Duryea Johnson died on September 11, 1912—not 1911, as it is commonly reported.)

The pugilist wept bitterly. "My wife was prostrated by overwork-—working over me when I was in the mood that she was when she killed herself," he said. "If it had not been for Etta I would have killed myself by leaping from a window of a hotel in Portland, Maine, a year ago." Only two days earlier, Johnson had presented her with a diamond ring and a sealskin coat.

Etta Johnson, the belle of Hempstead, L.I., but virtually friendless in death, was waked in the front parlor of Mrs. Tiny Johnson's home at 3344 South Wabash. Thousands of people packed the streets in front of the residence, hoping to catch a glimpse. They had to be restrained by a compliment of police from the Stanton Avenue station.

Etta's gray-haired mother, Mrs. David Terry, came all the way from New York with words of comfort that by now were meaningless. "She begged me not to forget her, not to put her out of my heart," she said between sobs. "And I have not. This is goodbye." Following a short service, Etta was interred in a vault at Graceland Cemetery on the North Side, where an equal number of spectators lined the route of the funeral cortege.

Jack Johnson babbled on for hours, almost incoherently, about his loss. He said many things in his sorrow, including a personal vow to quit the fight game and leave Chicago. But these were empty words. In truth, he was secretly romancing Lucille Cameron, a Minneapolis girl brought to Chicago by a Levee procuress named Jeannette Dorr. According to Johnson biographer Randy Roberts, she was "an experienced prostitute, having worked in Fannie Simpson's house in Minneapolis."

Lucille Cameron was barely eighteen years of age when she was driven down to the café to become better acquainted with Johnson. Enchanted, he moved Lucille into one of the spare bedrooms.

This was the final straw in a long line of humiliations foisted on the unhappy Etta by her faithless husband.

The brothel queens of Chicago had known all along the champ's zest for young white women, and his willingness to pay them handsomely for an "accommodation." But if Lucille was as experienced as Roberts claims, why did the mother put up such a determined fight to rescue her daughter from a life of immorality in the South Side vice dens?

When word leaked out about their latest discovery, the girl's deeply distressed mother, Mrs. L. Cameron-Falconet, charged Johnson with abduction.

GRACELAND CEMETERY

BURIAL PLOT OF JACK

ARTHUR JOHNSON AND

ETTA TERRY DURYEA

(BELOW), ANONYMOUS

IN DEATH.

(Photos by Lawrence Raeder)

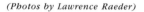

Angry whites hanged the champ's likeness in effigy from a lamppost at State and Walton, forcing Booker T. Washington, the courtly African-American leader, to denounce Johnson in the angriest of terms.

The girl was transferred to Rockford, Illinois, and detained in a jail cell while being examined by psychiatrists. Finding nothing wrong with Lucille other than the impetuousness of youth, authorities returned her to Chicago where she was compelled to appear as a witness against Johnson, who, by this time, had been arrested on charges of abduction and violating the Mann Act (the crime of transporting a minor across state lines for immoral purposes).

Famed criminal attorney Charles Erbstein, representing the aggrieved mother in the proceedings, blistered Lucille with questions, implying that she had been brought to Chicago against her will by the prizefighter. But the girl was adamant and declared her true affections for Johnson openly. Then one night she managed to escape from the Chicago hotel where her mother kept her sequestered. She returned to the South Side, but found the café closed and padlocked by order of the Police Department. Lucille combed the Levee dives and all of Johnson's usual haunts until she caught up with him.

The champ knew enough about criminal law to understand that if he were to make Lucille his wife, she would not be able to testify against him in the pending morals case. Johnson raced downtown with Lucille in hand to make it all legal.

After quarreling with clerk L. C. Legner, who was suspicious of the girl's legal age, Johnson managed to secure a marriage license after a direct appeal was made to City Clerk Robert Sweitzer. The couple were wed on December 3, 1912, inside the same Wabash Avenue parlor where Etta Duryea was waked only three months earlier.

To celebrate the festive occasion, Johnson wore a dazzling white-and-black-checked suit, and three diamond rings he had temporarily retired in the solemnity of his first wife's funeral. Upon hearing the news, Mrs. Cameron-Falconet, while in seclusion in her Minneapolis home, swooned and passed out. Interviewed by reporters, the girl's mother was prostrate with grief. "I had to give up the fight when Lucille disappeared," she said. "My battle is over. I feel sorry for my poor girl."

Six months later, the champ was convicted on Mann Act violations in the courtroom of Judge Kenesaw Mountain Landis, a white-haired southerner with a sour disposition who would later distinguish himself as baseball's first commissioner.

With Landis's steely-eyed gaze and angry frown focused squarely on the defendant, it was apparent to everyone in the court that the case was lost. Johnson realized his ploy to marry Lucille and avoid prosecution was all in vain.

While out on bond pending appeal, Johnson fled the country. He would remain abroad for the next seven years, fighting a succession of ringers in Paris, Central America, Buenos Aires, Cuba, and Mexico.

Having enough of this life, Johnson voluntarily surrendered to federal agents in July 1920. He was sent to Leavenworth Prison for ten months. Inside, he sparred with fellow inmates and counted the days till his release.

Lucille Cameron was waiting at the prison gates when her man got out, but they were divorced in 1924. She was in her thirties and cognizant of the many celebrity beauties buzzing about and smiling so seductively. Johnson satisfied his ravenous sexual appetite in Europe and Hollywood, where he was romantically linked to screen stars Lupe Velez and Mae West. In these final years, his conquests of "Great White Hopes" were mostly in bed.

Johnson died in a car crash twenty miles outside Raleigh, North Carolina, on June 10, 1946. He was sixty-eight years of age. It was said that he was driving too fast for conditions—which seemed to be the perfect metaphor of his entire life.

Bridgeport

Armour Square Park (between 31st and 34th Streets, east of Shields Avenue)

THE TWO SIDES OF BRIDGEPORT AND THE BEATING OF LENARD CLARK

March 21, 1997

Bridgeport is a working-class neighborhood unlike any other. Five of the last eight Chicago mayors lived here or had family ties in Bridgeport. Two generations of Daleys resided in a brick bungalow on Lowe Avenue, a stone's throw from Comiskey Park. In the 1850s Bridgeport was a port of entry for potato famine Irish and succeeding waves of Germans, Lithuanians, and Italians. The immigrants had to keep their wits about them working long hours dredging the Illinois and Michigan Canal or slaughtering hogs on the killing floors of Packing Town. The European tribes who came here seeking utopia did not always get along with one another, but the community adage was thrift and self-reliance. People managed to remain "close-knit" and bound together by tradition and old-world customs. Dominated by corner taverns, parish churches, social clubs, the White Sox, and the pageant of 11th Ward precinct workers and ward committeemen "turning out the vote" on election day, Bridgeport is anchored to its past. It is the fabric with which Chicago political history was sewn, but there is another side to this story. People of color, outsiders, even the fans of the beloved baseball team playing in the new Comiskey Park who trudge in from the distant suburbs, correctly sense that they are not always welcome here. Bridgeport, like suburban Cicero lying on the western border of the city, has become a symbol of racial intolerance and bigotry over the past decades, with the specter of organized crime lurking in the shadows. The senseless beating of thirteen-year-old Lenard Clark in Armour Square Park failed to ignite a storm of rioting and racial backlash as the police assault on motorist Rodney King did in Los Angeles, but the outside world took notice of this and asked the logical question, "Just what goes on down there on the South Side anyway?"

Turn south on any of the residential side streets of Bridgeport intersecting Thirty-first Street west of Bronzeville, and you are likely to run through a gauntlet of double-parked cars, especially in the warm summer months.

Nowhere else, in any part of Chicago, will you encounter this curious phenomenon. It is perfectly understandable if you know the way the "City That Works"
... works. With so many Chicago cops, city inspectors, bailiffs, union officials, and
wise guys clustered in the east end of Bridgeport, who would even dare to issue
the owner of the offending vehicle a ticket? The double-parked cars (none of them
with blinker lights flashing, incidentally) are a minor annoyance, but in small ways
they speak volumes about the nature of 11th Ward political "clout."

White Bridgeporters, fearing that their streets are about to be overrun by
blacks, Asians, and Hispanics and that they will be driven out of their homes, in
the process, resent the intrusion of outsiders into their insular neighborhood.
They gaze nervously over their shoulders and shudder at the ethnic diversity
they have witnessed in recent years along the Halsted Street retail corridor.
Newcomers pose a threat.

As every South Sider who does not fit the "acceptable" ethnic profile can tell
you from the wellspring of experience, there are a set of unwritten rules gov-
erning where minority people choose to walk, recreate, or shop in Bridgeport.
Stray too far and there are levels of intimidation ranging from a hostile glare, to
rude service, or to the fate befalling 13-year-old Lenard Clark when he rode his
bicycle into Armour Square Park, separating the parking lots of the New
Comiskey Park from the two flats and antique worker cottages of surrounding
white Bridgeport.

The park is a place for local residents to shoot hoops, watch the little ones
frolic in the playlot, or just hear the echoes of the cheering throngs inside
Comiskey, every time Frank Thomas cranks out another tape-measure home run.
A historic Daniel Burnham field house, constructed in 1904, faces Shields Avenue.

Clark and two friends believed that they had as much right to be there as

ARMOUR SQUARE

PARK, BRIDGEPORT

IN THE BACKGROUND.

anyone else. After finishing their game, they prepared to head back to the black neighborhood lying on the other side of Comiskey, when they were set upon by three white teenagers who singled out Clark after the other two managed to escape to the Stateway Gardens Housing Project. The three young men beat him into unconsciousness. Shouting racial insults, they kicked and pummeled Clark and left him for dead. The boy lapsed into a coma as a result of the assailant smashing his head into a wall.

Two days later, Frank Caruso Jr., Victor Jasas, and Michael Kwidzinski were charged with attempted murder, a hate crime, and aggravated battery. All were under the age of twenty-one. A fourth man who was witness to the beating disappeared from Chicago and was charged with a federal warrant for "flight from testimony."

An assistant state's attorney asked that bond be fixed at $1 million for the three boys, but a judge affixed bail at $100,000 to $150,000—sparking criticism and outrage from the black community. On March 27, four hundred men and women marched into Bridgeport chanting "No Justice! No peace!" They were met by angry white homeowners hurling insults at them, "Three innocent boys!" There were far worse epitaphs spewed that day.

Remember, this was not Selma, Alabama, circa 1965, but Chicago, Illinois, 1997.

Frank Caruso Jr. is the nephew of Bruno Caruso, former business manager of Local 1001 of the Laborers International Union of North America (LIUNA), representing a number of Streets and Sanitation workers in Chicago.

Bruno Caruso, his brother Frank Sr., and a cousin, Leo Caruso, long suspected of having close ties to organized crime, were all bounced from the union in January 2001 by an independent hearing officer following five years of careful investigation by the U.S. Justice Department into improprieties. It was seen as a major victory for a reform element eager to clean up a union that has been under the thumb of the mob for more than thirty years.

Bridgeport falls within the territory governed by the "26th Street Crew" (sometimes known as the Chinatown crew), one of seven identifiable street crews comprising the modern-day Chicago outfit. Frank "Skids" Caruso, grandfather of Lenard Clark's assailant, was alleged to have been the boss of that operation from the 1950s up through the 1970s. With deep and pervasive political ties to City Hall (through the late First Ward Alderman Fred Roti), this particular faction of the mob is heavily involved in chop-shop operations, extortion, labor racketeering, and gambling.

Was it any wonder, then, that the star witness in the Clark beating case conveniently chose to disappear?

Frank Caruso Jr. was sentenced to eight years in prison by Judge Daniel Localo after a prolonged delay in deliberations. Jasas and Kwidzinski pleaded guilty to aggravated battery and received thirty months probation. Lenard Clark's rehabilitation was long and painful, but he has since managed to recover. The boy was photographed side by side with Caruso at the medium-security Sheridan Correctional Center after a "reconciliation" had been effected between the two families. Frank Caruso Sr. offered to teach Clark how to drive and volunteered to help out with his school studies. Skeptics doubted the sincerity of the gesture, believing it was a shabby attempt to stir public sympathy for a reduction in the younger Caruso's sentence.

Meanwhile, back in Bridgeport the cycle of violence went on and on. The day before Christmas Eve, 1999, reputed mob figure Ronald W. Jarrett was struck by shotgun pellets as he was leaving his home in the 3000 block of South Lowe Avenue (five blocks north of the bungalow where the late mayor Richard J. Daley resided) en route to the funeral of "Guy" Bills, a former member of his burglary crew and a family relative. Jarrett's arrest record dated back to 1962 and filled five pages.

The assassin emerged from a Ryder rental truck and sprayed Jarrett with bullets before dumping the car in an alley in the 3200 block of South Normal Avenue. The car was on fire when police arrived. "Work cars" (as they are often called) are frequently torched in order to obliterate physical evidence. Jarrett died from his wounds a month later. It was the first murder attributed to organized crime since 1993, prompting speculation that a power struggle between rival mob factions was brewing.

Unrelated to organized crime, Lenard Clark, or the Carusos, was the vicious assault directed against Chicago radio personality Bill Simonson on June 9, 2000, following the conclusion of a Cubs–White Sox game. The sports talk-show host had just exited a neighborhood tap near Thirty-third and Wells when a gang of toughs, hanging out and "protecting their turf," assaulted Simonson and several other men walking through the neighborhood less than an hour later. This time, there was no racial provocation. The attack was directed against a group of white men who were heading back to the CTA Red Line trains following the baseball game because they happened to be strangers passing through an invisible tollgate in this strange land known as Armour Square Park.

In tough neighborhoods, the young men acting in this fashion are often taught from early age by hard-edged, bullying fathers that a man's worth is measured in physical terms, and not by acquiring social refinement or developing the coping skills necessary to lead an upstanding and rewarding life. The refrain goes something like this: "If a stranger looks at you funny, well, you know what to do, but remember to keep quiet. If the cops come around and start asking questions, as they sometimes do, justify it in the context of shoring up 'neighborhood pride.' They will understand. After all, you were only defending your turf."

Simonson was strident in his criticisms toward Chicago police, whom he accused of being slow to respond. Using his afternoon talk show on ESPN Radio as a public forum, the host lambasted the cops and the Bridgeport thugs responsible for the outrage.

The police had downplayed the seriousness of the attack all along, and closed ranks in a defensive posture. Instead of expressing sympathy and understanding for Simonson and the other men who wound up in Mercy Hospital for stitches after being kicked in the head while lying on the ground and vowing to get to the bottom of the matter, Superintendent Terry Hilliard castigated the radio host.

Stockyards District—Canaryville

Fortieth Street & Wallace, and various other locations

BATTLING THE BEEF TRUST: THE GREAT STOCKYARDS UPHEAVAL
December 5–9, 1921

Until 1971, the year that the Union Stockyards officially closed after 106 years of continuous operation, civic boosters touted the entire meatpacking industry as the "eighth wonder of the world." The Chicago Tribune *proclaimed in an 1889 editorial that "sufficient meats are there to feed the standing armies of Europe." Packingtown took shape in 1865 when New Yorker John B. Sherman purchased an abandoned tract of land west of Halsted Street between Thirty-nineth and Forty-seventh Streets. The Union Stock Yard and Transit Company opened on Christmas Day of that year, attracting cattle dealers and western stockmen to Chicago, thus establishing the city as America's great "Porkopolis" on the prairie. From the carcasses of the butchered cattle came all kinds of common household goods:, soap, lard, hairbrushes, oleomargarine, fertilizer, glue, gelatin, even violin strings. With the exception of moo or oink, every square inch of the cow and the pig (with the occasional swayback horse thrown in for good measure) was extracted for useful purposes. The early packing plants were situated on the South Branch of the Chicago River, where waste materials, offal, and debris polluted the sluggish*

*flow of the water. Bubbly Creek, near Thirty-fifth Street in the neighborhood
known as McKinley Park, was an open sewer conveying the sludge and muck
of Packingtown to the Chicago River. Sometimes a strikebreaker would be
thrown in the fetid pool by union workers, as was the case in 1921. The horrors of Packingtown are well documented by Upton Sinclair in his ground-
breaking 1906 novel* The Jungle, *based on his own firsthand observations in
the fall of 1905. From time to time the workers would rise up against the
deplorable conditions and ill treatment by management and walk off the job.
There was labor unrest in the early twentieth century as the stockyard strikes
of 1904, 1919, and 1921 attest. At issue in 1921 was an across-the-board 10
percent wage cut, something the "house union" (the meatpacker's handpicked
flunkies) acceded to. There were scenes of rioting and disorder in Canaryville
where the Irish lived, Back of the Yards (a Polish-Slavic settlement), and
McKinley Park all that month. The worst incident of violence, which perfectly
illustrates the means to which the Swifts, Armours, Wilsons, Morrises, and the
independent packers resorted to in order to break trade unionism and exploit
a tense situation, was the pitting of the working people of Chicago against one
another. An attack against a trainload of strikebreakers bound for the yards at
Fortieth and Wallace on December 8, 1921, was one of those terrible moments
brought on by the intransigence and venality of upper management. The
ancient viaduct, its masonry chipped away and eroded by time, crosses over
Wallace (a north-south street) amid the gloom of a decayed industrial area
scarred by boarded-up factories and rubble-strewn lots, where, in other days,
there used to be factories operating at full capacity.*

Philip Danforth Armour (1832–1901) was a Prairie Avenue aristocrat and the
king of Packingtown. "Through the wages I dispense and the provisions I supply,"
he boasted, "I give more people food than any man alive. I am just a butcher trying to go to heaven!"

Gustavus Franklin Swift (1839–1903) was a New England Yankee who
launched his meatpacking business in 1875, capitalizing on his ability to ship
dressed beef in specially designed railroad refrigerator cars all across the continent. "The secret of all undertakings is hard work and self-reliance," he exulted.

"You can be of the greatest benefit by employing lots of labor and helping
to maintain thousands of people, though you will never get any gratitude from
them, no thanks, but you will get satisfaction," echoed Nelson Morris, a livestock
dealer and one of the "big three."

These humble exponents of the virtues of thrift, perseverance, and old-fashioned ingenuity were the "Barons of the Beef Trust," though Upton Sinclair failed to mention them directly in his muckraking novel.

In 1903 the three firms merged into a giant conglomerate known as the National Packing Company. This lasted only until 1905 when the U.S. government ruled the beef trust a monopoly and ordered it dissolved.

Even then, these ruthless exploiters of labor went about their business; fixing prices, selling tainted and diseased beef to consumers and the U.S. government, driving down wages and enacting restrictive policies, buying off politicians, infiltrating the cutting rooms with spies and informants, and trampling on the rights of men and women to collectively bargain for even the most meager concessions.

And while they expected deep humility and Christian gratitude for the star-

POLICE AND STRIKERS CLASH DURING THE 1921 STOCKYARDS WALKOUT WHILE THE CAMERAS ROLL.

vation wages they paid and the filthy workplace they provided, in large measure the big meatpackers cared not a whit for the penniless immigrants from Europe who kept showing up at the Halsted Street gates each morning in the chill of winter and the deadly hot days of summer hoping to land a position.

By 1921, Packingtown's original founding fathers were all dead. Their sons, nephews, grandchildren, and family friends carried on the businesses and maintained the slaughterhouses and pens as one might expect them to do in a city like Chicago, where nepotism in politics, newspaper journalism, and commerce run rampant and the only way to succeed is to be born into it, or "have it in right" with those who are in a position to dispense favors.

Though some progress had been noted in 1921 since Sinclair's exposé first aroused the nation, conditions in Packingtown had not substantially improved, despite the enactment of congressional reforms aimed at correcting the interlocking corruption that spawned the shocking abuses.

During World War I, the labor shortage had artificially inflated wages, and a federally appointed arbitration board recognized the Amalgamated Meat Cutters Union as the official collective bargaining agent of the packinghouse workers. For the first time, labor and capital were managing to coexist, but the peace was shaky and it did not hold up after the term of Judge Samuel Alschuler, the federal arbitrator, expired on September 1, 1921.

A wage reduction was announced on November 18, owing to a general decline in revenue and a drop-off in postwar business. The union responded angrily, calling for a general strike the first week of December. The "shop representation committee," a toothless house union formulated by Armour & Company as a means of getting around the militancy of the Amalgamated Meat Cutters Union, sanctioned the pay cut as they were expected to.

The common laborers (constituting 45 percent of the entire Packingtown work force) were incensed at seeing their pay drop from 45 cents an hour to $37^{1}/_{2}$ cents. Within hours of the announcement, violence flared all over the South Side Stockyard District.

Rioting began near the front gates of the stockyards and spread north to Thirty-first Street and south to Fifty-first. Chief of Police Charles Fitzmorris ordered that all saloons be closed in the belief that demon rum and not intolerable working conditions sparked the violence.

Accompanied by Captain John Naughton, the chief proceeded cautiously, with his weapon drawn, through the riot district along Forty-seventh Street in a police flivver. At Forty-seventh and Elizabeth he ordered his car driven straight into a mob of strikers who were beating a Pole named Julius Jinski to death. Fitzmorris rescued the man from certain death.

SCENE OF RIOTING—THE VIADUCT AT 40TH STREET AND WALLACE. TODAY, IT IS AN ABANDONED INDUSTRIAL AREA (ABOVE). PACKINGTOWN, CIRCA 1921 (BELOW).

At Forty-eighth and Racine, a mob of 2,500 swarmed a streetcar, cutting the overhead trolley ropes and pelting the windows with rocks and stones. Many of the passengers were women, returning home from the downtown stores laden with packages. Police reserves had all they could do to contain the crowd, and were exasperated in their efforts when the strikers hurled red pepper in their faces.

The packers asked for an injunction against the strikers. In a defiant tone, John E. O'Hern, the general manager of Armour & Company, laid the blame on outside agitators and repeated management's hard line. "We are working with 95 percent full force and can add to this any time we wish. We turned away 600 applicants today."

Doubtless to say, O'Hern's offspring were not counted among the throngs of wretched poor "turned away" from the gates of Packingtown that afternoon. Nor could there be found in the whole miserable lot of them, a Swift, an Armour, a Morris, or a Wilson.

The poor souls waiting in line were willing to accept scab pay because they, like the angry strikers, were also starving. The easy availability of cheap foreign labor was the packer's frontline of defense. Without them, the packinghouses might have been forced to pay union scale wages or else shut down.

The scabs were vilified and threatened with death.

At the entrance of the Armour & Company glue plant at Thirty-first Street and Lock, replacement workers were showered with bricks at the end of the day.

Mobs of striking female workers attacked and looted homes of packing-house workers who crossed picket lines.

An African-American man who went to work as a strikebreaker was seized, beaten, and hurled into the Bubbly Creek cesspool. When he came up gasping for air, he was stoned to death, sinking into the vile ooze. The packers responded by ordering the work force to remain inside. It was the most charitable action they had undertaken for employees in thirty years.

By 7:00 P.M., on December 7, ten persons had been shot, and many more trampled by charging police on horseback. It was reported that the strikers were placing their children and wives in front of them as human shields. "Cossacks!" Cossacks!" they cried, many of them foreign-born Slavs and Poles who remembered the tyranny of czarist Russia.

Waves of police bluecoats charged a mob at Marshfield Avenue and Forty-fifth Street—Davis Square. "Don't shoot unless you have to," ordered Fitzmorris. "But treat 'em rough!"

The morning dawned clear and bright, but at 7:00 A.M., an elevated train loaded with strikebreakers was set upon at Fortieth and Wallace. Windows were broken and forty men trapped inside were struck with flying glass. The sullen throng at street level cheered lustily.

The courts came down hard on the union after that. Judge Denis F. Sullivan of the superior court granted the packers' request for a temporary injunction requiring them to cease interfering with the nonunion workers.

"I have come to the conclusion that there are no absolute rights in society today," he said. "All rights are relative. There is no denying that labor has the right to attract others to its ranks, but a line of demarcation must be drawn somewhere. It is only a question of whether we are to have civil government or civil war."

The union vowed to fight on, but the spirit of the workers had ebbed. The onset of winter, and the harsh economic realities the coming of the snows entailed, forced the defiant strikers to return to work, hats in hand, their gazes lowered.

By mid-January 1922, the packinghouses declared total victory, again proving to the Armours and Swifts that they were indispensable to the workmen, and not the other way around.

Meanwhile, the ringleaders of the strike were coldly informed that their positions had already been taken. The replacements were already on the line; men and women from distant corners of Eastern Europe and African Americans from the cotton South, who had the good common sense to accept their positions with profound expressions of . . . gratitude.

Washington Park

The Washington Park Bridle Path (near Payne Boulevard—one-half block west of the General Richard L. Jones National Guard Armory, 5200 South Cottage Grove Ave.)

THE GIRLS IN THE CLEARING: UNSOLVED AND FORGOTTEN
September 23, 1972

Washington Park was opened in time for the World's Fair of 1893 (the World's Columbian Exposition). America's foremost landscape architect, Frederick Law Olmsted, laid out the beautiful greensward, keeping faith with a municipal plan originally drawn up in the 1860s calling for a ring of parks to encircle the city. The intention was to show off the natural beauty of Chicago and preserve a rapidly disappearing agrarian ideal. Ten thousand acres of South Side real estate were duly set aside for the South Park commissioners, who were charged

with the task of developing a vista of fields, lagoons, footbridges, and prome-
nades for the enjoyment of the modern urban dweller. They succeeded in creating Central Park in miniature, extending from Fifty-first Street (Hyde Park
Boulevard) on the north to Sixtieth Street on the south; King Drive on the east
to Cottage Grove Avenue on the west. Amid the baseball diamonds, picnic
groves, and former sheep meadows of Washington Park there is a sense of
unworldliness in this pastoral setting. For the South Side Irish living in the tenement districts that sprouted around the edges of the park in the early 1900s,
the open fields, the greenery, and the trees were an escape from everyday living. The dream-like setting is best captured in the novels of James T. Farrell,
author of the Studs Lonigan trilogy chronicling the trials, tribulations, and
heartaches of South Side life poignantly told from the perspective of an embattled Irish family sliding down a slippery economic slope. The fictional Lonigan
is an unambitious street tough running with the wrong crowd. He dreams of
a better life, but sees no way out of his present difficulties. Only a few blocks
away, Washington Park sparks memories of a lost summer romance, passion,
longing, tenderness, and momentary relief, but these conflicted emotions are
perceived by Studs as dangerous signs of weakness. The parks are a refuge for
the people, as Studs Lonigan discovered for himself, but the people they serve
often choose to stay away, especially at night. The neighborhood surrounding
the park deteriorated—inexpensive three-flats built on the ragged edges at the
turn of the century turned into slums by the 1950s. In the tranquil setting of
Chicago's most beautiful open spaces, there is an implied danger. Crime has
been rampant in Washington Park over the years, though revitalization efforts
are ongoing. When crime is discussed by Washington Parkers, it is most often
within the context of muggings, purse snatchings, and gang violence until
something really serious occurs, like a double homicide. The Van Der Molen
and Kozlarek murders fit that description.

Why is it that no one remembers Carolyn Van Der Molen and Deborah
Kozlarek? In the cold-case file of the Chicago Police Department, this one gathers
dust.

Maybe it is because time has a way of erasing the pain and suffering. People
simply want to forget.

Or more likely, it is because friends, neighbors, and classmates of these girls
have all moved on. The Sherman Park neighborhood adjoining Garfield Boulevard
(Fifty-fifth Street) where the girls lived and played is 100 percent African-

SCENE OF THE KOZLAREK—VAN DER MOLEN MURDER IN
WASHINGTON PARK (TOP). THE MOTOR WORLD LOUNGE WHERE
DEBORAH KOZLAREK WORKED PART-TIME AS A WAITRESS IS NOW
THE CROSSROADS HOTEL PLAZA (BOTTOM).

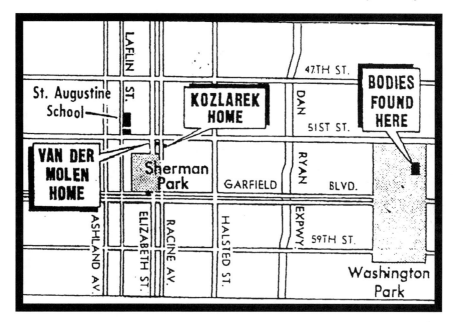

American, and those who lived in the St. Augustine Parish who might still remember the case are long gone.

No one was ever arrested or charged with the murder of these two girls. The police were even less sure of the set of circumstances that contributed to their disappearance.

The crime occurred at the beginning of the 1972–73 school year, a time when a deeply divided nation prayed for an end to the Vietnam War, but braced for a contentious presidential election pitting one candidate who guaranteed every American a monthly paycheck whether they chose to work or not, against an incumbent president who refused to divulge his "secret plan" to end the Southeast Asian conflict. The George McGovern–Richard Nixon follies were played out that fall against the backdrop of a "third-rate" burglary known as Watergate that would soon gain worldwide prominence.

In Chicago that year, police detectives were forced to contend with a rash of unsolved homicides involving young female victims who were turning up in roadside ditches, cornfields, and railroad viaducts. Between June and September of 1972, six women and an eighteen-month-old child were found in isolated city and suburban locations. The readily understood term "serial killer" had not yet seared the public consciousness as it would in the 1980s after we had the chance to glimpse John Wayne Gacy and Ted Bundy. Nor was there a hint or suggestion that these murders might have been related.

Thirteen-year-old Carolyn Van Der Molen was an eighth-grade student at St. Augustine Grammar School. She lived in a brick three-flat with her parents at 5131 South Elizabeth Street near Sherman Park, and was remembered by her principal as a "friendly girl, but a loner."

Carolyn's friend Deborah Kozlarek, age seventeen, was a high school dropout who lived with her parents and three siblings at 5160 South Racine. She was employed as a waitress at Motor World Lounge, a busy truck-stop motel with an adjoining coffee shop near Midway Airport. The coffee shop was located at 5300 South Pulaski Road. (*Author's Note:* The motel, composed of two four-story slabs, is now the Crossroads Hotel Plaza. The coffee shop has changed hands and is currently the Great Wall Chinese restaurant.)

It was reported at the time that the two girls were quarrelsome and rebellious and had difficulty getting along with their parents. Kozlarek dropped out of Gage Park High School after being stabbed in the leg during a racial altercation.

Tensions between whites and blacks ran high in those days. Sherman Park was the domain of the Gaylords, a tough white-ethnic street gang. Washington Park and points farther east were overrun by Black Gangster Disciples and the Black P Stone Nation (evolved from Jeff Fort's Blackstone Rangers).

In this cauldron of hate, Deborah tried to get along as best she could. Described as "worldly beyond her years," Deborah told her coworkers that she had worked in restaurants "all over the Loop."

They were all stunned to learn that she was only seventeen.

DOWN BEAT TAP, 52ND AND RACINE, WHERE THE POLICE BELIEVE THE GIRLS

BOUGHT POP AND CANDY BEFORE THEY WERE KILLED.

(Photo by Lawrence Raeder)

On the afternoon of her disappearance, Carolyn asked her father's permission to spend the night at Deborah's home, but he refused. Defiantly, she stormed out of the house to keep her appointment. She entered the Down Beat Tap to buy pop and candy around 9:00 P.M., and was last seen by neighbors walking with Kozlarek on Elizabeth Street around 11:00 P.M.

When Carolyn failed to return home the following morning, the anxious mother went to the Deering Police Station to file a missing person's report.

The next morning, a Sunday, a passing jogger found the two lifeless forms lying face-up in a clearing near the bridle path of Washington Park—one hundred feet south of a parking lot and directly west of the National Guard Armory.

The bodies were fully clothed. Ballistics tests showed that they had been shot to death with .32-caliber bullets. There was no evidence of sexual molestation, but an autopsy revealed that they had digested a full meal not long before they were killed. This fueled speculation that they either knew the killer or trusted a stranger long enough to buy them dinner. Both girls were in the habit of hitchhiking, but no one in their circle deemed it likely that they would stray into Washington Park so late on a Friday night.

Coroner Andrew J. Toman, whose father, John Toman, served as Cook County sheriff in the mid-1930s, concurred. He believed the girls were killed elsewhere and dumped in the park shortly after midnight.

Toman was censured for the misidentification of one of the girls. His office had released the erroneous information that the victim was a teenage runaway named Rosemarie Pilewicz. The embarrassed coroner had egg on his face and plenty of explaining to do the following day when the Pilewicz girl turned up alive and unharmed in the far North Side Foster Avenue police district.

Once proper identification was made, the grieving families laid the girls to rest in Resurrection Cemetery in south suburban Justice.

The Kozlarek–Van Der Molen case was an eerie rerun of the famous 1956 double homicide of Barbara and Patricia Grimes. Here were two pairs of South Side girls (separated by a generation) who disappeared under mysterious circumstances. In each instance, the victims were dumped in a secluded area by their killers. The lack of a suspect and compelling motive would haunt both case files with one important exception.

The disappearance of the Grimes sisters would be analyzed and debated for many more years to come, attaining near cult status among armchair crime buffs and devotees of the psychic paranormal. It is remarkable how this heinous and ghastly crime from the 1950s has managed to stir such intense public fascination all these years. It has evolved into a classic Chicago crime noir "whodunit."

Not so with the Kozlarek–Van Der Molen case. This one lies buried and forgotten by nearly all, except for the dogged efforts of crime researcher Lawrence Raeder to solve the puzzle. Raeder, who was twelve at the time of the shootings, grew up in the same neighborhood as the two girls. As a boy he played alley hockey with Deborah's brother Eddie (who was shot to death in 1979 while repossessing an automobile) and knew Carolyn's older brother only casually. To this day he wonders why there was such scant press coverage of the murders, and ponders the dearth of possible motives.

He discounts police theories that it was a robbery gone bad, or that the girls were the victims of a racially motivated killer, as was suspected by homicide detectives when their names were added to a lengthening list of white teenage girls who were turning up dead that summer.

"Nearly all racial killings involve extreme brutality and often some form of sexual assault. The racial theory is very unlikely," Raeder states. "If I had to write an ending to this story and speculate wildly, I'd say Deborah and Carolyn could have been involved in prostitution or in the making of porno movies. Carolyn had the lounge's phone number written on her hand when her body was found, and I have talked to people who say that prostitution went on in that place back then."

Taking this on as a personal crusade, Raeder has lobbied unsuccessfully to unlock closed doors and tap into Chicago police and FBI files under the Freedom of Information Act (FOIA). Thus far he has been stonewalled by federal and local law enforcement.

The trail is cold and he knows it.

Returning to the old neighborhood one last time, Raeder discovered that the homes of these two girls were both torn down long ago and the symbols of spreading urban decay are everywhere.

St. John of God Church, where Deborah Kozlarek's funeral mass was held, closed its doors in April 1992. Threatened with the wrecking ball, the historic church that once served a predominantly ethnic-Polish congregation is used today by neighborhood waifs as a gymnasium. In former days St. John of God was famous throughout the Midwest for the weeping icon of the Virgin Mary. The carved religious statue was brought here in 1984 and lured thousands of pilgrims to 1258 West Fifty-second Street hoping to glimpse a miracle in the making.

There are no more miracles left to deliver from the inside of the old church. Neighborhood crime drove the last of the parishioners away. And if there are tears to be shed, they should be shed for the senseless murder of innocents against the backdrop of the city and its rawness and brutality.

Hyde Park-Kenwood

Del Prado Hotel,

5307 Hyde Park

Boulevard

(southeast

corner, 53rd St.

and Hyde Park

Boulevard, one

block east of

Cornell)

SUNSET FOR IRVING VINE
May 6, 1963

Anchored by the University of Chicago, the community of Hyde Park–Kenwood extends along the south lakefront from Forty-seventh Street to Sixtieth Street. In many respects, it is Chicago's "island" neighborhood, with many beautiful old homes, neoclassical apartment-hotels, eclectic coffee houses, secondhand bookstores, student housing, and faculty residences. Surrounded by high-crime corridors to the north, south, and west, Hyde Park remains a delightful community in which to live and work. The political history of this integrated community of freethinkers, activists, economists, social psychologists, and theorists is equally interesting. Up until 1889, historic Hyde Park was a suburb within the township of Lake. Thereafter it was a Chicago neighborhood operating under the "protection" of Police Captain Nicholas Hunt, a head-cracking Irishman who curried the favor of the stockyard moguls by brutally suppressing labor gatherings. Hyde Park–Kenwood was the home of Gustavus Swift, reason enough for Captain Hunt to make things hot for union agitators. Hunt sent in columns of his meanest bluecoats who were unafraid to swing their hickory in the general direction of a workingman's cranium. While saving the city from the red menace of anarchy, Captain Hunt protected all of the Hyde Park "blind pig" saloons (Author's Note: *Places operating without a liquor license. Eleven square miles of Hyde Park remained in a Prohibition district after the 1889 annexation), gambling games, and short cons, as long as there were kickbacks made to the boys in the station. While Hunt ran riot in the first decade of the twentieth century, Hyde Park morals were vigorously upheld by Arthur Burrage Farwell, anti-saloon crusader and the driving force behind the Hyde Park Protective Association and the Chicago Law & Order League. With boundless energy, Farwell and his flock eventually succeeded in retiring Hunt, minimizing vote fraud, and keeping Hyde Park the God-fearing, tweedy bastion of ponderous philosophical thought we know today. Within this intense academic milieu, traces of the "real Chicago" and its attending larceny and villainy surface from*

time to time. There have been muggings, street crime, even the occasional mur-
der. One of them involving bookmaker Irving Vine occurred inside room 507
of the Del Prado Hotel, 5307 Hyde Park Boulevard, just east of the University
of Chicago campus. The Del Prado is a distinguished neighborhood landmark,
though it is no longer a hotel taking reservations and booking overnight
guests. For much of the first half of the twentieth century, it was the head-
quarters of visiting American League baseball teams coming into Chicago to
play the White Sox. Babe Ruth (1895–1948) lounged about the lobby smoking
fat Cuban cigars and reading his morning paper. Ayn Rand (1905–1982),
author, freethinker, and champion of the philosophy of "objectivism," was said
to have spent several nights here as a young Russian émigré about to make
her way out to Hollywood in the winter of 1926. Going even further back to
1895 when philosopher, psychologist, and educator John Dewey (1859–1952)
was an overnight guest, the Del Prado had already emerged as a symbol of
cordial South Side lakefront living. It was a time when things generally moved
at a slower, less uneven pace. Today it is an apartment house. The former ball-
room is the Hyde Park Art Center gallery, which is fine with me, just so long
as some insensitive developer doesn't take a swipe at history with a wrecking
ball.

Rosie Mitchell, a Del Prado Hotel housemaid, noticed that Irving Vine's door was slightly ajar. It was 9:45 in the morning, and Rosie was making the usual housecleaning rounds when she pushed back the door of room 507 and found the occupant of the room lying face-down on the floor, wearing only his boxer shorts. The apartment was ransacked. Scratch sheets and paper slips with the names of horses were littered about.

Vine's legs were bound with surgical tape, and there was tape slapped across his mouth and nose. A pillow covered his head. The killer must have labored under the belief that dead men tell no tales.

"He took a pretty good beating before he died," said Commander Robert Harness of the Hyde Park District police. The murder was committed between 8:00 and 9:45 A.M., because Rosie Mitchell was certain that she had passed by just before eight, and the door was closed at that time.

Three of Vine's ribs were broken. He had been smothered by a pillow. It was a tough ending for the old cardsharp whose ride on the merry-go-round ended after he lost the love of his life.

Vine was married to former dice girl Betty Jeanne Neibert from 1946–1952, until he lost her affections to Murray "the Camel" Humphreys, upper-echelon racketeer (discussed earlier in this book). Once the decree was granted, Vine moved in with Nathan "Butch" Ladon, a 250-pound gorilla who was Eddie "Dutch" Vogel's street enforcer.

Vine was a small-fry gambler who ran books for Vogel, the slot-machine boss of Cook County in the 1940s for the Capone mob. Arrested four times in Cicero and Chicago on bookmaking charges, there was only one possible explanation for the outfit to finish off the hapless bookie.

In 1959, Humphreys and Betty Jeanne purchased a sizable estate in Key Biscayne, Florida, for $65,000. The Chicago gangster spent large sums of money on landscaping, wiring, and the installation of a new swimming pool. In the belief that Humphreys had avoided paying his income taxes, the IRS demanded to know where the money came from. The money, Humphreys patiently explained to the agents, was received by Betty Jeanne long before they were married in 1957.

"That's a lie!" retorted Vine. "She never made so much as $75 a week as a dice girl!" He told the IRS he never had $50,000 to give, and was preparing to take the witness stand against Humphreys in his tax trial.

Telephone records showed that Vine had been in communication on a daily basis with syndicate heavyweights Gus Alex and "Dutch" Vogel.

Humphreys and his associates cajoled Vine into changing his story, but when he did not recant, he died.

Garfield Boulevard

A SWASHBUCKLER WHO DIED WITH HIS BOOTS ON: THE MURDER OF MOSSIE ENRIGHT
February 3, 1920

It is the conventional wisdom of crime historians that the murder of "Big Jim" Colosimo inside his café on May 11, 1920, officially inaugurated the thirteen-year reign of gangland mayhem in the streets of Chicago. For this dubious honor, I submit the name of Maurice "Mossie" Enright, and will let the reader decide. Enright was an assassin second to none in the labor rackets who made Big Jim look like a piker by comparison. Mossie drove a fog-gray touring car that chilled rivals to the bone. It came to be known as the "Enright pirate car," after reporters likened its owner to the swashbuckling buccaneers of old. When the vehicle pulled up to the front door of a labor meeting or a saloon where the workingmen gathered, it was a sure sign that trouble was brewing, perhaps even murder was afoot. Enright took no prisoners and brooked no interference from friend or foe. "Big Tim" Murphy was one such friend, but the two hoodlum bosses crossed swords, forcing Murphy and his henchmen to draw first blood (for which they would pay dearly). Moss lived like a king inside a fashionable brick home at 1110 West Garfield Boulevard. Today that area is 100 percent African-American. The housing stock has deteriorated and the area is plagued by poverty and other defining social problems.

For years, the Chicago newspapers kept close watch on Maurice Enright, expecting his death from unnatural causes to occur at any moment. When such a call was placed to the rewrite men by reporters on the street, the major dailies were ready with the full-page spread.

Even Mossie's own wife and two young children were trained to anticipate the day when the rattle of pistol fire would extinguish his life. When he lay dying on the sidewalk, Mrs. Enright gasped: "It's come! Oh Mossie, my man!" Her two sons, ages twelve and ten, stared dry-eyed at their daddy.

MOSSIE ENRIGHT IS

ANONYMOUS IN DEATH.

"MY JESUS HAVE

MERCY."

MOSSIE ENRIGHT WAS SHOT CURBSIDE IN FRONT OF HIS RESIDENCE AT 1110 WEST GARFIELD BOULEVARD.

(Photo by Lawrence Raeder)

Moss Enright was a product of the Back of the Yards neighborhood. He ran with the Ragen's Colts street gang, and was mentored by their leader, Frank Ragen, who rose to prominence in political circles as a Cook County commissioner.

Thugs and gunmen lacking requisite tradesmen's skills gravitated to union work—the intimidation of uncooperative employers, harassing strikebreakers, intervening in the jurisdictional fights between factions within a legitimate union local; this was the stock and trade of the feared "labor slugger."

The spectacular murder of slugger Vincent Altman, on a cold March day in 1911, introduced Moss Enright to Chicago at a time when the city was paralyzed by continuous labor strife of the slugging variety. Differences were settled by hired sluggers who sometimes worked together, or apart. Altman, a former Chicago police officer employed as an agent of the steam fitters union, was sharing a drink with Enright inside the Briggs House saloon when Moss jammed a pistol into the man's abdomen and fired. Altman died in the County Hospital refusing to name his killer.

Enright blamed his associate William "Dutch" Gentleman for the murder, but Gentleman was not available to defend himself against the charge. He was murdered by Enright inside Pat O'Malley's saloon three months after Altman was laid to rest. Mossie said the shooting was in self-defense and the cops let it go at that. The Altman matter was not so easily ignored.

A discarded gray coat belonging to Enright was found in one of the upstairs rooms, with a pistol tucked inside. Based on this bit of circumstantial evidence, State's Attorney John Wayman secured a life prison sentence amid the anguished cries of Enright supporters.

Moss told them all not to worry, and was shipped off to the Joliet penitentiary the following November, fully expecting commutation from the Democratic governor of Illinois, Edward F. Dunne, who was obliged to give it in 1913.

Dunne is praised by political historians for his endorsement of progressive causes, and championing the increased role of government. But to release an unrepentant killer like Enright back into society after only two years was foolhardy and irresponsible. His decision to free the gangster was based on a petition signed by forty thousand trade unionists from Chicago—forty thousand potential Democratic votes added to the roles.

They had no idea, of course, that the warden of the downstate prison was in the habit of granting Enright furloughs so he could return to the city from time to time to enjoy the nightclub districts.

Enright crept back into Chicago to resume operation of his downtown advertising agency, but his return signaled a renewal of labor union violence. (*Author's Note:* Twenty-three men were killed in Chicago in the name of labor between

1910 and 1920. Many suspects were arrested and tried but the juries were lenient and political influence was strong. Not one was sentenced to death.)

By this time Enright had parted company with his old friend from the North Side, "Big Tim" Murphy. The dispute was over control of the gas workers union. Murphy organized them into a local and collected the funds, but Enright received the charter and refused to give it up. There were threats of reprisal and bitter enmity, which Murphy denied. "D'ya know? I don't believe in enmity. If I were to punch a man in the nose I'll do it myself—then shake hands with him after we have fought it out."

The cops weren't buying it and braced for another shooting war. Samuel Insull, the morally bereft president of People's Gas, Light, & Coke Company, smirked and waited for the bullets to fly. He knew that if these two combatants destroyed each other, the final outcome might be no union at all or, at the very least, a cessation to the ugly practice of having to bribe corrupt union leaders to keep workers off the picket lines.

Things were at an impasse the night of February 3, 1920, when Enright drained a final glass of near beer at the saloon of former alderman Joseph Swift, 5428 South Halsted Street. "Got to get home for supper, boys," he remarked. With a casual wave of the hand to the men gathered inside the tavern, Moss exited the building and drove the short ten-minute distance back to his residence on Garfield Boulevard.

As he eased the car to the curb in front of his home, a second vehicle, trailing close behind, pulled in alongside Enright. It was customary for professional hit men in those days to employ touring cars with curtains concealing the gunmen in the back seat.

By the time two young boys playing in the street noticed that the curtains of the second car were parted, it was already too late to do anything to shield Moss from the line of fire. "Then there was a rattle like a pneumatic hammer and fire began darting from the car in streaks so fast and so many that we couldn't count them," said Frank Perlowski, a witness to the murder.

Enright slumped over the wheel. Ten slugs tore into the neck, jaw, and other parts of his body. The wife and kids raced out of the house, but it was already too late. "They didn't even give him a chance to defend himself!" lamented the widow.

Captain John L. Hogan of the Stockyards Police Station questioned Enright's brother at length. "Who shot him you ask?" Tom Enright chuckled nervously. "Why, he was robbed. Mossie didn't have an enemy in the world. It must have been a stickup!"

The usual 2:00 A.M. assortment of thieves and gunmen were hauled in for the showup. The cops were fairly certain that Tim Murphy or one of his men was behind it all. "Dago" Mike Carrozzo, twenty-six-year-old boss of the street sweepers' union and a henchman of Murphy, drove the death car. Vincenzo Cosmano, a Black Hand terrorist, was fingered as the actual assassin by James Vinci (one of the "Terrible Vincis"), who was also present inside the car. Vinci's confession (given under duress) resulted in the indictment of all four men.

The prosecution was led by Assistant State's Attorney James C. "Ropes" O'Brien, the hanging prosecutor who had sent more men to the gallows in Illinois than any other ASA before or since. "No human breast can contain knowledge of a cold-blooded murder," bellowed O'Brien. "It was Vinci's conscience—Vinci's God—that was breaking him down and not the state's attorney!"

He was opposed by the "Million Dollar Defense"—a 1920s legal "dream team" consisting of Clarence Darrow, Stephen Malato, and Frances Walker. Darrow, who never refused a case with a sizable check awaiting him at the end of the proceedings, put up a masterful defense.

The jury freed three of the defendants, but sentenced the whistle-blowing Vinci to fourteen years. Expecting the rope, the star defendant was exultant. "Happy as hell!" He laughed. "Didn't I miss the noose?"

Deputy Police Superintendent John H. Alcock resigned himself to the disappointing verdict. "Murder is murder. Inside a year, maybe sooner, the friends of Moss Enright will pay back. They think they have been personally wronged."

The bell was already beginning to toll for Jimmy Vinci and Big Tim Murphy.

From Tuckers to Tootsie Rolls: The History of an Infamous Idea, September 1946

7401 South Cicero (near Seventy-third Street and Cicero Avenue)

SIDETRIP

In the early days of World War II, when America was gearing up to full industrial capacity to counter the Axis threat, the Dodge Motor Company opened a gigantic manufacturing plant at 7401 South Cicero for the production of the B-29 engine. The factory, situated only a short distance from Midway Airport (then known as Municipal Airport), was surrounded by open fields.

When total victory in Europe and Japan was achieved in 1945, the B-29 plant closed and thousands of assembly workers were thrown into the unemployment line. The plant was emptied out, and the doors bolted shut. Then, less than a year after V-J Day (Victory over Japan), Michigan tool manufacturer Preston Tucker breezed into town to unveil a new motor-car, the rear-engine Tucker Torpedo sedan.

The inventor-designer was also a dreamer and a visionary; a living embodiment of Ayn Rand's fictional industrialist-hero John Galt. More important, Tucker was a voice of optimism in the disquieting postwar era and one of the few spokesmen of his time who instilled hope among the ranks of idled workingmen.

While other manufacturers bitterly complained of material shortages, and constant governmental interference, Tucker spoke passionately of future industrial prosperity. "I am coming into Chicago because it has everything we need!" he exclaimed. "We hope to start hiring around January 15, 1947. That force will number 7,500 persons, enough to operate a 200-car-a-day assembly line. Every major facility needed to manufacture a new automobile is here, raw materials, allied manufacturing enterprises, labor supply, and transportation."

Vowing to mass-produce 1,000 to 1,500 distinctively styled Torpedoes on his Chicago assembly line each day, Tucker leased the old Dodge plant for $500,000 a year for two years. The spacious facility, new, bright and airy as mills go, was to employ 42,000 workers at peak capacity according to Preston Tucker's wildly inflated projections.

Labor boss Walter Reuther of the C.I.O. United Auto Workers promised full-fledged support. A nationwide dealer network numbering 1,872 was standing by to pitch the advantages of the Torpedo to the American public even before the first automobile rolled off the line. All systems were go for the radically designed car.

Preston Tucker exuded boyish confidence in the free-enterprise system. The public was in the mood for something new. They had seen all of the hype, but the Detroit auto monopoly had other ideas about allowing this interloper into the field. They infiltrated the Chicago plant with company spies. Agents of the "Big Three" automakers attempted to bribe Tucker employees, while high-profile lobbyists exerted political pressure on Capitol Hill to forestall the sale of a Cleveland steel plant to the upstart. There were many other insidious traps to thwart Preston Tucker from seeing through his ambitious plans.

In a published letter appearing in the national press on June 15, 1948, Tucker wrote: "When the day comes that anyone can bend our country's laws and lawmakers to serve selfish, competitive ends, that day democratic government dies. And we're just optimistic enough to believe that once the facts are on the table, American public opinion will walk in with a big stick."

The big stick he was counting on turned out to be a broken twig. Before the dream died, only fifty-one Tucker Torpedoes rolled off the line. The plant (bounded by Cicero Avenue, 71st Street, 77th Street, and Crawford Avenue) was shut down and the structure was razed.

His life's dream shattered, Preston Tucker passed away in 1956 at age fifty-three. He is buried in Flat Rock, Michigan, with an engraving of his beloved Torpedo etched on the headstone. A beautifully crafted 1988 motion picture titled Tucker, A Man and His Dream, *starring Jeff Bridges as the inventor, preserved Tucker's name in history when it was in danger of slipping into the abyss of forgotten human failures.*

The main gate of the old Tucker plant at 7401 South Cicero is indistinguishable in the sprawl of the Ford City shopping plaza, the parking lot of a Holiday Inn motel, and the nearby Tootsie Roll factory. All of these commercial properties dotting the well-traveled Cicero Avenue (U.S. 50) trucking lanes have proved Preston Tucker to be not only a visionary but something of a prophet of his time when he predicted on September 28, 1946, "It looks as though there will be lots of life on Cicero Avenue."

South Shore

7225 Merrill Avenue (one-half block south of St. Philip Neri Church on 72nd Street)

GANGLAND AMBUSH CLAIMS A UNION LEADER'S WIFE
March 18, 1947

The housing boom in South Shore, whose natural boundaries extend from Sixtieth-seventh Street south to Seventy-ninth, and from Stony Island Avenue to the beaches of Lake Michigan, was largely the result of upward mobility among the ethnic Irish and German Jews of Washington Park in the 1920s and 1930s. The 1905 closing of the cherished Washington Park racetrack and its exclusive country club is offered as one excuse for the exodus of the wealthy elites and upper-middle-class residents into South Shore, but, in truth, the arrival of thousands of African-American families from the rural South triggered white flight and patterns of racial segregation that continued for decades. South Shore, once a Protestant enclave, absorbed a predominant Irish-Catholic and Jewish population throughout the 1920s and 1930s. Today, it is mostly African-American. One cannot help but be impressed by the magnificent apartment hotels, classically designed private homes, and the opulent South Shore Country Club (a symbol of the refinement and elegance of a lost age, but in the past very exclusionary). South Shore is where James T. Farrell settled after his family succumbed to real-estate pressure and moved out of Washington Park. The author of the Lonigan trilogy attended St. Philip Neri Church, a Tudor-Gothic-style parish constructed in 1928 at 2126 East Seventy-second Street (at Merrill). Less than a half-block south of the church on the east side of Merrill, stands the former residence of James D. Crowley, boss of the Chicago Bartenders Union, who lost his wife (and nearly his own life) in a hail of shotgun slugs. It is a lesser-known episode in the continuing saga of the Chicago underworld, but provides an abject lesson about the stupidity of labor union locals forging alliances with the mob. The home, an undistinguished two-story brown-brick structure, still stands at 7225 South Merrill.

Eyes wide in mounting horror, James Crowley shook his wife. "Betty! Betty!" he screamed. But Betty was slumped over the steering wheel, riddled with a lethal charge of shotgun pellets fired from a 12-gauge. Bits of her $3,000 silver-fox coat were showered throughout the car by the force of the blast. She did not move.

If not for blind luck, it would have been Crowley, and not his forty-four-year-old wife, Betty (the former Elizabeth Lorden), whom the ambulance driver would be carting off to the Cook County Morgue that night.

It was shortly after 2:15 in the morning when Mrs. Crowley eased the 1946 Cadillac sedan in front of the apartment house at 7225 South Merrill. They had lived here in the parish of St. Philip Neri since May 1942, and had purchased the building less than a year later to settle an estate issue.

The couple had just returned from a swanky party at the Morrison Hotel, where they had celebrated a rousing St. Patrick's Day in the company of the usual downtown revelers—cops, judges, bailiffs, and city workers, mostly of Irish descent.

There had been quite a bit of drinking going on—it wouldn't be a typical St. Patty's Day in Chicago otherwise.

Per his usual custom on festive occasions such as this, Crowley was in his cups by eight o'clock. He was a hard-drinking man and, with one DUI arrest already to his name, he suggested to Betty that it might be a good idea if she drove them back to the South Side, just to be on the safe side. Mrs. Crowley had given up imbibing intoxicating beverages in observance of Lent.

"We were unaware that any car followed us from the Loop. Had I known we were followed or in danger would I have permitted Betty to drive? As our car stopped in front there was a roar. I didn't hear another car or see anybody. I thought the sky had opened up and was raining shotgun pellets."

Crowley was the boss of Local 278 of the Bartender & Beverage Dispensers union (otherwise known as the Chicago Bartenders Union) and greatly admired for his courage and leadership in the fight against mob penetration of the union, though his dealings with Frank Nitti and other gangland minions who muscled their way in were at times suspicious. The labor racketeering squad of the Chicago PD termed Crowley "a fellow traveler" in mob circles, suave, affable— someone the boys out in Cicero thought they could always count on to play ball. Former Capone gunman Claude "Screwy" Maddox was the boss of Local 543, chartered in Cicero.

Like many other union toughs before him who forged expedient links with hoodlums only to kick the mobsters out when they were of no further use, Jim Crowley broke with Maddox and other syndicate overlords. He denounced mob rule and rode to power on the coattails of the reformers because it was in his best interests to do so.

In 1940, after five years of Louis Romano bleeding Local 278 dry, the members had finally had enough and drove him out. Romano was a Frank Nitti man, and a stone-cold killer.

Crowley, who had previously served under Romano as secretary treasurer of the Local, was elevated to the top spot under court supervision. Thereafter, he built a reputation for strong-arming the hoods by calling their bluff. Surrounded by his own goon squad, he began to feel invincible.

MR. AND MRS. CROWLEY, DEVOTED COUPLE, SHOWN AT THE RECEPTION FOLLOWING THEIR 1941 MARRIAGE. "I WISH IT WERE ME," MOANED THE HUSBAND WHEN INFORMED HIS MATE WAS DEAD. "SHE'S THE BEST FRIEND I'VE GOT. WHY, OH WHY COULDN'T IT HAVE BEEN ME?"

ELIZABETH CROWLEY WAS THE ACCIDENTAL VICTIM OF UNION POLITICS.
THE PHOTO DIAGRAM (ABOVE) OF THE 7200 BLOCK OF SOUTH
MERRILL ILLUSTRATES THE POSITIONING OF HER CAR (FACING NORTH,
TOWARD ST. PHILIP NERI CHURCH) AT THE TIME OF THE MURDER.

THE JAMES
CROWLEY
RESIDENCE ON
SOUTH MERRILL
AVENUE (CENTER
BRICK BUILDING)
AS IT LOOKS
TODAY.

That sense of invincibility was challenged in the summer of 1946. With six or eight helpers, Martin "the Ox" Ochs and Paul Labriola demanded huge advertising appropriations from South Side tavern owners for a carnival souvenir program they were plugging. This same criminal duet also demanded from Crowley that tavern keepers buy only a certain brand of pretzels and ginger ale, the kind the syndicate was distributing all over Chicago. Crowley sent word to his members to refuse to buy ads or pretzels, and challenged Ochs to do something about it. Ochs did nothing.

At stake for the Chicago mob in 1947 was control of the union. Crowley and Dennis Kelly of the Bartenders Union in Joliet were embroiled in a tough election fight to install C. T. McDonough of San Francisco as secretary treasurer of the international against Edward Miller of Kansas City. Crowley was slated for the vice-presidency of the international. The election of new officers was scheduled for mid-April.

The fight was bitter and contentious, and intra-union strife was the main reason police cited for the assassination attempt against Crowley, who staggered into his residence and managed to telephone the desk sergeant at the Grand Crossing District before passing out from loss of blood.

"Why couldn't it have been me alone?" he asked after regaining consciousness in Wesley Memorial Hospital. "Betty was my best friend."

At the southwest corner of Seventy-second Place and Merrill, police recovered five cigarette butts—telltale indicators that the killers had been lying in wait for quite some time.

It isn't often that gangland rubs out a woman, even in a moment of extreme

NOVELIST JAMES T. FARRELL LIVED ON THE SECOND FLOOR OF THIS BUILDING AT 2023 EAST 72ND STREET, A STONE'S THROW FROM THE JAMES CROWLEY MURDER SITE.

carelessness such as this one. But for the Chicago mob, now headed by the Jake Guzik–Paul "the Waiter" Ricca–Tony Accardo triumvirate, it was just another day at the office. And since they couldn't touch widower Crowley in his heavily guarded hospital room, they went after the number-two man instead.

On April 2, Dennis Kelly survived a syndicate ambush on Route 66A north of Joliet near Lockport, Illinois. A bullet perforated Kelly's lung, but he, too, managed to survive and move on with his life.

One would think that this level of intimidation would help bring out the sympathy vote among rank-and-file members. "I'm running for vice president against James P. Blakely and this shot-up arm isn't changing my mind!" Crowley vowed. But in an odd reversal of fortune for the so-called "reform" elements, the entire Crowley-McDonough slate was soundly defeated. Maybe the Chicago bartenders didn't consider them to be such great reformers after all.

On March 5, 1953, the twice-unlucky Dennis Kelly was mowed down by syndicate gunfire in Hammond, Indiana, after leaving the home of his mistress, Hazel Egdorf. He left behind a grieving wife and daughter in Joliet and a lot of unanswered questions.

Birthplace of Studs Lonigan
2023 East 72nd St.

Chicago novelist James T. Farrell (1904–1979) began writing the Studs Lonigan trilogy in 1929, while living in a second-floor flat at 2023 East Seventy-second Street, only a few blocks west of the Crowley crime scene (east of Jeffrey Boulevard). The four-story apartment house with the peaked roofs is typical of the residential architecture found in South Shore. Though James T. Farrell never drew personal satisfaction in his new surroundings (he was an exiled Washington Parker), he continued to live and work here until 1932. Farrell, a champion literary curmudgeon, made the decision to abandon Chicago for a Parisian junket before re-settling in New York City with his wife. Embittered and angry about the directions his writing career had taken him in later years, Farrell nevertheless managed to publish forty-two volumes of fiction in a busy lifetime, including the Danny O'Neill pentalogy (five volumes published between 1936 and 1953) and numerous short stories. Farrell's personal parting epitaph to the world: "There's one good kind of writer—a dead one."

SIDETRIP

South Shore & Back of the Yards

Various

South

Side

locations

A DEAD-END STREET IN AN ASPHALT JUNGLE:
THE SHADOWY LIFE OF A MURDERED BANKER
March 31, 1957

South Shore: 6760 Stony Island Avenue and 1243 East 71st Street. Back of the Yards: 2136 West 51st Street and 50th Street & South Campbell (between Artesian and Maplewood nearest the railroad embankment)

In 1950, Hollywood released the crime noir classic The Asphalt Jungle, *starring Sterling Hayden, James Whitmore, and a voluptuous ingénue named Marilyn Monroe, who was making her film debut. The contrived plot concerned a respectable businessman mixed up in the rackets. Scriptwriters, looking to draw inspiration from a real-life incident, would have found it in the secret life of South Side banker Leon Marcus, a foil for the Chicago outfit who dined at the Pump Room, lavished $10 tips on hatcheck girls (when ten bucks was a lot of money), and used the resources of his Southmoor Bank at 6760 Stony Island Avenue as a personal "cash station" for the pleasure of Illinois State Auditor Orville Hodge, a convicted embezzler who went to prison in 1956. The abduction-murder of Leon Marcus was one of the biggest crime stories of 1957. The cops had plenty to work with. There was no scarcity of motives or suspects after Leon Marcus's secret life and enemies list became a matter of public record. But as usual, pinning the crime on an actual person was beyond the ken of the homicide detectives. After nearly forty-five years, the crime is still unsolved, and the stately looking Southmoor Bank, fronted by massive Greek columns, is a boarded-up wreck at 6760 Stony Island Avenue. Such is the legacy of Leon Marcus. At 1243 East Seventy-first Street (east of Woodlawn Avenue brushing against the I.C. Railroad tracks), stands an unassuming three-story red-brick apartment house Leon used as his "love nest." Here, the sixty-one-year-old playboy entertained his common-law wife and other girlfriends while the estranged Mrs. Marcus picked up the pieces of her life down in Florida. We exit South Shore and drive north and west to the Back of the Yards neighborhood. On the sidewalk outside a frame house at 2136 West Fifty-first Street (still standing, near Hoyne), Marcus was dragged into an automobile and murdered with the crisp efficiency typical of the Chicago outfit. In the 1950s, the vinyl-sided home belonged to Marcus's closest friends and codefendants, Alfred and Joyce Rado, who ran a small construction business out of the first-floor* *storefront. This area has gradually been transformed from ethnic Polish and Lithuanian to a mostly Hispanic habitation. The final stop on the Marcus mystery tour takes us to Fiftieth Street and South Campbell Avenue, a dead-end intersection seven blocks from the Rado home. In 1957, the site was an open field (the killer pumped the fatal shot into the back of Leon's head). We easily deduced that the muddy field where Marcus was tossed out of the car was filled in with three single-family ranch houses sometime in the 1960s or later.*

D espite his money, his fine jewels, a Cadillac car, vacation homes in Lake Geneva, Wisconsin and Arizona, and other accouterments of wealth, Leon Marcus was a creature of the streets.

Those who experience poverty at so young an age are sometimes powerless to escape the hustle, even with a fortune in cash, securities, and real estate accumulated on the plus side of the ledger.

The fact that Marcus quit school in the third grade and accumulated a $3 million fortune made him no less imprudent in the company he kept or how he chose to manage his personal and professional life.

The son of a Latvian bookkeeper too poor to buy the boy eyeglasses when his sight failed, eight-year-old Leon Marcus trudged off to work as an errand boy in a clothing store to pay for his upkeep. Later, he became a partner in that same store. While in his early twenties, he branched out into the real-estate business and reaped the harvest of the 1920s bull market.

Marcus acquired the building at 6760 Stony Island Avenue and opened the Southmoor Bank in 1946. Several of his important customers were notorious South Side bookmakers and men of ill repute who skirted the fringes of the underworld.

His connection with the gambling syndicate came to light in 1950 when the Kem International Appliance Division, Inc., filed a Chapter 11 bankruptcy. The president of this concern was Lionel Ives (alias "Lionel Isaacs"), a racetrack tout and bookie who operated handbooks at several South Side addresses. Ives owed Southmoor Securities $127,162, but after the petition of bankruptcy was filed, the gambler sold his house and fled to Miami after being forewarned that syndicate hoodlums were after him.

Marcus enjoyed the company of men who lived over the top. He was a compulsive gambler who enjoyed the action that the card players and punchboard bookies provided him with. It has also been established that in later life Marcus derived his single greatest pleasure in life watching children's cartoons on the television with his grandkids perched on his knees.

By 1956, the Southmoor Bank & Trust had become a clearing-house for Illinois State Auditor Orville A. Hodge, who cashed more than $600,000 in fraudulent state warrants. Hodge, his aide Edward Epping, and Southmoor Bank official Edward A. Hintz were all convicted and sent to prison in a political scandal that scarred the administration of Governor William G. Stratton, a Lake County Republican.

During the Hodge investigation Marcus admitted that he had donated $4,600 of the bank's money to political fundraiser Charles Fleck, who was collecting money for Stratton's reelection campaign. Stratton hotly denied that Fleck was connected in any way with his campaign. The unauthorized donation was returned, but the public stink was costing the governor valuable support within his own party.

When the U.S. Senate Banking Committee convened hearings in Chicago, Stratton stormed into the chamber without invitation to remind panel members that in Illinois the state auditor is independent of the governor. Stratton saved his political hide and was reelected to a second term by 36,877 votes.

Leon Marcus was accused of misapplication of funds and falsifying bank records between 1953 and 1956. An eleven-count indictment charging Marcus, his brother Hyman, and his son-in-law Martin Rosene with conspiracy to divert $155,554 of federally insured bank deposits by false entries was filed on October 6, 1956. Marcus had repaid that entire amount only four months earlier and had sold his interests in the bank to a Detroit consortium, but the gesture was not enough to fend off government prosecutors.

Marcus was free on a $2,500 bond pending a September trial the evening of March 31, 1957, when he went to play a game of gin rummy and dine with Al and Joyce Rado, in their second-floor flat at 2136 West Fifty-first Street. Rado borrowed heavily from Marcus to finance his business. But the two men shared common interests and became friends thereafter. For the past three years, the Sunday night get-together had become a regular habit. The killers who were lying in wait knew their victim's daily routines and only had to linger there a few more hours before Marcus exited the building.

At nine-thirty in the evening Marcus said good night to his hosts and turned east. Rado described the chain of events to police and what happened next. "I had taken him down to the door and watched him start toward his car. Another car was double-parked. Two men left it and started struggling with Marcus." Rado dashed upstairs to call the police, hearing Marcus's plaintive cry for help.

"I'll give you anything! Don't do anything to me!"

The car sped away from the Rado home with Marcus jammed into the back seat. The abductors proceeded to an empty field at Fiftieth and Campbell. One

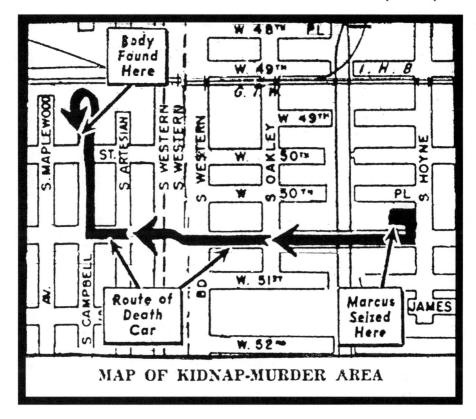

MAP OF KIDNAP-MURDER AREA

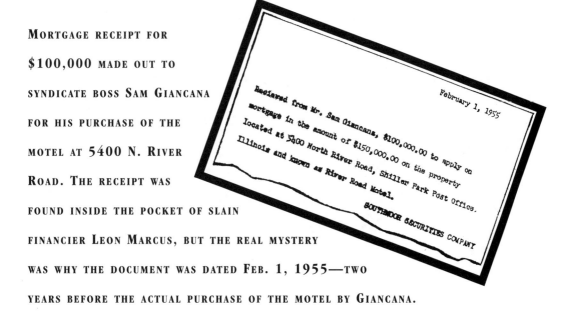

Recieved from Mr. Sam Giancana, $100,000.00 to apply on mortgage in the amount of $150,000.00 on the property located at 5400 North River Road, Shiller Park Post Office. Illinois and known as River Road Motel.

February 1, 1955

SOUTHMOOR SECURITIES COMPANY

MORTGAGE RECEIPT FOR $100,000 MADE OUT TO SYNDICATE BOSS SAM GIANCANA FOR HIS PURCHASE OF THE MOTEL AT 5400 N. RIVER ROAD. THE RECEIPT WAS FOUND INSIDE THE POCKET OF SLAIN FINANCIER LEON MARCUS, BUT THE REAL MYSTERY WAS WHY THE DOCUMENT WAS DATED FEB. 1, 1955—TWO YEARS BEFORE THE ACTUAL PURCHASE OF THE MOTEL BY GIANCANA.

BOARDED-UP SOUTHMOOR BANK, 6760 STONY ISLAND AVENUE (ABOVE). MOB
BANKER LEON MARCUS WAS KILLED ON THE SIDEWALK OUTSIDE THIS TWO-FLAT AT
2136 WEST 51ST STREET (BELOW).

local resident told police that he heard a shot, saw Marcus prostrate on the ground, and watched as a black Ford drove off at a rapid clip. Lieutenant James McMahon, chief of the Homicide Bureau, thought the whole thing was mighty queer.

"Both the fact that Marcus was killed with one shot and the fact his body was dumped in a dead-end street lead us to doubt the gang theory." McMahon believed it was a ransom kidnapping gone bad. "He knew gangsters and they knew him. If they were looking for a kidnap victim, this Latvian immigrant seemed a natural."

As investigators unraveled the tangled affairs of the slain banker, new facts came to light canceling out the abduction theory.

Found among Marcus's personal effects was a carbon copy of a receipt he had given to syndicate boss Sam "Momo" Giancana for the sum of $100,000. The money was to be applied to a mortgage held by Southmoor Securities (another Marcus holding) on the River Road Motel at 5400 North River Road, operated by Chuck Giancana in suburban Schiller Park. (*Author's Note:* The name of the motel was subsequently changed to the Thunderbolt Motel, then the Caraville.)

Giancana paid Marcus the $100,000 on March 28, just three days before the banker was targeted. The boss of the Chicago mob was in Havana, Cuba, on a gambling junket when Leon Marcus was slain.

Probing deep into his secret life, reporters from the *Chicago American* exposed Marcus as a two-timing Romeo whose common-law wife divided her time between the Hotel Luzern resort in Lake Geneva, Wisconsin; a ranch house in Phoenix, Arizona; and an elegantly furnished second-floor apartment at 1243 East Seventy-first Street in South Shore. This was Leon's "love nest," a secluded trysting spot with closets of mink stoles and full-length fur coats.

Blond-haired Ruth Weidner, the mystery woman in this South Side soap opera, was a former "26 dice girl" in a downtown cocktail lounge. She enticed Marcus while working as a waitress at Martin's Restaurant on Seventy-first and Jeffrey. The owner of the establishment, Al Martin, was another in a long line of Marcus acquaintances suspected of having close dealings with organized crime.

Leon and Ruth were often spotted sipping cocktails in a cozy little booth at the fabulous Pump Room of the Ambassador East Hotel on the Gold Coast. During a private tête-à-tête in the city, Marcus formally introduced the woman to business acquaintances as "Miss Worden." At other times, he kept Ruthie in the lap of luxury inside his Lake Geneva resort hotel, or the ranch house he built out in the desert. At the rear of the Phoenix residence, a parking space was reserved for "Mrs. Marcus."

She called Leon Marcus "Papa," and encouraged her adopted son Lee to do the same. Investigators wondered who the boy's natural father was.

Ruth entertained lavishly at the Seventy-first Street flat, a fact easily verified by another woman who was keeping steady company with Edward Glatt Sr., owner of the Morrison Hotel. She vividly recalled vacations to Lake Geneva, trips to the racetrack, and the dinner parties Ruth Weidner hosted for other elderly gents and their perky, doe-eyed "common-law wives."

"We've dined together in what is now called Leon's love nest where Ruthie was a wonderful hostess for Leon's guests," gushed the dark-haired beauty to reporters. "I'm happily married now. My husband, who was a car salesman, knows my past and says it makes no difference to him." When Glatt expired in 1955, the common-law wife won a $76,000 settlement after suing the family.

Weidner's affair with Marcus had been going strong for nearly twenty years, according to her own published statements. Ruthie was only forty-two years old when Marcus was murdered on the prairie. Leon was sixty-one.

Frances Marcus, the estranged wife and mother of Leon's grown daughters, returned to Chicago to attend funeral services and offer comfort to the five grandchildren. She remained in seclusion throughout the ordeal at her daughter's home at 7316 South Clyde Avenue. When the casket was placed in its cement vault in the "Eternal Life" section of Oakwoods Cemetery, the real Mrs. Marcus sobbed uncontrollably and threw herself upon it. "My Leon! My Leon!" she wailed.

Ruth Weidner was sequestered in Arizona throughout the ordeal, but retained the services of a downtown attorney after receiving news that Leon's will was filed in probate court. "Some people may call me a gold digger," she sighed. "But that is not true. The only thing I want is security for our son. Leon loved him dearly and I refuse to believe that he did not provide for him."

The Marcus heirs braced for a contentious "test of wills," literally and figuratively.

The probe into the dead man's financial improprieties continued. "The fact that such a man could become a banker and operate successfully in the field for some years seems to us to indicate that the moral standards required of bankers, both by bankers in general and by the State of Illinois have sunk dangerously low," editorialized the *Chicago American* on April 2, the day of the funeral.

As messy sex scandals go, this one was pretty raw given the turgid moral climate of the Eisenhower years. The afternoon newspapers had a field day baring secrets of the "love nest," but they could go no further in naming a suspect in the murder. With Sam Giancana mentioned so prominently, and the matter of the $100,000 of his money gathering interest in the Southmoor Bank, people drew their own inferences.

By the time the Orville Hodge investigation was consigned to history, the Southmoor Bank & Trust Company was reorganized and the name changed to the Guaranty Bank & Trust Company. In the 1960s it fell under the control of New York financier Victor Muscat, and Roy M. Cohn, former chief counsel for Senator Joseph McCarthy during the 1954 Army-McCarthy hearings. Cohn was every inch as unscrupulous as Marcus was indiscreet.

During a 1967 investigation of some $200,000 in unsecured loans made during the tenure of Muskat and Cohn, it was discovered that the $100,000 deposited in the bank by Marcus on March 28, 1957, went unclaimed.

Neither the executors of the Leon Marcus estate nor Sam Giancana attempted to recover the funds in the ensuing years. It is likely the one hundred grand in mob money ended up in the account of the State of Illinois (pursuant to the Unclaimed Property Act), because the old Southmoor Bank building stands empty and abandoned—the bitter epitaph to Leon's folly.

South Shore–Jackson Park Highlands Area

6834

South

Constance

"I MUST HAVE HAD SAND IN MY GEAR BOX": THE SUICIDE OF JOHN WAYMAN
April 17, 1913

Jackson Park Highlands is a corner of South Shore bordering Sixty-seventh Street that is unfamiliar to many North Siders and suburbanites. In some respects it is not unlike the Sauganash area, tucked into the remote northwest quarter of the city and brushing up against the suburbs. The professional elite of the city's commercial, cultural, and political life have, over the years, tended to live in both places. The Reverend Jesse Jackson and other notables settled into the Jackson Park Highlands. Some, like the good reverend, are remembered for the deeds they do, others are forgotten by history. John Wayman served as Cook County state's attorney from 1908 to 1912. He was a pragmatic and levelheaded politician who was unafraid of the political consequences of his actions. In his stormy term of office, Wayman attacked criminal wrongdoing head-on, even when it compromised his career and embarrassed his party. Honesty was his strong suit (ambition his downfall), but in the end it didn't get him to where he wanted to be. He lived and died in a spacious Prairie-style brick home on a residential side street (at 6834 South Constance) located in the Highlands.

In 1912, at the conclusion of his successful four-year run as state's attorney, no less of an authority on manliness than First Ward Alderman "Bathhouse" John Coughlin nominated John E. W. Wayman as the "handsomest man in Chicago." It was the sincerest flattery the Republican state's attorney could expect to garner from the irredeemably corrupt Democratic boss of the Levee District, whose empire of vice and liquor was nearly toppled by Wayman in October 1912.

SUICIDES OFTEN OCCUR IN AN UPSTAIRS BEDROOM. FORMER STATE'S ATTORNEY JOHN E. WAYMAN TOOK HIS LIFE BY ACCI-DENT OR DESIGN ON THE SECOND FLOOR OF THIS FINE OLD HOUSE IN SOUTH SIDE JACKSON HIGHLANDS.

(Photo by Lawrence Raeder)

John Wayman was something of a paradox in the eddy of Chicago politics in the Progressive Era, for Chicago was anything *but* progressive either in thought or deed during those roughhousing times.

Born in West Virginia, Wayman was a Greek scholar, and an educated open-minded realist who broke with the conservative wing of his party to campaign against Sunday closing laws and bluenose attitudes. In the 1908 election, he eked out a narrow victory over the incumbent State's Attorney John Healy after two grinding recounts. Healy was supported by the Woman's Christian Temperance Union (WCTU) and the Anti-Saloon League.

Wayman's strongest endorsement came from the German societies and city liberals who otherwise voted Democratic if not for their more pressing demand to keep the corner taverns open on Sunday.

Wayman interpreted his narrow victory as a mandate from the people, but in truth his noble intention and aggressive prosecutorial stance against some of the factions that helped elect him made him an anomaly in Chicago, where alliances are the only things that really count.

With noble bearing, he ruffled the feathers of his party masters by attacking the Fire Department cadre for graft and influence peddling in connection with kickbacks received from James P. Connery of the City Fuel Company.

At the center of this controversy stood Fred Busse (aka "Fat Freddie"), Chicago's first mayor of German extraction who squeezed into office in 1907. (*Author's Note:* Busse was warmly supported by both the *Chicago Tribune* and underworld characters like Christian "Barney" Bertsche. In this respect he seemed to be the perfect coalition builder.)

Busse had a stake in the coal company doing business with the Fire Department and other municipal agencies. He was perturbed by the cheeky attitude of the upstart state's attorney who set his sights on some very influential political personages.

Wayman's ill-advised decision to prosecute the slippery Edward McCann, a powerful West Side police captain who controlled the gambling privilege and collected payoffs from brothel keepers in the district surrounding Hull House, cost him valuable political support from the old guard of the Republican Party. (*Author's Note:* See my first volume for a discussion of the McCann case.)

He was indifferent to the powerful party boss, Congressman William Lorimer, who was expelled from his Senate seat in July 1912 for accepting bribes. And he prosecuted labor racketeer Maurice "Mossie" Enright for the murder of Vincent Altman in 1911. This cost him the support of labor.

By far his most controversial stance was to close the Levee in October 1912, after bowing to pressure from anti-liquor societies and church groups. Wayman was a pragmatist who subscribed to the belief that it is impossible to legislate morality, no matter how lofty the intent. Civic pressure was brought to bear. But Wayman kept resisting the impulse to close the Twenty-second Street dives until just before his term was scheduled to expire.

Then, armed with a box load of warrants, he sent in shock troops of police, telling them to close every house of ill-repute. He ordered the vice courts to remain open all night to handle the crush of prisoners rounded up in a series of spectacular raids into the South Side badlands. The Wayman raids climaxed the era of segregated vice districts in Chicago.

When it was all said and done, and the last clip joint, panel house, and dope den in Bathhouse John's bailiwick was padlocked, Wayman challenged his successor, the Democrat MacLay Hoyne, to keep them closed. In his campaign rhetoric, Hoyne had badgered Wayman to "do something before it was too late" about Chicago's intolerable vice conditions, but when it came time to enforce the closings on his own watch, Hoyne failed miserably and the Levee lived on for a few more years.

By now Wayman was embroiled in a bitter gubernatorial primary fight against four other candidates. His ambition for higher office got the best of him in a year when he stood little chance of winning. In the 1912 election, Wayman campaigned feverishly against the Lorimerites and Len Small, the scalawag farmer from Kankakee and one of the Republican Party's most disgraceful aspirants for high office. The crushing weight of the campaign sapped all of Wayman's energy. Though he was still a young man very much in the prime of life, he was also of nervous disposition and teetering on the verge of collapse. Ambition and the rigors of stump speaking had gotten the best of him.

Failing to muster support because he had managed to offend so many special-interest factions on both the conservative and liberal wing of the party, Wayman lost badly. Washed up politically, he returned to South Shore to launch a private law practice with Thomas Marshall, his former chief assistant state's attorney.

Unable to think clearly, Wayman suffered what friends and acquaintances termed a nervous breakdown. Only a couple of days earlier he had been diagnosed with a case of acute appendicitis. The doctors were on their way to his home to consult with him about the upcoming operation the afternoon of April 17, 1913, when a tragic accident occurred inside the house.

Mrs. Wayman and the three small children were in the first-floor living room when they heard two shots ring out from upstairs. The maids hustled the youngsters out onto the sidewalk. The wife raced upstairs and found her husband lying in the closet, a pistol at his side. The gun was on loan to Wayman from Charles Lund, a building contractor who had shot another man over labor trouble.

Wayman had taken it home to examine after Lund paid a retainer to engage him as private counsel in his upcoming legal battle.

Two steel-jacketed bullets pierced Wayman's thorax. "I don't know why I did it. I am very sorry," he gasped. "I guess I have sand in my gearbox." He joked and kidded with the attending physicians, but his complexion grew ever more pale. He was falling away.

Wayman clung to life until just past 10:00 P.M. Was it an accident or a suicide? That was the troubling question. The press had a hard time accepting the truth that such a forceful man so young and vigorous, could be emotionally troubled.

The next day, a gathering of two thousand people stood hushed and bowed outside the family home on Constance. The massed body of men and women followed the solemn procession from the Wayman residence, where the wake was held, to the funeral train conveying the casket to Mt. Greenwood Cemetery. Setting aside past differences, ex-mayor Fred Busse agreed to serve as an honorary pallbearer. The other Republican powerbrokers chose to stay away.

In death Wayman had many friends, but none of them in high places.

THE CASE OF THE CASTRATED PROFESSOR: A WACKY LOVE TRIANGLE
July 31, 1935

7124 Stony Island Avenue (71st Place & Stony Island Avenue)

The South Shore Line splices through the commercial heart of the business community along Seventy-first Street. It is generally regarded as the last electric interurban railway in America, with regularly scheduled service to Hammond, Gary, Michigan City, and South Bend. In the heyday of commuter rail travel, the South Shore line ran sixty-four trains a day along this busy corridor. Today there are not nearly as many, but the trains that pass through here each day, en route to the steel mills and Indiana cornfields, preserve the past and serve to remind us of a time when a more leisurely mode of city travel was still possible. In the 1930s, a gas station stood on the west side of Stony Island at Seventy-first Place, a block south of Seventy-first Street and the tracks of the South Shore railroad. Dr. Walter Bauer, professor of chemistry at the Kirksville Missouri College of Osteopathy and Surgery, was left for dead in the parking lot of this gas station by a berserk vengeance killer named Mandeville Zenge, who performed a slice-and-dice operation of his own inside a parked car. The Anderson Brothers filling station disappeared. Its proximate location is the parking lot of the busy Moo & Oink store—where sides of beef, ham bones, and spareribs are sliced up as routinely these days as the private parts of Mandeville Zenge's unfortunate victim.

A Missouri farmer, gnarled, weather-beaten, and as tough as an ox, strode into the Criminal Court Building to greet his son, held over to the grand jury on a charge of castrating and murdering the college professor who had stolen the affections of his sweetheart.

"It's a shame they suspect him of such a crime," sighed J. Andy Zenge. "Look at him! He needs a shave and he looks tired. Why, he never missed a day without shaving. He's a clean-cut, upright, and manly young man. My boy is innocent. I'll spare no expense to prove it!"

The elder Zenge was belligerent in the defense of his twenty-seven-year-old son, Mandeville, who maintained a stoic demeanor, even as he was forced to confront his childhood sweetheart, now the widow of the man he had savagely mutilated.

Mandeville seriously courted Louise Schaeffer, employed as a head nurse at Laughlin Hospital in Kirksville, Missouri, for seven years. The tall, dark-haired, and well-spoken young carpenter from Canton was to have married Louise on July 11, 1935. Three days later, Louise unexpectedly changed her mind and was betrothed to Dr. Walter J. Bauer in a quiet ceremony at her home. Mandeville, who had loved the young woman since the first stirring of adolescent passions, was devastated by the news.

Bauer was a professor of chemistry who was taking summer classes in osteopathic medicine at the University of Michigan in Ann Arbor. Three hours after the wedding ceremony was concluded, the professor left his bride on the doorstep of her Missouri home and returned to Ann Arbor to complete his semester's work. Louise had her trousseau packed in anticipation of a promised honeymoon, scheduled to begin on August 16 when the summer session ended.

Zenge brooded over the collective miseries and injustices of his life. The day before her marriage to Bauer, the heartsick young man had pooled his life savings and paid a Quincy, Illinois, jeweler the final balance on an engagement and wedding ring for Louise. In a last desperate attempt to change her mind, he appeared at her doorstep displaying the rings and threatening to kill himself if she did not change her mind.

"I have loved Dr. Bauer for more than a year, though neither of us had spoken of our feelings until a few months ago," she said in a cool, dispassionate tone. "I saw him daily at his wonderful research work for nearly four years. First I admired him. Then I knew I loved him."

Zenge accepted the news with quiet dejection, but was inwardly tormented and becoming increasingly desperate. He departed for Ann Arbor with a stopover in Chicago on July 26. He told his father he was going to the home office of his employer. Zenge worked for the general contracting firm of S. A. Healy, headquartered in Chicago, but his job was the farthest thing from his mind now.

Zenge appeared in Ann Arbor a few days later, registering under the name T. S. Jones at the Jennings House hotel where Bauer also happened to be staying.

A thought must have crossed the professor's mind that he was being set up to take the fall in a marriage swindle hatched by a pair of ingenious con artists. It appeared that way to police after they learned that Bauer had unexpectedly telephoned the merchants of Kirksville to cut off his wife's line of credit, this coming after only three days of marriage.

Dr. Bauer knew all about Zenge's fits of jealousy from Louise and was naturally concerned, but he had never actually laid eyes on his wife's former suitor until he was cornered outside the hotel by a stranger on the sidewalk of downtown Ann Arbor. Parked nearby was a green 1935 Chevrolet sedan. The car belonged to Zenge's father back in Missouri.

Zenge pointed a gun at Bauer, who stood motionless on the sidewalk. "Get in, we're going for a ride."

"What is this all about?" stammered the professor.

"You'd better do what I tell you because I am desperate. I am wanted all over the country and if I'm caught, it's the hot seat for me." Zenge ordered Bauer to keep driving, but was careful not to reveal his identity or the reason for the abduction.

Menaced by the gun pointed at his ribs, Bauer was forced to drive all night across lonely Michigan and Indiana back roads in the general direction of Chicago. On the way they stopped twice for gasoline and several times for sandwiches. They reached the vicinity of Oakwoods Cemetery on the South Side of Chicago at around one-thirty in the morning.

Bauer was ordered to drive down a deserted street brushing up against the stone walls of the cemetery and park the car. It was at that moment when the man beside him bound his wrists and ankles with a belt and some oily rags stashed in the car. Trussed up and helpless, Bauer watched in horror as Zenge drew out a pen knife and performed the emasculation on his love rival.

Bauer passed out from shock. In his sworn statement to police, Zenge said that he had not actually intended to kill Bauer, and fully expected him to recover. He said he just wanted to scare him.

At 2:10 in the morning, the Chevrolet rolled into the Anderson gas station at Seventy-first Place and Stony Island. Zenge bolted from the car and fled the scene, leaving his bloody, castrated victim behind. In his weakened state Bauer told the attendant Harold Anderson to summon a doctor. "You don't need a doctor, pal," Anderson said in a horrified tone of voice as he observed the blood in the car. "What you need is the hospital."

Rushed to the Jackson Park Hospital, Bauer issued a statement to Chicago Police Detectives Howard Doyle and Frank Murphy. "Before God I've never harmed anyone and I don't see why anyone should hurt me. My wife had been courted by a man for years before our marriage. I wouldn't know him if I saw him." At 6:20 the following morning Bauer died from shock and loss of blood.

A trace was done on the license plate number of the death car and J. Andy Zenge's name popped up.

Eyewitnesses said a cabdriver picked Zenge up at a hot dog stand at Sixty-seventh Street and South Shore Drive. It was revealed that the cabby drove him to Thirty-first and Indiana Avenue. There, Zenge flagged down a second taxi driven by William Leinnert, a talkative Chicago hack who made a few dollars on the side "recommending" strip clubs to single men. "How about letting me take you to this place I know called 'A Night in Paris'?

Leinnert received a cash tip for every john he delivered to the front door. It was an ancient custom in Chicago known as the "taxicab dancehall racket." Zenge kicked about the price, but eventually agreed. He was free of all concerns now.

During the course of their early morning sojourn to the strip club, Leinnert and Zenge became chums, and it wasn't long before he was providing his passenger with addresses of flophouses to hide out. Zenge confessed to the cabby what he had done, but he said that he expected Bauer would come out of it all right once the doctors got him on the table and sewed him up.

The press got a hold of the story the next day. Louise Schaeffer Bauer was hustled to Chicago for the inquest into her husband's death, and was asked to help police shed some light on the man they were seeking for murder. She supplied them with a photograph, details of her engagement to Mandeville Zenge, and her decision to split apart and marry Dr. Bauer.

"Every girl will understand. Those early loves often dim as we mature."

Meanwhile, Zenge was picked up at Rush Street and Ohio on the Near North Side and driven out to the edge of Navy Pier by Yellow Cab driver John Giannini. He left behind his bloodstained gray coat and a suicide note addressed to dad in the back seat of the cab.

Zenge handed over a one-dollar bill and told the driver to keep the motor running. When his passenger did not come back, the cabby shrugged and returned to his garage, with the incriminating gray coat and the little red book. By faking a suicide plunge, Mandeville hoped to convince the cops that the cold waters of Lake Michigan washed him away with the tide.

Louise Schaeffer Bauer broke under the terrible strain. In a frenzy of grief, she tried to pitch herself out of the twelfth floor of the Morrison Hotel. The Kirksville, Missouri, chief of police, who had escorted the woman to Chicago, pulled her back. Her jangled nerves were calmed after finding out from the police that Mandeville's suicide was ruled a hoax and that she did not have the blood of *two* men on her hands.

Acting on an informant's tip, Zenge was arrested inside a Chicago flophouse.

Confronting her former suitor hours later, the dry-eyed widow provided positive corroboration. "I know him so well," Louise lamented. "It's hard for me to believe he could do such a thing like that." It was painfully evident to Chicago Police Captain John Stege that Bauer's widow harbored deep and abiding feelings for her husband's slayer. Even at that sad moment in their lives, they remained devoted to each other in a spiritual sense.

Friends and family escorted Louise to Cleveland, Ohio, where Dr. Bauer was to be interred. Sobbing and in a state of near collapse, she tried to leap into the open grave as the casket was lowered. The mother-in-law she had never met pulled Louise back before she could hurt herself. Such were the raw and brutal emotions Zenge's knife-wielding act inspired.

The trial of Mandeville Zenge was convened in October 1935, before Acting Chief Justice of the Criminal Court Cornelius J. Harrington. (*Author's Note:* This was the same judge who decided the fate of "torso murderers" Blanche Dunkle and Evelyn Smith. At age thirty-seven, Harrington was the youngest jurist to serve on the circuit court bench.)

Cabby William Leinnert was the prosecution's star witness. Pointing a stubby finger at the defendant, Leinnert left no room for doubt. "Sure I sees him here. That's the guy there!"

Expert medical testimony provided by three doctors from Jackson Park Hospital established that the castration had occurred in Chicago, and not in Indiana as defense attorneys contended. The defense team's argument was mystifying to observers. Attorney Joseph Green denied that Zenge was responsible for this horrible act, but if it *had* occurred (he conceded as much), it must have been done in another state, and that his client was probably crazy anyway to want to do such a thing.

At one point, Green raised the possibility that Bauer and Zenge knew each other, and that Bauer had willingly consented to return to Kirksville where, presumably, Louise would choose between the two of them.

Judge Harrington and the twelve venire men had a hard time believing this tale, or understanding Green's circular logic, but with Leinnert and other eyewitnesses in general agreement, there was little room for doubt.

On October 18, 1935, after more than four hours of deliberation, Zenge was found guilty and sentenced to life in prison. While the foreman read the verdict, the convicted man remained upbeat and cheerful among reporters and a courtroom packed with swooning female spectators. They were charmed by the farm boy's dashing movie-star good looks, and very intrigued by his weird and fantastic tale of jealousy, passion, and murder that had left them spellbound all that summer.

"What will you do now, missus?" a reporter asked the widow.

Louise Schaeffer Bauer sighed. "I am going back to Kirksville to seek the position as chief night nurse at the Laughlin Hospital that I resigned. There is only one thing left for me to do in life—to devote myself to bringing comfort and ease to the sufferers—to those who are fighting against the misery of disease."

Mandeville Zenge was admitted to the state prison at Joliet on November 13, 1935. He served twenty-three years of his life sentence before being paroled to J. Andy Zenge, his devoted father who waited for him all those years, on December 12, 1958.

We can only guess at the thoughts that were racing through Louise Schaeffer Bauer's head at that moment.

"THEY DON'T CALL THAT GUY BUGS FOR NUTHIN'!" THE SHOOTING OF JOHNNY TORRIO

January 24, 1925

7011 South Clyde Avenue (between 70th and 71st Streets)

The tracks of the South Shore line lie only a half-block south of the former residence of Johnny Torrio, a tidy red-brick apartment house at 7011 South Clyde (south of Seventieth Street just before Seventy-first). In the hierarchical structure of the Chicago mob, Torrio was the second "boss," bridging the era of the "Mustache Petes" and Al Capone. Bred in poverty in the Cherry Hill section of New York City, Torrio was brought to Chicago from New York c. 1912–13 by his uncle "Big Jim" Colosimo, restaurateur, Levee brothel keeper, and titular head of the streetsweepers union. It was his task to protect Colosimo's interests from Black Hand extortionists.

Torrio came to the Windy City well armed. He was a hoodlum at an early age, running errands for Paul Kelly, boss of the Five Points gang, before moving uptown. He completed his criminal apprenticeship by participating in the murder-for-hire scheme to knock off New York gambler Herman "Beansie" Rosenthal in Times Square. The 1912 Rosenthal hit by "Gyp the Blood" Horowitz, "Lefty Louie," Torrio, and others was a watershed event in the New York underworld and front-page crime news in Chicago. It helped send a corrupt New York police lieutenant named Charles Becker to the electric chair three years later and was a compelling reason for Torrio to get away from the footlights of Broadway and lay low for a while.

George "Bugs" Moran and Earl "Hymie" Weiss were looking forward to the day when they could file past the cold, dead body of Johnny Torrio lying in state at Sbarbaro's funeral parlor.

The North Side gangsters were at war with the Torrio-Capone mob on the South Side, and they held Torrio personally responsible for the murder of their leader, Dion O'Banion, inside his flower shop in November 1924. They remembered the smirk on Torrio's face as he paid last respects to the stiff corpse of Deanie lying in state inside his silver-bronze casket. Revenge was uppermost in their minds every time they thought of Johnny Torrio daring to show up at the boss's wake and being so arrogant.

Not long after the funeral, the South Side gang leader and his Irish-American wife of twelve years, Anna McCarthy-Torrio, left Chicago for an extended vacation through Hot Springs, Arkansas, where they relaxed in the therapeutic waters. Then it was on to St. Petersburg, Florida, to soak up the winter sun before continuing to Havana, Cuba, for roulette. It was a grand and glorious tour, but with every roll of the dice or spin of the wheel an O'Banion associate was lurking in the shadows, waiting for the opportune moment to avenge Deanie. Somehow, the moment never seemed right, or maybe they never got close enough for a clear shot.

Unscathed, Torrio returned home to his Clyde Avenue apartment house in exclusive South Shore the first week of January 1925. Anna joined him in Chicago a few days later.

At age forty-three, Johnny Torrio was an elder statesman of organized crime. He had been knocking around Chicago for more than a decade, and had witnessed the evolution and expansion of the business from the Twenty-second Street red-light district where every form of vice was concentrated in one geographic zone, to the proliferation of prostitution, gambling, and bootlegging in far-reaching Cook County.

JOHNNY TORRIO ESCAPED

CHICAGO WITH HIS LIFE

AFTER BEING RIDDLED

WITH BULLETS OUTSIDE

THE VESTIBULE OF HIS

APARTMENT BUILDING AT

7011 S. CLYDE AVENUE.

Gentleman Johnny Torrio personally oversaw the gang's foray into Cicero, Stickney, Burnham, Chicago Heights, and Calumet City. Such moves were opposed by his uncle, Big Jim Colosimo, a cautious and conservative man who lacked the vision and foresight to realize that modern conveyances could transport the cash-paying clientele to suburbia where police interference was minimal.

But lately, it had become a young man's game, and Torrio wasn't up to mediating the endless territorial disputes arising from one faction's desire to control city and county bootlegging against another. The ambitious young gunmen he had to deal with on both sides of town were in their early twenties. They were quick with the trigger, unwilling to respect territorial sovereignty, and full of testosterone. It was a crazy world ruled by punks. Johnny Torrio had had about enough of the duplicity and betrayals.

Though gangland rivals perceived that Torrio was slipping, they also understood that until changes were made at the top of the pyramid, his word was absolute. If they had any hope at all of destroying the South Side gang, it had to begin with a calculated move against Torrio, and not Al Capone, who functioned as the number two man within the organization.

Al Capone had warned Torrio about the dangers of traveling around the city without protection. Less than two weeks earlier, on January 11, the crazy North Siders tried and failed to kill Capone.

A peaceable man since his early days in New York, Johnny Torrio never even bothered to carry a gun. The Moran-Weiss mob knew this and laid a trap.

It happened on a cold, clear Saturday afternoon in January 1925. Chauffeur Robert Barton (the brother of Capone's driver Sylvester Barton) drove the Torrios home from a downtown business meeting with former First Ward alderman Michael "Hinky Dink" Kenna and a busy afternoon of shopping. The rear compartment of the Lincoln was loaded with parcels. Anna chattered happily, while Torrio, unconcerned with the state of the world, gazed sullenly out the window.

The car was on loan to Torrio from Jake Guzik, brothel master and bookkeeper for the South Side mob. Guzik had been eternally devoted to Torrio ever since he had interceded with Illinois Governor Len Small to secure a parole for his brother Harry, who was convicted of criminal pandering. The use of the car was a gesture of his esteem.

At 4:30 P.M., the limousine drew to the curb outside the Clyde Avenue apartments. Anna Torrio climbed out of the back seat and walked toward the vestibule of the apartment building with the small packages tucked under her arm. Her husband lingered near the automobile, exchanging a few words with Barton while removing the heavier parcels from the car and placing them on the running board.

That's when Torrio spied two men running toward the front of the car at a fast clip from a Cadillac parked across the street at Seventieth Street and Clyde Avenue. One of them carried a pistol, the other a shotgun. Knowing at that moment he was marked for death, Torrio turned toward the entrance of his building, and safety. Shotgun pellets riddled the coachwork of the Lincoln, clipping Barton in the knee. The frightened chauffeur tore off down the street.

Caught in the middle of triangulated fire with packages in each arm, Torrio was unable to maneuver. He was shot in the arm with a .45-caliber bullet. Another slug tore into his jaw. The bullet came within one-fourteenth of an inch of severing the jugular vein. Two more shots struck him in the chest and a fourth blast tore open his abdomen.

The man with the pistol, believed to be George "Bugs" Moran, prepared to administer the *coup de grâce*, but was out of ammunition. He paused to reload, but the driver of the car warned them that there was no time left. Torrio was a lucky man. He must have been answering to a higher authority that day.

The three men sped rapidly away on Seventieth Street toward Stony Island where they turned north to Sixty-seventh Street. Laundry driver Walter Hildebrandt followed the escaping car, but lost them in the traffic congestion.

Hearing the shots, Anna Torrio rushed back outside and dragged her husband into the vestibule. A motorcycle policeman flagged down a passing cab. Torrio, drifting in and out of consciousness and rapidly losing blood, was taken to Jackson Park Hospital where Al Capone, assisted by Frank Ragen, the president of the institution, personally took charge of security arrangements.

Ragen was yet another in a long line of gangster politicians who crawled out of the sewers to make a name for himself in the straight world. Cofounder and organizer of the South Side Ragen's Colts street gang during the horse-and-buggy era, Frank Ragen rose from the status of saloon bouncer and newspaper slugger to an elected position on the Cook County Board of Commissioners, before receiving appointment to head a major Chicago hospital.

Comforted by Ragen, "Scarface" Capone could barely contain his sorrow as he gazed in horror at the bloody mess. "The gang did it! The gang did it!" he kept repeating. Moments later, Assistant State's Attorney John Sbarbaro (who, in his alter ego as mob mortician, owned a funeral parlor on Wells Street catering to the families of fallen gangsters) appeared at the hospital to question Torrio. His visit was more of a "courtesy call" than anything else. Capone slipped a comforting arm around his shoulder, whispering: "I'll tell you more when he gets better!"

Neither Anna Torrio nor her husband revealed the identity of the shooters. "I know who they are. It's my business, and I won't tell," Johnny told Sbarbaro.

The wife was even more candid. "I think I saw the persons who shot my husband. I'll talk to the right parties at the right time about that."

Deputy Superintendent Matthew Zimmer demanded to know just what she meant by that confounding remark. Mrs. Torrio smiled prettily and said nothing more. Meanwhile, Al Capone's request for round-the-clock armed protection was granted. Twenty-four uniformed Chicago police officers were posted to guard duty inside the hospital.

If gangland wasn't talking, a brave young lad who lived down the street from the Torrios picked "Bugs" Moran out of a police lineup and positively identified him as one of the two shooters. "Are you sure, son?" demanded Chief of Detectives William Schoemaker.

Standing off to the side, were the Guziks, Anna Torrio, and Al Capone. The formidable array of gangsters failed to intimidate seventeen-year-old Peter Veesaert, who never once faltered. "The fifth one from the east end," he repeated. When asked about this, Anna Torrio shook her head. "No, that's not the man I saw." She had a poker player's expression on her face, knowing that gangland justice would catch up with them all, in due course.

"Yer' nuts!" snarled Moran to the boy. The North Side racketeer was arrested in his home at 5128 Wolfram Street earlier in the day while in the middle of dinner with his wife and son.

It came as no surprise that the case against "Bugs" Moran collapsed when Torrio refused to press charges. Before it was over, Hymie Weiss and Vincent "Schemer" Drucci, leaders of the North Side mob, were paraded before Mrs. Torrio. But with a shrug of the shoulders she said that she had never laid eyes on either of these men. Within two years both Drucci and Weiss would be dead.

Torrio wavered between life and death for the next few days. Through the care of his personal physician, Dr. David V. Omens, the gravely wounded gang boss mounted a comeback. (*Author's Note:* The doctor told police he only worked on patients with "skin disease." Omens practiced at 1225 Independence Boulevard. He got into trouble later in the year for treating the gunshot wounds of Martin J. Durkin, master auto thief and fugitive murderer of a federal officer.)

Torrio fully recovered from his wounds and served out a nine-month sentence in the Lake County Jail for liquor-running violations in connection with his operation of the Sieben Brewery on Larrabee Street. Afterward, he left the Chicago business to his trusted associate Capone and fled to Italy with his personal fortune in tow.

Johnny Torrio and his wife leased an apartment in Naples, the city of his birth. Leading the life of a country squire had a soothing effect on his health and well-being until Benito Mussolini's fierce anti-Mafia crackdowns forced them to return to America in 1928. This time, Torrio permanently settled in New York, where he acted as consigliere to Charles "Lucky" Luciano, Meyer Lansky, Joe Adonis, and Frank Costello.

One by one, his old gangster pals died off or were driven into exile. Torrio avoided this fate and lived out the remainder of his days with Anna at 9902 Third Avenue in Brooklyn. He kept his name out of the newspapers and built on his existing fortune through shrewd real-estate investments.

On April 16, 1957, while seated in his favorite barber chair, Torrio slumped over—the victim of a fatal heart attack. He was rushed to Cumberland Hospital where he died at age seventy-five, unnoticed and minus all the Chicago-style fanfare.

Even in death, Anna continue to shield her husband from the prying eyes of the press. Torrio's passing was not disclosed to the outside world until three weeks later, by which time he was safely interred in Greenwood Cemetery.

Commented one Chicago newsman who lived through the violent Torrio-Capone era: "He could dish it out, but he couldn't take it."

Chatham

"A PILFERER OF GREAT SAGACITY": THE MANY FACES OF MARTY DURKIN
1925–1926

Various addresses: the Michigan Avenue Bridge over the Chicago River; 508 East 75th Street; 1057 West 80th Street; and 6237 Princeton Avenue

If not for the inescapable fact that Marty Durkin was a vicious killer who shot down a Chicago police officer and a federal agent, this debonair auto thief and compulsive seducer of married women might have become a truly legendary figure; a South Side Jesse James or John Dillinger perhaps. If only he had stuck to the small stuff, heeded his old Irish mother's protestations, and left the gunplay to the thugs, Durkin could have been elected to the City Council, where thievery was elevated to a science. He was indeed a Chicago original, but you don't hear much about him anymore except for the stories handed down by the old-timers and neighborhood folklorists. Durkin has been eclipsed by more cunning and ruthless criminals over the years. But in 1925 Martin J. Durkin was a bigger crook than Al Capone. He has left behind plenty of his footprints from one end of the old hometown to the other; places you can go and look at. In November 1925, Durkin's cousin faked his death underneath the double-leafed Michigan Avenue Bridge (built between 1918 and 1920), depositing a sorrowful suicide note on the walkway that fooled everyone, including his poor mother who lived at 508 East 75th Street in Chatham, into thinking he had gone over the edge. The Durkin homestead on 75th Street is a common brick apartment house with storefront businesses on the commercial block between Eberhart and Rhodes Avenues. Another corner apartment building at 1057 West 80th Street (an African-American residential neighborhood between Aberdeen and Carpenter) was the scene of one of Durkin's most famous shootouts. In December 1924, Chicago Police Officers John O'Keefe, Frank Schuler, and Cornelius Allen answered a burglar call at this address, after spotting Marty Durkin peeping into a window of an apartment. Durkin replied with a volley of shots. He wounded all three of the police officers and managed to flee the trap only slightly nicked. What catapulted this street criminal into the national spotlight was his "last-stand" shootout with a federal officer that ended disastrously for the government when Durkin killed Agent Edwin C. Shanahan inside a garage at 6237 South Princeton Avenue on October 11, 1925. In the ensuing commotion inside the smoky garage and out on the street, Durkin managed to elude his captors once more. The Department of Justice commenced a cross-country manhunt unprecedented for the times. The "Public Enemies" era was still several years away, and Director J. Edgar Hoover of the Bureau of Investigation had only been on the job for a little more than a year, but he was eager to make a good showing. The Durkin manhunt was Hoover's baptism by fire. Every able-bodied operative was pressed into duty. The order trickled down to the men in the field: Find Marty Durkin, or don't come back!

One of Marty Durkin's most profitable rackets was to wander off with some other man's wife, plunder the marital dowry, and leave the lady stranded and broke. The police caught wind of this scheme in January 1923. Durkin was arrested in Florida after "eloping" with a wealthy dowager from the Midwest. There was something about Marty the ladies found simply irresistible. His legitimate wife, whose maiden name was Ruth Fieback, said that when they lived together he was known around town as the "Sheik of Griffith, Indiana."

Durkin parted his hair down the middle. He sported a pencil-thin "William Powell mustache," and if you ran into him on a street corner one could easily mistake him for a high school sophomore duded up for prom night.

Marty was devoted to his elderly mother, Hattie Durkin, who fawned over her boy and couldn't come to terms with the fact that he had turned bad.

Apart from the playing the seduction game with skill and ease, Durkin's other great vice was his love of automobiles; high-powered Pierce Arrows, Packards, and Cadillacs. He couldn't afford them on a tinhorn's salary so he stole them from the dealer's showroom floor with alacrity. Durkin would present himself as a bona fide customer to the salesman, convincing the trusting fool of his sincere intention to return the following morning with cash or a check in the full amount.

"And by the way, I will not have time to wait for the car . . . pressing matters downtown you understand. Could you be a good man and have it oiled and gased up for me before I arrive?"

MARTY DURKIN'S SUICIDE NOTE, LEFT ON THE STEPS OF THE MICHIGAN AVENUE BRIDGE TO FOOL THE COPS. "I CANNOT LIVE WITHOUT YOU, AND OH MOTHER HOW I DID LOVE BETTY." DURKIN DUMPED BETTY AND MARRIED SOMEONE ELSE BEFORE BEING NABBED OUTSIDE OF ST. LOUIS.

The obliging salesman would, of course, comply with the request. A cash transaction is a powerful inducement. Later that night, while the salesman slept, Durkin would return with a jimmy in hand. Breaking into the showroom was never a problem. He had done it many times before, and always managed to drive off with his latest prize. Safely away, Durkin filed down the identifying serial numbers, procured license plates under assumed names, then drove it out of state for immediate sale. Within a few years, Marty Durkin was plying his trade all over the country.

FOLLOWING HIS ARREST AND INCARCERATION, THE *CHICAGO HERALD & EXAMINER* COMMISSIONED A STUDY TO ASSESS THE PERSONALITY TRAITS OF MARTY DURKIN BASED ON HIS FACIAL STRUCTURE. THE CONCLUSION: DURKIN APPEALED TO WOMEN.

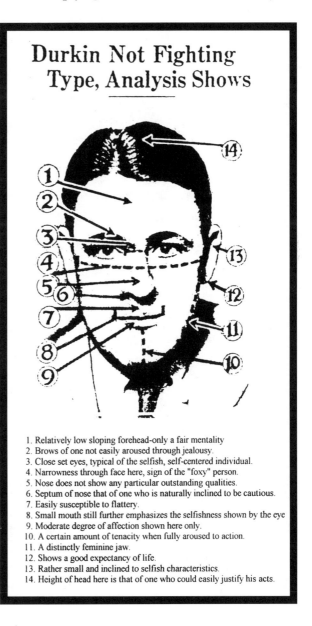

Durkin Not Fighting Type, Analysis Shows

1. Relatively low sloping forehead-only a fair mentality
2. Brows of one not easily aroused through jealousy.
3. Close set eyes, typical of the selfish, self-centered individual.
4. Narrowness through face here, sign of the "foxy" person.
5. Nose does not show any particular outstanding qualities.
6. Septum of nose that of one who is naturally inclined to be cautious.
7. Easily susceptible to flattery.
8. Small mouth still further emphasizes the selfishness shown by the eye
9. Moderate degree of affection shown here only.
10. A certain amount of tenacity when fully aroused to action.
11. A distinctly feminine jaw.
12. Shows a good expectancy of life.
13. Rather small and inclined to selfish characteristics.
14. Height of head here is that of one who could easily justify his acts.

508 EAST 75TH STREET. FORMER RESIDENCE OF MARTY DURKIN (ABOVE). DURKIN SHOT AND KILLED FBI AGENT EDWIN SHANAHAN AT A GARAGE AT 6237 SOUTH PRINCETON (THE VACANT LOT ON THE LEFT, BELOW).

(Photos by Lawrence Raeder)

A crime such as this violated the Dyer Act (interstate motor vehicle theft act). It was a federal crime that fell under the jurisdiction of the Justice Department. The Chicago police and other local agencies coast to coast kept the government informed. In Sacramento, California, one night, Durkin was being detained in the police chief's office on the second floor with his sweetheart from Chicago, Betty Werner. The lovesick young woman who had stolen Durkin's heart managed to draw the police far enough away so she could slam a door between them. Durkin took advantage of the security lapse and jumped out the window to freedom. There were many similar breaches of security in the months ahead.

In early October 1925, Agent Edwin C. Shanahan received confidential information that Durkin was due to arrive at 6237 South Princeton in a stolen automobile transported out of New Mexico. With Agent James D. Rooney, and Chicago Police Detectives Michael Naughton and James Rabbit assisting, Shanahan followed Durkin from Englewood to the garage address at 6237 Princeton.

Deciding that prudence was the better part of valor, the other officers split off and repaired to the Englewood station for backup, but Shanahan was fool-hardy and stupid. He pressed on alone, determined to bring in Durkin single-handedly, not fully realizing the caliber of the man he was up against.

Shanahan was killed instantly when Durkin produced an automatic pistol from under the seat of the stolen auto and drilled him through the chest. Edwin Shanahan is officially listed in departmental records as the first FBI agent to fall in the line of duty, though the agency was then known as the Bureau of Investigation.

Chicago Police Chief Morgan A. Collins posted a $500 reward for the arrest of Martin Durkin, but no one came forward to claim the money because the fugitive had already escaped the clutches of the law a second time. Five police officers were hiding out inside a flat at 240 Englewood Avenue where Betty Werner was living, in the belief that Durkin would not leave town without Betty and her infant son, Jack.

Marty Durkin was devoted to Betty, or so he had said many times. The couple planned to marry in Michigan as soon as they were able. To allay her uneasiness, Durkin promised to adopt Betty's son as his own. But plans ran afoul when Durkin landed in the middle of the police ambush. He had climbed in through a side window of the Englewood Avenue address, and was immediately fired on by police. In the exchange of gunfire that followed, Durkin shot and killed Sergeant Harry Gray (in self-defense, he insisted). Sergeant Naughton's errant bullet killed Durkin's first cousin Lloyd Austin inside the room, but he completely missed Marty, who disappeared into the vapors.

Shaking his fist, Chief Collins called it a "terrible piece of police bungling."

In the days that followed, Durkin resorted to subterfuge. He tried to lull the police into the belief that he had ended his life in a fit of remorse over the death of Sergeant Gray, the man he eulogized in a suicide note written to his mother. "I'm even sorry I shot Gray, not so much for myself but for his family." The note and a bloodstained overcoat belonging to Durkin were placed on the steps leading up the Michigan Avenue Bridge from the bank of the Chicago River. (*Author's Note:* Proximate location: northeast corner of the bridge, by Pioneer Court.)

Two Lincoln Park police officers recovered the coat and the death note, and for twenty-four hours the mood around headquarters was upbeat, just knowing the raffish gunman was dead. But before they could pop the champagne corks, an eyewitness came forward to volunteer the information that he had observed a woman placing the coat on the stone stairs underneath the bridge. The mystery woman was identified as Durkin's cousin from New York, Harriet Galow, who had arrived in town only a day earlier to assist Marty.

Unperturbed, the woman admitted that only a year earlier she had shielded Durkin in her New York home at a time when he was wanted for a score of automobile thefts.

The manhunt kicked into high gear. Special police patrols were dispatched around the city. The Hawthorne Hotel in Cicero, a hangout for the Torrio-Capone mob, was futilely searched, but Durkin was a lone wolf who had little to do with gangsters. This, police conceded, was the main reason why he was so elusive of a prey. He had no known associations and even fewer enemies willing to sell him out.

While the cops searched high and low from the Evanston border down to Calumet City, Durkin hid in plain sight. Without a care in the world, he drove around the city in his stolen Reo touring car. He revisited the garage where Agent Shanahan was slain only a few weeks earlier just to gloat.

With a gesture of contempt, Durkin parked his car outside the front door of the Englewood Police Station and sat patiently until the police had finished questioning his girlfriend, Betty Werner, inside the building. America's most wanted fugitive was finally evicted from his comfortable spot when a motorcycle cop told him he was parked too close to a fire hydrant. "Anything you say, officer," he said with a shrug.

Durkin enjoyed taunting his pursuers. He wrote a sarcastic letter to the *Chicago Tribune,* but the world-weary editors of highbrow affectations sniveled. "Durkin was a sort of a lone fox," wrote one *Tribune* correspondent, "wise beyond his years, a pilferer of great sagacity and one who fought with the desperation of a cornered rat."

Deciding not to press his luck any further, Marty Durkin slipped out of town. "He's a miracle man!" gushed his proud mother, upon receiving word that her boy made it out of town in one piece.

In late November, federal agents fired on his car in Masillon, Ohio, but the bullets harmlessly whizzed past his head. Durkin was a skilled high-speed driver and an expert marksman who won top prizes for accuracy on the pistol range while serving in the Canadian army. (Yes, the Canadian army.)

Durkin crisscrossed the country and remained at large for another two months before it ended with a whimper. Identified by a railroad conductor in El Paso, Texas, as a passenger on Southern Pacific train No. 10 bound for San Antonio, special agents from the local field offices were finally given something to work with.

Bureau agents traced Durkin's movements from Texas up through St. Louis, where he was due to arrive aboard the Texas Special at 11:00 A.M., January 20, 1926. The train was stopped in Webster Groves, a St. Louis suburb. A special detachment of St. Louis police and federal agents swarmed the stateroom of the Pullman car where Durkin was bundled under the covers with his wife of two weeks, Irma Sullivan, the pretty eighteen-year-old daughter of the Cornell, Illinois, village blacksmith.

"We've got you, Durkin! You picked a bad town to come to," said one.

"You're mistaken! I'm Valentino!" he replied unconvincingly.

"Get up now!"

"Well," the fugitive said, chuckling, "it took twenty of you guys to get me!"

The irons were clamped tight before he could reach for a weapon.

With Durkin finally in custody, the press clamored for interviews. The *Herald & Examiner* left no stone unturned. They were the first Chicago paper to locate Betty Werner for an exclusive. The young woman was prostrate with grief after they broke the awful news that Marty had jilted her for a younger woman. "I do not believe it!" she wailed. "He loved Jack so much!"

For a tidy sum (to buy Jack some new baby clothes), Betty gathered her thoughts and agreed to relate the life story of Marty Durkin for the readership of the Hearst chain, and promised to prepare a batch of his favorite recipes in the women's section of the paper.

Because the murder of a bureau agent was not yet a Federal offense (*Author's Note:* the law was amended in 1934), Durkin was tried and convicted in state court. His sentence for the Shanahan slaying was set at thirty-five years. Tried in Federal court for his string of automobile thefts, Durkin was ordered to serve an additional fifteen years.

He entered the Stateville Penitentiary in 1926, and remained there until

1946 when the government moved him to Leavenworth to complete the remainder of his sentence. Paroled on July 28, 1954, Marty Durkin was a free man at age fifty-three. He died in 1981.

South Chicago

Former site of Sam's Place, 11317 Green Bay Avenue (at 113th Street); Site of the Memorial Day riot, 116th and Burley Avenue

THE MEMORIAL DAY MASSACRE: A BLOODY EPISODE IN AMERICAN LABOR HISTORY
May 30, 1937

Once the bulwark of heavy industry in Chicago, the Southeast Side has suffered a devastating economic downturn as the great steelmaking firms disappeared, sapping the lifeblood of a community. The giants have fallen. Wisconsin Steel is but a memory. Gigantic U.S. Steel, the backbone of industrial America, dwindled away. What is left are decaying infrastructure, rows of worker cottages whose occupants rode the crest of prosperity and plumbed the depths of despair, and Republic Steel. It is bitter irony that the one company most opposed to the collective bargaining process is open for business in a field littered with abandoned factories. The Republic Steel strike was a bellwether of the violent struggles between labor and capital that reached a crescendo of fury in the 1930s.

Inhumanity was laid bare in an empty field that straddles the gates of the modern-day Republic/LTV Steel plant at 116th and Burley Avenue. Gaze across this open field, and in the distance you will observe smokestacks and foundries and parking lots. It is all so perfectly quiet now, a still life of pain and suffering, and killing bathed in the sunlight of a golden afternoon. What began as a nonviolent march at Sam's Place, a neighborhood saloon that used to be a dancehall, ended in massacre. Sam's Place at 113th and Green Bay, where the strikers went to receive information about their picketing duties, has since been demolished. Small one-story bungalows reminiscent of the post–World War II "Levittowns" of America line the residential side street. This, too, is a very quiet place. About the only visible reminder of the massacre is Memorial Hall at 11731 South Avenue O, roughly five hundred yards from the scene of the riot. The building was dedicated in 1969 with a bronze plaque mounted underneath the flagpole. The names of the dead are inscribed on the plaque, but the concrete base has chipped away and deteriorated with age.

The combatants in this deadly drama sparred over technicalities. And when it was over, ten good men who toiled in the mills lay dead in the morgue.

The central issue precipitating a nationwide walkout of steelworkers on May 26, 1937, was the refusal of a consortium of five independent companies known as "Little Steel" to sign a contract recognizing the Steel Workers Organization Committee (SWOC).

In early 1937, U.S. Steel broke ranks and recognized SWOC, which had been organized in 1936 with the help of the fiery John L. Lewis (1880-1969) of the

WITH DRAWN REVOLVERS AND UPRAISED TRUNCHEONS, CHICAGO POLICE MAIMED AND KILLED STRIKING STEELWORKERS, NOT THE OTHER WAY AROUND AS COLONEL ROBERT R. MCCORMICK'S *TRIBUNE* ASSERTED.

United Mine Workers. (*Author's Note:* SWOC was a part of a larger federation of unions then known as Committee for Industrial Organization, CIO. In 1938 the name was changed to the Congress of Industrial Organizations.)

A raise in wages and overall improvement in working conditions for these men soon followed, but Little Steel remained defiant. They would not sign a contract with SWOC.

Little Steel was led by the doughty Thomas Girdler, hard-line president of Republic Steel, a company founded in Youngstown, Ohio, in 1899. Girdler was supported by Bethlehem, Youngstown Sheet and Tube, Inland, and Weirton—all nonunion shops willing to draw up a blacklist, send in company spies, and recruit replacement workers when necessary.

"I have never seen John L. Lewis except at a distance, and I hope to God I never do," snarled Girdler, the anti-union rottweiler dispatched to Chicago to manage the affairs of Republic by the genteel patricians of big steel; the union leaguers and men of affairs who owned all of the plants, the mills, and the foundries.

Girdler was a self-made "Horatio Alger" character who had come up through the ranks of workingmen as a steel salesman. He was not a blue-blood Ivy League aristocrat, nor did he own company stock. But in order to stoke the fire of ambition, he sided with the barons of the steel trust over the interests of the laborers. He became the monopolists' shill, willing to employ whatever means necessary to end union agitation in his shops.

Tom Girdler was paid $130,000 a year by the invisible men in the eastern boardrooms who dared not sully their expensive linen suits with the blood of labor. They employed Tom Girdler for that purpose. And if not Girdler, then someone else.

TREES GROW WHERE DAZED AND BLOODIED MEN STAGGERED TO THEIR FEET DURING THE 1937 MEMORIAL DAY MASSACRE.

THE WAGNER ACT OF
1935 PROHIBITED
EMPLOYERS FROM
SETTING UP COMPANY
UNIONS OR DISCRIMI-
NATING AGAINST
WORKERS WHO JOINED
UNIONS. THIS
CARTOON, PUBLISHED
ON JUNE 2, 1937,
URGED PEACEFUL
NEGOTIATION, BUT
IT WAS ALSO A
SUBTLE JAB AT
REPUBLIC STEEL'S
INTRANSIGENCE.

When 25,000 Republic workers emptied the plant in a show of union solidarity with Local 1033, Girdler hired scabs and brought in crates of weapons and ammunition for the coming fight. Asked about this later, he did not mince words. "I never knew a steel plant that didn't have guns. We have to protect our property and our workmen. I'm not saying our workers are armed, but our police are."

In his public pronouncements, Girdler branded President Franklin D. Roosevelt a "communist" and volunteered the prediction that if he were to be reelected in 1940 there would be a civil war. This was an example of Girdler's befuddled logic, but he was correct about one thing: The cops were at his beck and call.

On May 28, eighteen strikers and six sympathizers clashed with Chicago police outside the main gate, despite assurances from Mayor Edward Kelly that they would be allowed to picket without interference.

Inside the plant, production continued at 40 percent capacity. The more scabs Girdler pulled off the street, the angrier the union men became.

On Memorial Day, a crowd gathered outside Sam's Place to hear the comments of Nicholas Fontecchio, SWOC district director, and thirty-three-year-old Joseph Weber, a SWOC organizer, urging them to march on the plant to drive out the scabs. "We have a right to go to the plant and tell the men inside that the strike is won and tell them to join the union!"

At the head of the column (an estimated fifteen hundred persons followed the procession), two men marched with American flags. Behind them, men, women, and children hoisted a forest of picket signs, chanting "CIO! CIO!"

They advanced slowly down Green Bay Avenue toward the Republic plant where the cops had routed them only two nights earlier. Near 117th Street, two hundred police officers under the command of Supervising Captain James L. Mooney were thumping their batons into the open palms of their hands in anticipation of the melee to come.

Mooney was a veteran line officer. He joined the department in 1894. He rose to the rank of chief of detectives and deputy commissioner in an event-filled career spanning forty-six years. Captain Mooney lived at 6721 South Merrill Avenue in the Jackson Park Highlands, and for most of his life was an ordinary workingman, like the striking steelworkers slowly approaching his column from the north.

Mooney did not recognize the steelworkers as South Side neighbors, but only as subversive "Reds." Goaded to madness, he imagined that he had heard the strain of the "*Internationale*" ringing in his ears, when in fact some of the younger girls bringing up the rear were singing folk songs of the labor movement. Mooney was convinced that communist infiltrators and provocateurs were behind this march. "Go on back if you know what is good for you!" one of his men cried out.

What happened next is open to interpretation, and depends on the political point of view being expressed. Colonel Robert Rutherford McCormick's conservative *Chicago Tribune* and several afternoon city newspapers described a vicious mob action directed against the police.

> The police stood their ground and made no effort to harm the attackers until pelted with brickbats and bolts. The police then defended themselves with tear gas. When the rioters resorted to firearms the police said they were forced to draw their revolvers to protect themselves. Peter Cleary, 58, of the Chicago Lawn station saw a comrade beaten to the ground by one hoodlum, armed with a metal rod. Even then they first fired into the air as a final warning, according to James L. Mooney.

This version of events reported by the *Tribune* completely contradicts eyewitness reports and what Chairman Robert LaFollette's Senate Civil Liberties Committee later observed in newsreel footage of the rioting.

It was demonstrated that the strikers were quickly put to flight by charging police who freely swung their hickory clubs and fired their service revolvers. Broken and bleeding marchers were dragged into police wagons. The remaining injured were dragged from the field by makeshift ambulances supplied by SWOC. It was over in less than ten minutes.

Police halfheartedly threw a tear gas canister in the direction of the remaining spectators lining the road, then one of them chuckled and said to another, "You've earned a good day's pay today," clapping the younger officer on the back.

When the injuries and fatalities were added up, ten strikers were dead and ninety persons injured (twenty-six as a result of gunfire).

If the marchers were as heavily armed as the *Tribune* insisted, then it stands to reason that at least one of these cops would have been treated for a gunshot wound, but their injuries were only minor.

Captain Mooney said that the strikers had been rehearsing riot tactics for several days. In light of the bloodshed and mayhem, he called the actions of his officers "lifesaving." "If we hadn't stopped those men, there would have been 200 killed."

From Washington, D.C., John L. Lewis denounced the police tactics. "The nation knows that the Chicago Police Department is corrupt. It is the same force that for years protected the thug and the hoodlum. It now aids Republic Steel. This company and the police are guilty of planned murder."

Throughout its checkered history (riddled with nepotism, scandal, and public corruption), the Chicago Police Department has been guilty of egregious overreaction to groups exercising their right to free speech and public assembly in a democratic society. The 1968 Democratic National Convention melee, the most recent example, was termed a "police riot" by a future governor of Illinois.

In every instance of extreme police brutality in Chicago, one or two overzealous members of the cadre, convinced that dreaded agent provocateurs were set loose in the city to foment a revolution, reacted with blind fury. During the Haymarket Riot of 1886, Michael Schaak and John Bonfield suspended constitutional guarantees against unreasonable search and seizure in their citywide dragnet for "anarchists" until the mayor was forced to put a stop to the nonsense.

The Stockyards Strike of 1904 exposed Captain Nicholas Hunt as a power-mad sadist, "rented" by the beef trust to dampen the resolve of the trade unionists. His private dealings with a gang of jewel thieves nearly cost him his career two years later.

Captain Mooney's description (taken under oath) of the Memorial Day disturbance down at Republic was nothing short of an outright lie.

Nevertheless, a coroner's jury sided with the police and returned a verdict of justifiable homicide in the deaths of Earl J. Handley (fractured skull), Otis Jones (bullet in the back), electrician Kenneth Reed (bled to death in the paddy wagon), WPA employee Joseph Rothmund (shot in the back), Lee Tisdale (died of blood poisoning from a neglected wound), Anthony Tagliori (abdominal wounds), Swedish immigrant Hilding Anderson (blood poisoning from gunshot wounds), carpenter Alfred Causey (four bullet wounds), Leo Francisco (shot in the back), and Sam Popovich (as a result of wounds to his head from police batons).

Funerals for the first six victims were held at Eagle's Hall, 9233 Houston Avenue. (*Author's Note:* The building is located at Houston and East 92nd Street. It is now the Neighborhood Opportunity Center for the City of Chicago.)

While plans were being finalized to bury the dead, Tom Girdler reaffirmed the company's hard-line stance, vowing never to sign a contract recognizing SWOC, the CIO, or any other representative body of workingmen. Mayor Kelly responded by ordering the Republic Steel Corporation to evacuate all strike-breakers from the premises within forty-eight hours. It was a violation of the law, Kelly countered, to quarter employees overnight in the South Chicago plant. Van Bittner, regional CIO organizer, praised the mayor's actions but even this measure did not compel Republic to back down.

In July the steelworkers went back to work without a contract. Local 1033 ran out of strike funds in November, forcing cancellation of the job action. Emboldened by his victory, Girdler filed a lawsuit against the organizing committee seeking $7.5 million in compensation for lost revenues. Deputy U.S. marshals served papers on the organizers, many of whom were too poor to patch the holes in their roofs, let alone pay Girdler the compensation he demanded.

The setbacks and hardships of the strikers ended on August 12, 1941, when the National Labor Relations Board (NLRB) found Republic Steel guilty of unfair labor practices and ordered 617 discharged workers reinstated with full back pay. Tom Girdler's lawsuit was overturned a month later.

On August 11, 1942, with the company backed into a corner as a result of an acute wartime labor shortage and massive government contracts to fulfill, officials from Republic Steel were forced to rethink their antiunion stance. By now, they were most eager to sign a contract with the United Steelworkers of America, granting full union recognition.

Captain James L. Mooney, who must share the burden of guilt with Tom Girdler for this shameful episode in Chicago police history, passed away at the ripe old age of eighty-seven in his Merrill Avenue home on September 20, 1960.

Republic Steel remained prosperous through the 1950s, but as the demand for foreign steel increased and environmentalism placed new restrictions on the domestic producers, company profits declined in a soft economy. In 1984, Jones & Laughlin, a subsidiary of the Cleveland-based LTV Corporation, merged with Republic to form LTV Steel.

It was with the Jones & Laughlin firm that Tom Girdler had risen to prominence decades earlier.

Southeast Side: Calumet Region & Hammond

Burnham

Avenue

and 120th

Street

WOLF LAKE: A PLACE TO PICNIC, FISH, WINDSURF, AND DUMP BODIES
Various Dates and Locations

The William W. Powers Conservation Area (better known as Wolf Lake), is a wetlands and wildlife refuge straddling the Indiana-Illinois border where Hammond and Chicago converge. Located east of Avenue O/Burnham Avenue between 120th and 134th Streets on the Southeast Side, Wolf Lake was discovered by the French voyageur Father Jacques Marquette in the seventeenth century. Long before the Civil War, Lieutenant Jefferson Davis, the future president of the Confederate States of America, surveyed the area for the U.S. government. According to another popular legend (the origin of the story is highly suspect), Abraham Lincoln visited the area during his young and impressionable years, and was caught up in the wild beauty of the lake and the surrounding woods. Today, Wolf Lake is a recreational oasis for outdoorsmen and picnickers. The prevailing winds buffeting off Lake Michigan to the east make it an ideal location for water-skiers. In wintertime the ice fishermen drop their lines into the frigid waters, never really knowing what they might pull up.

T here is a haunting resonance to these ancient woods where the Native tribes once roamed. The imprint of sinister acts committed by desperate men have long marked the Powers Conservation Area and Wolf Lake as a notorious spot in southern Cook County. There have been periodic reports of young children straying too far out into the lake and drowning in the cold waters. Two crosses standing on the shore mark the spot where two boys, ages six and ten, fell into a drop-off on June 19, 1998, and drowned. Now and then victims of foul play turn up in the marshes. A phalanx of Hammond and Chicago police tramp through dense underbrush in the eternal quest for evidence and clues.

In Prohibition days, the most talked about gangland murders occurring at or near Wolf Lake involved Al Capone's two pet gunmen, John Scalise and Albert Anselmi, and a third man, Joseph "Hop Toed" Giunta, Tony Lombardo's successor as president of the *Unione Sicilione*. Their gun-shot bodies were found on May 8, 1929, inside a car that had nosed into a ditch at Sheffield Avenue and Hohman Street, an undeveloped real estate subdivision just across the Illinois line in Hammond.

Accused of complicity in the St. Valentine's Day Massacre and brought in for questioning by the Cook County state's attorney, the Sicilian-born cop-killing Mafia assassins Scalise and Anselmi were out on bond when they were overtaken by rival gangsters believed to be working for George "Bugs" Moran.

Others hold fast to the theory that Capone, alerted to the existence of a

THIRTEEN-YEAR-OLD BOBBY FRANKS, VICTIM OF "THRILL KILLERS" NATHAN LEOPOLD AND RICHARD LOEB, WAS FOUND NEAR THIS RECENTLY PAVED-OVER RAILROAD BED IN A DESERTED REGION OF WOLF LAKE ON MAY 21, 1924.

murder plot directed against him, bludgeoned the pair to death with a baseball bat in the presence of a roomful of horrified party guests. The story cannot be verified one way or another, but if it happened according to Hollywood's depiction in the 1967 movie *The St. Valentine's Day Massacre*, the likely location was either the Stockade speakeasy in Burnham, managed by Sonny Sheets, or the Plantation resort in Hammond.

The coroner concluded that the death car had been transported to the Hammond intersection to throw police off the trail. Desolate Wolf Lake, where there was no one around to hear their screams, remains another possibility.

The murder-at-the-banquet scenario is given additional credence by ballistics expert Calvin Goddard, who determined that Scalise had tried to shield his face from a gunshot fired at close range. Part of a finger on the left hand was torn off by a bullet. This could only have been accomplished while he was sitting down.

Wolf Lake will forever be linked to the "Crime of the Century," the abduction and "thrill killing" of thirteen-year-old Bobby Franks by Nathan "Babe" Leopold and Richard Loeb on May 21, 1924. The lad was picked up outside his house at 5052 South Ellis in the fashionable Kenwood section of the South Side by two wealthy young idlers from the University of Chicago who convinced themselves that as "superior beings" they could commit the perfect crime and get away with it. Struck over the head multiple times by an iron chisel, Franks's trussed-up body was covered by a rug and transported to a culvert underneath the Pennsylvania Railroad tracks near 121st and the Calumet River. The killers removed the boy's clothes and poured hydrochloric acid on the remains in order to make identification difficult.

Within twenty-four hours the body of Bobby Franks—and an incriminating pair of glasses carelessly left behind by Leopold—were found. Ten days after the abduction, Leopold and Loeb, the compulsion killers, were in custody and the "perfect crime" was easily unraveled by the Cook County state's attorney with the help of two reporters from the *Chicago Daily News*. (*Author's Note:* See my first volume, *Return to the Scene of the Crime*, for additional details of the Leopold-Loeb case.)

Wading through tall grass, thickets, and dense underbrush in search of the seventy-six-year-old crime scene is almost an impossibility. The Pennsylvania railroad tracks have been completely torn up, but the imprint of the track is visible to the naked eye. The culvert near 121st Street is obliterated, but during an exhaustive search of the marshlands, we managed to locate (within five hundred feet) the general area of where the body of Bobby Franks was recovered. The silence that particular autumn afternoon was unsettling and eerie. Overhead the buzz of the electric power lines, an occasional passing vehicle in the distance, and the gentle rustling of the trees and tall grass were the only audible sounds. It was time to retreat to the car, and leave the restless stirrings of that tragic event far behind us.

Down through the years there have been other ghastly discoveries made in Wolf Lake, though none as famous or internationally known as the Loeb and Leopold case.

The severed torso of Ervin Lang, victim of the vengeful female "vampire killer" (see page 165), was dumped in low-lying water in 1935. More recently, on May 22, 1988, off-duty Chicago Police Officer John Matthews was horribly beaten to death by three men, two Hispanics and a white, after they were ordered out of the park. Matthews lived at 131st Street and Avenue M and was trying to preserve the peace of his neighborhood.

On March 27, 1997, the bullet-riddled remains of thirty-one-year-old Antonio Fort was found floating in the shallows on the Hammond, Indiana, side by a fisherman on the shoreline. The victim was one of seven children sired by Jeff Fort, imprisoned gang chieftain of the former Black P Stone Nation (later known as the El Rukns). Who left the young man there remains a mystery.

Andrew Urdiales, prime suspect in the murders of eight women, dumped two of his victims in Wolf Lake in 1996. Urdiales was a security guard who lived in the 9700 block of South Commercial Avenue in South Chicago until he was picked up in April 1997. The neighbors said he always "kept to himself."

There are other Wolf Lake legends and curiosities. A Nike Ajax missile base with sixteen launchers was located in an area proximate to Avenue K and 133rd Street near the lake. The five-decade heritage of the Cold War is embedded in four concrete radar towers, now overgrown with weeds and underbrush, about three-quarters of a mile off the main road.

Do not attempt to explore the site on your own or stray too far into these woods without first consulting the park rangers, especially after dark.

TOUR 6

Suburban Living . . . and Dying:

South Suburban Chicago

The suburban communities lying beyond the southern boundary of Chicago reflect the art and science of post–World War II mobility in America. The city of Park Forest, for example, is due south of Chicago Heights and is an older, blue-collar town that was notorious throughout the 1920s, 1930s, and 1940s as a haven for gangsters and their women. After WWII, Park Forest became one of the planned residential communities designed for GIs returning from the battlefields of Europe.

Chicagoans in large numbers poured into the suburbs in the 1950s and 1960s for affordable housing, better schools, and other quality-of-life issues that often had more to do with racial attitudes than with anything else.

As the inner-city neighborhoods west of the lakefront changed from white to black, the former residents headed in a west and southwesterly direction. Evergreen Park (where we'll learn the Unabomber grew up) lured thousands of people away from Chicago because of stable housing and affordable amenities. In short, it was a nice place to live.

To the southeast, along the Lake Michigan shoreline, is a high concentration of steel-processing plants, heavy industry, and refineries that extend into north-west Indiana. In the 1920s, as the automobile took root in American culture, the purveyors of vice and gambling established "road house" districts in Burnham, Chicago Heights, and Calumet City, rural towns that were mostly free of police interference. Whatever police presence there happened to be was easily bought off, and the bawdy attractions flourished in these locations for many years. On any given Saturday night, the workingmen answered the clarion call of the tawdry nightclubs, burlesque bars, low-end gin joints, and houses of prostitution.

Until quite recently the lurid attractions of Calumet City continued to accentuate the "sin in sincerely," and even attached a whole new meaning to the word.

1. Boyhood home of the Unabomber, 9209 S. Lawndale, Evergreen Park.
2. Village Courtyard Restaurant (now Hobknobs), 8101 West 123rd St. (Palos Park).
3. Chicago Sanitary and Ship Canal—where Dianne Masters was murdered.
4. Stateline Road sin strip—Calumet City.

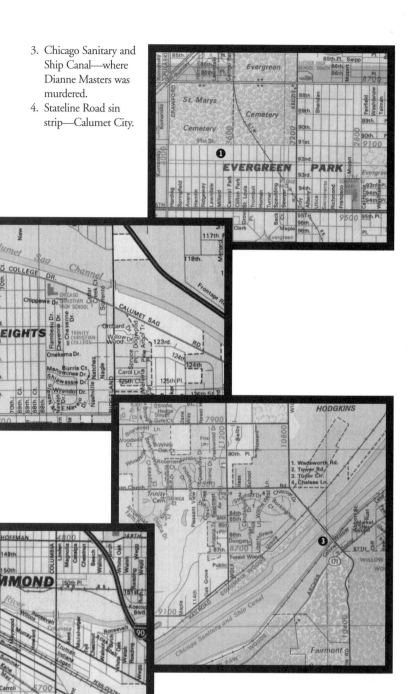

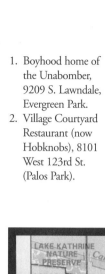

Evergreen Park

THE BOYHOOD HOME OF THE UNABOMBER
1950s

9209

South

Lawndale

Imagine Mayfield, television's answer to Levittown, where Wally and the Beaver walked home from school each afternoon in a blissful depiction of America in the late 1950s. Incorporated in 1893, Evergreen Park was mainly truck farms and roadside fruit stands out in the country until the end of World War II, when suddenly acres of modest red-brick homes sprouted on the prairie. Again, try to imagine Mayfield, then experience the real thing in this placid blue-collar bedroom suburb just beyond the Beverly section of Chicago along bustling Ninety-fifth Street. In many respects the community was the quintessential utopia for thousands of working-class GI's coming home from World War II. Evergreen Park, all three-plus square miles of it, embodied everything held sacrosanct in the God-fearing 1950s—PTA meetings, backyard barbecues, sock-hop dances, bowling leagues, Georgian-style homes with neatly arranged flower beds, a Meister Brau on Saturday night, and Mass the following morning. Theodore John Kaczynski, known to the rest of America as the soulless "Unabomber" responsible for the mail-bomb deaths of three randomly targeted people, lived in an average brick Cape Cod house at 9209 Lawndale Avenue with doting parents, who placed a premium on education. The former Kaczynski residence is located due south of St. Mary's Cemetery, where Chicago Bears legend Brian Piccolo and Edward "Spike" O'Donnell, a tough bootlegging bird from the Prohibition Era, have found their eternal rest. The neighbors could hardly believe it when they heard the Unabomber lived down the street. Of course, he was a lot younger then, and people do change. What was it that made a smart boy like that become an ecoterrorist and murderer?

Theodore R. Kaczynski, the Unabomber's dad, worked in a stockyards factory at Forty-ninth Street and Ashland Avenue manufacturing Polish sausage. It was honest but uninspiring work, allowing the family to maintain a comfortable middle-class existence in the suburbs. Kaczynski and his wife, Wanda, were well-read, liberal-minded citizens of the community who placed a premium on education for their two growing boys, David and Ted.

Neighbors recalled that David was polite and outgoing, but young Ted was introspective—a self-conscious loner who shunned the companionship of other boys for a safe haven in the academic world. While his classmates were buying up Batman comics down at the corner candy store for twelve cents, Ted was devouring *Romping Through Mathematics from Addition to Calculus*—not exactly run-of-the-mill reading for an eleven-year-old boy.

The neighbors remembered Wanda Kaczynski doting on her sons. On summer nights, she and the boys were observed reading *Scientific American* on the front steps of the house on Lawndale. A stickler for early education, Wanda opened a neighborhood preschool, a concept years ahead of its time.

A psychological report prepared by Dr. Sally Johnson for Court TV (following Kaczynski's imprisonment for the sixteen Unabomber attacks between 1978 and 1995) revealed Kaczynski to be "highly intelligent, but socially withdrawn." These tendencies were manifest early in life when he withdrew from his peers. According to Johnson, two triggering incidents in childhood sparked inner depression and contributed to his alienation from society.

At age fifteen, an older woman told him he was a "beautiful boy." Kaczynski took it to heart, but as time went by, he found that he could not sustain a meaningful relationship with women. Later in life, a female acquaintance blunted his elevated self-image by telling him his looks were only "run-of-the-mill."

Kaczynski's brilliance of mind did not go unnoticed. He was jumped from the fifth grade to the seventh, but was unable to cope with the relentless teasing and bullying of his older classmates. The bully syndrome is a neglected form of child abuse. Educators and parents are often at a loss as to what they can do to ease a child's suffering. Most youngsters experiencing these tortures live through it with their egos and self-esteems scarred, but intact. Kaczynski, it seems, did not and retreated further inward.

In his chemistry class at Evergreen Park Community High School, Kaczynski mixed iodine and ammonia together and constructed a pipe bomb, but no one seemed terribly concerned, chalking it up to one of those "boys-will-be-boys" episodes of adolescence. He was, after all, one of the school's five 1958 National Merit Scholarship finalists.

At age sixteen, Ted Kaczynski entered Harvard on a scholarship, and his experiences living with the "preppies" at Eliot House seemed to accelerate his withdrawal from society as a whole.

Kaczynski imagined science and technology as his personal enemies and the scourge of the world. In a lifetime of journaling, he made many references to his "Luddite" anti-techno-philosophy, and his anger against mankind. "I'll just chuck all of this silly morality business and hate anybody I please," he wrote. "... I have never had any interest in or respect for morality, ethics, or anything of the sort."

In 1967, he moved to Berkeley, California, where he taught mathematics to undergraduates as an assistant professor. While others of that politically galvanized generation were turning on and tuning in, the future Unabomber was preparing to drop out. He resigned from the university in 1969, wandering from one place to another in search of himself through much of the 1970s.

He eventually settled in a cattle ranching area of Montana near the Blackfoot River (the focus of the movie *A River Runs Through It*). There he lived the frugal life of a mountain man, a regular Grizzly Adams, in an unheated shack with walls laden with books and empty cans of Van Camp's pork and beans. The residents of Lincoln, Montana, considered him a nut, but as long as he kept to himself and didn't stir up trouble, few people paid him any mind.

The first Unabomber attack was directed against Northwestern University in Evanston, Illinois, on May 26, 1978. A security guard was injured in the explosion. A second bomb targeting Northwestern exploded at the Technological Institute on May 9, 1979, injuring one person.

Kaczynski singled out the airlines, the computer industry, and higher education—symbols of the evils of the modern age. On November 15, 1979, outside Dallas, he nearly downed an American Airlines jetliner when one of his infernal devices exploded in the cargo hold, forcing an emergency landing. Twelve people suffered smoke inhalation.

Kaczynski accused his parents of "emotional abuse," and pleaded with his brother, David, to help him sever the remaining family ties. Wanda and her husband sold the house in Evergreen Park in 1966. They eventually settled in west suburban Lombard. The father committed suicide in 1990, by which time Ted was a hermit camped out in the wilderness. Such was the unraveling of a 1950s all-American family.

After the Unabomber's rambling diatribe against the technological age was published in the *New York Times* as an "appeasement" to induce him to end the terrorism, David Kaczynski recognized his brother's prose and notified the FBI.

The hermitic Kaczynski was arrested inside his Spartan cabin near Lincoln on April 3, 1996. David pleaded with the government not to seek the death penalty against his brother.

In January 1998, Theodore Kaczynski acknowledged his role in the mail bombings and agreed to a plea-bargain arrangement calling for four consecutive life sentences in exchange for his guilty plea. The Justice Department had originally asked for the death sentence, but agreed to a life term after a court-ordered psychiatric evaluation concluded that the Harvard-trained mathematician was a paranoid schizophrenic.

"The defendant committed unspeakable and monstrous crimes for which he shows utterly no remorse," commented U.S. District Judge Garland Burrell Jr.

Palos Park and Willow Springs

8600 South

Willow

Springs Road

and 8101

West 123rd

Street

MASTERS OF DECEIT: JEALOUSY, CORRUPTION, AND MURDER IN THE SOUTH SUBURBS

March 19, 1982

Chicago Sanitary and Ship Canal, 8600 S. Willow Springs Road; and the Village Courtyard Restaurant (now Hobknobs in the Park) at 8101 W. 123rd Street

In 1962 there were just three policemen, a rundown shack, and four thousand people nestled between the golf courses and trees of Willow Springs, a suburban municipality located about seventeen miles southwest of Chicago. The suburb is best known for the Willowbrook Ballroom (8900 S. Archer Avenue) and the legend of Resurrection Mary, the hitchhiking ghost who danced the Charleston underneath the twirling silver ball back in the Roaring Twenties. "Willow Springs . . . where, from beneath the willow tree, a bountiful spring leaped into the air, its dancing waters sparkling and flashing, spewing forth its rich treasure of life-giving mineral. Rejuvenescence!" Putting that bit of nineteenth-century doggerel aside for now, the murky waters of the northern portion of the glacial valley forming the Chicago Sanitary and Ship Canal yielded something far more sinister than life-giving minerals on December 11, 1982. A car was pulled from the pitch-black depths, and in the trunk of that car, human remains protruded from the odd assortment of discarded junk. Forensic investigators did not have much to work with, however. The body was badly decomposed, but it was soon established that the deceased was pretty Dianne Turner Masters, who was reported missing by her husband, the facile Palos Park political fixer and shyster lawyer Alan Masters. The 1978 Cadillac was pulled from its watery grave near 8600 South Willow Springs Road, under the Sanitary and Ship Canal Bridge where at least seventy other cars were dumped in an insurance scam that went undetected for years. It's a creepy, secluded area where "murder most foul" is only a slight exaggeration. The killer finished Dianne off with two shots to the head, then pushed the car into the drink, where it would remain for the next nine months. You must be careful in these woods with birds chirping, campers picnicking, and hikers communing with nature. If something should happen, no one can hear the scream.

An icy glaze covered the fallen leaves and thick underbrush of the forest preserve that lined the banks of the Willow Springs section of the Chicago Sanitary and Ship Canal. The killer stood beside a yellow-and-white Cadillac underneath the overpass spanning the slow-moving canal, dug by Irish potato famine immigrants in the late 1840s. The canal used to ferry industrial barges southward from Chicago to the locks in Lemont. Now it covered the rusting carcasses of junked automobiles.

Two shots pierced the nighttime calm. Dianne Masters—the golden girl who dreamed of romantic settings and an uncluttered life surrounded by educated sophisticates, but instead settled for fat, insensitive Alan—was gone. The trunk hood was slammed shut and the car was slipped into gear. Dianne's car lurched forward and bounced noisily down the muddy embankment before sliding beneath the water line.

The inner circle of plotters responsible for this dastardly crime believed they would never be troubled by her kind again. This inner circle included at least two men who had taken solemn oaths to protect and defend the public as sworn officers of the law.

Alan Masters could fix anything. From his law office on Sixty-third Street in Summit, Illinois, the paunchy, middle-aged lawyer received referrals from Willow Springs Police Chief Michael Corbitt and Lt. James Keating of the Cook County sheriff's police. In return, Keating was paid $300 per month by Masters (between 1972 and 1984) for allowing low-level vice and gambling clubs Masters had an interest in to flourish in southern Cook County. Masters also paid them to "fix" state criminal charges tried in southwest suburban courts.

"Masters is a terrific lawyer who can get anybody off any beef because he pays the cops, the judges, and everyone else!" an FBI agent testified in the corruption trial of James Keating in 1986.

Alan knew everybody. He fed on the collegiality that existed between the judges of the Cook County Circuit Court and defense lawyers in the pre-Greylord era when everyone was on the take. (*Author's Note:* The Operation Greylord scandal broke in 1983. Fifteen judges were eventually convicted of taking bribes.)

Keating, who was praised as an improvising undercover investigator with a knack for donning clever disguises by one of his Cook County supervisors that the author had occasion to interview, was brought into the sheriff's police in 1964, two years after he was bounced out of the Chicago Police Department. He was on the job less than a month before he was pink-slipped. (For many years, the Cook County Sheriff's Police Department functioned as a quasi-employment agency for discredited city cops and out-of-work suburban castoffs. The present sheriff, Democrat Michael Sheahan, has done a pretty good job of improving the image, integrity, and overall efficiency of the department.)

Keating came in with a positive recommendation from Richard Cain, a less than sterling mob "double agent" who served as chief investigator before he was shuttled off to prison after being implicated in a $240,000 drug warehouse burglary.

Until Jim Keating was dismissed from the department in 1986 (following his bribery conviction), he headed an elite, ten-member Criminal Intelligence Unit (CIU) charged with investigating major organized crime and drug-trafficking rings. In the ten-year period following its inception in the 1970s, the CIU never cleared a homicide in its jurisdiction. Not one.

In an August 1989 exposé probing the rotten inner core of the sheriff's police, the *Chicago Tribune* concluded that Keating "was secretly controlled by the mob" and had "obstructed the inquiry of at least two [other] murders and suppressed evidence that police, prosecution, and judges had fixed dozens of criminal cases in Chicago and the suburbs."

Within the spider's web of cover-ups, squelched evidence, murder-for-hire schemes, suburban whorehouses, card games, chop shops, and sheriff's cops who turned a blind eye because of indifference, incompetence, or flat-out greed, there was a more personal side to all this anguish.

There were plenty of unhappy housewives, Little League moms, and desperate women like Dianne Masters who were slapped around, abused, and chained to egomaniacal wheeler-dealers like Alan. Some of these battered women were married to cops. For numerous reasons, the badge and the gun breed incidences of spousal abuse. But Alan Masters was always there to rescue the wife-beating bully from financial ruin once papers were served on the lout. He also specialized in the DUIs and low-level criminal defense work that drew him into contact with corrupt suburban judges. It was a "volume" business they all shared in.

Masters, a flabby, baggy-pants lawyer who grew up in Lawndale (among the racketeers and gamblers of the "Jewish faction" of West Side organized crime), represented Dianne Turner in a divorce proceeding against her first husband, Ronald Mueller. Until Dianne met Alan, she lived day-to-day, striving to make ends meet. More than anything, Dianne yearned for a different kind of life, one free of the financial worry and hardships of poverty. She dreamed of vacations in Acapulco and the chance to flash a Diners Club card at pricey boutiques. Mueller could not possibly provide the thrills and excitement she craved on his workingman's salary. At the same time Mueller was struggling to hold his marriage

DIANNE MASTERS,

SHORTLY BEFORE HER

BRUTAL MURDER.

(Photo courtesy of Barbara Schaaf)

together, albeit from a distance (he was serving his country in Vietnam as an army engineer), Dianne was illicitly carrying on with other men.

Dianne's marriage to Mueller was over by 1970.

By moving in with Alan (before finally marrying him in 1980), Dianne crossed the great economic divide separating the tract house from the penthouse.

Her financial woes all but ended. Suddenly there was money for diamonds, Cadillacs, and resort vacations and the Diners Club bill was paid on time; but her chance for a lifestyle where she was free to make her own decisions was gone forever.

Alan kept Dianne on a short leash while he ran around with a succession of women. His jealousy was monumental, and his ill treatment of his beautiful young trophy wife was perverse and cruel. According to a former south suburban police officer close to the investigation, Masters was guilty of repeated infidelities and, on at least one occasion, forced his wife to perform oral sex on one of his police officer pals while vacationing at a Florida beach.

In the fall of 1981, Dianne began a romantic affair with an economics professor at Moraine Valley Community College in Palos Hills, where she served on the board as a trustee. Being married to Alan had driven her into the arms of other men.

The following January, she hired a female divorce attorney from Chicago to initiate proceedings against her husband. Emboldened by her rising sense of self-confidence, she decided it was time now to make a clean break from Alan. (*Author's Note:* In 1979, Dianne launched a twenty-four-hour hot line for abused women in the kitchen of her home. This later evolved into the Dianne Masters Shelter. By now she was also politically ambitious, volunteering her services as an unpaid campaign worker in the office of State Treasurer Jerome Cosentino.)

"Dianne was a late bloomer who came to terms with her past mistakes and was looking forward to a second chance at life," explains Barbara Schaaf, author of *Shattered Hopes: A True Crime Story of Marriage, Murder, Corruption and Cover-up in the Suburbs.*

"She knew she was in danger from her corrupt lawyer husband Alan, and she told friends and members of law enforcement of her fears. Her friends believed her, but the authorities either ignored her or tattled on her to Alan."

Vowing to "destroy" Dianne before it ever got to the point of splitting up marital assets, Masters hired a private investigator to eavesdrop on his wife. The P.I. came back with a taped phone call between Dianne and her lover. In it, the two of them recalled in explicit detail a recent sexual adventure, sending Alan

THE VILLAGE COURTYARD RESTAURANT AT 8101 WEST 123RD STREET, WHERE DIANNE MASTERS ATE HER LAST MEAL BEFORE SHE DISAPPEARED, IS TODAY HOBKNOBS.

into a dizzying tailspin of anger and revulsion.

Backed into a corner and blinded by his jealousies, Alan Masters reacted violently. He drew Keating and Willow Springs Police Chief Michael Corbitt into a plot to kill Dianne, although none of the three would face charges of murder when the initial indictments were handed down. They were instead accused of conspiring to defraud an insurance company of $100,000 on the policy Dianne had taken out through Moraine Valley Community College. This was to have been their shared reward for doing away with the feckless wife.

On the night of March 18, 1982, Alan remained at home with their four-year-old daughter, Anndra, while Dianne went off to attend a board meeting at the college (10900 South Eighty-eighth Avenue). It was customary for the board members to adjourn to a local restaurant for food and drink after the formal meeting concluded. On this particular evening, Dianne and five colleagues had gone to dinner at the Village Courtyard Restaurant at 8101 West 123rd Street in Palos Park. (*Author's Note:* For the past nine years, this restaurant has been called Hobknob's in the Park and features a gourmet menu, fireplace, and sense of rustic intimacy amid the forest preserve woodlands of Palos.)

At 1:10 in the morning, the party of six broke up. Dianne was observed driving west on 123rd Street (McCarthy Road). She then turned south heading in the direction of her home at 12460 Wolf Road and a rendezvous with death.

Of course, the story Alan concocted did not jibe with the reconstruction of events prosecutors would later bring before the court. Masters claimed his wife had not come home that night at all. "Probably out chasing after that damned professor!"

When the professor was interviewed at length in the sheriff's police district headquarters, he expressed doubts as to whether or not the CCSPD investigator was conducting a valid police investigation or acting as an agent of Alan Masters.

The Cook County Sheriff's Police Department was investigating a crime it had helped commit.

Sheriff Richard Elrod, son of the 1940s Twenty-fourth Ward political sachem Arthur X. Elrod, did not have the proper law enforcement background necessary to efficiently administer the duties of this office or rein in the malefactors of graft who had brought continuous shame and disgrace on the department.

A career politician from the old school, Elrod was a dupe, oblivious to the intrigues afoot in his own department and the manner in which certain line officers like Keating tacked "for sale" signs on the scales of justice. Incredibly, Dick Elrod was faithfully elected to four terms of office (sixteen years total) by an electorate that was either blind or naive or both.

Clyde Snow, a forensic anthropologist assisting the Cook County medical examiner, determined that Dianne Masters was struck on the front and back of the head with "a considerable amount of force," likely with a tire iron, baseball bat, or butt end of a pistol.

Assistant U.S. Attorneys Thomas Scorza and Patrick Foley contended that Dianne was assaulted by her husband as she prepared to retire for the evening, though the sequence of events occurring inside their house that night may never be known. Whether or not Keating was summoned by Masters to advise him about what he should do next is a matter of conjecture. Alan refused to submit to a lie detector test, giving the excuse that they were "unreliable."

Half-dressed and unconscious, Dianne was dragged outside and dropped into the trunk of her car. Despite all her work on behalf of battered women, there was no one to help her. The vehicle was driven to the banks of the Sanitary and Ship Canal, not far from the Willow Springs Police Department. Before discharging two shots into her head, the killer may have fondled the genital area of his victim. Her panties were missing, and the blue skirt she had worn the last night of her life was pushed above her naval.

Six days after Dianne's murder, Keating and Masters fabricated a story to deceive the press and other law enforcement agencies into thinking Alan's wife was abducted and being held for a $25,000 ransom payment. To lend credibility to the deception, Keating, Masters, and investigators from the Criminal Investigations Unit drove to the Seville Restaurant in distant north suburban Waukegan, Illinois, to await further "instructions" from the imaginary kidnapper dialing in to the restaurant pay phone.

On March 31, James Keating personally typed the CCSPD Supplementary Report, signed his name, and concluded the narrative account of their Waukegan foray with the following statement: "According to Mr. Masters when he got on the phone the same unknown caller told him he was being followed (at no time during the operation was Masters' vehicle followed). Masters again indicated he wanted to cooperate with the caller and he (Masters) wanted to speak to his wife. At this time, according to Masters, the unknown caller said 'he would send Masters his wife's head through the mail tomorrow'; the unknown caller then hung up.—Lt. James D. Keating, star #22."

Government prosecutors accused Michael Corbitt (who served as Willow Springs Chief of Police from 1974 to 1982) of pulling the trigger, but this has never been proved beyond a shadow of a doubt. The indictment filed against Corbitt in June 1988 charged racketeering, racketeering conspiracy, and mail fraud. This came on the heels of his earlier conviction for conspiracy and extortion in connection with his role in the federal anti-corruption probe, "Operation Safebet."

"Safebet" was a sweeping four-year undercover probe carried out by the FBI into vice conditions in Suburban Cook County and the layers of protection afforded the owners of seamy strip clubs and massage parlors by corrupt sheriff's police officers.

An FBI-operated credit card service in Palatine processed $30 million in claims for several of the after-hours gentlemen's clubs suspected of soliciting prostitution. James Keating and Sergeant Bruce Frasch, a sixteen-year veteran who headed the vice control unit from 1978 until 1983, were convicted on eighteen counts of racketeering, conspiracy, extortion, income tax fraud, and bribery.

The jaunty Keating, who did everything in his power to derail the Dianne Masters murder investigation for Alan, was sentenced to fifteen years in prison. It took the jury only six hours to convict both Keating and Frasch.

Author Barbara Schaaf is not satisfied with the outcome of the Cook County corruption trials as they related to Dianne. "Jim Keating is keeping mum in his federal pen," she reports, "and Mike Corbitt, who admitted his complicity after the fact and who is a three-time federal loser, was able to flimflam the FBI into a get-out-of-jail-free card so that he can enjoy his Florida condo and oceangoing yacht."

Alan Masters, who kept insisting that Dianne had absconded with her jewels to Florida, remained in the clear until December 11, 1982, when the Cadillac was dredged from the bottom of the chemically polluted Sanitary and Ship Canal, following the removal of seventy other vehicles disposed of at the request of their owners for the insurance money.

If there is a happy ending to this sordid tale, it is the satisfaction of knowing that Alan Masters, the "master fixer," drew a forty-year prison sentence in 1989 after Federal Judge James Zagel ruled that he had conspired with Keating and Corbitt to murder his wife.

"It would be nice to say that the revelations surrounding Dianne's murder led to a cleanup of suburban corruption, but it would be inaccurate," sighs Schaaf. "After a handful of prosecutions, the lid was firmly clamped back on the cesspool that is the judicial-law enforcement system in the suburbs."

Alan Masters, age sixty-five, died on October 11, 2000, at the Federal Medical Center in Rochester, Minnesota, after being transferred there from the Pekin (Illinois) Federal Correctional Institute. He lived just long enough to see an actor portray him in a made-for-TV movie titled *Deadly Matrimony*, based on Barbara Schaaf's fine book. Alan Masters was played by Hollywood hunk Treat Williams, who bears no resemblance to the fat, political attorney from Summit who wore a toupee and was convinced of his own invulnerability.

Calumet City (formerly known as West Hammond)

THE VAMPIRE WOMAN OF WEST HAMMOND AND OTHER STORIES OF VICE AND DEPRAVITY
1912–2001

Stateline Road from the 500 block through the 800 block and State Street in the vicinity of Inghram

Certainly Al Capone cannot be blamed for everything that was evil, corrupt, and banal in Chicago. Prostitution, dope dealing, gambling, and badger games existed long before Capone laid claim to Johnny Torrio's empire of sin and sleaze, which extended from the Levee and Chinatown down to Hammond, Indiana. Stateline Road divides Calumet City from Hammond. In the days of high-button shoes, handlebar mustaches, and Stanley Steamers, Calumet City (then known as West Hammond) was about as dangerous a place for a high-steppin' dude to venture into as anything this side of the Pecos. Study the history of urban America, and you will come across many such towns whose histories parallel that of West Hammond/Calumet City. With an invisible boundary line separating one state from another, jurisdictional rivalries between gangs of pernicious politicians and crooked cops compromise the peace and stability of overlapping communities. It is an open invitation to the proprietors of whorehouses, gambling hells, penny arcades, pawnshops, and all-night saloons to move into the peripheral areas of town, throw open the doors, and hang out a shingle in a blaze of red light. For nearly one hundred years, West Hammond/Calumet City was a no man's land suffering under the yoke of unchecked vice. The seeds were transplanted from the South Side Levee District of Chicago around the turn of the last century despite the best efforts of reformers like the impassioned Virginia Brooks, whom they laughed out of town. Police crackdowns were haphazard, and prosecutions ended in suspended sentences. The main artery of all this evil-doing was a four-block stretch of State Line Road, augmented by areas in and around State Street. (Author's Note: *On the Hammond side, State Street was once a bustling commercial center. Today it is a ghost town full of outdated buildings preservationists are fighting to save.*) *In the 1990s, conditions in Calumet City changed—in a hurry. A young and ambitious mayor named Jerry Genova vowed to clean up the city's East Side and tear down all the objectionable places where prostitution and girlie shows flourished. Genova was given high marks for his efforts. Owners of legitimate places heaped praise on him as the walls of the seedy Sodom-and-Gomorrah dives came tumbling down. In the 800 block of Stateline Road on the Illinois side, there are empty lots, one after the other, where only the grass grows. The only sign of activity on a listless Saturday night is the occasional appearance of an ambulance pulling up to the emergency room of St. Margaret–Mary Hospital across the street in Hammond. Otherwise, you could throw bowling balls down the street and not expect to hit anything. The "Whoopie Era" is clearly over in Cal City. Is the city better off for it? At the very least, there has been a sharp drop-off in liquor licensing revenue in recent years. As to the fate of the young Lohengrin fighting for the virtue of a town, a federal grand jury in Chicago returned a nine-count indictment against Genova in July 2000, charging him with using city money to finance his political career and the remodeling of his home.*

Paul Prince, custodian of the vicious West Hammond dive owned and operated by Henry Foss, pointed to a doorway leading to the backroom. "Eleven of them under that floor—all bodies—once livin' men like you and me, but all dead now!"

Attorneys for the widow of the man who came to an untimely end in the assignation room above the saloon registered shock, but the cackling, toothless barkeep prattled on, as if it were a perfectly natural occurrence in the course of daily life. "Death chamber here all right! And I got a gun. I take it in my hand and when the eleven get too loud . . . I can't fight them spirits with no human gun. Them's spirits I says! Eleven of 'em, all under that floor where their bodies were put."

Reports of a mass grave underneath the Foss saloon brought in a police raiding party from Chicago. They were ordered in to lend assistance to Virginia Brooks, a crusading young suffragette and amateur sleuth from the silk-stocking district who had been fighting a vicious gang of "white slave" traffickers and a cabal of corrupt city politicians for nearly two years. Brooks, dubbed the "Joan of Arc" of West Hammond, was ignored and shunted aside until she came into possession of an anonymous note linking barkeep Foss to the death of wealthy engineer John Messmaker, who perished inside the resort on August 13, 1912. His death was "unnatural," the result of poison mixed with alcohol, the note went on to say.

Messmaker was poured a fatal dose the morning after a night of debauchery with Frankie Ford, his favorite consort. Writers from the yellow press, who

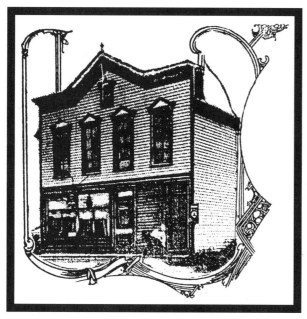

ARTIST'S SKETCH OF HENRY FOSS' SALOON AND ASSIGNATION HOUSE IN WEST HAMMOND, SEPTEMBER, 1912. IT WAS RUMORED THAT ELEVEN MEN WERE BURIED UNDERNEATH THE FLOORBOARDS AFTER THEY WERE DRUGGED AND KILLED BY FOSS AND HIS FEMALE ACCOMPLICES.

had a special flair for sensationalizing the exploits of underworld characters, identified Ford to the reading public as the "Vampire Woman of West Hammond."

Virginia Brooks, an earnest young woman desirous of ridding the town of Foss and his henchmen in city government, forced a confession out of Frankie Ford, otherwise known as "Mrs. Fasting Dutch."

She said she had been with Messmaker the night he strolled into the saloon, and was showing him affection. "I did not kill him," she insisted. "It was Henry Foss who said I was getting too familiar with Messmaker. Foss told me the night that Messmaker died, and he told several other girls in the place, that he would stop Messmaker from calling on me."

Frankie Ford divulged to Virginia Brooks that her real name was Ethel Parker, and for two years she had been working in shame as a West Hammond prostitute to satisfy a morphine habit.

She had come from wealthy and refined parents who owned a beautiful home in Lake County, Indiana. At fifteen, she ran off to Chicago to strike a fortune, but found misery instead. Unlike Theodore Dreiser's fictional small-town heroine in *Sister Carrie*, who achieves theatrical stardom in the big city, Parker was a victim of her own savage innocence. She fell into bad company after marrying and giving birth to a baby girl.

The husband cast her to the mercies of the world. The going was hard, and she drifted from bad to worse. Parker's only comfort came from a hypodermic

ETHEL PARKER (AKA "FRANKIE FORD"), MORPHINE ADDICT, PROSTITUTE, AND THE "VAMPIRE WOMAN OF WEST HAMMOND."

syringe loaded with morphine and the demimonde congregating inside Henry Foss's saloon and whorehouse. It was Parker's task to lure victims to the second floor with the connivance of Robert Clayton, a cabdriver who was paid a percentage for every "joy rider" he safely delivered to the doorstep.

Before a fortnight had passed, Clayton had also turned up dead. Like Messmaker, the official cause of death was listed as "stomach trouble."

Behind the bar, Henry Foss concealed a bottle of unbonded whiskey laced with knockout drops. If the customer did not spend his money fast enough to suit Foss, he was given a drink from that bottle until his face turned black and he passed out. The victim would then be robbed and dumped in an alley nearby.

According to wild rumor circulating through the district, not all of the victims managed to recover from their temporary slumber. It was alleged by Prince and others close to Foss and his band of cutthroats that the bodies were buried under the floorboards of the saloon.

You would think that sooner or later the stench would have made things hot for Foss if the story were indeed true. Apparently the West Hammond police did not smell anything, because they made no further inquiry into the matter. At that moment, they were interested only in getting to the bottom of the Messmaker murder, because the widow had complained to the press that the cops were not on the square.

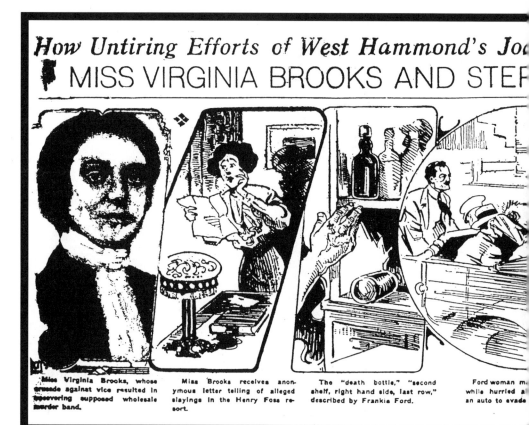

How Untiring Efforts of West Hammond's Jo[

MISS VIRGINIA BROOKS AND STEF

Miss Virginia Brooks, whose crusade against vice resulted in uncovering supposed wholesale murder band.

Miss Brooks receives anonymous letter telling of alleged slayings in the Henry Foss resort.

The "death bottle," "second shelf, right hand side, last row," described by Frankie Ford.

Ford woman m[while hurried a[an auto to evad[

With the hand of Miss Brooks pressing down upon city officials in the court of public opinion, a roundup was ordered by Mayor K. M. Woscynski, who admitted that he did not trust his police to carry out the task.

The beleaguered Woscynski requested immediate assistance from Chicago Mayor Carter Harrison II, who sent in a detachment of bluecoats to preserve order and a contingent of top detectives to investigate rumors of multiple homicides. (*Author's Note:* It is a highly unusual and controversial step for a Chicago mayor to order city police officers into adjoining cities and suburbs to preserve civil order. The only other time this would occur in the twentieth century would be during the April 1924 general elections, when the Capone mob threatened Cicero voters.)

Twenty professional sluggers, aided and abetted by a throng of angry men loyal to Foss, engaged the Windy City raiding party in a free-for-all when an attempt was made to padlock the Colonial Hotel, a notorious place owned by Cornelius "Con" Moore.

f Arc Exposed *"Death Chamber Horrors"*
N ARREST OF FRANKIE FORD

Assistant County Attorney Thomas J. Johnson searches the Ford woman's apartments after her arrest.

"Vampire woman" formally arrested, arraigned before Judge Owens and held under heavy bond.

Ethel Parker, alias Frankie Ford, whose revelations may clear up a score of death mysteries.

Henry Foss and "Con" Moore, ringleaders of the West Hammond vice ring that paid off Police Chief John Kulczyk for the privilege of operating gambling and bordellos around town, were arrested by federal authorities on September 7, 1912.

When Foss woke up in the county jail the following morning after being charged with the murder of Messmaker, the first words out of his mouth were "Fake! Fake!"

"I was a respected citizen once and sheriff of my county," he boasted. "They made the mistake of not re-electing me, and they put a good officeholder to the bad. I saved up enough money to get a license and then I opened my own place. There hasn't been much money in that. The reformers and the screech owls like this Ford woman spoiled the game."

Ethel Parker, only twenty-two years of age at the time, admitted that she had administered shots of morphine to Messmaker the night before he died, but she kept insisting that he was in good shape the next morning, at least up until the very moment he was served the poisoned whiskey by Foss or his son.

Cook County Coroner Peter Hoffman, a perfect fool of a man who inspired playwright Ben Hecht to howling laughter as he wrote him into the script of the Broadway smash *The Front Page*, placed the blame for the deaths of Messmaker and prostitute Esther Harrison squarely on Ford's wilted frame and rather stooped shoulders.

Under a curtain of secrecy, Parker and Foss were shuttled to the Sheffield Avenue Police Station in Chicago for questioning. By now, however, Virginia Brooks had softened her attitudes concerning the culpability of the "Vampire Woman" in the Messmaker murder. For nearly two hours, she described Parker as a pathetic junkie and traced the vice problem back to the police chief, who allowed seven West Hammond whorehouses to remain open in defiance of the law.

"The story told by this woman has scarcely any parallel in the history of Midwest towns and cities," Brooks testified. "It shows that crimes innumerable have been committed in West Hammond by vice keepers and their men and women slaves while the police looked on and winked."

After three weeks in the lockup, both Parker and Foss were released ... with a wink and a nod.

The West Hammond police chief was tried by the City Council, found guilty of allowing vice to proliferate, and discharged from duty. Miss Brooks was elated and claimed total victory in her righteous crusade.

It would be nice to say that West Hammond became a better place for law-abiding residents to live after that, but when the row was ended the dives were thrown open. The eastern end of the city would remain a ferocious cesspool of vice ruled by the Capone gang for the next eighty years. Vice-mongering in the steel-mill district was the charge in March 1953 when State Senator Arthur J. Bidwill of the Seventh Illinois District launched an investigation into conditions along "Strip Row"—this is what an eight-block section between Stateline Road and 215 State Street (inclusive of 100–350 Plummer Street and the forever-notorious three-block stretch from 500 to 800 on Stateline Road) in Calumet City had become.

Forty years had passed since Henry Foss, Ethel Parker, and Chief Kulczyk divided up the nightly swag. In all those years, nothing had changed except the names and the faces of the politicians and the crooks. Foss and his gang were succeeded by a more vicious element who were running things out of Chicago.

In the 1950s, Frankie LaPorte (née: Francesco Liparota) was a rising star of Calumet City and Lake County, Indiana, organized crime. LaPorte worked through Jim Emery (née: Vincenzo Ammeratto), the syndicate overlord of the steelyard district who ran the operation from Chicago Heights. After Emery passed away in

1957, Frankie LaPorte was the man to be reckoned with.

LaPorte and Tony Accardo were partners in the Owl Club gambling casino, one of the main attractions along Stateline Road providing Las Vegas–style action, until LaPorte's sister Connie Franze and her husband, Tony, bought out Accardo's interests. The Owl Club was written up in police reports for years. It was the cash cow of Cal City.

Author Ovid Demaris calculated the *daily* take from gambling and prostitution as $50,000. In the 1950s, Calumet City was the clearing-house for the distribution of pornography. One night, Paul Newey and his state's attorney's raiders seized 50,000 obscene photos, 100 reels of sexually explicit film, and obscene novels to be sold on the street for $25 apiece at 104 State Street. Today, of course, smut can be purchased over the counter, but fifty years ago pornography was as "hot" as cocaine, and purveyors of X-rated entertainment and the strip palaces faced

THE WORLDS OF SHOW BUSINESS AND GANGLAND CONVERGE AT CALUMET CITY'S INFAMOUS OWL CLUB. LEFT TO RIGHT, SEATED: PAUL "THE WAITER" RICCA, LOUIS "LITTLE NEW YORK" CAMPAGNA, FRANKIE LAPORTE, AND COMEDIAN JIMMY DURANTE.

(From the collection of John Binder and Matt Luzi)

long jail sentences unless they enjoyed the protection of obliging politicians.

The new Cal City mayor, Frank Kamminski (who doubled as liquor control commissioner), had shown no interest in complying with directives to enforce closing times, not with so much syndicate heat emanating from the north. It was estimated that in Cal City there was one bar for every forty-six residents—the highest percentage of saloons in the nation up to that time. (*Authors Note:* According to 1953 statistics, there were 365 saloons in a town with a population of 16,825 citizens.)

The strip joints catered mostly to Polish and Lithuanian workers from the South Chicago–Gary–Hammond steelyards, hard-living bachelors who wandered into town to blow their paychecks and live riotously one or two days out of the week.

Military personnel from Great Lakes Naval Training Station and the local Coast Guard who patronized the "B-girl" saloons like the Riptide Tavern at 101 State Street, the Play House, Al Pilotto's Club Palace, Ciro's Saloon, the Ron-da-Voo, the Ozark, and the 21 Club down the street were ordered to keep out by their post commanders.

"By this method I hope that some of our youngsters can be kept out of the Calumet City dives," said Cook County Sheriff John Babb.

That wouldn't happen until 1993, when the entire district was ground to dust. By then most of the steelyards were out of business and vice districts like "Strip Row" in Hammond were a thing of the past.

"The Curse of the Doomed Circus Train"

Hammond, Indiana

S I D E T R I P

Over the years, ghostly tales have been told of the famous circus-train wreck occurring outside Hammond, Indiana, in the closing months of World War I. One of them, all but forgotten now, points to a curse that may or may not have contributed to a succession of calamitous events befalling the Hagenbeck-Wallace Circus long *before* the deadly train crash of June 22, 1918.

Ben Wallace launched his Midwestern wagon show in 1886, bringing a colorful array of circus performers, magicians, and clowns to sleepy small towns in the rural backwashes of Indiana, Wisconsin, Minnesota, Iowa, Missouri, and Illinois. Business was good—the country people especially enjoyed the rousing parade down the main street. So, by 1894, the Wallace operation branched out as a railroad show, eventually becoming the nation's third largest circus.

On August 7, 1903, two sections of the Wallace Circus train collided with another train at Durand, Michigan, killing twenty-three people (most of them workmen). It was a tragic human error, presaging the nearly identical disaster at Hammond by fifteen years.

Three years passed. In 1906, after all the lawsuits stemming from the earlier wreck had been settled and the furor had died down, Wallace merged with Carl Hagenbeck, a celebrated showman with an exceptional collection of wild animals to show off to the gaping populace. Not long after the deal was closed, a fire in Peru, Indiana, nearly put the entire circus out of business. By now, the show-biz world began to gossip about Hagenbeck-Wallace. Surely they were jinxed. How else could you explain continuous bad luck? No one could remember a more ill-fated operation.

If all this wasn't bad enough, a flood of the Wabash River in 1913 drowned many of the prized circus animals. Ben Wallace had finally had enough. He sold his interests to Edward Ballard of French Lick, Indiana, who was joined by a consortium of former circus performers and businessmen. Together, they decided to challenge fate.

Having passed through the plagues of fire and flood, what more, pray tell, could possibly happen to the circus train? They were soon to find out.

Shortly before 4:00 A.M., the morning of June 22, 1918, the Hagenbeck-Wallace Circus train was parked on a rail siding on the outskirts of Hammond (near Ivanhoe, Indiana), awaiting clearance to proceed into the city when disaster struck. The engineer had stopped the train in order to cool an overheated wheel bearing, but was now awaiting the flagman's signal to continue.

On board, three hundred circus performers were sleeping soundly, or preparing for the next day's show, scheduled to take place at 150th Street and Calumet Avenue (present site of the A. L. Spohn School). The previous day, they had put on a splendid show in Michigan City, Indiana.

An empty military troop train bound for Chicago from Kalamazoo, Michigan, followed close behind. Engineer Alonzo Sargent was at the throttle of the transport train, but apparently he had failed to spot the red warning lights or the cars of the Hagenbeck-Wallace Circus lying in a direct path on the same Michigan Central tracks.

Sargent later admitted that he had dozed off, exhausted from a heavy workload. The troop train plowed into the rear of the circus train at a speed of 60 miles per hour, destroying three cars before finally stopping. Sheets of fire tore through the performers' cars, incinerating eighty-six people. The impact of the crash jarred loose the kerosene lamps, igniting the interiors of the wooden Pullman cars.

Powerful explosions lit up the night sky. Within seconds, the entire train was a raging inferno. The Gary (Indiana) Fire Department was hampered by lack of water. All they could do was silently observe the carnage.

Said one eyewitness: "I was awakened by a crash that was so terrifying I thought the steel mills had blown up. It did not seem like two railroad trains to me, but a huge pile of kindling wood. I could hear people screaming and shouting, and I knew something terrible had happened."

Those trapped under the wreckage died horribly, and it would be days before the last of the bodies were pried loose by civilian volunteers from Hammond.

The doomed Hagenbeck-Wallace Circus missed only that one performance in Hammond. With the assistance of Ringling Brothers and Barnum & Bailey Shows, supplies, equipment, and replacement performers were rushed in, allowing owner Ballard to resume his hectic schedule of performances in Wisconsin the following week. Engineer Sargent was dragged into a court of law on a charge of manslaughter, but was released when the jury could not agree on a verdict.

A large funeral plot was purchased by the Showman's League of America at Woodlawn Cemetery in West Suburban Forest Park. A mass funeral for the victims of the crash was held on June 25, only five days after the conflagration.

Over the years, there have been reports of the trumpeting of elephants and the roar of lions coming from deep inside the cemetery. Local ghost hunters were convinced the restless dead from the train wreck were crying out for salvation, until one of the local geniuses figured out that the unearthly animal sounds were coming from nearby Brookfield Zoo and could only be heard when carried on the wind from that direction.

The curse, you ask? As a result of his latest misfortune, Edward Ballard became one of the true believers. He put the circus up for sale before the first spade of dirt in the Woodlawn Cemetery was turned.

Life and Death in the City:

The West Side from Maxwell Street to the Suburbs

At the close of the nineteenth century, the West Side of Chicago was a picture-perfect ideal of gracious town and country living. The greenery of Garfield Park, Douglas Park, Humboldt Park, and a ribbon of spacious boulevards laid out by city planners, suggested to outsiders that a utopian oasis was an attainable dream in the interior of the rough Midwestern industrial corridor. But as Jane Jacobs noted in *The Death and Life of Great American Cities*, "Parks are volatile places . . . they can grow more beloved and valuable with the years, but pitifully few show this staying power. For every Rittenhouse Square in Philadelphia, or Rockefeller Plaza, or Washington Square in New York, or Boston Common, or their loved equivalents in other cities, there are dozens of dispirited city vacuums called parks, eaten around with decay, little used, unloved." The natural beauty of the West Side park system has been eroded by decades-long poverty, crime, and racial polarization. The panic peddling and white flight of the 1950s and 1960s accelerated patterns of racial segregation and class division evident in the decaying infrastructure of the neighborhoods. David Fremon pointed out in his book *Chicago Politics Ward by Ward* that in the Lawndale community, the white population dropped from 87,000 in 1950 to 11,000 in 1960. Today, it is near zero. Three times in the 1960s, these economically dispirited West Side neighborhoods went up in flames. The worst episode of inner-city rioting occurred in March 1968 as a violent epitaph to the assassination of Reverend Dr. Martin Luther King, who had visited the area only a few years earlier urging non-violent protest against long-standing injustices, and moderation in the face of hate. Buildings were burned to the ground. Businesses moved away. Housing was substandard, and there were fewer social welfare agencies and churches to uplift the poor than on the South Side of the city where the African-American population was older, firmly entrenched, and more prosperous than the refugees from the Mississippi Delta and "Jim Crow" South who migrated north to Lawndale in succeeding waves in the 1950s and 1960s. By the 1980s, West Side block clubs

1. Amos Snell Washington Boulevard residence.
2. Alderman Albert Prignano was murdered here.
3. "Samoots" Ammatuna slaying at Halsted & Roosevelt.
4. The Tunnel Inferno, 22nd and Laflin.
5. Brach Candy Company fire (Kinzie & Kilpatrick).
6. Church of the Holy Ghost (Adams & Kildare).
7. Headquarters of "Zookie the Bookie."
8. "Zookie the Bookie" murder site at 4042 Wilcox.
9. The West Side Riots, 1966.
10. 1954 Mars Oldsmobile shootout, 5817 West Madison.
11. Cicero Race Riot, 6139 West 19th St., Cicero.
12. Taxi Dancehall Girls of Stickney (Vicinity of Harlem & Ogden).
13. Residence of Paul "the Waiter" Ricca, 1515 Bonnie Brae, River Forest.
14. Horwath's Restaurant, 1850 North Harlem Ave.
15. Ken Eto was shot outside the Montclare Theater, 7129 West Grand Ave.

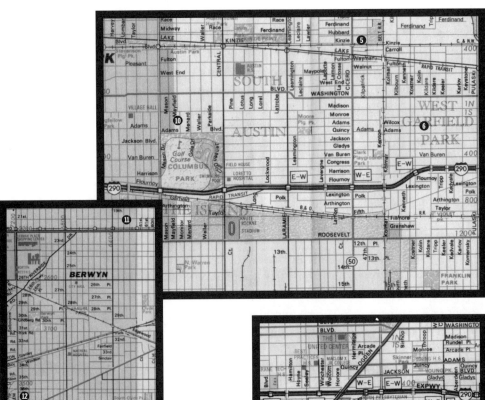

were formed to battle the malignant scourge of street gangs and the open-air drug markets in the Harrison Police District pandering to city and suburban clients. Driving through Garfield Park and Lawndale, one senses growing despair bordering on hopelessness. The West Side has never fully recovered from the trauma of the 1960s, but there is a rich history here, if you look closely. The visible reminders of past and present are found in the historic graystones, the churches, and former synagogues converted to other purposes. Tragically, many of these old buildings surrounding the swath of green parks are boarded-up, burned-out hulks awaiting demolition. Once destroyed, they are rarely replaced. Thus, in any exploration of the historic West Side parks and boulevards, you run across considerable "prairie space" on the side streets and commercial thoroughfares where buildings ought to be. Crime has always been transcendent, assuming different shapes and forms over the years. At the beginning of the twentieth century, tenement conditions along Halsted Street on the Near West Side were Chicago's shame. Prostitution, vice, and robbery flourished in the shadow of Hull House, the social relief agency founded by Jane Addams in 1889. By the 1920s and 1930s, organized crime progressed steadily westward along Twelfth Street (Roosevelt Road), invading Douglas Park and Lawndale where Eastern European Jews from Maxwell Street had settled. Lawndale spawned assassin Jack Ruby, the terrible Miller brothers, "Zookie the Bookie," Lenny Patrick, and lesser vassals of gangland's "Jewish Faction," whose names are listed separately on the Chicago Crime Commission's mob organizational chart. Today, one is left with the numbing feeling that the West Side has been forgotten and the utopian vision of the landscape architects invalidated. It is a side of Chicago where the Gray Line tour bus is rarely seen.

Near West Side

425 Washington Boulevard (now 1326 West Washington, at Ada Street, Northwest corner)

THE SNELL CASE: A FAMOUS GASLIGHT ERA MURDER MYSTERY
February 8, 1888

Echoes of the near-perfect crime reverberated around Chicago for nearly fifty years. Crime reporters, like fishwives and gossipmongers, love to spin yarns and tell tales. In the reporters' room adjoining the Detective Bureau in the old City Hall, speculation as to the whereabouts of the villain who murdered the wealthy real-estate plunger Amos Jerome Snell in the foyer of his Washington Boulevard man-

sion was a fruitful topic of conversation long after the century turned and automobiles replaced the horse as the preferred mode of transportation. Amos Snell lived in a mansion described by the Chicago Times *(a long-defunct sheet) as "... one of the most beautiful and striking on the fine West Side boulevard which it graces. There are handsome well-kept grounds about it, where flowers blossom and fountains play in summer. It has broad, delightful piazzas where the happy grandchildren of the dead man have many times romped in child-ish glee." With a heavy sigh, we can only imagine such a time and place. The home of Amos Snell was one of many showy private residences lining the boulevard. It was a fifteen-room, spired Victorian built in 1870 at substantial cost by a wealthy recluse who could easily afford the trappings of money. By the turn of the last century, Washington Boulevard was already beginning to slip as a "millionaire's row." Once the elderly owners of these drafty old man-sions had expired, the Gilded Age palaces of another age were partitioned, sub-divided, and turned into shabby rooming houses renting to the indigent and downtrodden. The properties decayed and went to seed sooner than anyone had expected. Thus, in the name of urban renewal (a euphemism for slum clearance), the old Victorians were demolished, one by one, and the last ves-tiges of a more refined and elegant era of Chicago living vanished forever. A one-story red-brick lithographing company crowds the street corner where the Snell mansion once stood. A few doors east, at 1304-1308 West Washington, a handful of surviving brownstones remind us that amid the decomposition of Chicago's historic districts, traces of humanity—history's gift to the present generation—manage to hold on.*

The air was bleak and biting, and frost hung in the air. Outside the residence of Amos J. Snell, the stillness of night was punctuated by the gentle clip-clopping of carriages rolling along the lighted street, and the laughter of the coachmen as they drove the young people home from an evening dance at Martine's.

The hour was late, and the Norwegian governess, Miss Ida Bjornstad, had just put Snell's grandchildren to bed for the evening. Snell, a white-haired but spry old gent of sixty-five who owned more prime Chicago real estate than any other man in Cook County, was in his study reading a book.

From his bedroom, five-year-old Chester Snell Coffin cried out in terror, "Ida, there won't be any burglars here tonight, will there?" The governess assured him there would not. The boy had a vivid imagination, but she had also heard disturbing stories that Chief of Police Frederick Ebersold was being criti-cized for his mishandling of cases during a recent crime wave. Burglaries and thieving were occurring at alarming frequency all across the city, and Ebersold, who was held accountable for the public relations fiasco surrounding his department's bungled investigation into the 1886 Haymarket Riot bombing, was on the hot seat.

Amos Snell's wife, Henrietta, and his daughter, Grace Henrietta, were in Milwaukee and not scheduled to return for a few days. Only the servants and the children were present that night when an armed intruder broke in through the front door and crept along the darkened parlor-floor hallway toward the basement, where the safe full of valuables was located.

Snell, clad in a white sleeping gown, heard the disturbance coming from the downstairs parlor and reached for his bedside gun. Creeping down the stairs with his loaded revolver in hand, the old man called out to the thieves, "Get out! Get Out!" Upstairs, Rosa Bergstuhler, the German cook, and Ida Bjornstad heard their employer's commands, and clung to each other in fright knowing that a prowler was loose in the house.

Snell fired blindly into the dark, but his errant shot passed harmlessly through a silk decoration and lodged in the wall. The thief returned fire, fatally striking Snell in the head and midsection. The millionaire was dead before he hit the floor. Having already pillaged the contents of the safe, the assassin turned and exited through the front entrance, taking with him $2,000 in securities and bonds. The neighbors knew that the deceased was something of a recluse. Snell was born in Upstate New York, but he had earned his millions buying up empty farmland in the unincorporated Northwest Side of Chicago after the Civil War, and used part of his fortune to improve the West Side neighborhood he resided in. He disdained pretentiousness and avoided society gatherings at all cost.

AMOS SNELL WAS SHOT WHEN HE INTERRUPTED A BURGLAR.

GEORGE W. HUBBARD,
SUPERINTENDENT OF POLICE
1888–1889. HE WAS
APPOINTED CHIEF AFTER THE
INVESTIGATION INTO THE
MURDER OF MILLIONAIRE
AMOS SNELL FOUNDERED.

Amos Snell was every inch a Yankee blue-blood with the mannerisms and stubborn mindset of a Puritan but possessing the business sense of a Rockefeller. Snell, Marshall Field, Potter Palmer, Levi Leiter, William B. Ogden—these were men with a head for business who built frontier Chicago from the ground up and reaped the whirlwind. "He was a great home man and cared absolutely nothing for society," commented one afternoon newspaper, which partly explains the absence of Snell's name alongside Chicago's monied elites in the city social registers and history books.

Amos Snell was not in the habit of talking in his sleep or roaming about, which refuted the far-fetched tale concocted by the cook and maid, who told police they did not immediately rush downstairs to investigate because they believed that their employer was experiencing bad dreams and had fired his bedside gun at nocturnal phantoms while half-asleep. Suspicion fell immediately on the domestic help, but in truth, the two young immigrant women were paralyzed by fear and had locked themselves in their fourth-floor bedrooms until dawn, daring not to peak over the edge of their quilted blankets till the light of day illuminated the bedchamber.

The body was discovered early the next morning by the coachman of nineteen years, dutiful Henry Winklocke, as he began his daily rounds.

The mystery that shrouded the brutal murder of Amos Snell was solved less than eleven days later, but not before the newspaper editorialists had pressured the Republican mayor, John A. Roche, to dismiss Superintendent Ebersold for incompetency. Matters in the police department had reached a crisis level, and Ebersold's day-to-day status was complicated by what the papers began calling "The Snell Affair."

The department personnel were badly demoralized, complaining of low pay and lack of appreciation. Embittered detectives, paid half of what their counterparts in New York City were earning at the time, grumbled that the City of Chicago refused to provide them with "walking-around money" to pay tipsters and informants for useful items of gossip to help them crack a high-profile case like this one.

The mayor promised a speedy resolution to the murder, and fortunately for his reform administration, it came less than a week later. On February 19, the incoming superintendent, George W. Hubbard, was exceptionally pleased to announce the identity of the abysmal fiend who was responsible for killing poor Mr. Snell.

Finding that fiend, at this late hour, was another matter all together.

On a bitterly cold February morning, three thousand persons from all walks of life gathered in front of the Snell mansion to pay their respects or simply gawk at the spectacle. From inside the rear parlor there could be heard on the street the strains of the traditional church hymn "Nearer My God to Thee," sung with tenderness and empathy by Miss Abbie Carrington, soprano and pianist.

Nearly 150 carriages in the Snell funeral cortege passed through the gates of Rosehill Cemetery for the interment. In one of them sat Mrs. Ella Wick, proprietress of a rooming house at 474 West Madison Street. (*Author's Note:* Now 1343 West Madison. It is a parking lot, adjoining loft apartments between Ada Street and Loomis.)

Before the long line of somber black carriages departed from the Snell mansion, Mrs. Wick confided to police detective John "Sandy" Hanley that she had recently rented a room to a stylish young man calling himself "Mr. William Scott."

"There is something I must show you!" she whispered. "Please come by this evening!"

The man in question had vacated his room the morning following the murder in the company of a stranger. When asked by Mrs. Wick if he would return for his things, Scott replied: "Yes, I may come back in two weeks and it may be two months. While I am gone, I want you to take care of my things. I will want the room when I come back."

Mrs. Wick's curiosity eventually got the best of her, and with the passkey, she entered his room and began rummaging through the closet. Expensive silverware and other items belonging to a rich person were found, and only on the day of the funeral did she choose to confide her suspicions to the police. Some of the papers taken from the Snell safe, including Cook County scrip, were later found under the bed.

Probing further, the police learned that Scott had recently worked as a night reporter for the *Chicago Times*, but was fired for incompetence. Before that he had served time in the federal prison at Frankfort, Kentucky. Detectives established his real name as William B. Tascott, wastrel son of James Tascott, owner of a manufacturing plant on Canal Street. The elder Tascott was respected as a man of good character and social standing. His son was an accomplished thief and con man before his twenty-first birthday.

Wanted posters were circulated across the Midwest, and the passenger lists for the thirty train routes leading out of the city of Chicago were scoured by police to see if Tascott had purchased a ticket using one of his many aliases. Chief Hubbard warned out-of-town police to be on the lookout for a blond-haired man whose ankles were scarred by the wearing of prison leg irons.

The owner of a newsstand in St. Paul, Minnesota, reported spotting a man matching Tascott's physical description. He said that the suspect presented himself as the advance man for a itinerant theatrical troop performing *Around the World in Eighty Days*. But when Chicago police headed north to investigate, the only thing they could come up with was his gold-headed cane offered for sale in a pawnshop.

Despite earnest efforts to track down every reported lead, Tascott vanished into the abyss of history. His whereabouts remain a mystery to this very day. The sizable reward money offered by the Snell family was never claimed, despite more than three hundred sightings of the fugitive in the years following the murder.

The case faded from view. The Snell mansion was sold, its beautiful oaken interior subdivided, and its rooms converted into cheap rooming-house lodging. Not much more was heard of the unsolved murder mystery in the twentieth century until a frail old woman staggered into Judge James Fardy's courtroom in the Superior Court of Cook County on May 31, 1937, seeking her rightful share of her late father's estate.

Mrs. Grace Henrietta Snell Love, age seventy-one and married six times (three times to the same man, her first husband, Frank Nixon Coffin), complained that she could not live on the $400 a month stipend paid to her by the trust. And as the sole surviving child of Amos Snell, she believed she was entitled to much more. Her daughter, Mildred S. Engelke, begged to disagree. Brought before the court, she was asked to provide a vivid description of her mother, whose marital difficulties were grist for the Gaslight Era gossip sheets for many a year.

Summing it all up, Mildred pined: "Why, she is the cruelest mother a girl ever had!"

722 Bunker

Street

(now 722

Greenshaw)

MARKED FOR DEATH: GANGLAND MURDERS ANOTHER POLITICIAN
December 29, 1935

By the middle of the 1920s, the Italians were the predominant ethnic group residing in the poor, working-class slums west of downtown Chicago. The Near West Side, apart from the fading mansions of Washington Boulevard, was a gloomy urban jungle defined by political struggles, blood feuds, poverty, and creeping despair. The Italian quarter, centered around Taylor Street due north of the Maxwell Street Jewish ghetto, was a spawning ground for career criminals and organized crime chieftains. In the days of National Prohibition, when much of the entire area was a bootlegging battlefield, the downtown politicians, the cops, and even the local residents called this Near West Side Ward the "Bloody 20th." Alternately known as "the West Side Valley," the 20th Ward was firmly under the thumb of the Al Capone gang. The criminal organization he founded backed a succession of aldermanic candidates and state representatives favorable to their interests. For a time, Albert Prignano was a vassal of the gang. He was a likable politician who curried the favor of syndicate bigwigs and was seemingly destined to rise even higher—until he fell out of favor with his sponsors. The Prignano murder, coming in 1935 when the winds of change blew ill for the Chicago crime syndicate, was a signature mob hit prominently reported in the local media. Today, it is an episode overlooked and forgotten by crime researchers and devotees of the Capone period of Chicago history. The residence of Albert J. Prignano, and all the other homes that lined Bunker Street (renamed Greenshaw in the 1940s), disappeared when the area was rezoned and converted to light manufacturing. Greenshaw is an east-west street sandwiched between Clinton and Jefferson (it is a block south of DeKoven Street where the 1871 Chicago Fire started). Given what we already know about the Near West Side high residential density of former times, it is hard to imagine that in such an ugly, surreal rust-belt setting like this one, families with real concerns actually lived there. A Marathon gas station, factories, and an asphalt parking lot are all you will find on Greenshaw today. If the spirit of

Albert Prignano wanders about the street seeking reconciliation with past events, he will surely find himself hopelessly lost.

Al Prignano was married to the former radio singer Jean Gibson for thirteen years when plans for a joyous second honeymoon were scuttled by the clatter of bullets on a quiet side street in the dead of night.

It was a cold-blooded gangland execution no less, crudely disguised as an armed robbery. The cops suspected that the killing was ordered by Frank Nitti, heir and successor to Al Capone, who languished inside the Alcatraz penitentiary in January 1935. Proving the theory was another matter.

The slain politician was a force in the maelstrom of 20th Ward Democratic politics for a number of years, beginning as a secretary to Municipal Court Bailiff Dennis Egan. At the time, the 20th Ward was controlled by City Collector Morris Eller, his son Emmanuel (a circuit court judge), and sixteen political satraps loyal to Mayor William Hale Thompson.

The Eller gang was notorious for digging their fingers into everyone else's racket, and they did not cotton to the motives of reformers or good-government types. Octavius Granady, an African-American lawyer who opposed Morris Eller in the race for Republican committeeman, was assassinated in 1928. Seven men, including four policemen, stood trial for the Granady murder. All seven were acquitted.

In his rise to power, Prignano took a more conciliatory attitude toward Capone than Granady, and in fact was quite chummy with old "Scarface." Prignano was an overnight guest of Capone in one of Havana's fabled gambling hotels, and was even photographed side by side with Capone at the Notre Dame–Northwestern football game at Soldier Field on October 10, 1931.

Neither the Ellers nor Capone brooked interference from Democrats or Republicans in their rush to throw weight behind Prignano in his 1927 race for alderman. His tolerance of gambling, booze, and vice squared him with the mob. But as violence escalated in his ward, Alderman Prignano reconsidered his alliances. "Those boys are going too far," he remarked. The Municipal Voters League commended him for his hard work and tireless efforts to improve sanitary conditions and rid the neighborhood of crime.

Al Prignano had made a clean break from the hoodlum faction, but that ill-advised move cost him his reelection bid in 1929. Prignano's Republican cousin William V. "Wild Bill" Pacelli received support from the Eller gang and easily defeated Prignano at the polls amid threats of violence and election terrorism.

Still, Al Capone retained a measure of fondness for Prignano and wished him no harm. But within two years, Capone was sent to prison and Prignano's immunity waiver was lifted by Nitti.

In the fall of 1934, when the Democratic Party swept the ticket and the last vestiges of the corrupt cabal of former Thompson supporters were driven from office, Prignano was elected 17th District State Representative to the Illinois General Assembly. He crusaded for old-age pension bills and legislation to remove elderly firemen and police officers from the department as a means of improving efficiency. He hinted to Detective William Drury that "he knew plenty" about mob operations in Chicago, and would expose it all in due course.

Aware of Prignano's reformer overtones, crime boss Nitti demanded that he grant the syndicate wider leverage in patronage appointments, and ordered him to get behind a scheme to allow gambling in the new South Water Wholesale Market, opened in 1925 at Fifteenth Street and Aberdeen. Prignano retained his post as Democratic ward committeeman, and was in a position to do these favors. But when the request was denied, Frank Nitti marked Prignano for death. He was fired on by two gunmen at Twenty-second and Wentworth in the middle of Chinatown late one night, but the assassins had poor aim. The mob's high council demanded swift, effective action.

The plot to kill Prignano was hatched by James D'Angelo, a dice-and-card-room operator out of St. Louis, and Michael Genovese, a Chicago gunsel. They enlisted two minor safecrackers named Michael Novak and Henry Szelangowski, who were led to believe that it would go down as a routine stickup of a political bigshot who wouldn't report the incident to police.

D'Angelo did not accompany the other three to 722 Bunker Street, but he was confident that Genovese would accomplish the hidden motives behind the bogus holdup attempt.

That night, Prignano, his wife, their eight-year-old adopted son John, and Prignano's mother-in-law, Julia Beardmore, were returning home from a family party when they were accosted by the three men just as Jean turned the key in the front door. The family chauffeur, Victor Galante, followed them halfway up the walk.

"This is a stickup, Prignano. Keep quiet and you won't get hurt!" shouted Genovese. They removed $2,000 in cash from his pockets and an expensive diamond ring from his finger. Prignano was ordered to turn around and the women were told to proceed with the boy up the stairs.

Terrified at the request, the wife pleaded for her husband's life. "Don't make him turn his back!" she cried.

The gunmen ignored her, and a shot was fired into the back of the politician's head. He tumbled headlong into the vestibule. Genovese finished him off with five more shots.

Novak and Szelangowski panicked and ran to the getaway car. They had not counted on any of this, and wondered why they had been used as unwitting pawns in so obvious a murder plot. The chauffeur Galante drew a pistol and winged Genovese in the leg as he ran toward the car, while the shaky Szelangowski flooded the engine. All three were forced to ditch the vehicle and flee on foot.

Chicago police fingered a fugitive Mafia hoodlum named Angelo Lazzia (aka Santo Virusso) for the killing. Lazzia had recently escaped from fascist Italy, where Benito Mussolini's recent anti-Mafia crackdowns had temporarily driven murderers out of the country and disabled operations. At first the cops believed Lazzia had engineered a Mafia–Black Hand "vendetta" for personal reasons. This was not the case, however.

As it developed, Novak was later arrested on burglary charges and sent to the Joliet penitentiary. Facing extradition to Missouri, Novak implicated Szelangowski in the Prignano holdup. Both men pleaded guilty to the murder, but were given reduced fifteen-year sentences after the judge was convinced that they knew nothing about the murder plot beforehand.

Michael Genovese disappeared from the public eye and was never found. The trussed-up body of the plotter Jimmy D'Angelo was removed from inside the trunk of his automobile on LaSalle Street, March 11, 1944.

Albert Prignano died broke and was waked at his home on Bunker Street. A requiem high mass was held at the Church of the Guardian Angel at 717 West Forquer Street—the first Italian Catholic parish on the West Side. (*Author's Note:* The famous church was built in 1899 and razed in 1959.)

High city and state officials were notable by their absence. The taint of the underworld was a powerful inducement for them to stay away.

Summing up the life and times of the amiable but troubled West Side politician, the Chicago *Herald & Examiner* editorialized: "He goes to his grave the victim of underworld bullets—bullets that were messengers from the strata of life into which he had allowed himself to be drawn. The very manner of his death is a sermon to the voters of this city. Through the ghastliness of the murder is revealed the ghastliness of some of Prignano's associations."

804 Roosevelt

Road (Halsted

Street &

Roosevelt,

northwest

corner)

THE BOOTLEGGING BEAU BRUMMEL: RECALLING THE LIFE AND DEATH OF SAMUEL SAMUZZO "SAMOOTS" AMMATUNA
November 10, 1925

From the 1880s onward, this historic Near West Side intersection represented the symbolic port of entry for tens of thousands of Eastern European Jews (Orthodox in belief), fleeing the pogroms of Russia. A West Side immigrant ghetto (or "shtetl") took shape, displacing the Germans and Irish who once lived here. Its natural boundaries extended north to south from Polk Street down to Sixteenth Street, and from Canal on the east to Blue Island Avenue on the west. Pushcarts and open-air vendors flooded into the Maxwell Street market, while the needle trades and large clothing manufacturers like Hart, Schaffner & Marx flourished on Roosevelt Road. The Jews accounted for 68 percent of the city's tailors in 1910. The whole area was a swirling mass of impoverished humanity; a commercial bazaar and way station for the poor and disenfranchised, offering spectacular and peculiar sights, old-world custom, kosher foods, and eclectic charm. Living conditions were squalid as one might expect, and crime was a natural byproduct of the cramped and outmoded infrastructure of wooden tenements with backyard privies. Davy Miller, Maxie Eisen, Samuel "Nails" Morton, Jake Guzik, and other criminal heavyweights from the Jewish ghetto learned the ropes on Roosevelt Road and were often visited by Italian hoodlums from the Taylor Street quarter nearby. "Samoots" Ammatuna purchased his custom-made suits from Jewish tailors, and received his haircuts and shaves from Isadore Paul, whose barbershop stood at 804 Roosevelt. The barbershop, like much of the surrounding Near West Side, has been swallowed up by the University of Illinois Chicago campus. The old buildings were flattened. Neighborhood life, as it existed up until the late 1950s when the bulldozers moved in, has been eviscerated. The University of Illinois athletic field replaced the sidewalk storefronts in the 800 block of Roosevelt where "Samoots" laughed and joked with his barber. Across the street stands St. Francis of Assisi Church, once an Italian parish, but not much of anything anymore. The people have all moved away.

The floral arrangements were ordered. The jittery young bride had packed her trousseau, and the final preparations were underway for gangland's swankiest and most highly anticipated nuptials of the fall 1925 social season—the union of Samuel Samuzzo "Samoots" Ammatuna and Rose Pecoraro, sister-in-law of the dearly departed but long-remembered Mike Merlo, boss of the *Unione Sicilione*.

Samoots Ammatuna was a Prohibition original who first came to the attention of Chicago police in 1921, when he masterminded the vendetta killing of Paul Labriola, a court bailiff loyal to 19th Ward Alderman Johnny "de Pow" Powers during the "war of Italian succession." The Taylor Street gangsters were trying to end long-standing Irish political control of the district.

Ammatuna was an accomplished Charleston dancer and opera devotee who exercised his musically correct tenor voice inside the Bluebird Cafe on Halsted Street. Much admired and looked up to by the immigrant Sicilians living in the district, Ammatuna was a glib storyteller who personally recoiled from violence and wandered the dangerous streets of the West Side without protection in his expensive suits, diamond watch, diamond stickpin, and diamond watch chain.

He refused to carry a gun, believing there were more practical ways to resolve disputes. Nevertheless, the pacifist possessed a certain bravado and feared no one. According to one contemporary account, he was "always ready to hurl defiance into the teeth of his enemies."

His courage was never questioned, even among the five "Terrible" Genna brothers of Taylor Street, who viewed Ammatuna as a natural threat and hated him on general principles. When he showed up one day in front of their liquor depot unarmed and expressing the desire to take them all on, man to man, they brushed him off as crazy. But they did not emerge from the garage to take him up on the challenge either.

The Gennas provided the necessary supplies to an army of home-grown Italian moonshine cookers making whiskey inside their two flats butting up against Taylor Street. But when the rival gangs picked off three of the Gennas and forced the other two into exile, Samoots saw an opportunity to move up in the world. He proclaimed Taylor Street as open territory and recruited Eddie Zine, proprietor of a Willow Springs roadhouse, to help convince the inner council of the Italian secret societies to anoint him rightful heir and successor to Mike Merlo.

The presidency of the *Unione Sicilione* carried with it enormous prestige and influence. As president, Ammatuna would be in a position to checkmate the ambitions of Al Capone, a rising star in 1925, and not the all-powerful boss he was destined to become two years later.

His marriage to Rose Pecoraro was a calculated move, though he was forced to postpone it for one year out of respect to Mike's memory.

With four dress circle tickets to the Chicago Lyric Opera presentation of

Aida tucked inside his suit pocket, Samoots settled into his barber's chair for a haircut and manicure. Had he paid closer attention to the calendar this early evening of November 10, 1925, he would have known that it was *exactly* one year to the day of Mike Merlo's funeral and the assassination of Dion O'Banion in his North State Street flower shop. Thoughts of the grim reaper coming back to repeat history on this important gangland anniversary were the farthest thing from his mind as he happily gossiped about the upcoming baseball season, his wedding, and the opera with Bertha "Birdie" Drake, the pretty manicurist, and the barber, Vincenzo Gloia.

As Ammatuna arose from the chair to begin a festive evening of wine and song, two men burst through the door of the shop with their pistols leveled at Samoots. The attackers, one tall, one short, and both dark-complected, fired a series of eight shots, sending the patrons and barbers scurrying for cover. A bullet tore through Ammatuna's neck, narrowly missing his spine. When the smoke had cleared, and the gunmen safely away, Samoots was dragged to an awaiting taxicab by cohorts loitering outside.

The cabby drove the mortally wounded gangster to a cigar shop at 814 Taylor Street for a strategy conference, and then on to the Jefferson Park Hospital, where it was thought that he might still have a chance for recovery.

A vigil formed at the bedside. "Diamond Joe" Esposito, a Taylor Street gangster-saloon politician, conferred privately with Ammatuna. It is believed that Samoots whispered the identity of the gunmen to only two people: Esposito and Ammatuna's brother Luigi, recently arrived from Italy. Out of respect to the code of "Omerta," Samoots said nothing to Assistant State's Attorney Joseph F. Savage; Police Captain Daniel Lynch, commander of the Maxwell Street precinct; or the assembled multitude of reporters.

Ammatuna called for his fiancée and summoned a priest to perform the wedding ceremony, once the doctors decreed that there was no hope for recovery. Rose wasn't thinking clearly, and her eyes were full of tears, but she nodded in agreement to her darling's dying wish. Before the exchange of vows could begin however, Samoots lapsed into unconsciousness. He died moments later, and Rose Pecoraro would remain Rose Pecoraro for the time being.

No one was ever brought to justice for the murder of Samoots Ammatuna, but there was little doubt in gangland who was behind it all. Samoots had gotten too big for his pants, and Al Capone wished him dead. The presidency of the *Unione Sicilione* was too big of a prize to go to an amateur like Samoots who was not solidly aligned with the Capone interests. Tony Lombardo, a man of old-world refinement, and not Samoots Ammatuna, was the man Capone designated for the job.

Less than five days later, on November 18, Eddie Zine was finished off in the south suburbs by the same two gunmen who had killed his boss. Only four hours earlier, Zine was attending Samoots's funeral and wondering how he was going to protect himself. That same week, he was betrothed to the rich widow of Tony Blinstrop, owner of the Village Gardens roadhouse. Gangland's newest widow recalled how Eddie had predicted his own death, even as they were preparing to tie the knot. "If someone should shoot me, see, I want to be cremated," he said.

Marriage, like death, is inevitable for most men. But you usually do not expect one to come so soon before the other.

Pilsen

22nd Street and Laflin

THE TUNNEL INFERNO
April 13–14, 1931

Throughout much of Chicago's early history, residents were forced to contend with the menace of cholera, a deadly plague spawned in the fetid water of the Chicago River. The lack of proper drainage, and the generally unsanitary conditions in the frontier city made it less likely for residents to die from gunplay, venereal disease, or some other urban horror than from contaminated drinking water. The problem was not adequately addressed until 1889, when the Metropolitan Sanitary District of Chicago was created by legislative fiat in order to find the means necessary to send the accumulated pollution away from Lake Michigan and down to the Mississippi River via the Des Plaines and Illinois Rivers. With the opening of the Chicago Sanitary and Ship Canal in 1900, the district scored a stunning triumph of modern engineering by reversing the flow of the river and sending the sludge and backwash twenty-eight miles south to Lockport, Illinois. The Metropolitan Sanitary District of Greater Chicago is recognized as one of the most reliable and innovative municipal agencies in the science of sewage treatment in our country today. But like any other great technological achievement of mankind, there is an ominous flip side to the equation. Forgotten in the history of this great engineering gift to the City of Chicago is the 1931 West Side tunnel explosion at Twenty-second Street and Laflin, just east of Ashland Avenue in Pilsen. The site of the disaster stands opposite Benito Juarez High School on the south side of Twenty-second Street. The infrastructure of the neighborhood hasn't changed much in the intervening years. It is still gray and dismal. This particular section of the West Side approaching the shopping district of Pilsen (a Mexican-American barrio since the close of World War II) is a sparsely settled and grimy industrial corridor punctuated by weather-beaten factories, abandoned railroad tracks, broken sidewalks, heavy equipment, and the presence of factory workers grimly huddled on forlorn bus corners at 5:00 P.M. waiting to go to their residences farther west. A used car parts warehouse and tractor trailers stacked like cordwood are situated in the location where the death tunnel was dug. You do not expect to find a commemorative marker in such a place as this, nor has one been erected. The rusting hulks of the trailers will have to suffice for now.

Ten thousand anxious persons whispered silent prayers while firemen carried on the work of rescue in a scene of pandemonium and chaos—thirty-five feet below ground.

A seventeen-foot-high sewage tunnel running the length of a full city block entombed eleven city workmen, including four firefighters, when a sudden explosion, deadly fire, and noxious fumes cut off all effective means of escape. The tunnel was part of the Metropolitan Sanitary District underground system, and was only half completed when a candle carried by a city plasterer looking for a reported leak in the concrete walls ignited a pile of sawdust.

Albert Martino told a coroner's jury in a barely audible whisper that he was carrying out repair work in the customary way. "I hunted all along the tunnel with the candle in my hand. I stopped up a number of leaks, but continued to find more. Then I saw what looked like a lump of concrete and I examined it closely, but found it was sawdust. It caught fire from the candle then I saw a number of fires starting all around me."

The only means of ventilation was supplied by a forty-foot-wide steel tube and air compressor. A narrow shaft leading to the street level provided the only means of escape.

With little regard for the safety of the workmen, the incomplete tunnel was "corked" at both ends by steel protection walls. By modern-day Occupational Safety and Hazard Act (OSHA) standards, it seems incomprehensible that Sanitary District inspectors would be carrying lit candles into poorly lighted, dangerous shafts fortified by wooden beams with construction sawdust scattered about, but the lack of concern for proper safety measures was very typical of the period.

Chicago firefighters faced a daunting task—burrowing down into the deadly enclosure with walls of fire on all sides. Rescue efforts were hampered by the firefighters unfamiliarity with the layout of the tunnel, the dense, choking smoke, and the droplets of scalding water pouring down from fissures in the walls. Time and time again, firemen and city workers battling the blaze returned to the surface gasping for air, their faces blackened with soot.

"It's hell down there!" reported Maurice Cahill, superintendent of the construction company in charge of the project. "The electric lights are on, but they don't penetrate five inches. The smoke and gas are like a blanket. The only way we get those bodies is to stumble over them."

Hopes soared when a smoke-ejecting gadget recently invented by one Peter

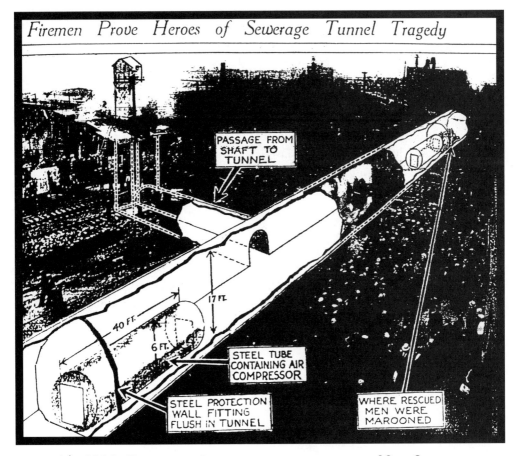

Firemen Prove Heroes of Sewerage Tunnel Tragedy

PASSAGE FROM
SHAFT TO
TUNNEL

17 FT.

40 FT.

6 FT.

STEEL TUBE
CONTAINING AIR
COMPRESSOR

STEEL PROTECTION
WALL FITTING
FLUSH IN TUNNEL

WHERE RESCUED
MEN WERE
MAROONED

APRIL 14, 1931. ELEVEN MEN KILLED IN A TUNNEL FIRE AT 22ND ST. AND LAFLIN. PHOTO DIAGRAM ILLUSTRATES THE UNDERGROUND CHAMBER WHERE DISASTER STRUCK.

Pirsch of Kenosha, Wisconsin, began to do its work. The blower of the smoke ejector helped clear a path of escape from one of the sealed safety chambers inside the tunnel. A dozen men spent the entire night inside the chamber awaiting imminent death from suffocation. "It seemed a long time until we heard the blower of that smoke ejector. Then we noticed that the air seemed to be getting clearer," said one. As the flames and smoke subsided, a carriage was lowered and the survivors were elevated to the surface, where wives and children and fathers and mothers were overwhelmed by tears of joy.

For those who were not so fortunate, the grief of anxious relatives aboveground was etched in the faces of the families of the missing. One young woman, recently married to a firefighter, was told that her husband had perished in the flames. She broke through a police cordon and was about to hurl herself into the pit before police officers pulled her back. "If my husband can die down there, so can I!" sobbed the widow of Edward Pratt of Engine Company #23. Captain James O'Neill of Hook and Ladder Company #14 was also lost in the tunnel disaster.

A hellish night ended on a somber, quiet note, but the coroner's jury of experts demanded to know what steps could be taken to prevent a recurrence. When testimony was concluded, the jurors recommended modest proposals—tacking up clearly posted maps to assist firemen in future emergency calls and the addition of a proper ventilating system with a telephone line reaching all parts of the tunnels.

Cigarette smoking and open flames were banned, which makes perfect sense in dangerous underground tunnels. In fact, it was so painfully obvious to anyone with half a brain that one only wonders how these guidelines managed to elude the Sanitary District dunces in the first place. But then again, political hacks who feed at the trough of public works kickbacks are never unduly concerned until the hue and cry of public opinion turns against them following an entirely preventable calamity such as this one.

Garfield Park

4656 West

Kinzie Street

(Kinzie &

Kilpatrick

Avenue);

main offices

at 401 North

Cicero

DEATH IN CANDYLAND:
THE BRACH CANDY COMPANY FIRE
September 6, 1948

With ninety confectionary companies and 13,000 skilled laborers boiling the chocolate and coating the jelly beans, the city of Chicago produces more candy than any other place in the world. Hog butcher to the world, stacker of wheat, maker of sweets ... or so it has been said. The most acclaimed local candy maker of them all was, of course, E. J. Brach & Compan. After five generations of family ownership, the company merged with Brock's Candy Company of Chattanooga, Tennessee, in 1994, following a decade of prolonged labor strife, cutbacks in sugar imports, and assorted industry upheavals that left a bitter taste in the mouths of most workers. Left behind was an enduring old-world legacy. Family patriarch Emil J. Brach began manufacturing his famous pan caramels in a North Avenue shop he called the "Palace of Sweets" in 1904. With a modest investment of $1,000, Brach began packaging and selling his confections to school stores and corner groceries. His two sons, Edwin and Frank, were kept busy after school distributing their father's famous caramels all across town. By 1916, the Brach company was churning out 250,000 pounds of sweets each week. Family fortunes soared in the 1920s when Frank Brach grew the business spectacularly with the help of brother Edwin, who hired commercial artists to draw the famous Canterbury silhouettes that became the company's trademark on boxes and cartons. The uptick in business conditions convinced Brach to expand his manufacturing operation. In 1924, he built a spacious new West Side plant from the ground up at the northeast corner of Kinzie and Kilpatrick. (The most current mailing address was 401 North Cicero.) Five separate buildings arose on the site, costing the firm an estimated $5 million. Brach malted milk balls, StarBrite mints, chocolate stars, Swedish fish, bull's eyes, and two hundred other varieties of penny-candy favorites more than made up for any cash-flow shortfall, and for years were popular items for the kids at grocery store checkout counters. By 1948, the year the West Side plant exploded into a fireball, the Brach Candy Company produced eight million pounds of confections *a week—by far the largest industrial output of candy in the nation. In the 1990s, Brach employees churned out more than five hundred million pounds of candy each year from a huge complex of thirteen factory buildings, towering over the intersection of Kinzie & Kilpatrick adjacent to the tracks of the Chicago & Northwestern Line and the CTA Lake Street elevated line. They were the seventh largest confectioner in the United States until January 11, 2001, when Brach's president Kevin Kotecki announced the shutdown of the entire plant. Kotecki blamed the high cost of domestic sugar and the outmoded West Side facilities. Dismayed officials from the mayor's office said they were told only three weeks earlier that Brach had no intention of closing. The work force was caught by surprise. More then eleven hundred people were informed that they would lose their jobs in a gradual three-year phaseout. It wasn't the first time the candy manufacturer had been guilty of callous insensitivity, but it would probably be the last, now that Brach's Chicago is no more.*

A strange whistling sound preceded a terrible predawn blast that ripped apart large chunks of the wall on the east end of the Brach factory. The blast shook two square miles of the Garfield Park neighborhood, sending thousands of people into the streets convinced that the Russians had finally invaded Chicago.

It was shortly after 4:00 A.M., Labor Day weekend, and only forty-five of the three thousand workers employed inside the plant were on duty. It was divine providence that most people were at home with their families, but of the unfortunate forty-five employees working that holiday weekend fifteen perished in the blast.

"The place was a holocaust," said Monsignor William J. Gorman, Fire Department chaplain. "I saw men with the skin completely burned off their faces and hands huddled amid the wreckage."

The Brach factory was in shambles. Broken candy racks were strewn about. Twisted fire debris and broken glass littered the grounds. Nearby, the side streets were brown with chocolate-colored water after firefighters responding to the 5-11 alarm trained their hoses on the devastation. Injured workers, coated with sugar and chocolate, were rushed to three area hospitals.

The origin of the blaze was traced to the third-floor cream department where starch used to make candy spontaneously exploded, blowing out walls and ejecting workers into the parking lot two stories below. "The skies suddenly lit up as though a meteor had burst," said one eyewitness. "There was shattered glass everywhere."

HELEN BRACH'S FATHER-IN-LAW, AND FOUNDER OF THE BRACH CANDY COMPANY, RESPECTFULLY CARICATURED IN THIS 1923 CARTOON ORGINALLY PUBLISHED IN THE *CHICAGO EVENING POST*.

BROKEN SIDEWALKS, WEEDS, AND SECURITY FENCING CREATE A STILL-LIFE EERINESS AT 4656 W. KINZIE WHERE THE BUILDING ON THIS SIDE OF THE E. J. BRACH FACTORY COMPLEX CAUGHT FIRE IN 1948.

While relatives of the dead and dying grieved inside the emergency room of Loretto Hospital, management's attitude bordered on callous indifference. Edwin Brach, who was enjoying his vacation, communicated his intention to resume production inside the shattered factory within forty-eight hours. Forty percent of the work force were ordered back to work immediately. Part of them were assigned the daunting task of clearing away fire debris where fifteen of their friends and colleagues had died.

Before another fortnight had passed, construction crews were busy applying new brick and fresh mortar.

West Garfield Park

Adams Street and Kildare Avenue, one block south of Madison

THE FINAL MIRACLE OF THE CHURCH OF THE HOLY GHOST
Good Friday, March 28, 1929

In the annals of murder, there is nothing more foul than the senseless slaughter of innocents. Child murders, and the killing of the weak, the elderly, and the defenseless tug at the heartstrings. Rarely, though, do we find killers targeting the feeble-minded, the insane, or men of the cloth. I am sure there is a good reason for that, for even in the darkest corners of the netherworld there must surely exist a semblance of honor. I strongly suspect that it would require years of investigative research to uncover more than a half-dozen homicides committed against members of clergy within the Catholic Archdiocese of Chicago. There is at least one documented incident involving the attempted murder of a priest, and it occurred on the West Side at the Church of the Holy Ghost. The shooting of Reverend Charles A. Erkenswick is a long-forgotten episode among laypersons; but a crime like this speaks volumes about hard times and the lives of the weak and downtrodden of the community who reverted to crime out of desperation bordering on insanity. The Church of the Holy Ghost was a German parish, founded in 1896 by Archbishop Patrick Feehan (known among mirthful German Catholics as an "FBI"—Foreign Born Irish) and attended to by the Sisters of St. Agnes who came down from Fond du Lac, Wisconsin, in 1898. The tiny West Side parish struggled to keep its doors open, and was always on the brink of being swallowed whole by nearby St. Mel's and its eternally ambitious spiritual leader, the Right Reverend Francis A. Purcell. The merger became a reality in 1941, when the two parishes were consolidated into one and renamed St. Mel's–Holy Ghost. In 1965, the Chicago Board of Education acquired the church building and renamed it the Nathan Goldblatt School. It stands opposite a deserted weed lot on the northeast corner of Kildare and Adams. It is here in a place abandoned by time that the priests and nuns of the Holy Ghost served the religious devotions of the German Catholics of the West Side. Today, the area appears as an economically depressed war zone. The desperation is written in the faces of young and old African Americans who live here in the Fillmore District, a dangerous side of town menaced by gangs and drug traffickers.

They were hardly geniuses of crime. Paul Menna and his brother John were half-wits from south Damen Avenue who were accused of looting the church poor box. The crime was repeated twenty-five times, against neighborhood parishes scattered all over the city during the cold winter months of 1928–29.

The boys were arrested inside Reverend Charles A. Erkenswick's church on March 20, 1929, after their actions aroused the priest's suspicion. Frightened of the likely consequences about to befall them, the Menna brothers provided police with a full confession before being locked away inside the Cook County Jail. Once inside their cells, the underage boys scribbled a note to their mother:

> Just a few lines to let you know we are well and hope you are the same. Me and John are in the county jail. We got picked up on Wednesday afternoon. Me and John was caught in Holy Ghost Church, and we didn't touch nothing. And as we was walking down the street, we was caught by Fillmore police. My cause will be up in the boys court next week and if you want to find out when my case is up, go to the boy's court and if you want to send me $2 and some cigars. Your son, Paul.

Police records showed that Paul Menna had previously been sent to a special school for the mentally impaired at Lincoln, Illinois. (*Author's Note:* The Lincoln school in those days was a snakepit. Untold horrors, including Nazi-style medical experiments, were routinely conducted on the bedeviled inmates. The incidents are well documented.)

Incensed that a priest gave up his boy so easily to the cops, Gaetano Menna stormed the church with a gun in one pocket and the soiled, pencil-written letter in the other. Menna thrust the letter into Reverend Erkenswick's hand and demanded that he read it. "I can't do anything for the boys," shrugged Erkenswick with a sigh. "They have confessed to other robberies. It's up to the police now to dispense justice."

The priest turned away. God's mercy for sinners was one thing. Robbing from the church poor to satisfy personal greed was another matter.

Pastor Erkenswick was well up in years by this time, and was not in the frame of mind to consider mitigating circumstances, if indeed someone could manage to come up with a reasonable excuse for these two street punks.

Erkenswick was ordained around 1880 and had served the parish of St. Dionysius in Cicero for more than a quarter-century, from 1895 until June 1924, when he was transferred to Holy Ghost. There were less than three hundred families in the entire West Side congregation when he arrived. And by the standards of enrollment set forth by the Archdiocese of Chicago, the church was insignificant, except perhaps, to the priests and their parishioners.

"But they knew survival tactics—and they thrived on it," explains Timothy Unsworth, scholar, historian of the Catholic Church, and author of *The Last Priests in America*. "Holy Ghost was one of several smaller area churches in Chicago that survived on novenas (devotions). In this case, the novenas were made to the German saints. Occasionally that could bring 12,000 people out on a Sunday."

Erkenswick struggled to keep his church open against long odds, and these concerns were uppermost in his mind. The murderous intent of Menna was probably the last thing he expected, as he stared into the man's hate-filled eyes and tried to make some sense of the hand-scribbled note.

Then, without warning, Menna whipped out the revolver he had concealed in his coat pocket and shot the priest in the eye. The first bullet spun Erkenswick around. The next two hit him in the back and sent him sprawling to the pavement face-down. A Park District police officer summoned an ambulance and the priest was dispatched to St. Anne's Hospital, barely clinging to life. There was little hope. The wounds appeared to be fatal.

Gaetano Menna ran east to Keeler Avenue, then darted over to Madison Street where he was intercepted by a police officer and taken into custody. By now, the rage that had coursed through his veins only moments earlier had dissipated with the realization that he had shot a priest down in cold blood.

"My God, what have I done?" implored Menna. But this time God would not answer. The newspapers made much of the fact that Erkenswick was not expected to survive so vicious an attack. He was a goner, predicted the *Daily News*. No one could survive a bullet to the head and two to the back, not even the tough gangsters of Roosevelt Road.

There must have been one last devine miracle left inside the hallowed walls of the doomed old church, a novena or two reserved especially for Reverend Erkenswick, because over the next few weeks he staged a miraculous recovery and managed to survive the near fatal Good Friday shooting.

Erkenswick returned to the church and lived another nine years before being summoned by the Creator on October 20, 1938.

Lawndale-Douglas Park

"ZOOKIE THE BOOKIE" ROLLS SNAKE EYES
January 14, 1944

3216 West Roosevelt Road & 4042 Wilcox (west of Pulaski and east of Karlov)

Politics and crime are intermingled themes in the long and bloody history of the 24th Ward, comprising much of the Lawndale-Douglas Park neighborhood. Due west of the old Maxwell Street ghetto, Douglas Park is a fully landscaped patch of greenery in a residential and commercial setting. Designed and laid out by architect William LeBaron Jenny in 1880, the actual park and its surrounding West Side communities absorbed an influx of Eastern European Jewish families fleeing the over-crowded and intolerable conditions of the Maxwell Street ghetto. By 1920, Lawndale and Douglas were predomi-nantly Jewish. Political control was vested in Moe and Max Rosenberg, owners of a junk shop and scrap-iron yard. The Rosenbergs rose to power by forging necessary alliances with an emerging criminal fac-tion that in time would come to be known as "the Jewish Faction" of the Chicago outfit. Their cloak of authority eventually fell on the shoulders of their protégé, Jacob M. Arvey, principal architect of the Chicago Democratic Machine of legend. In the rough-and-tumble days of Prohibition, when Arvey was still finding his way as an attorney for Moe's junkyard, Davey Miller and his broth-er Herschie brokered political favors from Republican Mayor William Hale Thompson. They courted favor with the North Side bootlegging gang headed by Dion O'Banion and Samuel "Nails" Morton (discussed in Tour 3) and ran the gambling rackets on their side of town. But as tough as they were, Davey and his crew were forced to surrender control to a rising faction of Young Turks, headed by Ben "Zookie the Bookie" Zuckerman, Ben Glaser, Willie Tarsch, "Flattop" Weinberg, and their senior advisor, Julius "Loving Putty"

Anixeter, a throwback to the South Side Levee vice district of the early 1900s. The politics of the 24th Ward gradually shifted from Republican to Democrat, and Arvey became its committeeman, political king maker, and protector of gangster rackets. Zookie's role in the politico-criminal paradigm of the 1940s was tenuous. What happened to him is a textbook example of the fate awaiting most cocky and ambitious gangsters who believe they are invincible. Sooner or later it all catches up with you, and likewise the former syndicate battlegrounds these men purported to represent never remain the same. Beginning in the 1950s, Douglas Park and Lawndale lost their Jewish identity all together when African Americans by the tens of thousands began pouring in. Today, poverty and crime reign supreme in the 24th Ward, only now it is mostly black-on-black crime and not the incessant gunplay of outfit hoodlums fighting for control over the West Side Jewish rackets. Zuckerman set up his headquarters at 3216 West Roosevelt Road, south of the old Sears Roebuck catalog plant at Homan Avenue & Arthington. He took over for Davey Miller, who ran the storefront address as a poolroom for the neighborhood hustlers. Zookie converted the place to the R & K Restaurant, allowing the backroom card game to go on without interruption. The downtown politicians understood that he who ruled the roost at that address spoke for the entire Jewish underworld, and acted accordingly. In the heyday of the 24th Ward (the 1930s and 1940s mostly), R & K was an important underworld clearing-house, but the years passed and the entire block was destroyed by time. The Lawndale Plaza (a strip mall), with acres of parking, covers the former crime site today. You can locate Zookie's residence at 4042 Wilcox (a narrow east-west side street). It is a sagging four-story, yellow-brick apartment house, east of Karlov Avenue. The building, like the dilapidated neighborhood surrounding it, has obviously seen its better days.

Homicide investigators familiar with a particular stretch of Roosevelt Road from Kedzie Avenue to Pulaski Road called it "Murderer's Row" for the many unsolved gangland killings occurring in the span of ten years (1935–45). Ben Zuckerman, a gambler and bookmaker with a penchant for committing murder, was behind many of the nightly assaults.

Zookie's predilection for violence was legendary. During a minor traffic altercation with Northwestern University football hero John C. Archer in November 1928, Zuckerman pulled out a gun and drilled the young man at point-blank range. Charges against Zookie were dropped when Archer and his brother were unable to identify him in a police lineup. Archer died of his wounds six months later.

Active as a bootlegger during Prohibition days, Zuckerman survived three shotgun slugs in the face after rival gunmen blasted him in March 1927. Following repeal, Zookie and his crew plunged headlong into the gambling racket, operating a card and dice room at 3223 West Roosevelt Road. The preferred game was five-card draw poker. The customers were mostly neighborhood residents—middle-aged and elderly Jews who were provided high-interest loans when their luck turned bad. According to investigator Art Bilek, the syndicate loan officer was known as the "three-for-five" guy. "You pay me five for every three I give you!"

After Julius "Loving Putty" Annixter was snuffed out in December 1943, Zookie claimed supreme control of the 24th ward, and that didn't set well with Arthur X. Elrod, the stand-in for Arvey while he was off fighting the Japanese in the South Pacific. Elrod, who peddled low-cost insurance up and down Roosevelt Road, was a political schemer with designs on a bigger slice of the pie than remaining Arvey's top precinct captain and vote getter.

Zuckerman was spinning out of control, and the political divisions in gangland were splitting the ward organization apart. There wasn't much Elrod could do to curb gang warfare until Arvey's soothing presence eased tensions. Mediation was not Elrod's strong suit.

It was around this same time that Zookie concocted a scheme to peddle diluted alcoholic spirits in order to cash in on public demand for scarce booze during the crunching wartime shortage. He bought up a string of liquor stores with large inventories of good whiskeys in the backroom, then used these liquors to color the illegal rotgut his gang of ex-bootleggers were distilling in hidden vaults and basements. Zuckerman was listed as part owner of the Central West Beer Distributors, at 2408 South Pulaski Road. When he began pushing his swill into "Dago" Lawrence Mangano's territory west of Sacramento Avenue in the guise of a Central West salesman, Zookie was warned to lay off the black market rackets or risk reprisals.

Detectives from the Fillmore Police District believed that this was the contributing factor in the decision to eliminate Zookie. Actually, there was much more to it than petty disagreements over diluted intoxicants. Zuckerman was about to be summoned to testify before a grand jury, and a cabal of younger, more ambitious men, aware that the state's attorney was closing in fast, decided the time was right to exploit Zookie's vulnerabilities.

Late in the evening of January 16, 1944, Zuckerman was walking toward the front door of his apartment house at 4042 Wilcox when a slightly built man with a turned-up collar raced toward him, gun in hand. Before Zookie could defend himself, the gunman fired at close range, dropping his intended victim to the ground.

Zuckerman gasped: "Don't shoot! Don't kill me!" The killer fired two more shots, then turned and fled. Zookie was dead at age forty-nine, and you can bet there were those who said that he could have been a statesmen, a rabbi, a businessman, or a shining example to youth, instead of a dead gangster stretched out on the sidewalk. Two young boys, William and John Carroll, were the only eyewitnesses to the murder, but they could not tell the police very much.

Later that day, upon being informed of his partner's death, sixty-year-old convicted rapist Ben Glaser dropped dead of fright. His ticker gave out under the strain of knowing that he would probably be next.

A trio of gunmen, Dave Yaras, Lenny Patrick, and Willie Block, were strongly suspected of carrying out the Zookie hit on orders from syndicate boss Jake "Greasy Thumb" Guzik, an important link for the isolated West Side Jewish gangster faction hoping to curry favor with the Italians in the outfit.

Gambling oddsmaker Lenny Patrick emerged from the shadows to reign as the all-powerful chieftain of the Jewish faction. He followed the exodus of West Side Jews to the Far North Side of the city and transferred the entire gambling mechanism to Rogers Park, once Douglas Park and Lawndale were no longer tenable as a home base for the white hoodlums and their political sponsors.

THE LONG HOT SUMMER
June 12–16, 1966 & July 12–16, 1966

Damen & Division Streets, Humboldt Park and Roosevelt Road & Throop Street (and other West Side locations)

There was a time in the mid-1960s when the arrival of the warm summer months carried with it the scent of danger in the overcrowded inner cities of the industrial North. The image of National Guard troops in military transport vehicles rumbling past burned-out riot districts in Chicago, Los Angeles, Newark, and Detroit defined a decade and painted a picture of America under siege and teetering on the brink of class warfare. The "long hot summer" was a modern American metaphor for violent confrontation, racial polarization, and separate societies drifting farther apart, one black, one white. The struggle to achieve open housing, closure to long-standing patterns of discrimination in public education, and simmering resentments directed against police for acts of brutality triggered some of the worst rioting of the decade on the West Side of Chicago in 1966. In June of that year, the grievances expressed by the black community spilled over into the Near Northwest Side Puerto Rican community in several nights of rioting and looting. When it was at last over and sanity restored, Chicagoans were advised by a dazed and shaken Mayor Richard J. Daley that the looted store-fronts, the bloodshed, the Molotov cocktail attacks, and the general street may-hem were the work of "outside agitators" and communists spurred on by the preachings of Reverend Dr. Martin Luther King, who had brought his nonvio-lent movement to Chicago that year. It was inconceivable Daley argued, for Chicagoans of any race, creed, or color to lead an armed insurrection against his city. The "long hot summers" of the 1960s are in the rearview mirror of our history, but the deeper sociological implications that sparked these episodes are very much with us, even today.

Damen and Division Streets, June 12, 1966. The disturbance started shortly before nightfall in the Wood Street Police District. Patrolman Thomas Munyon and his partner, Raymond Howard, observed a street fracas in progress at the south-west corner of Damen Avenue and Division. Amid jeers and insults hurled at them from a hostile crowd of Spanish-speaking men and women, Munyon got out of his squad car and approached the combatants, intending to break up the fight and arrest the instigators.

Officer Munyon later reported to his supervisors that he glimpsed a young man reaching for a gun. Certain that he was about to be fired on, Munyon turned and drew, firing a bullet into the leg of nineteen-year-old Arcelis Cruz. Some eye-witnesses confirmed that Cruz reached for a gun first; others disputed it. But in the heat of the moment, an angry and emotional mob had already formed, and they did not much care to sort out the particulars.

Within minutes the crowd swarmed the squad car. The glass was shattered and the dispatch radio yanked from the dash. Another car was splashed with gasoline and set on fire. The size of the crowd swelled to several thousand. Rioters were met by two hundred helmeted police summoned by their superiors to check the disturbances in the area. A command post was set up in a grocery store parking lot at Damen and Le Moyne Avenues.

Overhead, bricks, bottles, rocks, and other heavy objects rained down from the open windows and rooftops of businesses and two flats. A bullet struck Officer Casimir Golosinski in the leg. A street brawl had escalated into a riot, and the police were quick to close ranks and defend their actions. "There was noth-ing racial about this," said Acting Deputy Police Superintendent John Hartnett. "It

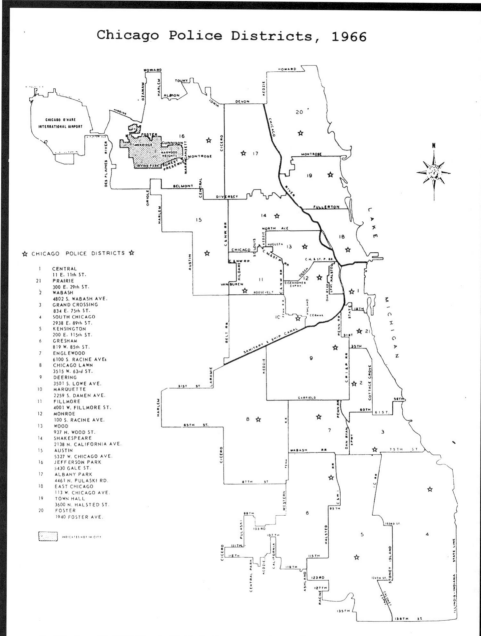

Chicago Police Districts, 1966

☆ CHICAGO POLICE DISTRICTS ☆

1   CENTRAL
    11 E. 11th ST.
21 PRAIRIE
    300 E. 29th ST.
2   WABASH
    4802 S. WABASH AVE.
3   GRAND CROSSING
    834 E. 75th ST.
4   SOUTH CHICAGO
    2938 E. 89th ST.
5   KENSINGTON
    200 E. 115th ST.
6   GRESHAM
    819 W. 85th ST.
7   ENGLEWOOD
    6100 S. RACINE AVE.
8   CHICAGO LAWN
    3515 W. 63rd ST.
9   DEERING
    3501 S. LOWE AVE.
10 MARQUETTE
    2259 S. DAMEN AVE.
11 FILLMORE
    4001 W. FILLMORE ST.
12 MONROE
    100 S. RACINE AVE.
13 WOOD
    937 N. WOOD ST.
14 SHAKESPEARE
    2138 N. CALIFORNIA AVE.
15 AUSTIN
    5327 W. CHICAGO AVE.
16 JEFFERSON PARK
    5430 GALE ST.
17 ALBANY PARK
    4461 N. PULASKI RD.
18 EAST CHICAGO
    113 W. CHICAGO AVE.
19 TOWN HALL
    3600 N. HALSTED ST.
20 FOSTER
    1940 FOSTER AVE.

INDICATES NOT IN CITY

*   The June 12, 1966 Humboldt Park riot occurred in the 13th District (Wood Street)

*   The July 12-16 West Side riots occurred in the 11th District (Fillmore) and the 12th District (Monroe). Sporadic incidents of rioting were also reported in the 10th District (Marquette) was a battle against the police."

Three squad cars were burned. Five false fire alarms were pulled during the first night of rioting. Two hundred windows were blown out, including the plate glass of the San Juan Theater. *Chicago Tribune* photographer Ray Foster was beaten and kicked while taking pictures. The crackling of sporadic sniper fire from the upper floors of the buildings was heard throughout the night. At least seven people were treated for gunshot wounds.

Before dawn three men were already in custody and hauled before Judge Benjamin Kanter of Boy's Court on charges of disorderly conduct, burglary, and grand theft.

The rioting continued for a second consecutive night along Division Street between Damen and California Avenues in the Humboldt Park community. More than one hundred demonstrators blocking the intersection of Division Street and Oakley Avenue had to be forcibly ejected, and three more newspaper and TV reporters were injured in the melee.

In an effort to soothe escalating tensions, Police Superintendent Orlando W. Wilson ordered the immediate transfer of Officer Munyon to the 16th District in Jefferson Park—a conservative, all-white bungalow-belt neighborhood where he was not likely to clash with minority people because there were no minorities to be found this far north in the city.

According to Wilson, the master of the understatement, Officer Thomas Howard was "unlucky," and had to be shifted out of Wood Street. In a widely publicized case cited by Wilson, Howard had been censured by Judge George N. Leighton for using excessive force in an earlier arrest of two Hispanic men on the North Side.

In disgust, Howard turned in his star and resigned from the department. The response from the rank and file was swift and predictable. Officer Daniel Green, head of a fledgling (pre-union era) grievance committee known as the Confederation of Police, promised to award the two officers a plaque for "devotion to duty in the face of overwhelming odds."

In July, the Chicago Commission on Human Relations convened a meeting in City Hall with community representatives. The Reverend Ramos Mendez outlined the modest agenda of his people. He called for the appointment of Puerto Ricans to the various city commissions, additional park space for the children, an end to the deployment of police attack dogs, and elimination of rat-infested tenement housing.

These aims were beyond the ken of the worthy members of the Confederation of Police and other militant cop groups who automatically close ranks when one of their own is censured. Whether the accused happens to be right or wrong is immaterial.

• • •

Roosevelt Road and Throop Street. One month later. While the city prepared to open a dialog with Puerto Rican community leaders, rising tensions between white cops and black residents on the West Side spilled over into the streets, igniting the city's worst race riot since 1919.

July is a deadly month in Chicago. Summer heat and humidity turn un-air-conditioned homes and apartments into infernos, driving people with time on their hands into the streets, where they soon get into trouble. The elderly die from heat exhaustion. Tempers flare. When there is no relief, there is often chaos and violence.

The July 1919 race riot erupted on the shoreline of the segregated 29th Street beach where white and black South Side residents had gone to cool off in the waters of Lake Michigan. A 14-year-old African-American boy named Eugene Williams accidentally crossed the invisible boundary line and swam into the white side of the beach. The boy was stoned by angry whites lining the water's edge. He floundered in the water, then disappeared below the waves.

In the days that followed hundreds more were killed or injured. Sand-bag bunkers manned by National Guardsmen armed with machine guns maintained order on the stricken neighborhoods.

Nothing of this magnitude would occur again in the streets of Chicago until the long hot summers of the 1960s.

"Long hot summer, nothing! It's going to be a real cool summer," exclaimed Sergeant John S. Brown of the police civil rights unit ten days before the explosion on the West Side. Sergeant Brown was an O.W. Wilson appointee who invited representatives of the Woodlawn Organization, the NAACP, and the Urban League to devise strategies to adjudicate problems between police and the community.

While the social scientists, activists, and police liaison officers pondered the issues of race and poverty in closed-door meetings, a petty disagreement ignited major civil unrest in the streets. On the night of July 12, neighborhood youths in the vicinity of Roosevelt Road and Throop Street turned on a water hydrant to cool themselves off in the miserable 90-degree heat that had lingered for five days.

There was a city ordinance against this kind of activity—water pressure would be lowered in the neighborhood—and the police responded accordingly by shutting off the hydrant. Six African-American men were arrested after they defied police and reopened the spigots. In the process, one of the Chicago cops used a nightstick, inflaming an angry mob to ransack a Jewish-owned Rexall drugstore at 1259 Roosevelt Road.

After detectives from the traffic warrant section arrested a screaming ex-convict outside a liquor store at 137 South Pulaski Road that same night, a peevish crowd of hecklers encircled the officers, demanding his release. With the help of reinforcements, the detectives managed to load the balky prisoner into the squadrol as the familiar cries of "police brutality," and "black power" went up.

These incidents touched off a week of sporadic looting, rock throwing, arson fires, and burglaries that resulted in the call-up of seventeen National Guard Units to assist one thousand Chicago police officers sent into the area by O.W. Wilson, who admitted that his men could no longer control looting on 16th Street from Central Park Avenue to Pulaski.

Sixteenth Street was known as the "Street of Dreams" because of heavy narcotics trafficking. This was the territory of the Vice Lords—a powerful street gang formed in the 1950s at the Illinois State Training School for Boys in St. Charles, Illinois. The "VLs" and their various satellite gangs were heavily involved in narcotics dealing, extortion, murder, and drive-by shootings. Over a period of years they turned the Altgeld Gardens, Eden Green, and Golden Gate housing projects into hells on earth for the residents.

Fifteen hundred Guardsmen, fanning out from six city armories, patrolled a 140-square-block area of the West Side. They carried fixed bayonets and tear gas canisters.

By the fourth day, tensions eased and order was restored. But the finger-pointing was only beginning. Mayor Daley traced the blame to the Reverend Dr. Martin Luther King, who had addressed a rally at Soldier Field only a few days earlier. Dr. King admonished his listeners ". . . to decide to fill up the jails of Chicago if necessary in order to end slums."

Daley interpreted the remark as inflammatory provocation to riot. Dr. King called for boycotts and mass demonstrations, which, in Daley's way of thinking, could mean only one thing. "Outside agitators," possibly communist sympathizers, were afoot in the city fomenting racial hate.

Symbolic of his campaign to improve the quality of life for West Side blacks was King's decision to move his family into a $90-a-month apartment at 1550 South Hamlin in Lawndale ("Slumdale"), where living conditions were intolerable. The family was shocked by the surrounding squalor and omnipresent danger. Dr. King recalled with grim irony Daley's now-famous utterance: "There are no slums in Chicago, only bad housing."

As conditions worsened, the mayor denounced the politics of confrontation, but agreed to meet privately with Dr. King and various ecumenical leaders from the city to come up with the practical means to end the rioting.

Reasoning together, Dr. King, Daley, and Archbishop John Cardinal Cody hammered out an agreement to affix sprinkler attachments to city fire hydrants and provide city firemen with the ability to regulate the discharge of water. The mayor readily agreed to build ten community swimming pools—a simple, cost-effective measure consistent with the larger objectives of his urban-renewal agenda. Daley promised "special emphasis" on furthering relationships between the community and the police, and retreated from his earlier remarks castigating Dr. King.

"I think you cannot charge it directly to Martin Luther King, but surely some of the people came in here and have been talking for the last year in violence and showing pictures and instructing people in how to conduct violence," he said at his press conference.

On July 25, a twenty-three-member citizen's commission was appointed to study police community relations.

With peace restored and matters moving forward in a positive direction, Dr. King moved on to other battlefronts of the civil rights movement. The peace agreement was more of a temporary truce than a solution, however, and the work of the blue-ribbon panel seemed to have only a desultory effect on police-minority relations. Two years later, the West Side would once again be plundered and pillaged by angry mobs following the assassination of Dr. King in Memphis. That is when the mayor issued his famous "shoot to kill" order.

The realization was beginning to sink in among the practical-thinking men in City Hall that fire hydrant sprinklers and public pools alone were not enough to appease growing black militancy. The problems would not go away. A new and more vocal coalition of African-American leaders were beginning to revolt against Chicago's political plantation system governed by West Side Bloc hoodlum-politicians with close ties to City Hall, the State House, and the mob.

Richard J. Daley's secular way of running Chicago; his narrow 11th Ward Bridgeport bungalow culture revolving around the parish, corner social clubs, family devotion, and his indifference to the concerns of a hostile minority community were coming under increasing attack from political gadflies, activists, and extremists. The political landscape of Chicago would never be the same once the chinks in the armor were exposed to the world.

The year of reckoning was 1968.

Austin

5817 West

Madison Street

(between

Menard Avenue

and Mayfield)

"GET 'EM—ALIVE OR DEAD!" ANOTHER TURKEY SHOOT FOR THE "TOUGHEST COP IN AMERICA"

September 24, 1954

The crime-ridden community of Austin, on the Far West Side, bears the visible signs of urban decay; empty storefronts, the notable absence of national retail chains, and residential side streets that have been "cul-de-saced" in recent years in order to keep gangbangers with an eye to committing a drive-by out. The low-income African-American residents who moved here in overwhelming numbers in the 1960s and 1970s have weathered the accumulated social problems of drugs, gangs, public indifference, and poor policing. The Austin Police District has been rocked with two major corruption scandals, once in 1973 and again in 1996. Indicative of the changing times, the scandal in 1973 involved kickbacks from local tavern owners to Captain Mark Thanasouras and eighteen other officers serving under him. (Author's Note: *See* Return to the Scene of the Crime *for coverage of the Thanasouras case.*) *Austin was dealt another black eye in 1996 when seven police officers from the tactical unit were charged with robbing and extorting local drug dealers. In moments of valor and frequent times of shame, the Chicago Police Department has endured periodic criticism from outraged community activists against those perceived to be at odds with the interests of the community. The late Captain Frank Pape, who died in the year 2000 after living to the ripe old age of ninety-one, certainly falls into this category. His biographer and other admirers of this hard-edged old crime fighter, who boasted that he never lost a single night's sleep over the nine pitiful men he dispatched to local cemeteries, label him "the Toughest Cop in America." Is this necessarily a badge of honor, or is it a mark of shame? That depends largely on the political viewpoint expressed and the times in which you have lived. Retired cops from the pre-Miranda era who pine for the days when an officer could draw down on a criminal suspect with impunity, minus all the liberal fuss, eulogize Pape and his South Side counterpart, Sylvester "Two Gun Pete" Washington, as the last of a venerable breed of street cop. They admire Pape for the nine notches he carved on his gun handle and wonder why it still can't be that way today. Others (liberals; activists; blacks; younger, more enlightened college-edu-cated officers; and humanitarians) hold fast to an entirely different view. Opponents of his harsh methods branded Pape a sadist and a killer. Some (like author Ovid Demaris) have gone so far as to allege that he may have con-sorted with organized crime figures—a serious charge that has never been substantiated one way or the other. We await the final verdict of history and recall with a shudder one of his most infamous shootouts. It occurred in broad daylight in the alley in back of the Mars Oldsmobile agency at 5817 W. Madison Street (between Menard on the east and Mayfield on the west). The area changed from white to black in the 1960s and the dealership pulled up stakes long ago. Since then, the former show room has been converted into a delicatessen, Mario's Butcher Shop—a busy neighborhood place on Saturday mornings. But with imagination, it is still possible to visualize Pape's ambush in the alley in back of the place. In fact, the garage where the two crooks walked to their doom is still functioning as a repair shop. Ironically, Jack Metnick, founder of the West Suburban auto show room, died in Arizona only a few months after Captain Pape had expired in Chicago.*

In the course of his thirty-nine-year police career dating back to 1933, Frank Pape used a .45-caliber Thompson submachine gun only twice in the line of duty, but with deadly efficiency each time.

The weapon came into his possession in the early 1950s, and he cherished it, the same way a concert violinist cherishes his Stradivarius. Pape was always quick to point out that in the good old days every unmarked detective car carried one because you never knew who you were going to run into. The Thompson, like the Stradivarius, was only played by its owner on rare, special occasions.

Frank Pape, born and raised in Bucktown by Irish-German parents, headed a legendary robbery detail that inspired admiration from Hollywood scriptwriters and earned the respect of the great silent generation of patriotic young Republicans living in John Wayne's America. It was the 1950s, and each week the fictional TV cop, Lt. Frank Ballinger of *M-Squad,* patrolled the streets of Chicago in his fedora hat and trench coat, spewing nonstop blood-and-guts action.

Frank Pape was the inspiration for Frank Ballinger. The bad guys that the two Franks (one fictional, one real) tangled with on the streets of Chicago every week were not "outfit" bosses, clever con men, master swindlers, or men of exceptional intelligence, wit, or cunning. They were, for the most part, mentally stunted career criminals whose thuggery and lack of imagination made it possible for the major crime units headed by line officers like Frank Pape to cashier them easily and quickly.

It was no different with Chris Kanakes, who had been in and out of the Joliet penitentiary many times since 1936, or his partner, Spiros Demitralis (alias George Manos and John Springer), wanted for bond forfeiture.

The pair were sought for a string of armed robberies, including recent holdups at two Near North bistros, the Tradewinds at 865 Rush and the Singapore at 1011 Rush. The fact that these smalltimers would dare point a gun inside either one of the syndicate-controlled show lounges gives you pause. They must not have been very bright, or they simply did not know the rules of conduct by which the underworld operated. Freelance thieves who molest residences, businesses, girlfriends, or wives of outfit hoodlums rarely live long enough to collect their pension.

Frank Pape was on to them from the moment his robbery detail had captured the third member of the gang, Thomas Kostas, who implicated his partners during an all-night grilling at headquarters. (In those days, police detectives routinely slept on the tops of their desks or on the floors during round-the-clock interrogations.)

T W O S M A L L T I M E C R O O K S W E R E A M B U S H E D I N T H I S N A R R O W A L L E Y

I N 1 9 5 4 B Y L I E U T E N A N T F R A N K P A P E ' S F E A R E D R O B B E R Y D E T A I L .

Kostas was released on bond and ordered to report back to Pape the moment he heard something. You can laugh all you want. There was no way Kostas was going to skip town—and risk crossing Frank Pape. That wasn't going to happen, but in hindsight he would have been far better off making a run for it.

Through information gleaned from Kostas and two of his plainclothesmen, Pape learned that Demitralis and Kanakes were planning to bring Demitralis's new car into the Mars Oldsmobile agency for a one-thousand-mile tune-up. On the afternoon of September 22, ten members of Pape's unit, disguised as laborers and mechanics, took up positions in the alley in back of the dealership and in three panel trucks near the garage, poised for a shootout. The robbery unit was up to the task. Their leader had already participated in thirteen gun battles leading up to the showdown at the Mars auto corral.

Pape's men waited thirty-five grueling hours for the dull-witted hoodlums to show up.

After the police cover was nearly blown by a local merchant alarmed by the presence of suspicious-looking men lurking about in the alley, the robbers showed up at 4:10 P.M.

They parked their vehicle at the mouth of the alley east of the dealership and walked toward the service door. That's when Detectives Bryan Connolly, Charley Fitzgerald, Marty Flynn, and Alfred Friedl, trailing close behind, ordered them to halt. Kanakes made the fatal mistake of drawing a gun from his coat pocket.

It was a spontaneous reaction, and Frank Pape's cue to unleash a fusillade of bullets into the backs of the fleeing gunmen, opening fire from a concealed position in the back of a panel truck.

Morgue attendants counted thirteen bullet wounds in Demitralis. Kanakes took nine.

"This was the first time I used a machine gun," Pape told reporters. "We were eleven men against two today. They decided to shoot it out, and that's where they made their mistake."

Years later, from the comfort of his easy chair in his Park Ridge home, Pape told the author that his primary concern was for the safety of the children in the nearby grammar school. Pape feared that Kanakes would seek refuge inside the school, resulting in a tense hostage standoff.

Curious about this, I managed to locate the Robert Emmet Academy during my visit to the West Side crime scene, and was surprised to discover that it is situated at Madison and Central, two and a half city blocks east of the Mars car dealership. Even with the wildest stretch of imagination, it is impossible to conceive of Kanakes or anyone else escaping from that narrow alley, ringed by ten heavily armed cops under Pape's command and making it to the school.

Instead, the neighborhood children and their parents gaped in awe at the brave police officers standing over the chunks of torn flush and rivulets of blood streaming into the alley as they posed for newspaper photographs. It was a never-to-be-forgotten image.

Pape was becoming quite a media celebrity. He was on friendly terms with Mayor Richard J. Daley and a half-dozen aldermen and judges, and he command-ed the attention of *Chicago American* columnist Nate Gross, who molded him into the archetype of the last fearless cop in America.

Police Commissioner Timothy O'Connor never referred to him by rank, but always as "Francois," a term of endearment.

Accolades and testimonials continued to pour in for a few more years at least, until Pape ran afoul of the African-American community as a result of a civil rights action involving his erroneous arrest of a black man named James Monroe during a homicide investigation. The plaintiff in the racially charged lawsuit alleged that Frank Pape and his men had broken into his house, and that Pape had struck him with the butt end of a revolver. There were suits and countersuits. But in the end, Pape was ordered to pay $8,000 in damages to the plaintiff in what amounted to a case of mistaken identity.

Frank Pape rose to the rank of captain and no farther. He often said that he harbored no secret ambitions for higher rank in the police cadre and would be content just to be called "Captain" by friends and well-wishers until the end of his days. Though embittered by the outcome of the Monroe case, he offered no apologies for the actions he had undertaken against crooks and often said that he felt no personal remorse for the nine dead men. "They deserved to die," he dead-panned.

There is one curious footnote to this story, however. Not long after the Mars Oldsmobile ambush, the third suspect, Thomas Kostas, was found dead in the trunk of his car.

Cicero

<table>
<tr><td>

6139 West

19th Street,

Cicero, Illinois

(Lombard

Avenue and

19th Street)

</td><td>

ANATOMY OF A RACE RIOT
July 11–13, 1951

The definitive volume of history concerning the town of Cicero has yet to be written. I have been told that the publication of a manuscript recounting the legendary organized crime tie-ups between local politicians and organized crime minions dating back to Al Capone's takeover of the town in 1923 was canceled at the last minute because the author had expressed legitimate concerns for his personal safety. Anyone who is familiar with Cicero and the history of its reputation knows what I am talking about. Journalist and author Ray Hanania is intimately acquainted with the character of the town. He offered a sage piece of advice to the effect that in Cicero one should never stand directly in front

</td></tr>
</table>

of an open window. You never know who might be driving by. With its all-night taverns, whorehouses, and gambling games, the Cicero of legend achieved worldwide notoriety as the only town in America governed by the mob. Conditions are not nearly as raucous and wide open today, as they were, let's say, in the 1920s and 1930s (continuing through the 1970s), but one must also pity the decent, hardworking people living in the bungalows and two-flats off Twenty-second Street, the main business corridor. They have fought hard to maintain their properties and raise children in safe, crime-free neighborhoods unencumbered by the soap-opera politics of Town Hall and the stain of organized crime. By the same token, the white ethnics of Cicero historically fostered racial discord, and to this day have succeeded in keeping African-American residents of the adjoining West Side from spilling across the invisible boundary line separating the two races. A particularly shameful chapter in the volume of Cicero history we anxiously await concerns the efforts of Harvey Clark, an African-American man, to settle his family in a twenty-flat, three-story red-brick apartment building at 6139 West Nineteenth Street. The street where the race riot occurred is peaceful and quiet these days, the building well-maintained, and the surrounding working-class bungalow neighborhood is a safe place to live if you aren't black. In recent years, large numbers of Hispanics have moved into Cicero alongside the white residents of European descent, and by all accounts they have managed to get along with one another without resorting to civil unrest.

T he post–World War II housing shortage was an economic problem that cut across all sectors of society—white and black, rich and poor. For the returning white GIs who had served their country in the recent conflict, the easy availability of low-interest loans made it possible to move to the spacious, outlying areas of the city and the suburbs without undue concern.

For African Americans residing in the congested South Side and dismal West Side tenement districts, matters were not quite that simple. Hemmed in by decades-old patterns of discrimination, redlining, and societal attitudes, blacks were squeezed together, often in intolerable conditions.

Harvey E. Clark Jr., a twenty-nine-year-old CTA bus driver and war vet, confronted the dilemma by signing a lease agreement with Camille de Rose, owner of a large apartment house at 6139 West Nineteenth Street in Cicero. Neither the landlord nor the Clarks seemed overly concerned about what the neighborhood reaction might be to the arrival of the first black family in this tough, white ethnic worker's town. As far as anyone could recall, no African American had ever settled in Cicero before.

Clark and his wife, Johnetta, previously lived in a cramped one-room flat at 921 East Forty-fourth Street in Chicago. They were eager to begin anew in Cicero where the streets were clean and crime was effectively dealt with by a presumably honest police department. The sordid politics of the town that everyone else had heard of for years was apparently lost on the Clarks in their eagerness to relocate.

When it came time to move their belongings into the third-floor apartment on June 7, a "welcoming committee" of Cicero police officers was on hand to greet them at the front door of the apartment building. While neighbors jeered and hissed the couple from across the street, the cops kicked and beat Clark without provocation, warning him that he had better reconsider his ill-advised decision before it was too late.

Manhandled by police, Harvey Clark was even more determined than ever to stake his claim among the bigots of Cicero. He filed a $200,000 damage suit against the eighty-member police department. When it came before the court on June 26, U.S. District Judge John P. Barnes reprimanded the town. "You are going to exercise the same diligence in seeing that these people move in as you did in trying to keep them out."

Tensions escalated as the days passed. At first, small knots of Cicero residents gathered on the street each night after supper. In low tones, they talked

Shaded streets form boundaries of Cicero area policed by National Guard troops. Arrow indicates building at 6139 W. 19th.

WHEN AN AFRICAN-AMERICAN COUPLE ATTEMPTED TO MOVE INTO THIS CICERO APARTMENT HOUSE (BELOW) IN 1951, A VICIOUS RACE RIOT ERUPTED IN THE STREET.

among themselves about the economic calamities and hardships that awaited them if the Clarks were allowed to move in.

The age-old argument against open housing went something like this: There would be more and more *of them* coming each year. All the white people would soon be forced to move out. Property values in the neighborhood were certain to plummet. The neighborhood would be wracked with crime and no longer safe for "decent people" to live in.

"We have worked all our lives to build something for ourselves and our children, and now this!"

All across the northern cities this familiar lament was beginning to be heard in borderline communities with racial attitudes mirroring those of Cicero. It was called panic peddling, very often fueled by fast-buck real-estate agencies playing one race off against the other. Before the government intervened and enforced existing open housing laws, unscrupulous realtors often relocated exploited black families into temporary residences in white neighborhoods, paid their rent, and awaited the recurring pattern of "white flight" to stimulate fire sales of residential property.

The dawning of the civil rights movement in America was at hand, and what happened to the Clarks came as a fire bell sounding in the night.

Sensing the coming fury, other residents of the 6139 building quietly moved out, taking with them a few meager possessions.

"Burn 'em out!" "Teach 'em to stay out!" The slogans and epitaphs grew louder each day, as hundreds of Cicero residents living in remote corners of the town descended on Lombard and Nineteenth Streets to demonstrate, intimidate, and frighten away the newcomers.

The crescendo of escalating violence was reached on July 11, 1951, when the mob swelled to four thousand, and the brick-throwing melee began. Trees were pulled down, and items of furniture looted from the Clark's half-furnished apartment were thrown out the window and set on fire. The idea was to torch the entire building, but a Cicero hose cart arrived on the scene and prevented that from happening.

The Cicero police, under the command of Chief Erwin Konovsky, made a feeble, half-hearted attempt to preserve order. When the mob disregarded their directives, the cops stepped aside and allowed the rioters to ransack the entire building. One of the vandals found the Clarks' marriage certificate inside the apartment, and threw it into the fire amid loud, raucous cheers.

Cook County Sheriff John Babb, affectionately known as "Two Gun" because of the set of pearl-handled revolvers he carried under his trench coat, sent in thirty deputies to quell the disturbance, but they proved as useless as the Cicero cops.

The deputies stood a safe distance away, smoking cigarettes and joking with the uniformed town cops. In mounting desperation, Babb called on Illinois Governor Adlai Stevenson to send in the National Guard. Conditions were fast spinning out of control. The request was granted.

The combined resources of police and guardsmen formed a phalanx around one square block of Cicero, cutting off access to the apartment house. But the mob broke through once again, and the building sustained more property damage. Tear gas canisters thrown into the rank of rioters finally discouraged further hooliganism.

The riot ended on a whimper. The Clarks abandoned the idea of moving into Cicero, and the task of affixing responsibility for the devastation was left to a federal grand jury, convened by Assistant U.S. Attorney Leo F. Tierney in November 1951.

Attorney George N. Leighton, who rose to prominence first as a civil rights activist and later as a federal judge, represented the Clarks in their fight against Cicero. He was among the first to be indicted for conspiring to start a race riot. "To the credit of the Chicago bar, lawyers rallied around me," he said. "And the *Chicago Tribune* wrote editorials denouncing the indictment." Thurgood Marshall, general counsel for the NAACP and a future Supreme Court justice, was summoned to Chicago where he successfully argued for the indictment to be dismissed.

In June 1952, Police Chief Konovsky and two of his men were convicted of violating Harvey Clark's civil rights. Town President Henry Sandusky was cleared of any wrongdoing, but Camille de Rose, the embattled owner of the property, was institutionalized after showing up in court brandishing a loaded gun and demanding justice.

The Cicero Police Department, at times racist and brutal, was among the very first law enforcement agencies in the state of Illinois to walk off the job and strike for the right to be represented by a union in the collective bargaining process. They took their fight to the people and stormed Town Hall in 1968–69. Pounding on the desk the union organizers demanded concessions from the same ramrod Republican machine that had controlled Cicero since 1918.

How bitterly ironic it all seemed. The police struggled to attain decent working conditions, a good salary, and a higher standard of living—unalienable rights that they seemed only too willing to deny to others.

Stickney

THE TAXI DANCEHALL GIRLS: "DIRTY DANCING" ALONG THE STICKNEY STRIP

Prominent 1925–1945

6923 Pershing Road, 3958 South Harlem, 4232 South Harlem (vicinity of Harlem and Ogden; Harlem and Pershing Road)

Before the City of Chicago stepped in and annexed half of the original town in 1889, Cicero encompassed thirty-six square miles. Deciding that was just too much acreage for the local magistrates to manage, various ordinances and public referendums eventually whittled Cicero down to five and three-quarter miles, its present size. What Chicago did not absorb into the city limits, was siphoned off to two new municipalities, Berwyn and Oak Park. Ernest Hemingway's boyhood home is in Oak Park—and it remains one of the most popular tourist destinations in Cook County. What is not generally known is that "Papa," the rugged adventurer and novelist, was actually born in Cicero in 1899 just before that part of the town was ceded to Oak Park. But that's another story for a different day. The Village of Stickney, home of the Hawthorne Park Race Track, where many a dishonest bookie clocked bets on the nags before thoroughbred wagering was outlawed by the state legislature in 1904 (the moratorium was lifted in 1922), was yet another municipality carved out of the belly of Cicero and under the "protection" of Johnny Torrio and Al Capone. In the 1920s and 1930s, Stickney was a sparsely populated roadhouse district. It was a place to go for fun-seekers, gamblers, and lonely men in search of female companionship without fear of having to appear in a police "showup" the following morning on charges of soliciting a prostitute. The "taxi dancehall girls" recruited from the surrounding city and suburbs earned their living in the vicious dives operated by Capone and his brother Ralph. The automobile, paved roads, and easily corrupted suburban mayors and police chiefs allowed vice to spread to the four corners of Cook County following the breakup of the South Side Levee District around the time of World War I. Stickney remained notorious for nearly four decades. But all that has changed, at least for the most part. The famous vice dens of yesteryear that caused so much consternation among "Committees of Fifteen," crusading Puritan blue bloods, and idealists vowing to clean things up are all gone. A row of 1970s vintage commercial buildings and the Southwind Saloon replaced the "Rendezvous" at 6923 Pershing Road (three blocks east of Harlem). Tough Tony Capezio's "Silver Slipper," 3958 South Harlem, straddled the border of neighboring Lyons near Harlem Avenue. A shopping center anchored by a Marshall's clothing store is all you will find at that address. I would have to guess that the proximate location of the "Slipper" is the asphalt parking lot for Marshall's customers, which seems to be the commonly shared fate of many infamous places I have visited over the course of the last three years. And finally, Ralph Capone's "Harlem Nut House" at 4232 South Harlem, south of Joliet Road, is Cook County Forest Preserve land. Dense underbrush and trees obscure the location. The 5,800 law-abiding residents who live in this tiny bedroom suburb may have even overheard the stories passed down through the generations by the old-timers about places like this, but that is a slice of history–based folklore the writers of community history would just as soon forget.

To back up the sensational and occasional ribald testimony presented to a Cook County grand jury in March 1936 by former "taxi dancehall girl" Marcia O'Hare, Assistant State's Attorney William Lancaster had no choice but to summon sixty more inmates who had worked inside Stickney's most notorious dive, the "Silver Slipper." One by one they repeated the same shocking story of depravity, and dirty dancing.

On trial for criminal malfeasance of office was Village President William C. Loeffler, a lackey of the Al Capone gang who permitted vice and gambling to flourish in his remote suburban bailiwick, which had been a satellite of Chicago organized crime operations since the early years of Prohibition when Johnny Torrio expanded operations westward from Twenty-second Street.

Loeffler had argued unconvincingly that he was being made the scapegoat of the Cook County state's attorney. "I don't know of anything wrong out there," he protested. "I don't know nuthin'!"

Stickney Chief of Police Louis Marek, fired by Loeffler for raiding one of the sin spots under his protection, said that his hands were tied and there was nothing he could do once Loeffler sent word to "lay off."

Ralph "Bottles" Capone, the older brother of "Scarface," was the prime mover of vice in the isolated Western Suburb beginning in 1931 when Al went off to prison for income tax evasion and his "Harlem Inn" (4225 South Harlem) was padlocked.

Ralph Capone's money "fronted" the "Harlem Nut House," where gambling and a lewd form of dancing known as the "shake" (obscene by the standards of decency set forth in 1935) prevailed. Decorously loose young women known in the business as "taxi dancehall girls" entertained the gentlemen customers each night beginning at 9:00 P.M. and continued uninterrupted until dawn. Dance tickets were sold at the door for a quarter a piece with two-thirds going to the house. The taxicab figured prominently when it came time to repair to a more private

CHICAGO RAP SHEET

AND POLICE MUG

SHOT OF RALPH

"BOTTLES" CAPONE.

*(Courtesy of the Chicago
Crime Commission)*

trysting spot, and whatever else the girl could earn at that point was pin money.

Marcia O'Hare, the twenty-year-old brunette who decided it was in her best interests to cooperate with the state's attorney, provided jurors with a revealing glimpse into the trials and tribulations of working as a taxi dancer inside the Silver Slipper for $6.91 . . . a week. "They told me I would have to have an evening gown when I reported for work. I said I had one. They said it would have to be cut down to be more revealing, and we were instructed to wear nothing under our dresses."

The dancing became licentious when the manager of the place, one "Al Brown" (*Author's Note:* For many years, Al Capone's preferred alias, but it is doubtful that this person was Capone), ordered the lights lowered; a high sign for the men to lead the girls to a dimly lit corner of the road house for some after-hours "dirty dancing."

"For certain dances Al Brown would give the limit signal and the dance from then on was thoroughly indecent," explained O'Hare. "I saw one man pick a girl up and let her slide down his body."

The girls were known by the company they kept, and the hangers-on at the "Silver Slipper" were veteran Capone gunmen from the Prohibition wars of the 1920s. Claude "Screwy" Maddox and "Tough" Tony Capezio established their headquarters at the Silver Slipper.

"I don't know nuthin' about that either," Mayor Loeffler said, shrugging.

Before the Depression drove down wages, the taxi dancehall girls were paid $12 to $35 a week. "The highest paid girl is generally envied," the former manager of the Silver Slipper disclosed to investigators. "There is much professional jealousy among taxi dancehall girls. It often comes to blows, hair-pulling matches and scratching of faces. The girls are given instructions to use aliases, and if anyone asks questions about the place or its owner, they are told to reply: 'I don't know, I've only been here a couple of days.' They are also told what door to use in case of a raid."

Those who refused to "shimmy" with a patron were fired on the spot if the "john" complained to management.

I often wonder what happens to young women lured into this sordid kind of life after youth and beauty fade? Do they live out the rest of their days hustling on the streets for some gangster pimp they eventually marry, or were they already dead by age fifty? History does not tell us much about the wasted, pathetic lives of the throwaway people—the "taxi dancehall girls."

There was an air of unconcern for the common good and well-being of the residents of Stickney who lived through this riotous era. The "Ace of Clubs" was a wide-open gambling casino, standing catty-corner from the only public school in the village at 4038 S. Oak Park Avenue. The "Rendezvous" at 6923 Pershing Road offered the double attraction of girls and card games.

"Sensuous twisting of bodies, wild liquor orgies, and unrestrained shimmy dancing in the wee hours were some of the features that enticed hundreds of patrons to the 'Silver Slipper' and other taxi dance dives in the Village of Stickney," the *Chicago Times* reported in 1936.

All of this shaking and shimmying seems rather tame compared to the Roman circuses inside the strip joints of Rush Street in the 1960s, or the lurid spectacle of naked strippers "lap-dancing" for cash-paying customers at the gentlemen's clubs that define the modern era of vice.

River Forest

1515 Bonnie Brae Place, River Forest

THE "INS" AND OUTS OF PAUL "THE WAITER" RICCA—A VISIT TO HIS FORMER RESIDENCE

When he wasn't serving time in prison for income tax evasion, fighting deportation, or hiding behind the Fifth Amendment, Paul "the Waiter" Ricca lived a life of luxury in his baronial three-story home at 1515 Bonnie Brae. The sleek lines of the white building, situated half a block south of North Avenue and a block west of Harlem, are distinctive in this graceful West Suburban setting, renowned for its historic mansions, spacious front yards, and elegant estates. Without a major business district slicing through the village, River Forest consistently maintains a high standard of living. In other words, the well-to-do continue to build luxurious homes without fear of sagging property values. In the 1940s, an influx of cash-paying West Side hoodlums began moving in. Ricca lived in an apartment at 312 Lathrop during the time of his movie studio difficulties. Once out of prison, he paid $170,000 for his mansion on Bonnie Brae, where he lived quite contentedly from the time the U.S. government revoked his citizenship in 1957 until his death in 1972. For more than a decade the Immigration and Naturalization Service (INS) tried unsuccessfully to ship him back to Italy, but each time the gangster boss outwitted them. Sage advice given to him many years earlier by Meyer Lansky of Murder Incorporated rang true. "We'll make you rich. Play the waiting game. Keep your name out of the newspapers and build your own organization." He was neither flamboyant nor *showy, preferring to keep things close to the vest. Paul Ricca ruled the Chicago mob with precision from 1941 until 1957.*

Born Felice DeLucia in Naples, Italy on July 10, 1898, the rackets boss known as Paul "the Waiter" Ricca was a hunted fugitive before his seventeenth birthday. He was accused of murdering Emilio Perillo, his sister Amelia's beau. For this crime, DeLucia served a two-year prison sentence. Upon his return to the outside world, he tracked down the only eyewitness to the Perillo murder and killed him, too. In 1934, the Italian courts convicted him of murder in absentia.

DeLucia fled his native land in 1920 under the assumed name of Paul Maglio, who just happened to be the former town clerk in Apricena, Italy. When the time came to apply for U.S. citizenship in 1927, Ricca lied about his identity and true circumstances. Years later, the INS cited his perjury as the basis for initiating deportation proceedings, but in June 1968, the government was stunned to learn that Italy didn't want him, either.

"The Italian Embassy has refused to issue travel authorization for us to send Ricca to Italy," disclosed William Dozier of the U.S. State Department. "We tried but a spokesman for the Ambassador turned us down."

Ricca cleverly obtained an Italian judge's affidavit, stating that he had lost his citizenship when he was granted naturalization in the U.S. Through his attorney, Ricca next sent a secret dossier to nearly every nation in the world detailing his criminal past. The publicity derailed efforts to have him sent back as an undesirable, allowing the outfit boss to live out the remainder of his golden years in his River Forest home.

It was a long and bumpy ride from the Taylor Street Italian quarter, where Ricca worked as a waiter at "Diamond Joe" Esposito's famous Bella Napoli Cafe (*Author's Note:* the restaurant address was 850 South Halsted Street. It is now a part of the University of Illinois campus), to River Forest and national prominence.

In between fame and obscurity, Paul Ricca ingratiated himself with Al Capone, serving as a bodyguard and personal emissary to the New York mobs. However, tales like this are impossible to verify and are often hatched in the overactive imaginations of sensationalist crime writers planting deliberate disinformation in their books to see where it will next be picked up.

In the case of Paul "the Waiter" Ricca, it has been alleged from time to time that he was dispatched to New York by Capone to mediate differences between Joe "the Boss" Masseria and Salvatore Maranzano, and bring an end to the Castellammarese War of 1930. If true, it would have been quite a weighty assign-

UNHAPPY GANGSTER PAUL RICCA (CENTER) IS TAKEN INTO CUSTODY BY DEPUTY U.S. MARSHALS AL WOHLERS (LEFT) AND WALTER SHANAHAN (RIGHT) ON JUNE 16, 1949.

(Courtesy of the Chicago Crime Commission)

ment for a young man still learning the ropes in Chicago and, therefore, all together unbelievable.

A clearer picture of Ricca begins to emerge in the 1940s, when he became entangled in the Hollywood extortion case—the mob's attempt to shake down four motion picture studios (Paramount, Loew's, Warner Brothers, and Twentieth Century Fox) through direct control over the International Alliance of Theatrical Stage Employees (IATSE).

Gangster Willie Bioff, a chubby, myopic, and thoroughly despicable Chicago pimp, coaxed stage union chief George E. Browne into becoming a willing accomplice in the coast-to-coast shakedown scheme. Backed by Chicago "muscle," Bioff netted the mob overlords $1 million until screen actor Robert Montgomery exposed the whole sordid affair in the press, which resulted in indictments.

PAUL "THE

WAITER" RICCA'S

FORMER DWELLING

IN RIVER FOREST.

Paul Ricca was one of seven Chicago hoodlum bosses indicted by a New York City grand jury on March 18, 1943. Up until this time, he had received only passing mention. His name cropped up in the 1934 murder of gangster "Three Finger" Jack White, but apart from attempts to take over the bartenders union, Ricca's rap sheet was clean.

The day after the indictments were read aloud, Frank Nitti, Capone's successor as boss, staggered onto the Illinois Central Railroad tracks west of Harlem Avenue near Cermak Road in North Riverside not far from the former municipal sanitarium. (*Author's Note:* Chicago ghost hunter Richard Crowe alleges that Frank Nitti's restless spirit haunts the site to this day.)

In the presence of an IC trainman, Nitti fired two shots into his head. The first one missed the mark. The second one did not.

Nitti was despondent over the prospect of a return visit to Leavenworth, where he had already served an eighteen-month sentence for income tax evasion in 1930. At a private confab held at 712 South Selbourne, Nitti's North Riverside home, Paul Ricca advised him to stop complaining and "stand the pinch"—meaning that he should be prepared to take it like a man and accept responsibility for the failure of the movie studio caper. Nitti respected Ricca, and saw in him a "good businessman" who avoided trouble. He may have also sensed that Ricca was a man of coming importance on the local scene.

Nitti left the world in a veil of tears. He was suffering from stomach cancer, and his last-ditch effort to save himself from prison stripes was coldly rebuffed by Prosecutor M. F. Correa, who flatly refused to be bribed by him or any other Chicago gangster.

Police recovered a pitiful $1.03 in loose change from the dead man's pock-

FRANK NITTI NEVER

APPROACHED HIS

DUTIES AS BOSS OF

THE CHICAGO RACKETS

WITH THE SAME ZEST

AS HIS FORMER

MENTOR AL CAPONE.

ets. When told by an aide that Frank Nitti killed himself, Chicago Mayor Edward Kelly was exultant. "Good riddance!" Kelly chirped.

It was a high moment in the life of Paul Ricca. Nitti's decision to blow his brains out rather than go to prison thrust Ricca into the spotlight as the new boss of the Chicago outfit, lately governed by the rule of committee. He chose the quiet and self-effacing Tony Accardo to serve as his underboss, and for the next thirty years, Ricca and Accardo groomed a new generation of gangsters and shaped the destiny of organized crime in Chicago.

After serving only three and a half years of a ten-year sentence, Ricca and four coconspirators in the extortion case were paroled from the Leavenworth penitentiary on August 13, 1947. It was a national scandal, sparking a federal inquiry into corruption and payoffs at the highest levels of government.

The three-member Federal Parole Board voted unanimously to release the four crime bosses amid shocking allegations that New York gangster Frank Costello guaranteed the postmaster of the United States, Robert E. Hannegan,

$250,000 if he could "influence" the Truman White House to free Ricca, Charles "Cherry Nose" Gioe, Louis "Little New York" Campagna, and Phil D'Andrea. Supposedly Jake Guzik, political fixer and gambling czar of Chicago, kicked in $300,000 to sweeten the pot.

A House committee failed to find evidence of bribery, but Attorney General Thomas Campbell Clark ordered FBI Director J. Edgar Hoover to seal all records pertaining to the sensitive investigation. Neither Hannegan nor Clark (who appointed all three parole board members) remained in the cabinet very much longer. Hannegan was a Missouri political hack and a loyal election year campaigner who quietly bowed out in 1947 in order to assume the presidency of the St. Louis Cardinals baseball team.

President Truman nominated Clark to fill a vacancy on the U.S. Supreme Court on July 28, 1949. It amounted to nothing more than a political payoff for "services rendered." Clark, a former Eagle Scout from Texas who directed the systematic wartime relocation of Japanese-Americans into concentration camps in the Southwest, remained on the high court until June 12, 1967, when his son Ramsey Clark was appointed attorney general by President Lyndon Johnson.

When asked years later about his biggest mistake as president, Harry Truman was unequivocal. "Tom Clark was my biggest mistake. No question about it. That damn fool from Texas that I made Attorney General, then put on the Supreme Court. I don't know what got into me. He was no damn good as Attorney General, and on the Supreme Court … it doesn't seem possible, but he's been even worse."

It must also be remembered that "Give 'em Hell" Harry Truman, whom admiring historical revisionists rank alongside Abraham Lincoln for character, decency, and mental toughness, was a product of the oily Kansas City political machine ruled by "Boss" Thomas Pendergast and a local criminal gang responsible for the 1933 Union Station Massacre, one of the watershed events in twentieth-century organized crime history.

In light of the parole scandal, the generation of the 1940s was forced to reassess their support of Truman having glimpsed the machinery of the federal government at work and cabinet members giving succor and comfort to crime bosses. "Give 'em Parole" Harry might have been a more appropriate moniker for the nation's thirty-third president who surrounded himself with men of mediocre ability and questionable character.

With a new lease on life, Paul Ricca returned to Chicago and ran the outfit for another decade until the INS and the IRS began probing into his private affairs. In 1957, he appointed Sam Giancana interim boss, in order to devote his full time to staying out of prison. This time, Ricca was not nearly so successful.

On June 11, 1958, Federal Judge Julius Miner sentenced Ricca to three and a half years in the federal prison at Terre Haute, Indiana, on the federal tax rap. The house on Bonnie Brae and all of his property were subjected to a tax lien.

Ricca quietly served twenty-seven months and returned to civilian life as a "retired man living off his investments." The government could go no further, despite loud and anguished cries of protest from the Chicago Crime Commission, the FBI, the INS, and the IRS who tried and failed to bring him up on income tax evasion charges a second time in 1963.

Thereafter, this elder statesman of Chicago gangdom avoided air travel at all costs, fearing that it would be his bad luck to be on board when some nut-job commandeered the jetliner and directed the pilot to fly to Cuba. Ricca expressed real concerns that he would be denied reentry into the U.S. were that to happen.

When asked what he was doing to keep himself busy, Paul Ricca told the IRS that he liked to watch the planes take off and land at O'Hare Airport. Otherwise, he made his money at the track betting on the sure thing. And the odds remained with him right up to the end.

The former busboy, waiter, and shakedown artist died of a heart ailment at Rush-Presbyterian St. Luke's Hospital on October 11, 1972, and was buried at Queen of Heaven Cemetery near fellow gangsters Sam "Teetz" Battaglia and Tony Accardo.

Elmwood Park

Horwath's Restaurant, 1850 North Harlem Avenue (Cortland & Harlem)

JUKEBOX BOSS SLAIN IN RESTAURANT PARKING LOT
February 13, 1985

Chuckie English, bodyguard and best buddy of the garrulous rackets boss Sam Giancana, was slain in the parking lot of Horwath's Restaurant, straddling the boundary line separating West Suburban Elmwood Park from the Montclare neighborhood of Chicago. Horwath's is a friendly neighborhood place that has managed to remain open all these years, despite being twice bombed in May and August 1982. The reasons were never disclosed, and business went on as usual.

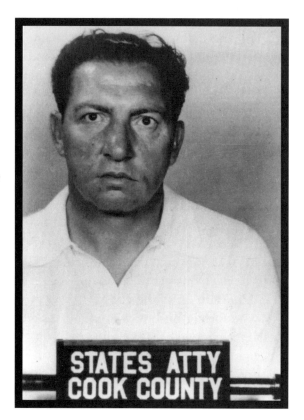

CHARLES "CHUCKIE" ENGLISH, "ROUGH AROUND THE EDGES."

HORWATH'S RESTAURANT: ENGLISH WAS SLAIN IN THE PARKING LOT.

No one was exactly sure why a semiretired gangster who had been told to "get lost" by mob hierarchy would wind up dead in the parking lot of Horwath's. Chuckie English (née: Charles Carmen Inglesia) served Sam "Momo" Giancana faithfully as his top mob lieutenant from 1957–1966, among the most violent and deadly years in Chicago mob history. But when Giancana was murdered in the basement of his Oak Park home while cooking a pan of Italian sausage, the ride was nearly canceled for Chuckie English.

Police and FBI might have even suspected that English was behind a palace coup to overthrow "Momo," but the outfit bosses and Antoinette Giancana, daughter of the slain mobster and the author of *Mafia Princess,* knew better. Questioned about Chuckie's death by *Sun-Times* crime writer Art Petacque, Antoinette expressed anger and dismay upon hearing the news. "I don't have nice things to say about those guys anymore. I'm tired of these ruthless greedy animals who would kill a nice man like Chuckie."

Antoinette related to the author that while she was growing up she had "spent a lot of time" in Chuckie's West Side home. The English family lived next door to the Giancanas in the 2800 block of Lexington in the heart of the old Taylor Street Italian ghetto before moving farther west. As they made their way up the rackets, Sam and Chuckie were inseparable companions. Antoinette made friends with the English children.

"I was at their home three times a week," she remembered. "Let's say that Chuckie was a guy who was rough around the edges. They were *all* rough around the edges!"

English, whose criminal record dated back to 1933, was a wheel horse in the syndicate's lucrative vending machine and jukebox racket—an iron-clad monopoly cultivated by gangster Eddie "Four-by-Four" Vogel in the late 1930s with the help of "Umbrella" Mike Boyle, boss of the Associated Phonograph Owners, one of many mob-tainted union locals heavily involved in the entertainment industry.

Chuckie English owned and operated Lormar Distributing, a jukebox and record company with offices at 5954 West Roosevelt Road in Cicero, the "capital city" of organized crime in Cook County. The Intelligence Division of the Chicago Police Department and the Chicago Crime Commission described the place as a front for the mob's loansharking business. Chuckie English was a feared juice loan collector, when he wasn't pressing counterfeit music tapes for sale and distribution on the streets of Chicago, or trading on his useful political connections to further the business.

During the McClellan Senate Rackets Committee proceedings (investigating the mob's penetration of bigtime labor and the recording industry), Senator Robert F. Kennedy, then chief counsel, called English a front man for Sam Giancana. Chuckie replied by taking the Fifth Amendment fifty-six times.

In the 1960s, Chuckie English spread his wings and flew off in all directions, following the scent of the dollar. He was in charge of all illegal gambling operations in the Austin District (the 29th Ward), extending into Cicero.

Chuckie had an older brother whose name also happened to be "Sam." In the early 1950s they operated a bookie parlor at Fifth Avenue and Jackson—the "Fifth Jack." As always, they reaped the benefits of the friendship and patronage of Sam Giancana.

By 1963, the brothers were living off the fat of the land. Sam "Butch" English was overseer of a sprawling dude ranch in Yavapai County, Arizona. In order to lend a distinctive Chicago flavor to the operation, Sam and Chuck purchased a vanload of salvage furniture from the basement of the Cook County Building.

The sale of the furniture (for $57 plus $2.28 in taxes) was arranged through State Senator Bernard S. Neistein, Democratic Committeeman, political boss of the 29th Ward, and member of the hoodlum-dominated West Side Bloc. Neistein listed his address at 4123 West Harrison Street in a ragged slum district, but his actual residence was a Gold Coast condominium.

Also present on moving day were three toughs identified as "29th Ward precinct captains" and Berwyn Alderman George Vydra, a lifelong friend of the English brothers who ran a Cicero supper club with "Mad" Sam DeStefano and his brother Mario. The supper club was opened for the purpose of showcasing the talents of Vydra's girlfriend and latest discovery, Miss Jane Darwyn, a nightclub chanteuse trying to become the next Helen Morgan. Vydra worked very hard trying to make Jane a star, but Helen Morgan was passé and rock 'n' roll was in.

Things turned sour for Vydra after that. They always do when your landlord and business partners are mobsters.

The nightclub was put out of business, and Vydra was found dead (under mysterious circumstances) in the cab of his pickup truck on Christmas Day 1964. The cause of death was listed as suicide by carbon monoxide poisoning—Vydra was understandably despondent over his failed romance and business reversals. One thing was puzzling, however. If it was a suicide, why was the engine of the pickup truck turned off, and the door slightly ajar?

It was never proved that foul play contributed to the cause of death, but given Vydra's shady connections, anything was possible.

Chuckie English carried on his business in a ten-room, two-story Mediterranean-style mansion on Lathrop Avenue in River Forest, not far from scores of wealthy crime bosses who could afford luxury living in safe, affluent, and amenable surroundings.

In 1976, a year after Giancana's death, English was demoted and stripped of his ownership in the jukebox company by Joe "Nagall" Ferriola, juice loan extortionist and a rising star in mob circles. Chuckie sensed that it was the right time to lay low for a while—in Hallandale, Florida, where he could partake in deep-sea fishing and golf. Invited back to Chicago by Joey "the Clown" Lombardo, English crept into the city sometime in the early 1980s to supervise a small bookmaking operation—for old time's sake—nothing more.

That's why investigators were stymied by the apparent lack of motive for the February 13, 1985, murder. He was no longer a boss worthy of government attention, but a fringe player running a card game here and there.

It was shortly after 6:00 P.M. when two men wearing ski masks approached him in Horwath's parking lot as he walked toward his Cadillac. Chuckie had just finished his dinner, allowing another restaurant patron to pick up his tab. Being a wise guy, even a washed-up wise guy, carried with it the usual entitlements.

Fifty feet from the entrance of Horwath's, one of the masked assassins shot English between the eyes, then fled between two homes on Seventy-second Court behind the restaurant. The murder weapon must have been a revolver, because no spent shell casings were found in the blood-stained snow.

A half-hour later, the aging gangland kingpin was pronounced dead at Gottlieb Memorial Hospital. Paramedics might have saved themselves time and trouble by simply transferring Chuckie across the street—to the funeral home opposite Horwath's.

While homicide investigators sifted through the dirty snow looking for spent shell casings, no one commented on the grim irony of Chuckie's time of passing. For in a few short hours it would be Valentine's Day and the fifty-sixth anniversary of the Clark Street garage massacre that made Chicago famous.

Montclare—A Chicago Neighborhood
at the Crossroads

Former site of the Montclare Theater, 7129 W. Grand Avenue, one block east of Harlem Ave.

SYNDICATE BULLETS COULD NOT KILL THE "MAN WHO KNEW TOO MUCH"

February 10, 1983

Driving in a northerly direction on Oak Park Avenue away from the village of Stickney, the motorist passes through the heart of West Suburban Berwyn and Oak Park before entering Montclare, one of the few remaining all-white, all-ethnic European bastions left in modern-day Chicago. "Mad Sam" DeStefano, one of the most feared out-fit assassins of all time (more about Sam in Return to the Scene of the Crime*), lived in a ranch home at Sayre and Wabansia. Some years back, the late FBI agent William F. Roemer conducted a late-night clandestine meeting with the "Chicago godfather," Anthony "Big Tuna" Accardo, in the parking lot of the Sears Roebuck store at Harlem and North Avenue, where it was agreed in prin-ciple that the Feds would desist from surveilling family members of the hood-lum gangsters in return for a guarantee from Accardo that the Chicago outfit would not molest or intimidate the wives and children of the Chicago bureau agents. The two men shook hands and parted. The Italian presence in Montclare is everywhere, and gangsters like Accardo who passed through are in no way reflective of the community and the pride in home ownership resi-dents feel. Harlem Avenue from Irving Park on the north to North Avenue on the south is called the Corsa Italia (Italian Boulevard) because of its many Sicilian and Neapolitan restaurants, bakeries, and butcher shops. This is also the 36th Ward, former outpost of the grandiloquent Alderman John Aiello, who summoned reporters to his office one day to happily announce that he had found a pearl in his clam pizza. There are all kinds of dark tales and amusing stories to relate, but one of the most famous concerns gambler Ken "Tokyo Joe" Eto, a local legend who took three syndicate bullets to the head and walked away unhurt. His assailants were not nearly so lucky once Eto began opening up to the Feds about mob gambling operations. Eto was shot in the parking lot of the Montclare Theater, a famous neighborhood popcorn palace whose 1990s death knell was sounded by TV, the VCR, video games, and children's general lack of interest in going to a Saturday afternoon matinee. An*

AutoZone parts store occupies the oversized lot at North and Neva Avenue where the movie house once stood. The entire appearance of the block has radically changed with the sad and disheartening disappearance of this old theater. Without the Montclare defining the North Avenue landscape east of Harlem, a slice of quaint neighborhood charm has also vanished.

Before the Illinois state legislature arrived at the dumbfounded realization that there was more money to be made in a legalized variation of the old South Side numbers racket than continuing to close down every rigged game of chance carried on in mob-controlled bars and restaurants, there was "*bolita.*" The literal translation is "little ball," and for a time, the game was enormously popular in the Hispanic and Asian communities on the South and West Sides of the city.

The daily winning number was picked by drawing numbered balls from wire cages. By 1968, the daily take was estimated to be $100,000—a fabulous sum in those days. Six years later, in 1974, the Illinois State Lottery was legislated into existence, and many of the *bolita* players had the good sense to fork over their gambling money to the state politicians. Others continued to pay Ken "Tokyo Joe" Eto, who ran *bolita* operations as a trusted associate of the syndicate for many years.

Ken Eto was unique in the inner circle of mob factotums. He was the only Japanese-American in the Chicago crime cartel. The "outfit" remained an equal opportunity employer, quite unlike the rigid caste system prevailing in New York, where one must first be Italian by birthright and a "made member" of a "family" to qualify for old-age pension benefits.

Ken Eto was born in Stockton, California, in 1919 to Japanese parents (*Nisei,* or second generation), and was recognized as a smart gambler and a "good earner" by Chicago mob overseers, who charted his progress almost from the very moment he was pinched by the cops in a September 1944 gambling raid at 837 North LaSalle Street.

While Ken Eto emerged from the shadows as a reliable lieutenant for gambler William Goldstein, Eto's older brother Joseph (the original "Tokyo Joe") was categorized by the Chicago Crime Commission as a "frontman" for North Side boss Jimmy "the Monk" Allegretti and Joseph "Caesar" DiVarco. "Tokyo Joe" Eto ran the notorious Cadillac numbers wheel for Ross Prio, labor racketeer and Rush Street mobster.

By the early 1960s, Ken Eto's name began appearing more frequently in newspaper accounts of illegal gambling activity on the Near North Side. After

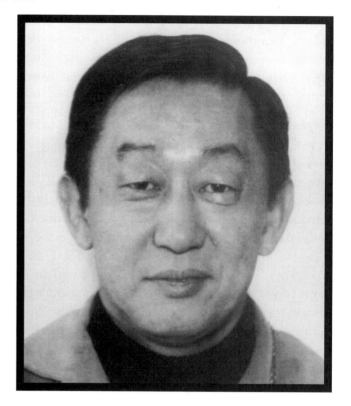

KEN ETO, THE

MAN WHO KNEW

TOO MUCH.

(Courtesy of the Chicago
Crime Commission)

"Monk" Allegretti died in 1969, gambling operations were consolidated under DiVarco, Big Joe Arnold, and Eto, who were still charted with Ross Prio. A 1972 Chicago *Sun-Times* report described Eto as "the mob's man at the racetracks—fraternizing with certain jockeys and trainers" on behalf of Tony Accardo and Paul "the Waiter" Ricca, elder statesmen of the Chicago mob, and the closest approximation to the mythic "Godfather," if indeed this shopworn movie cliché can rightfully be applied to any of the Chicago outfit hierarchy.

By the early seventies, Ken Eto was well known to Chicago journalists, the Crime Commission, and the Intelligence Division of the Chicago Police Department, even though he had managed to elude serious prosecution and lengthy jail time. Formal indictments were issued in March 1978 on charges of syndicated gambling—a felony in Illinois—but the warrant was improperly served and the evidence seized was inadmissible. In August 1980, motel rooms in the Melrose Park Holiday Inn were searched by FBI men who uncovered enough gambling records to pursue another indictment.

The impounded records indicated Eto was running a *bolita* game that grossed $3 million a year, and employed 100 people in Chicago and northern Indiana. The Chicago police took a second look and cracked down in January

KEN ETO STAGGERED
INTO THIS PHARMACY
AT 7029 WEST GRAND
AVENUE MOMENTS
AFTER BEING SHOT IN
THE HEAD AND LEFT
FOR DEAD BY TWO
BUNGLING MOB
ASSASSINS.

VINCE SOLANO,

THE MAN ON THE

RIGHT, ALLEGEDLY

TARGETED ETO FOR

DEATH.

1982. An indictment in January 1983 and conviction on gambling and racketeering charges followed. Believing that Eto was not strong enough to "stand the pinch," the upper echelon of the Chicago outfit experienced sudden convulsions of fear and a prolonged anxiety attack.

Ken Eto worked the streets quietly in some dangerous times. And despite some highly publicized capers, he was never considered "high profile" in the same sense as Sam Giancana, or the other Rush Street habitués. He paid a $2,000-a-month street tax to labor boss Vince Solano (of the hoodlum-infested Laborers International Union) through DiVarco for the privilege of running a sports bookmaking operation.

Eto was not a "muscleman," just a gambler who calculated the odds and rolled sevens for much of his life until his luck turned for the worse on February 10, 1983.

While seated behind the wheel of his late-model Ford Torino in the parking lot of the Montclare Theater, Eto, now sixty-three, was shot and left for dead by his two companions. Moments earlier they were casually discussing business with him in the car.

Three pistol shots fired at close range bounced off his head. A faulty silencer on the .22-caliber pistol apparently reduced the muzzle velocity of the bullets, or the bullets were defective. The police were never sure.

Eto played dead until the shooters were safely away. Dazed and staggering from the concussion of the shots, but otherwise not seriously hurt, he dragged himself out of the car and made his way into the Terminal Pharmacy at 7029 West Grand Avenue (opposite the CTA bus turnaround), where one of the clerks telephoned the police.

Within the next seven days, Eto was delivered safely into the arms of the U.S. government, where he worked out the final details of an agreement to enter into the Federal Witness Protection Program. The gambler interpreted the shooting as salvation; and a divine signal from a higher authority that it was time to renounce the gangster life and travel the path of the righteous. "I am now a new person with a new life," he proclaimed. Citing his devotion to Japanese karma and religious spiritualism, Eto said that his near death experience "released" him from any lingering obligations to those who tried to have him killed.

To his FBI handlers, Ken Eto fingered Joseph Gattuso, a Cook County deputy sheriff from Glenview, and Jasper "Jay" Campise, a sixty-seven-year-old loanshark and gambler who was a prime suspect in several unsolved gangland homicides in Kansas City, Missouri, dating back to the late 1950s. Campise's money bankrolled three tables at a Las Vegas–style gambling room inside a Rosemont hotel. (Rosemont, Illinois, is a border town, brushing up against O'Hare Airport. Very few families live there. It is laid out for conventioneers, partygoers, and transients. Mob influence in the union locals servicing the convention business has long been suspected, but rarely investigated.) Gattuso operated several syndicate honky-tonk taverns, gay bars, and restaurants.

On the day of the attempted murder, DiVarco and Big Joe Arnold, acting under orders from Solano, advised Eto to confer with Gattuso and Campise. Ken Eto was told that they had expressed an interest in buying a Lyons, Illinois, cocktail lounge belonging to Eto's wife, Marilou, a Philippines-born singer.

Eto agreed, and caught up with them later in the day at a Northwest Side American Legion Hall. It was suggested that they proceed immediately to a restaurant at Grand and Harlem

"Gattuso and Campise steered me into a parking lot," Eto related. "As I went into the parking lot they told me where to park. That was when Joe Gattuso shot me three times in the head."

Never before had outfit assassins botched a "hit" as miserably as this one. This was unforgettable, and it must have been an embarrassing effrontery to the downtown bosses who meted out swift justice as the punishment for failure.

Gattuso and Campise were indicted on a charge of attempted murder but the case never went to trial. Reported missing on July 12, 1983, the pair were taken for the proverbial one-way ride.

The mangled bodies were wrapped in plastic bags and stuffed into the trunk of Gattuso's car, later recovered in the parking lot of the Pebblewood condominiums at 55070 Pebblewood Lane in West Suburban Naperville. The motive was clearcut. The outfit was afraid that these two birds were about to join Eto in the Witness Protection Program. Gattuso was laid to rest in Queen of Heaven Cemetery in Hillside before one hundred mourners who remembered him in better days.

With a eye for detail, Ken Eto spilled mob secrets dating back to the early 1950s. He appeared in a succession of high-profile mob trials, supplying the Feds with six hundred pages of information.

As the star witness before the President's Commission on Organized Crime in 1985, Eto laid bare the inner workings of syndicate gambling. He told of payoffs to politicians, juice loan operations, and filled in the missing names on incomplete mob organizational charts.

Eto's defection was costly because it severely disrupted Chicago crime syndicate operations for years to come. The impact of the Federal RICO statutes and the work of the regional Organized Crime Strike Force helped demolish one prominent Chicago "street crew" involved in "juice loan" shakedowns in the 1980s, and sent a score of top-ranking hoods to prison. Ken Eto was one of several important ex-gangland figures who helped the government build its case during this important time.

Japanese karma, and not blind luck, may have had a whole lot more to do with it than one might imagine.

SUPPLEMENTAL READING

Asbury, Herbert. *Sucker's Progress: An Informal History of Gambling in America from the Colonies to Canfield*. New York: Dodd, Mead & Company, 1938.

> A colorful and richly detailed survey of the changing fashions in gambling from the eighteenth century up through the celebrated era of the New York *bon vivant* Richard A. Canfield, successor to Mike McDonald as America's reigning king of the cardsharps. Long out of print, the heavily illustrated tome is probably Asbury's most ambitious and enduring work. Asbury was one of the first "crime historians" to write for the popular market. He was a prolific storyteller who traveled from coast to coast chronicling the wickedness of Chicago, New York, San Francisco, and New Orleans.

Aylesworth, Thomas G., and Virginia Aylesworth. *Chicago: The Glamour Years, 1919–1941*. New York: Gallery Books, 1986.

> A simple narrative with an eye-catching gallery of photographs, many of them rare and unusual, make this out-of-print, coffee-table-sized book one of my personal favorites.

Brannon, William Tibbetts. *Yellow Kid Weil: The Autobiography of America's Master Swindler*. Chicago: Ziff-Davis Publishing Company, 1948.

> Republished in 1974 by Dover Publications as *The Con Game and Yellow Kid Weil*. The author claims to have followed Weil "all over Chicago," and "far from finding the Kid a man of superficialities, I discovered he has many real accomplishments." Apart from a nimble mind and the ability to exploit human foibles in ruthless ways, I can't imagine what these sterling "accomplishments" might actually be. The author is painfully in awe of his subject and fancies him to be a cavalier figure, but he never gets around to revealing the so-called strength of the con man's character. Yellow Kid Weil was the inspiration for the 1973 movie *The Sting*. He pulled off many colorful and outrageous capers during his 101 years of reckless living. However, I cannot help but believe that Brannon and other fawning crime writers who have written of the Kid with glowing affection in the ensuing years were themselves the victim of a subtle, but ingenious con aimed at transforming Weil into an antihero. The Kid relates to the author that on a "hot summer night" he stood at the bar of "Bathhouse" John Coughlin's Randolph Street saloon "quaffing a glass of beer." It is an interesting reminiscence except for one important fact. Alderman Coughlin *never owned* a saloon. He was instead the proprietor of two Turkish bathhouses, hence the famous nickname.

Casey, Robert J. *Chicago Medium Rare: When We Were Both Younger*. New York: Bobbs-Merrill, 1949.

> Personal memoirs like this are always a delight to read. Their factual accuracy is another matter. Casey surveys the years 1890–1910, carving out a series of short

sketches that wrap the era in the warm sunlight of happy memory. A gentle and pleasing book, providing a snapshot glimpse of the city as it appeared before our time, nothing more.

Cohen, Adam, and Elizabeth Taylor. *American Pharaoh: Mayor Richard J. Daley, His Battle for Chicago and the Nation.* New York: Little Brown, 2000.

A finely crafted textbook biography of America's last big-city boss, emphasizing issues of race and poverty, political control, and patterns of segregation in Chicago that brought Daley into sharp conflict with the forces of history. Neither Cohen nor Taylor grew up in Daley's Chicago—the Chicago of bungalows, parishes, baseball teams, and corner taverns. Absent, therefore, are the anecdotal sidelights that can only come from intimate firsthand knowledge of the subject; which is the unifying thread found in the work of earlier Daley biographers—Bill Gleason, Mike Royko, Eugene Kennedy, and Frank Sullivan. The Cohen-Taylor entry is a fact-engorged volume, tirelessly researched, heavily footnoted, and an impressive first effort from two younger journalists who were colleagues at *Time* magazine.

Crowe, Richard, with Carol Mercado. *Chicago Street Guide to the Supernatural: A Guide to Haunted and Legendary Places in and near the Windy City.* Oak Park, IL: Carolando Press, Inc., 2001.

Richard Crowe is the dean of a growing legion of Illinois ghost hunters who have turned to book writing. In this category, we read with interest the recent volumes of Ursula Bielski, Dale Kaczmarek, and Troy Taylor, the latter a prolific author and publisher headquartered in downstate Alton, Illinois. Tales of the supernatural are in vogue just now, with more and more paranormal researchers publishing newsletters and books, hosting lively and entertaining symposiums, and running guided bus tours in and out of every graveyard in the Midwest. They work hard, and are entitled to whatever success may happen to come their way, but a tip of the chapeau is certainly due Crowe, who invented this cottage industry more than thirty years ago and made it pay off. The author is a font of information, but I can't help believing that he should have published his findings in book form ten, fifteen, or maybe even twenty years ago, before the "second generation" of Chicago ghost gatherers began work on manuscripts that essentially troll the same waters as Richard. Some of the stories he chose to relate in this volume stretch the limits of imagination, but I have talked to enough people associated with these dark and spectral tales of the paranormal to know that logic and science cannot always account for the unexplained. What seems to be missing from the spate of ghostly tour guides appearing on the shelves at your local bookstore these days, however, is evidence of hard research into property records and death certificates, examination of old newspaper copy, and verification of historic events. Too often the authors tell us of "a murder that happened here long ago, and ever since that time, weird lights have been observed . . ." Okay. So *who* was killed, and *when* exactly did it happen? Rather than blindly accepting gossip, faulty memories, and unverifiable secondhand yarns (which seem to be the tendency among authors writing about the paranormal, hearkening back to Hans Holzer and continuing up through the modern age), researchers need to dig deeper. Give us names and dates, please. Flesh out a complete story. I am not specifically targeting Richard's volume for this criticism. It seems to be a universal problem among *all* the recently published ghost books. Indeed, Richard and Carol have published an eminently readable and enjoyable book. It just needs a *little more* seasoning in the soup. That's all.

Demaris, Ovid. *Captive City: Chicago in Chains*. New York: Lyle Stuart, 1969.

My dog-eared copy of *Captive City* needs replacing. What a superb book this is! About the only people who could possibly find fault with Demaris's "tell-it-like-it-is," staccato-style crime coverage were the injured parties who ran screaming to their lawyers with fedora hats and trench coats pulled snugly over their guilt-singed faces. I speak with no fond affection for the dramatis personae of crooked cops, union bosses, syndicate hoods, flesh-peddlers, and pinky-ring politicians who figure so prominently in a running narrative that at times lapses into this great satire of Chicago, the "City that *Almost* Works." *Captive City* cries out for a sequel. Mr. Demaris, are you listening?

Drummond, John. *Thirty Years in the Trenches: Covering Crooks, Characters, and Capers*. Louisville, KY: Chicago Spectrum Press, 1999.

Television news reporters come and go. Most of them have not lingered long enough in Chicago to tap into the soul of the city beyond the usual Michigan Avenue pastiche of boutiques and bistros. A few of them might have even aspired to cover the Chicago crime beat, but none of them, I can assure you, come close to matching the thoroughness and insight of "Bulldog" Drummond, inducted into the Chicago Journalism Hall of Fame in 1997. From City Hall to the Federal Building, down to Skid Row and up "the Drive" to Gold Coast destinations, John Drummond, in his unmistakable deadpan style, revealed more subtle truths about Windy City living than all of the coffeehouse poets and barroom philosophers combined. His retirement memoir is a fanciful collection of tales of the famous and obscure. This anthology contains rich material about Chicago's down-and-outers, late-nighters, and shady characters galore. You might even spot one of them lying under the viaduct.

Englade, Ken. *Hot Blood: The Money. The Brach Murders. The Horse Murders*. New York: St. Martin's Press, 1996.

A veteran private investigator of good repute confided to me one day that there was a logical explanation why the Chicago mob never penetrated the aristocracy of horse breeding. Certainly there was big money in it. Wealthy widows never abandon their girlish love of equestrianism. They often become, therefore, easy targets for predatory con men tied to the mob, do they not? Of course, my wizened friend replied, but the hoodlums understood that these champagne-sipping peddlers of horseflesh were stone-cold *crazy*. Who could transact business with Silas Jayne and his mercenary gang of dopesters, cutthroats, and assassins, this suburban "horse mafia," and reasonably expect to come out ahead? Author Englade has crafted a diabolical tale weaving together the Helen Brach murder (she was a voice from the grave), a gigolo named Richard Bailey, and the slaughter of old and sickly horses carried out in the name of human greed.

Gibson, Edie, Ray Gibson, and Randall Turner. *Blind Justice: A Murder, A Scandal, and a Brother's Search to Avenge His Sister's Death*. New York: St. Martin's Press, 1991.

When the Gibson book was first published in 1991, a *Chicago Sun-Times* reviewer condemned this true-crime volume as a "clip job," which is the unkindest cut of them all for one journalist to bestow upon another. A clip job is the retrieval of old articles from the newspaper morgue for rewrite purposes. When the case is still fresh, like the 1982 Dianne Masters murder was in 1990, it is a relatively simple task. Try scrolling through blurry newspaper microfilm from 1875 at the Chicago Public Library. That's when "clip jobs" become serious editorial research. We have to take into account that Gibson is a veteran *Chicago Tribune* reporter, and the reviewer happened to work for the other paper located just across the street. The Gibson book is not a prize-inner (it cries out for another edit), but it's not that bad, either. *Blind Justice* is a competent straightforward retelling of Dianne's story with the family perspective thrown in. For my money, however, I give the nod to Barbara Schaff's volume, *Shattered Hopes: A True Crime Story of Marriage, Murder, Corruption, and Cover-up in the Suburbs*.

Halpern, Rick. *Down on the Killing Floor: Black and White Workers in Chicago's Packing Houses 1904–1954*. Champaign, IL: University of Illinois Press, 1997.

Books about packing town are surprisingly scarce given the richness of the subject matter. Few writers seemed willing to tangle with the stockyards trust after Upton Sinclair had his fill of them. Attacking entrenched monopolies was a daunting prospect and, moreover, what else could possibly be said? Halpern's premise is the "dynamic of race" and how white and black managed to struggle through the miseries of the yards. Racial tension flared up many times in the early twentieth century, but the problem has seldom been addressed. The Halpern volume combines oral history and narrative with refreshing new insights.

Hansen, Henry. *The Chicago*. New York: Farrar & Reinhart, 1942.

Vistas of the Chicago River from the earliest days of settlement up through the commercial boom of the late nineteenth and early twentieth centuries. Part of the Rivers of America series, this hard-to-find, illustrated edition was edited by Stephen Vincent Benet, which may partly explain how a city reporter's dry prose was transformed into such lyrical sonnet.

Helmer, William, with Rick Mattix. *Public Enemies: America's Criminal Past 1919–1940*. New York: Facts on File, 1998.

Two solid reference books stand out in the popular genre of Chicago crime. One of them is Ovid Demaris's singularly engrossing volume, *Captive City*. The other was recently published by former *Playboy* magazine Senior Editor Bill Helmer, who is not only a meticulous researcher but a marvelous storyteller and founder of the "John Dillinger Died for *You* Society." Helmer's *Public Enemies* is a *tour-de-force* almanac of crime (head and shoulders above all others) that verifies facts without repeating hearsay, spreading gossip, or reinventing truth for dramatic purpose.

Howard, Robert P. *Mostly Good and Competent Men: Illinois Governors 1818–1988.* Springfield, IL: Illinois Issues Magazine and Sangamon State University, 1988.

Howard's survey of Illinois governors is a soothing and inoffensive tome, filling a gap in the historiography and political literature of the state. Howard was a longtime statehouse correspondent for the *Chicago Tribune.* The book is informative but bland. One is left with the feeling that there is a whole lot more to be said about the thirty-nine "good and competent men" who have sat in the governor's chair than what is presented in this volume. But I suspect you won't hear it from the gentlemanly Mr. Howard, unless it is repeated from behind closed doors by someone else and strictly off the record.

Jacobs, Jane. *The Death and Life of Great American Cities.* New York: Random House, 1961.

Our understanding of how cities are shaped is greatly enriched by Jacobs' 1961 masterpiece that still has something important to say to us in the modern day. Chosen as a 1993 selection for the Modern Library of the World's Best Books, Jacobs' beautifully written volume was praised by the *New York Times* as "perhaps the most influential single work in the history of town planning."

Koenig, Rev. Monsignor Harry C., ed. *A History of the Parishes of the Archdiocese of Chicago.* 2 vols. Chicago: Archdiocese of Chicago, 1980.

An excellent source book for researchers tracing genealogies or the consolidations and demises of Chicago's neighborhood parishes.

Krammer, Arnold. *Nazi Prisoners of War in America.* New York: Stein & Day, 1979.

Krammer, a professor of history at Texas A & M University, interviewed 250 POWs in preparation for a book on this little-known chapter of World War II history. Exquisitely detailed and thoroughly researched, the author leaves no stone unturned and presents a balanced account of the internment program. The POWs were so well sequestered that many American citizens were oblivious to the presence of former soldiers of Hitler's *Wehrmacht* living close-by in their communities.

McPhaul, John L. *Deadlines & Monkeyshines: The Fabled World of Chicago Journalism.* New York: Prentice-Hall, 1962.

Jack McPhaul was a talented and cunning reporter. He spanned the era of the *Front Page*, right up through the slow and agonizing decline of Chicago newspaper journalism in the 1950s and 1960s. McPhaul helped secure the release of Joe Majczek from the penitentiary for a crime he did not commit at a time when the reporters *made* news through their sheer inventiveness and back-alley guile. McPhaul's book is a roll call of the famous names from the city desk, along with their nightly drinking escapades, practical jokes, and gallows humor that transcended the job. Like most anecdotal memoirs of this sort, it is light reading, and one only wonders how many second- and third-generation yarns repeated by the author ever really happened.

Miller, Merle. *Plain Speaking: An Oral Biography of Harry Truman*. New York: Berkley Publishing, 1973.

A praiseworthy biography based on hundreds of hours of taped interviews with the nation's thirty-third president. Truman was candid and outspoken about his poor cabinet choices, and never deflected blame to subordinates for elevating Tom Clark to national life.

Morton, Richard Allen. *Justice and Humanity: Edward F. Dunne, Illinois Progressive*. Carbondale, IL: Southern Illinois University Press, 1997.

The title of this political biography is interesting, wouldn't you say? It leaves little doubt as to where the author's sympathies lie with respect to his subject matter. Edward Dunne is the only Illinois politician to serve as mayor of Chicago and governor of the state. He is an engrossing subject for a biography, and with more objective reporting than what Morton serves up in this book, a clearer picture will likely emerge. Dunne championed a number of statewide reforms while serving as governor from 1913–1917, but the author fails to hold him accountable for pardoning labor racketeer and convicted murderer Mossie Enright and other crooks. The pardon of Enright was as smelly a backroom political deal in its day as Bill Clinton's pardon of fugitive financier Marc Rich in 2001. In fact, Morton sidesteps the entire Enright episode. Morton is an effective apologist for Dunne, who was permanently branded a tool of the Hearst press. Governor Dunne was never so far above reproach that he didn't accept the help of the crooked politicians he openly assailed in his public pronouncements.

Murray, George. *The Madhouse on Madison Street*. Chicago: Follett Publishing, 1965.

A hard-drinking journalist, playwright, and author from the Missouri Ozarks, Murray recounts the rise and fall of the Hearst papers in Chicago from 1900 up through 1956, and his own adventures as a cub reporter breaking into the news racket in 1933. Murray speaks with fondness of "the Chief" and insulates the squire of San Simeon from history's unflattering judgment, as a number of press veterans who worked under William Randolph Hearst have done over the years. Like so many other newspaper writers who turn to book writing, Murray's historical research is often slipshod and unreliable. Murray's account of the Marty Durkin manhunt and capture is laden with fiction. In fact, I don't know where he came up with some of this stuff! Unless the history he chooses to survey is a collection of short newspaper clips sent up from the morgue in a manila folder, the reporter-turned-author very often struggles to comprehend events occurring outside his limited frame of reference. Few of these reporters/authors ever marked time at the library, and it shows up in the quality of the finished product.

Orth, Maureen. *Vulgar Favors: Andrew Cunanan, Gianni Versace, and the Largest Failed Manhunt in U.S. History*. New York: Delacorte Press, 1999.

It is doubtful the author would have found much of an audience for a book such as this except for the Versace cachet. Nor would the self-absorbed pretty boy Cunanan have become a national media curiosity in his own right if he had limited his killing spree to Minnesota, Chicago, and New Jersey. The shelf life for these kinds of true-crime potboilers is very limited. It is obvious the book was produced in great haste while Cunanan was still fresh in the public eye. But the book manages to pass muster only because the author has attempted to interpret Cunanan's motivations, while shedding light on the killer's troubled home life and even more disturbing associations in the gay community.

Pacyga, Dominic A., and Ellen Skerrett. *Chicago: City of Neighborhoods*. Chicago: Loyola University Press, 1986.

An invaluable tour guide with an emphasis on sacred space, patterns of immigration and settlement, and the historic evolution of neighborhoods. A gentle, reaffirming statement about the strength of Chicago.

Patterson, Lt. Colonel J. H. *The Man Eating Lions of Tsavo*. Chicago: The Field Museum of Natural History Zoological Leaflet, 1925.

Published to coincide with Colonel Patterson's visit to Chicago, the firsthand account of the lifesaving Kenya lion-hunting expedition is a worthy adventure story in the tradition of *King Solomon's Mines, Call of the Wild*, and the other yarns that once thrilled younger generations before the deluge of television and computers.

Peterson, Virgil W. *The Juke Box Racket*. Chicago: Unpublished report, 1954.

Ex-FBI man Virgil Peterson was the driving force behind the Chicago Crime Commission for nearly four decades. Mr. Peterson was more than a just a top-notch investigator and staunch foe of the mob. He was a profiler of organized crime, and his typewritten reports, notes, and miscellaneous papers could easily fill volumes were they to be published. (Actually they fill hundreds of bulging cardboard cartons and rusting filing cabinets crammed inside the CCC offices.) Peterson was unafraid of lawsuits or controversy. In fact he thrived on it. He tarred and feathered scores of public officials as corrupt. He published the names and home addresses of Chicago hoodlums, and threw a spotlight on crime that has dimmed since his passing in 1984. In 1954, Peterson turned his attention to the jukebox and recording industry, exposing criminal ties between crooked union officials, manufacturers of jukeboxes and coin-operated devices, and the mobsters who tapped a plentiful revenue stream from this industry.

President's Commission on Organized Crime. *Organized Crime and Gambling: Record of Hearing VII, June 24–26, 1985*. New York.

Created by Executive Order 12435 of July 28, 1983, the President's Commission on Organized Crime conducted a region-by-region analysis of organized crime activity, tracing sources of income, with a major focus on how the mobs are able to infiltrate and profit from legal gambling. Testimony concerning the failed assassination attempt against Ken Eto was delivered by Sergeant Donald Herion of the Cook County Sheriff's Police, who is recognized as a foremost expert on sports gambling and illegal bookmaking in the State of Illinois, and Judith Dobkin, a member of the Department of Justice, Chicago Strike Force.

Roberts, Randy. *Papa Jack: Jack Johnson and the Era of the White Hopes.* New York: The Free Press, 1983.

Raised in the streets of Galveston, Texas, Jack Arthur Johnson had an overpowering right hook that forced America to take a hard look at itself—in and out of the boxing ring. Johnson toppled many racial barriers and social taboos during his extravagant and reckless life. He became a hero of the civil rights movement by default. Joe Louis shunned him; Booker T. Washington castigated him; the 1960s generation celebrated him. Taking a closer look, we observe an ego-driven man victimized by obsession and other self-destructive tendencies. The author of this flattering biography builds a strong case for his subject, but I question some of his conclusions concerning the moral character of Louise Cameron and Belle Schreiber. The evidence suggests that these impressionable teenage girls were seduced and lured away from respectable homes by Johnson, a compulsive romancer. Roberts's assertion that they were inmates of notorious brothels before hooking up with Johnson is dubious. If moral turpitude is taken into account, Jack Johnson is not likely to qualify for sainthood anytime soon.

Roemer, William F., Jr. *The Enforcer: Spilotro—The Chicago Mob's Man Over Las Vegas.* New York: Donald J. Fine, 1994.

Roemer's foray into the publishing world earned him national acclaim. His *Man Against the Mob*, published in 1989, was a finely crafted memoir of his FBI career in Chicago, and it thrust him into the national spotlight as an expert spokesman on the battle against organized crime. For several years, Roemer traveled from city to city picking up bits of useful information here and there about local mob activity from veteran bureau agents. He used this information to great advantage during on-air chat sessions with radio-talk-show hosts during scheduled stops on national book tours. Consequently, there was always a certain amount of resentment and jealousy directed against Roemer among the law enforcement fraternity. He was often accused of being a publicity hound and exaggerating his own importance. Bill was a convincing spokesperson nevertheless and a sincere man of the "hail-fellow-well-met" variety. Having edited his material for a quarterly column he prepared for the *Illinois Police & Sheriff's News,* I was impressed by the character and stature of the man, but disappointed with the quality of his later writings. He really only had that one book in him, and neither the Spilotro or subsequent Tony Accardo biography measured up to *Man Against the Mob.* Both volumes rehashed the same old material. Familiar anecdotes were repeated, and Roemer never managed to tell us very much about the early backgrounds and private lives of either Spilotro or Accardo beyond what we already knew from newspapers and magazines.

Shea, Robert. *From No Man's Land to Plaza del Lago.* Chicago: American Reference Publishing, 1987.

Real-estate developer Joseph Moss commissioned veteran magazine writer Shea to conduct a research project and write a book about the twenty-two acres of disputed land straddling the Wilmette-Kenilworth boundary line. The resultant one-of-a-kind community history project is obscure, but fills a valuable "niche" in our understanding of suburban land development.

Sinclair, Upton. *The Jungle*. New York: Doubleday-Page, 1906.

There is a tendency to overlook all the good that unions have done. Far too often, we read about organized crime penetration of labor; the corruption of Teamster officials in camel-hair coats squired around town in Cadillacs; cop unions that make it impossible for municipalities to suspend or fire police personnel for malfeasance and brutality; and the outrageous contract demands foisted on management forcing smaller shops to throw up their hands and close down or move to parts of the world where the work can be performed cheaper. Then a reading of Sinclair's masterful, muckraking exposé of conditions in Chicago's packing houses reminds us of the world of our ancestors, when work was a euphemism for the callous exploitation and children as young as six were allowed to toil from dawn till dusk in canning factories and sweatshops. Sinclair's book is a powerful wake-up call for America as we begin the twenty-first century. It reminds us that we cannot afford to look the other way—ever.

Stonehouse, Frederick. *Went Missing: Unsolved Great Lakes Shipwreck Mysteries*. Marquette, MI: Avery Color Studios, 1984.

Peruse the souvenir shops of Michigan's rustic Upper Peninsula and you will certainly run across a whole series of these obscure titles detailing the hidden histories of ghost-ship sightings and nautical disasters dating back more than 120 years. They are often well researched and finely illustrated, but limited regional distribution prevents the authors from reaching wider audiences.

Tarr, Joel Arthur. *A Study in Boss Politics: William Lorimer of Chicago*. Champaign, IL: University of Illinois Press, 1971.

In this one-party town, it is hard to conceive of the Republican Party as a force in city elections. There have only been two Republican mayors in twentieth-century Chicago—Fred Busse and William Hale Thompson. Neither of them inspired the City Council to appropriate funds to hire a sculptor to chisel commemorative statues in their likeness. In the first decades of the last century, however, the GOP of Cook County was powerful in certain city wards, and Republican bosses like William Lorimer were equally as voracious in their political plunder as their Democratic counterparts. Tarr's political biography is at times dry reading, but it is one of the few volumes of urban history that scrapes the minutiae of the bloody intraparty squabbles, the electoral process of Illinois in the first decade of the last century, and what, if anything, these people really stood for.

NEWSPAPERS

Chicago American (1900–1907; 1951–69)

Chicago Daily Journal (1900–1910)

Chicago Daily News (1875–1978)

Chicago Evening Post (1922–23)

Chicago Herald & Examiner (1922–39)

Chicago Herald-American (1940–48)

Chicago Inter-Ocean (1890–1915)

Chicago Sun (1941–45)

Chicago Sun-Times (1948–   )

Chicago Times (1934–48)

Chicago Today (1969–74)

Chicago Tribune (1855–   )

Crain's Chicago Business (1990–   )

Daily Southtown Economist (1982–88)

Northwest Herald (1983–   )

MISCELLANY

The Chicago Crime Commission. Annual Reports on Chicago Crime, 1953–1968.

Organized Crime Digest: An Independent News Summary of Organized Crime Activity. Various years, 1990–.

"A TOWN WITH A QUEEN ANNE FRONT AND A MARY ANN BACK."

—*Paul H. Douglas, 1977*

ABOUT THE AUTHOR

Author, historian, and journalist Richard Lindberg was born and raised in Chicago, the backdrop for ten earlier books all dealing with aspects of the city's history, politics, crime, ethnicity, and sport.

Over the course of a twenty-five-year writing career, Lindberg served as head writer and senior editor for the Edgar Award–winning, six-volume *Encyclopedia of World Crime*, published in 1990. As editor of the *Illinois Police & Sheriff's News* for six years, Lindberg cast a searchlight on many controversial issues within the law enforcement community. He presently serves as marketing director for Search International, a worldwide investigations and research firm headquartered in the Chicago suburbs.

Among his ten published volumes is *"To Serve and Collect: Chicago Politics and Police Corruption From the Lager Beer Riot to the Summerdale Scandal."* It is the first history of the Chicago Police Department to appear in book form since 1887. The volume was subsequently released in paperback by Southern Illinois University Press in 1998.

In addition, Lindberg has served the Chicago White Sox as their official team historian since 1985. In this capacity, he has appeared before numerous fan groups, assisted the team in various marketing and promotional campaigns, conducted statistical research, and authored numerous articles and publications. In 1988, he acted as a historical consultant to John Sayles's film crew during the production of the motion picture *Eight Men Out*.

Over the years, Lindberg's byline has appeared in numerous publications including the *Chicago Tribune Magazine*, *Chicago History*, *Inside Chicago Magazine*, *Screen Magazine*, *The Reader*, *U.S.A. Today* magazine, and others.

As an author and Chicago historian, Rich has been featured on various TV and radio programs of local and national origin including A&E's *American Justice*, *CBS News Overnight*, the Travel Channel, *The Hidden History of Chicago*, and *History's Mysteries* for the History Channel. He is a member of the Chicago Crime Commission, the Illinois Academy of Criminology, the Chicago Press Veterans, and is a past president of the Society of Midland Authors.

Mr. Lindberg participated in the development of an interactive visual display depicting significant events from Chicago history. The exhibit was unveiled atop the Skydeck of the Sears Tower in April 2000. He was responsible for the editorial content in the sports section. The Chicago displays are expected to be viewed by several million visitors from around the world within the next two to three years.

Books by Richard Lindberg

- *Stuck on the Sox*, Sassafrass Press, 1978.
- *Who's On Third: The Chicago White Sox Story*, Icarus Press, 1983.
- *The Macmillan White Sox Encyclopedia*, Macmillan, 1984.
- *Chicago Ragtime:Another Look at Chicago 1880-1920*, Icarus Press, 1985.
- *To Serve and Collect: Chicago Politics and Police Corruption from the Lager Beer Riot to the Summerdale Scandal, 1880-1960*, Praeger Press, 1990 (reprinted in paperback by Southern Illinois University Press in 1998).
- *Passport's Guide to Ethnic Chicago*, NTC/Contemporary Books 1992, second edition 1997.
- *Stealing First in a Two-Team Town: The White Sox from Comiskey to Reinsdorf*, Sagamore Publishing, 1994.
- *Chicago By Gaslight:A History of the Chicago Netherworld 1880-1920* (a paperback reprint of *Chicago Ragtime*), 1996.
- *Quotable Chicago*, Wild Onion books, 1996.
- *The White Sox Encyclopedia*, Temple University Press, 1997.
- *The Arm Chair Companion to Chicago Sports*, Cumberland House, 1997.
- *Return to the Scene of the Crime:A Guide to Infamous Places in Chicago*, Cumberland House, 1999.

Contributing

- *A Kid's Guide to Chicago* (1980).
- *The Baseball Biographical Encyclopedia* (1990).
- *The Encyclopedia of Major League Baseball Team Histories* (1990).
- *The Encyclopedia of World Crime* (1990).
- *American National Biography* (1999).

INDEX

H

I

J

Wemette, William "Red," 232
Werner, Betty, 319, 321
West Side, 357–424
    maps of, 358–359
Whitechapel Club, 45–48
Willard, Frances E., 7
Williams, Eugene, 390
Wilner, Emma, v
Wilson, Orlando W., 389–391
Wing Foot, 36
Winkler, Gus, 156
Woman's Christian Temperance
    Union (WCTU), 7
Wonderful Wizard of Oz, The, 10
Wooldridge, Clifton Rodman, 15
Wright, Frank, 123

Y

Yarrow, Philip, 54

Z

Zenge, Mandeville, 303–308
Zine, Eddie, 373
Zuckerman, Ben, 384